Joseph Malet Lambert

Two Thousand Years of Gild Life

Joseph Malet Lambert

Two Thousand Years of Gild Life

ISBN/EAN: 9783744723886

Printed in Europe, USA, Canada, Australia, Japan

Cover: Foto ©ninafisch / pixelio.de

Two Thousand Years

OF

GILD LIFE;

OR AN OUTLINE OF THE HISTORY AND DEVELOPMENT OF THE GILD SYSTEM FROM EARLY TIMES, WITH SPECIAL REFERENCE TO ITS APPLICATION TO TRADE AND INDUSTRY;

TOGETHER WITH A FULL ACCOUNT OF THE

GILDS AND TRADING COMPANIES

OF KINGSTON-UPON-HULL,

FROM THE 14TH TO THE 18TH CENTURY.

BY

REV. J. MALET LAMBERT, M.A., LL.D.,

Vicar of Newland, Hull; and Chairman Hull School Board.

"For, as on the one side, it cannot be doubtful but that the too studious Affectation of bare and sterile antiquitie, which is nothing els but to bee exceeding busie about nothing, may soon descend to a Dotage; so on the other, the neglect or only vulgar regard of the fruitfull and precious part of it, which gives necessarie light to the Present in matter of State, Law, Historie, and the understanding of good authors, is but preferring that kind of ignorant Infancie, which our short life alone allows us, before the many ages of former Experience and Observation, which may so accumulate yeers to us as if we had lived even from the beginning of Time."—*Selden.*

HULL:

A. BROWN & SONS, SAVILE STREET;

LONDON: SIMPKIN, MARSHALL, HAMILTON, KENT & CO., LIMITED.

1891.

ILLUSTRATIONS.

CONTENTS.

Chapter XII.

Chapter XIII.

Chapter XIV.

Chapter XV.

Chapter XVI.

Chapter XVII.

CHAPTER XXXI.

CHAPTER XXXII.

CHAPTER XXXIII.

CHAPTER XXXIV.

CHAPTER XXXV.

CHAPTER XXXVI.

APPENDIX I.

APPENDIX II.

INTRODUCTION.

THE following book is an attempt to sketch in outline, so far as is possible in a single volume, the origin and course in this country of that peculiar principle of association which has its typical form in the mediæval Gild.

It is not simply the history of benefit or of trades' societies, or of religious associations. It is rather the history in outline of a form of union which has not been limited to any age, or to any of the special objects for which men band themselves together. If man is above all a social being, the mould in which the lesser social organisations of so many ages took their form and character must be an object of curious interest. The natural association of the family in its various forms of development has become a part of the science of sociology; political union is a science in itself. The class of intermediate associations, chiefly to be found in the sphere which has lately come to bear in a special sense the term social, and which lent itself readily to industrial and mercantile concerns, has been noticed incidentally by many writers, but has hardly had the attention which from many and various aspects it has deserved.

This design is worked out chiefly on the basis of the extant documents, mostly hitherto unpublished, of the Gilds, and especially the Merchant Companies and Craft Fraternities of Kingstown-upon-Hull, thus in part furnishing a chapter in the history of general English economic progress which it is thought will not be without special interest at the present day.

There is indeed hardly any subject more inviting to the student of social history or economic development than that of the ancient and mediæval Gilds. The field of enquiry open to the enquirer is both extensive and to a large extent unworked. In almost every town of England in the 13th century was there a Merchant Gild including in its membership nearly all the principal inhabitants, exercising most important functions with respect to trade, and closely bound up with the municipal government. Within a century afterwards, and probably long before this, every craft in addition had its own separate gild organisation, and these Gilds included every regular worker in the crafts. At the same time, connected with every town and with very many of the larger villages, were great numbers of others whose objects were purely benevolent or religious and funereal, and which embraced all classes of the community.

Thus the whole municipal, industrial, and social life of the Middle Ages, if we except the industry of agriculture, moved in the circle of the Gild. Not alone the public, but also the social and private, the moral and municipal interests of the townsfolk centred therein. They were very largely the Chambers of Commerce, the Friendly Societies, the Trades Unions, the Freemasonry, and in some degree the Joint Stock Companies, of times when the merchant lived in his warehouse, which was also his factory as well as his shop: when the apprentice sat at his master's table for his seven years, somewhat after the fashion of an adopted son; and when to attain the membership of the Gild was to gain a recognised and honorable position in the land. They were no mere formal organisations for purposes which ended with the hard toil of the working day. The warm blood of the life of the time circulated in them. Their members sat together at the feast, stood by each other's honour in the mart, lived in the same quarter, shared the same purchase, marched side by side in the pageant, acted together in the play, and fought together in the part of the city walls committed to their care. The esprit de corps was as strong among them as among the knights of higher rank. Honesty and fair dealing were dear to them, and they followed the bier of the departed and paid wax for the rest of his soul in peace. It is plain that to enter into the current of this ancient life is to become familiar with no small part of the true history of the people.

Nor is the interest which the study evokes one merely of history or archæology. It also opens out a most important chapter in economic history. The extension of the historical method into the field of economics promises on the one hand to revolutionise the social science of Political Economy, and on the other to lead gradually to a recognition of the true factors in a most important department of social life. The condition of the dreary science indeed, at the present time, may be compared not inaptly to that of science in general when the aerial structures of the mediæval schoolmen were beginning to totter as their slender *a priori* foundations were dissolving in the flood of Baconian naturalism. As Mr. Bagehot pointed out, the postulates of the "fluidity" of capital and labour required by our standard books on Political Economy are inapplicable, while their application even to the economics of to-day is subject to very wide and subtle limitations. The earliest conditions of the creation and exchange of wealth in its fullest sense were determined by contemporary social institutions, partly the inherited methods of social life, partly the tentative and timorous adaptation of these to the changing needs of the day. If we would set in a clear light the principles and practice of ancient trade, we must search out the origin and early development of the social institutions with which they were combined. If this be possible much is accomplished: not only the true meaning of a great deal which remains in the economic present becomes plainer, but also in the larger social laboratory of to-day, when the old bonds are fast ceasing to hold, and the liberated elements of society are crystalising afresh round those centres to which their natural tendencies attract them, the possession of examples of these same elements in mankind forming in simpler combinations but in accordance with the same laws may render aid in the solution of the problems of our own time. It will not be necessary to pursue this line of thought further at present, as it is developed in greater detail in the chapter on the economic position of the

Gild. Enough has been said to show the value of a fuller study of the ancient trade societies than has yet been made in order to help on a better understanding on the subject.

Yet notwithstanding both the historic and economic interest involved, there is hardly any field of enquiry which has less attracted the labours of historians. Until the last few years the short essay by M. Brentano attached to the volume of the Early English Text Society on Gilds, edited by Mr. Toulmin Smith, constituted not only the classic but also the literature of the subject. There are a few valuable local volumes on individual Gilds, and the pageantry and mystery plays of the Corpus Christi festival, which have been studied chiefly for the history of the drama, and have brought into some notice the various trades which took part in the display, but if we except Herbert's account of the London Livery Companies, and the other monographs dealing with the same, as having an interest peculiar to themselves, the records of the old fraternities have been left mostly disregarded or unknown. Their place in history has been either altogether vacant, or has been unworthy of that which was its due. In Hull the very existence of the ancient ordinances of the societies, if known, was ignored by the historians of the town. The buildings formerly connected with them have departed and left no trace. If we except one or two obscure indications left us in the names of streets, the societies have left no memory behind them. Yet probably no documents hitherto made public can vie with these ordinances in bringing back into view the every-day life of the town in the centuries of which they treat. As we study them we can mingle again in the vigorous life of the narrow streets. We can learn how it was that the men of that time built houses of which the mortar stands to-day as hard as stone; we can picture the barber looking askance at the upstart man who presumed as surgeon to molest his ancient right of letting the blood of his customers at the fall of the leaf; we can look into the mysteries of the brewing vat as it was before tea had usurped the time-honoured place of the pewter at the breakfast tables of society; we can see the shipwrights who made the ships of Elizabeth at work; we can walk as it were along the small booths and shops and judge of the quality of the goods which had come from Hamburg or Muscovy, or which had been fashioned with such care in the workshop behind the parlor. We can hear the jealous counsel of the merchants as they banded themselves together to defeat the machinations of the "men of divers occupations and crafts, tailors, shoemakers, and others," who aspired to be merchants as themselves; and sometimes a sentence will remind us of principles which are being whispered to-day as discoveries of 19th century reaction against Adam Smith.

The long neglect of these old records in Hull is but a sample of the neglect of the subject with which they deal in the national literature. In his volume on "Economic History," published in 1889, Mr. Ashley prefixes to his chapter on "Merchant and Craft Gilds" a useful bibliography of the most important works of reference relating thereto; but the books named are nearly all Continental, and inaccessible to English readers. Neither Mommsen's "de Collegiis" nor Gross's "Gilda Mercatoria" could be procured in this country. His own chapter places many new facts before his readers, and has the merit of recognising that these Gilds lay at the foundation of the beginnings of English trade, and I am the more glad to notice the value of his work, as from some of his conclusions I have felt myself compelled to differ (1). This scarcity of information upon this subject has been the reason why this work has taken a wider scope than was at first intended. Being, as I believe is the case, the most complete publication of the records of mediæval Craft Gilds which has as yet been offered to the public referring to any of the provincial towns of England, it seemed not inappropriate that it should be accompanied by a somewhat fuller account of what can be learned respecting their origin and history, and of the many curious and interesting analogies with similar institutions which can be traced in more ancient times, especially also their connection with the earliest forms assumed by the Christian Church.

(1) His English list does not include the book on Gilds by the late Mr. Walford, and Dr. Gross gives a list of works which is fuller for the department with which he deals. For further information on this head see the Bibliography at the end of the book.

There are, however, several additional reasons which render the collection of Hull ordinances not an unfitting basis for a general consideration of the subject of Gilds, mediæval, town, and trade. The Humber district, known in the Scandinavian Sagas as *Humra*, and equally well known in the literature of the Cymry, was from a very early period an important seat of trade with the districts of northern Europe. The changes in the geographical features of the coast within historic times have indeed been so great as to have not only altered the comparative importance of the towns formerly existing, but even to have buried both towns and villages under the waves of the North Sea. Not only is Hedon left high and dry, but Ravenspurn has disappeared as completely as Winetta in the picturesque legends of the Baltic. But the same broad estuary remains which was familiar to the Cymry and the Romans, and was dark many a time with the long-ships of the Vikings, as it had been with the keels of the Saxons. Grimbsbœr, or Grimsby, too, is well known to the reader of the Sagas, and the muddy stream of the Markflót, or Marfleet, which awaits the devouring approach of the town on the east, bears the name of the Icelandic stream which witnessed the leap of Skarphedinn (2); and the gatherings of the great Thing, or popular assembly of the Norsemen, an assembly at least as worthy of remembrance by Englishmen as the Curia at Rome, or the Demos at Athens.

Whatever we may think of the theory of the origin of the

(2) There was a feud between Thrain and Skarphedinn. The Flót, or river, which in its semi-frozen state was from 18 to 26 feet broad from side to side, separated the two parties, there being four with Skarphedinn and seven with Thrain. "Skarphedinn sprang up as soon as he was ready and had lifted his axe—'the ogress of war'—aloft, and runs down to the Fleet. But the Fleet was so deep that there was no fording it for a long way up or down. A great sheet of ice had been thrown up by the flood on the other side of the Fleet, as smooth and slippery as glass, and there Thrain and his men stood in the midst of the sheet. Skarphedinn takes a spring into the air, and leaps over the stream between the icebanks, and does not check his course, but rushes still onwards with a slide. The sheet of ice was very slippery, and so he went on as fast as a bird flies. Thrain was just about to put his helm on his head, and now Skarphedinn bore down upon them, and hews at Thrain with his axe—'the ogress of war'—and smote him on the head, and clove him down to the teeth, so that his jaw teeth fell out on the ice. This feat was done with such a quick sleight that no one could get a blow at him; he glided away from them at once at full speed. Tjorvi indeed threw his shield before him on the ice, but he leapt over it, and still kept his feet, and slid quite to the end of the sheet of ice. . . . 'This was done like a man,' says Kari."—Dasent, *Burnt Njal*, *II.*, p. 63.

English race put forward by M. Du Chaillu in his recent work, there can be no question as to the evidence of the high grade of civilisation possessed by the Scandinavian and Danish people. Some of the industrial arts were undoubtedly in an advanced state at the period to which we are alluding, and "many-colored English cloth," among other things, was much prized by the people. The instinct of trade was strong among them, and though the records of it have mostly perished, there can be but little doubt that before the Conquest there was a very considerable intercourse between the people of Yorkshire and the Baltic. As Montesquieu has said, "The history of commerce is the history of the intercommunication of peoples"; and to-day the square sails of the Humber "keels" are almost exact reproductions of the ones which are figured in the Tapestry of Bayeux. We shall return to this hereafter. It is alluded to here as giving additional interest to the study of the early traffic of the port, which, now that a thousand years have gone by, is the chief seat of the Baltic and Scandinavian trade. Not a week passes but many hundreds of the descendants of those Norsemen who were the first of Europeans to set foot on North America, land on the Humber bank at Hull, on their way to colonise that land which their forefathers discovered 900 years ago. The late Mr. Frost has shown clearly that Hull was a town of great commercial importance long before its charter by Edward I., and the present is not the only century in which it has been placed third in the list of the seaports of the kingdom. It was from the earliest time one of the staple towns. In the 14th century it was the scene of the commercial enterprise of the De la Poles, afterwards Earls of Suffolk (8), who also appear in the records of the trade of London. The Merchants of the Staple, the Merchant Adventurers, the Hanseatic League, the Eastland and Russia Companies, had their branches here, besides the Chartered Merchants' Company of the town; and the town itself was the first in the kingdom to receive a charter of incorporation. In 1698 De la Pryme records in his Diary that "it is a very fine

(8) See their History, by J. Travis Cook, F.R.H.S. (A. Brown & Sons, Hull.)

town, exceedingly well governed, and kept in very great awe (4)."

It is true the trade ordinances existing are not the most ancient in existence, and in their present form they all date from a period subsequent to the great economic revolution which resulted from the Black Death in the 14th century; but it will be seen that they bear evidence of much greater antiquity than the actual documents in which they have come down to us. It must be also borne in mind that the actual history of trade and industry in the period from the 15th to the 18th centuries is not only of more importance to us as being the immediate progenitor of the present, but is also apparently almost as "dark" in current economic history as mediæval times. We are told, for instance, that "The Crafts' Gilds of England, generally speaking, received their death-blow in 1547. . . . Had the condition of industrial life been such that they were really required, they would certainly have escaped, though shorn of their wealth; but they were no longer necessary for regulating industry wisely and effectively; and if they were not broken up, they had not vigor enough to maintain a useless existence (5)." The following pages will shew how far this answers to the facts. In reality, the principle of close association, which was the life of the more ancient Gilds, dominated industry and commerce for good and evil right down to the last century. Not only was this so, but the evidence now published shews the form of association as well as the spirit which animated it to have been continuous. Thus these records form a not unfitting basis for a summary of Gild history from the first traces of its appearance in the economic history of England.

The plan of this work is as follows:—Chapters I. and II. discuss the current theories as to the origin of Gilds, and their position in ante-Christian times and in Imperial Rome. Chapter III. traces their first appearance in this country in Anglo-Saxon times, and the probable sources of their origin. The obscure questions relating to the Gilda Mercatoria and

(4) Diary, Surtees Society, p. 197.

(5) Cunningham, *History of Industry*, pp. 465-6.

Hanse, especially with respect to the influence of the Continental towns, are then considered with some fulness in Chapters IV., V. and VI. The second part deals first with the remains of the religious and social Gilds of the town of Kingstown-upon-Hull from the Record Office and the archives of the Borough, and other independent sources. These range from the 14th to the 18th centuries. For this subject, in some cases, the only authorities are those external to the Borough records. In others, however, the books and charters of the Merchant Companies which remain have been studied, and shed a new and interesting light on the commercial history of the period to which they refer. The copious records of the still living Merchant Companies of York have been consulted, and afford no small help in realising the actual course of traffic in the 17th and 18th centuries. The ordinances of the Crafts are then given from the original documents either in the archives of the Corporation, or in the hands of several private owners and public institutions, together with an explanatory comment. The dates of these records are from the 15th to the 18th centuries. A chapter has been added on the place of these Gilds in economic history and their relation to modern industrial and social problems; also one on the legal and constitutional position of the Gilds; and another on the interesting question of the connection of the Gild principle with the Christian Church.

For the transcription of the "Compositions" in the archives of Kingstown-upon-Hull, I am indebted in a large degree to the Hull Literary Club and its indefatigable Secretary, Mr. William Andrews, F.R.H.S., who succeeded in obtaining the services of Mr. T. Tindall Wildridge, the Keeper of the Records, whose ability is a guarantee for the accuracy of the work, and from whom I have also received some valuable notes.

For the transcripts or translations of some of the deeds of foundation of the Religious Gilds, of the Charter and Court Records of the Merchants' Company, the references to the York archives, the account of the Coopers' Book, and the Bricklayers' Ordinances, none of which have before been published, I am myself responsible. It is a pleasure to acknowledge the kindness of many friends. The Corporation of Hull has granted me access to its Records. To Mr. Councillor Fewster I am indebted for the loan of the Coopers' Book; to the Hull Subscription Library for permission to use the MS. copy of the Bricklayers' Book; and to E. S. Wilson, Esq., F.S.A., for his kind response to my enquiries relating to the Trinity House, and the valuable MSS. of De la Pryme now in his possession. H.B.M. Vice Consul at Nisch, R. Macdonald, Esq., most courteously undertook some enquiries for me respecting the Servian Esnaifs, and M. Stogan Novakovitch, the Servian Minister at Constantinople, who is preparing a historical book on the Bulgarian towns, forwarded to me some most valuable information relating to the Gilds in that city. M. P. du Chaillu also replied very kindly to my enquiry respecting the existence of Gilds in the early history of Scandinavia. To the Rev. H. E. Maddock, M.A., I am indebted for his assistance in the translation of the Ordinances of the Collegium of Diana and Antinous. Of the shortcomings of the work I am painfully aware. In part, other duties of an exacting kind may be alleged as the reason, although they are by no means pleaded as an excuse. The authorities quoted, unless when otherwise stated, are at first hand, and are, I think, correctly referred to.

The book is made public in the hope that it may not alone be of some service in elucidating the past history of this great seaport, but may also help somewhat in stimulating a deeper and truer interest in those social and industrial problems which confront us, indeed, to-day, but which had their part to play also in days gone by.

CHAPTER I.

SOCIOLOGICAL THEORIES AS TO THE ORIGIN OF GILDS.

WHEN the townsmen of Stratford-on-Avon were required in the year 1381 to make a return to the King's Government as to the ordinances of their Gild, and the date of its foundation, they made reply that as to its origin it was "whereunto the memory of man reacheth not." The saying was a wise one. There is no institution which has had a wider distribution, or which reaches further back into the mists of ancient history. It is this well-nigh universal distribution which renders the task of estimating their historic position one of great delicacy. It is a task which may be compared with the one which confronts the student of Biology in his attempt to classify and trace the connection of the various organs of animals and plants in the light of the modern theory of evolution, and the terms which are technically used in these sciences apply equally to the subject of enquiry in a different field. As we study the social institutions of different peoples and continents we find some performing analogous functions, but in no way historically connected; others we find which have taken to themselves diverse forms, but which can be traced to a common origin and a typical progenitor. The Chinese Gild of to-day may be performing functions similar to the English Trades' Unions, but may have a completely independent origin. The ancient Phœnician Gild may have had a diverse form from the Hanseatic League, but if a historic connection can be traced, the relationship affords a basis of interest of another kind. This distinction, upon which Mr. Freeman has insisted, should be clearly drawn.

In considering the evidence which early records show as to different forms of the Gild, the problem then consists in estimating the amount of historic continuity between them, and distinguishing it from the element which is simply an independent development from the same factor in human nature. Let us then, firstly, ask what is the account sociologists have given of the natural tendencies which go to produce the general organisation of the institution known in early English history as the Gild (6), and which govern the course of its development; and secondly, enquire how far the records of the actual progress of society during historic times accord with the theory which has been laid down.

As we might expect, so universal an organisation has not escaped the encyclopædic enquiry of Mr. Herbert Spencer. His account may be summarised as follows. The combination of men in society proceeds necessarily, just as the combination of separate cells in the organic world gradually evolves the higher and complex organisations of living beings, culminating in man. Slight individual aptitudes arise among men, increase by exercise, and are transmitted by heredity; as society develops, the demand for the work produced by these individuals becomes regular, and requires a regular supply. A father naturally trains his son in the same aptitude which in time is transmitted as a hereditary tendency; and it grows into custom and law that each man shall bring up his family to his own trade. It was thus in Peru and in Egypt: skilled occupations descended from father to son, and where circumstances were favourable to that development, hardened into castes. It was so in European nations in early times. In the Theodosian codes a Roman youth "was compelled

(6) It may be as well here to justify the spelling of this word here adopted. "Guild," says Mr. Skeat, "is as false as it is common." There can be no doubt that this is so. Either in its Anglo Saxon or Latin form the u has no place. But there is something to be said for it. It will be seen that it has been in use for 260 years, and thus, like many an etymological monstrosity in our language, has acquired some of the rights of prescription. Still it is not too late to assert the earlier and better right; and it is to strengthen this that it is here written "Gild."

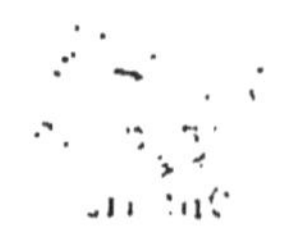

to follow the employment of his father, and the suitor who sought the hand of the daughter could only obtain the bride by becoming wedded to the calling of her family." So in mediæval France, crafts were inherited, and also in England. Then the "branching of the family through generations into a number of kindred families, carrying on the same occupation, produced the germ of the Gild," and formed a distinct cluster in towns. Then in process of time followed apprenticeship into the family circle, to learn the trade. By and bye, with increase of trade, the master developes into the trader, and the workman into the citizen. Thus the Craft Gild is the typical form of the institution (7).

The late Sir Henry Maine arrives at a somewhat similar conclusion in his memorable works on the comparative jurisprudence of the archaic forms of society. After showing that the fundamental assumption of such early states was that every man not related by blood was either an enemy or a slave, he goes on to show how this condition of "*bellum omnium contra omnes*" was modified by the fictitious relationships produced by adoption. Other tribes or families not related were admitted, and were counted as kin, and to this co-partnership he attributes in part the probable origin of Gilds. He finds an indication of this in the Roman ancient contract "*Omnium bonorum*," by which all the goods of each were brought together, and considers it probable that it was probably a survival of ancient gilds arising from these customs. In the same manner he accounts for the peculiar form which the early Irish monasteries took under purely Keltic influences. They bore strong traces of these early ideas of kinship, being called by the name of some parent saint or founder, as "The Family of Columbkille," and their membership, like that of a gild, tended to become hereditary. As is well known, the Abbacies were commonly fixed in one family or sept (8). Mr. Spencer and Sir H. Maine may be taken as representing the standard scientific and sociological opinion in the country at the present time. If

(7) H. Spencer, *Principles of Sociology*, p. 490.

(8) Maine, *Early Institutions*, Section viii.

we take in addition the words of a great German, who in accord with the wide range of his national philosophy, starting from a more metaphysical standpoint, seeks to place in due order and symmetry the various tendencies which have assisted at the historical evolution of society, we shall have a fairly complete view of the current state of theory as to the origin of Gilds in general ([9]). The author is Hermann Lotze.

> Hereditary callings are natural to dawning civilisation. Partly with the object operated upon, as in the case of the tiller of the soil, partly with the instruction which coincides with family education, where the transmission of knowledge by schools separate from the home is as yet non-existent, the calling of the parent is transmitted to the children. Free choice of some other employment is prevented by the narrowness of men's intellectual horizon, which embraces only that which is familiar, and forces them to attach themselves thereto, and by the natural jealousy with which not only the different classes of society, but also the various trades, strove to keep themselves exclusive. These customs have, however, swayed in many ways the civilisations of later times. They occurred in the dawning culture of Egypt and India, but it was only in India that the contrast between the conquering race and the native population (which was here greater than in the valley of the Nile), and moreover the influence of priestly views, developed such customs into those irremovable distinctions of Caste, which while they made certain callings obligatory, oppressed all lower castes with the graduated contempt of those which were above them. China alone never laid these fetters of Caste and Status on its industrial population, knowing no hereditary differences of rank and calling, and all being under general State guardianship: this was perhaps a happy incidental effect of the absence of religious fanaticism or warlike thirst for glory.

And here it is perhaps necessary to note the distinction lately so strongly insisted upon by Mr. H. Spencer between abstract political theory and its realisation in historical fact. We must be careful in attempting to apply these *a priori* theories to account for the origin of the gild system of any countries whatever. There is such a thing as perspective in historical theory and enquiry. These growths from the family to the trade, and from the trade to the Gild, belong to the primary strata of historical science. Only where the conditions of national life have been such as to allow of unchecked growth for long centuries together,

9) Lotze, *Microcosmus*, Vol. II., p. 351.

can we hope to find anything like a consecutive development on the lines of the ideal theory. India is the only modern country which affords such a field, and it was upon Indian experience that Sir Henry Maine largely based his conclusions. In ancient Egypt we know of little which can be said to correspond with the Gilds of Europe, and so far as I am aware, of nothing of this kind in ancient Babylon or Nineveh. Of Mexico and Peru we know too little to speak. The only other indigenous civilisation, if such it be, and not an early offshoot from the Accadian stock of Babylon, is that of China. It is true that the prevalence of secret associations and trade gilds is a strongly marked feature of the modern Chinese people. But what we know of these trade gilds tends to show that they are of quite recent development, and probably of comparatively recent origin. So far as our present information extends they present no evidence of being a stage in social evolution from family life.

As the theory rests then upon the case of India, it will be useful to give in full Sir William Hunter's very interesting account of the present system of Gilds in that country (10), especially as it may be convenient for future comparison.

> Each caste is to some extent a trade guild, a mutual assurance society, and a religious sect. As a trade union it insists on the proper training of the youth of its craft, regulates the wages of its members, deals with delinquents, and promotes good fellowship by social gatherings. The famous fabrics of mediæval India, and its chief local industries in our own day, were developed under the supervision of caste or trade guilds of this sort. Such guilds may yet be found in many parts of India, but not always with the same complete development. In Ahmedabad District each different trade or manufacture forms a separate guild. All heads of artisan households are ranged under their proper guild. The objects of the guild are to regulate competition among the members, and to uphold the interest of the body in any dispute arising with other craftsmen. To moderate competition the guild appoints certain days as trade holidays, when any member who works is punished by a fine. A special case occurred in 1873 among the Ahmedabad bricklayers. Men of this class sometimes added 3d. to their daily wages by working extra time in the early morning. But several families were thrown out of employment, and accordingly the guild met and decided that as there was

(10) *Indian Empire*, pp. 183-185.

not employment for all, no man should be allowed to work extra time.

The decisions of the guild are enforced by fines, and if the offender refuses to pay, and the members of the guild all belong to one caste, the offender is put out of caste. If the guild contains men of different castes, the guild uses its influence with other guilds to prevent the recusant member from getting work. The guild also acts in its corporate capacity against other crafts. For example, in 1872 the Ahmedabad cloth-dealers resolved amongst themselves to reduce the rates paid to the sizers or tagias. The sizers' guild refused to prepare cloth at the lower rates, and remained six weeks on strike. At length a compromise was arrived at and both guilds signed an agreement on stamped paper. Besides its punitive fines the guild draws an income from fees on persons beginning to practice its craft. This custom prevails at Ahmedabad in the cloth and other industries, but no fee is paid by potters, carpenters, and inferior artizans. An exception is made too in the case of a son succeeding to his father, when nothing has to be paid. In other cases the amount varies in proportion to the importance of the trade from £5 to £50. The revenue derived from these fees and from fines is expended on feasts to the members of the guild and in support of poor craftsmen and their orphans, and in charity.

A favourite device for raising money in Surat is for the members of a trade to agree to keep a certain date as a holiday, and to shut up all the shops except one: the right to keep open this one shop is let by auction, and the amount bid is credited to the guild fund.

Within the guild the interests of the common trade sometimes overpower the race element of the caste. Thus in Surat each class of craftsmen, although including men of different castes and races, combine to form a guild with a council and head man, and a common purse for charity and entertainments. But indeed in Ahmedabad, Broach, and many industrial centres the trade organization into guilds exists side by side with the race structure of caste. The twofold organization also appears in the village community. Caste regulates the theoretical position of any family within it, but the low castes often claim the headship of the village government. In the Básárat Sub-district in Bengal of 5818 enumerated village heads, only 15 were Brahmins or Rajputs, 4 were Kásyaths, while 3524 belonged to the Sudra or inferior castes down to the detested cowskinners and corpse bearers; the balance being Mohammedans, with 13 native Christians. In Southern India the village head is sometimes of so low a caste that he cannot sit under the same roof with his colleagues in the village government. He therefore hands up his staff, which is set in the place of honour, while he himself squats on the ground outside. The trade guilds in the cities and the village communities in the country act together with caste as mutual assurance societies, and in ordinary times allow none of their members to starve. Caste, and the trading or agricultural guilds concurrent with it, take the place of a poor law in India.

In this account are several points worthy of notice. The caste system and the gilds are not coterminous. A Gild contains men of different castes, and this in the same village community. Caste we know is not one of the most ancient institutions of Indian life, but it is nevertheless very ancient. The Craft Gild for its development requires, on the other hand, a considerable development of town and industrial life. The hereditary smith or carpenter exists long before he can organise his descendants into a gild; for a gild means a considerable supply and demand. For this course of uninterrupted development to occur an undisturbed growth of society must take place for long centuries. Even in India the requisite conditions seem wanting. There may well be an historic connection between Caste and Gild; direct descent of the latter from the former is certainly not proved. On the other hand, the close interaction of the two, at any rate in their later stages, is clear enough. But the course of growth between the hereditary trade of the members of the village community and the fully formed Gild is a long one, and the proof of its actual occurrence is wanting. Many another influence must have intervened in the formation of the Gild as it now appears.

The Gild appears in maturity while the family retains its ancient strength. Its bond of unity intersects the circle of the kin, natural or extended, it does not coincide with it. If the course of evolution be as has been suggested, it is hidden in archaic times—it does not form a page in history.

The remark which would doubtless be made by Mr. Spencer would be that the explanation is to be found in the analogy of animal life. Just as one of the higher animals, such as man, does not actually pass through the complete series of lower forms through which the race has reached the result of the human organism before it arrives at maturity, so with the higher social organism. The traces of these successive steps are to be found if we watch the development of the embryo, but they are traces only, yet from germ to vertebrate the series is the same. So it may be with a higher grade of social organism. We cannot see that a mediæval gild passed through the series from family to hereditary calling, and the rest; but we shall be able to trace the same course of development in the psychological and social processes which have produced it. It may be so. Our present position is that for historical purposes of enquiry within our 2000 years we shall be compelled practically to treat the process as non-existent.

The importance of these considerations will be immediately evident. The question which we have to solve is practically the origin of the mediæval Gild of Central and Western Europe. Is it possible to account for the development of these institutions in any of these lands by the foregoing theory of normal evolution? Setting aside for a moment the treatment of the Roman and Greek civilisations, and their origin, we can lay down with very fair accuracy the periods between which, if at all, it must have taken place. It must have occurred between the periods of the dissolution of the Roman Empire and the dawn of a new epoch in the 9th or 10th century. There were no such indigenous institutions among the Germanic tribes at the earlier period, and they appear fully formed at the later. The exact evidence as to this country we shall see at a later stage. At present it is enough to point out that the duration of time, and the known circumstances of Europe at the time in question, render such an orderly development simply impossible. We might as well attempt to cram the separation of the English coast from France into the period between the foundation of Rome and the landing of Julius Cæsar. On the other hand, both in France and England, at the beginning of the period, there were beyond question throughout each country many examples of fully-formed and highly-matured Gilds, which owed their existence to an earlier civilisation. In the face of these, a purely indigenous origin from these natural causes could not take place. There may well have been a complex indigenous development of the associative principle; in any case, if there were even an adaptation of a foreign institution, there must have been a strong infusion of native elements, and an adaptation to new conditions, but there would not have been a purely natural development from the archaic forms of the family and the tribe. As Dr. Gross says, the dissolution of the family was the occasion, perhaps, but not the origin, of the Gild. Leaving now the discussion of *a priori* principles we will endeavour to trace the historical facts which have come down to us respecting the Gild in its earliest forms.

CHAPTER II.

GILDS IN GREEK AND ROMAN ANTIQUITY.

THE earliest extant written code of Aryan laws is said to be that contained in the twelve tables of Rome. It is indeed held to be only a reduction to writing of customs and laws, of some of which we have independent evidence in ages long previous; and it contains also evidence of the strong idiosyncrasy of the Roman state, but its witness is on any subject irrefragable for the 5th century B.C. It provides:—"Sodales legem quam volent, dum ne quid ex publica lege corrumpant, sibi serunto." Thus early did the Roman law lay down the principle which we shall find enunciated in our law courts in England nearly 2000 years after as an exposition of the law and customs of England. As Blackstone says, every corporation has "the right to make bye-laws or private statutes for the better government of the corporation, which are binding upon themselves unless contrary to the law of the land [11]." In his statement, however, that the world owes to Roman law the origin of the conception of corporations, Blackstone goes too far. A classical example to the contrary, though not the earliest that might be quoted, is to be seen in the foundation of the School of Plato. On his death, he bequeathed his garden and appointments in the place called after the hero Hekademus, to his followers. "But he was obliged to do it in the only way possible at Athens. He made it a religious foundation, on the basis of a fixed worship of the Muses—a Mouseion—which was to be perpetually rendered by his school in *monthly offerings*, accompanied by a reunion of the members, and *a common feast*. As Williamowitz has shown in an

(11) Blackstone, Book II., Chapter 18, 2.

interesting appendix to his "Antigonus of Karystos," this was the form of all private clubs and associations at Athens, and was the thoroughly legal cloak under which very illegal and immoral objects were often concealed. The right of private association, with fixed contributions, which the society had the same right of enforcing as our clubs have, appears to have dated from the days of Solon. The head or president of Plato's "Association of the Muses" "was the treasurer and manager of the common fund, who invited guests to the feasts, to which each member contributed his share (ερανος). . . This, then, was the first academy, so often imitated in so many lands, and of which our colleges are the direct descendants ([12])." Similarly, Grote speaks of the Eikadeis, "an association the members of which are bound to each other by a common oath, as well as by a curse which the mythical hero of the association, Eikadeus, is supposed to have imprecated. They possess common property, and it was held contrary to the oath for any of the members to enter into a pecuniary process against the Koinon, or community ([13])." Here we have the monthly feast, the offerings, the perpetual succession, the presiding genii or saints, and, in Plato's case, the perpetually handed down craft, the philosophic craft, which were the characteristics of a gild, either social, or religious, or craft, in Hull in the 14th century.

There are thus two collateral types of this kind of association, in Greece and in Rome, which we can trace from certain evidence down from the 5th century B.C., but which, on their first appearance in historic form, appear as already fixed social institutions, and, by presumption, of considerable antiquity. Each of these must claim a share of our attention. The institutions of Greece had not any direct influence on those of Teutonic Europe. It was not till many centuries after the political importance of Hellas proper had vanished, that the larger Hellas, the Greek-speaking people of the Mediterranean, began to influence the Western world. We shall have occasion, shortly, to note of what

(12) Mahaffy.

(13) Vol. VIII., p. 23.

kind this influence was. This, however, is by anticipation. Our first course must be to give a short account of the Roman societies.

According to Mommsen, eight gilds of craftsmen were numbered among the institutions of King Numa, that is, among the institutions which had existed at Rome from time immemorial. These were as follows :—

Flute-blowers,	Goldsmiths,
Coppersmiths,	Carpenters,
Fullers,	Dyers,
Potters,	Shoemakers,

a list which probably exhausts the class of contemporary tradesmen working to order and for the purposes of sale. It bears evidence of great antiquity. There is no gild of bakers, whether from the fact that the baking of bread was not known, as Mommsen thinks, or from the fact that it was performed by the women of the household. There was no professional art of healing, though possibly the colleges of the priests, if such existed, performed what was customary at the time. Wool was spun into clothing in the household. There was no gild of workers in iron, probably because the time had not yet arrived when iron had taken the place of copper. The importance of these societies in the urban life of Rome was very considerable, and not to be measured by the depressed condition of Roman handicrafts in later times when slavery so largely supplanted free labour. "The oldest lays of Rome celebrate not only the war-god Mamers, but also the skilled armourer Mamuvius, who understood the art of forging for his fellow burgesses shields similar to the divine model shield which had fallen from heaven ; and then in the earliest Rome, as elsewhere, the art of forging and of welding the ploughshare and the sword went hand in hand, and there was none of that arrogant contempt for handicrafts which we afterwards meet with there." After the Servian military re-organisation, the artizans, probably from the lack of a freehold qualification, very largely lost the position which they had previously possessed, only the carpenters, coppersmiths, and musicians, as directly subsidiary to military life, were attached to the army. The ordinances of these early Roman societies are unknown. That there was some mode of excluding unskilful persons, Mommsen thinks probable, but no traces are to be met with either of monopolising tendencies, or of protective steps against inferior manufactures; he adds, however, that there is no aspect of the life of the Roman people respecting which the information is so scanty as that of the Roman trades (14). Such as it is, however, it is clear and irrefragable as to the existence and importance of the societies in question. The stirring political life of Rome, and the constant influx of the spoil and luxury of conquered peoples, would necessarily interfere with the natural progress from organisation to monopoly which has everywhere marked their progress where scope has been afforded to their development. Rome lacked the noble fruit as well as the abuse of artizan life. In Mommsen's noble words, "When man no longer finds enjoyment in work, and works merely to attain as quickly as possible to enjoyment, it is a mere accident that he does not become a criminal."

We have one other isolated mention of a Gild among the higher class of trades, though as to its exact historic value it is impossible to speak with certainty. Livy (II., 27) tells us that B.C. 493, "There was a contest between the consuls as to which of them should dedicate the temple to Mercury. The Senate refused to decide the matter and referred it to the people, passing a vote that to whichever of them the dedication should be granted, the same should preside over the markets, should institute a college of merchants, and join the pontiff in the performance of the ceremonies usual on such occasions. The people gave the dedication to Marcus Lætorius, a centurion of the first rank." After this the Collegia and Sodalicia almost disappear from sight until the mists of storm and battle and revolution began to clear away, and the calm of the Roman peace to settle over the vast Empire which owned the rule of the Cæsars. There is no reason to suppose that they ceased to exist. Their life continued

(14) Mommsen, *History*, I. p. 208.

to flow like a subterranean stream till its level should be reached once more in the sight of men. It was merely that there was no place for them in the great drama of the history of the age.

Although, however, the scope for free organisation among artizans was narrowed, the tendency towards those associations which were peculiarly social and religious in aim seems to have survived and acquired greater force. It is not possible to draw a hard and fast line between the two. Some Collegia were partly craft and partly religious gilds, some were religious only, but none so far as I am aware were entirely destitute of religious form and ceremony. The relationship seems to have been more nearly that prevailing in the mediæval Gilds of England, where the two ran imperceptibly into each other, and every Craft Gild had its religious side, than that of France where the Gild of the craft and the fraternity for religious observance tended more to be kept separate, and the members of the one were often independently members of the other. Brentano and Toulmin Smith have discussed at some length the question whether the old English Gild, which had no trade significance, is properly to be described as social or religious, and the same question meets us when we consider the Collegia and Sodalicia of Rome. The decision favoured by Mr. Smith was that the social element preponderated. It will be well, however, to observe that the distinction is one which in both cases arises simply from modern ideas. Among all ancient people, and up to a period in Europe even subsequent to the Reformation, no such division was in fact possible, and to apply it to the old institutions partakes of an anachronism. The social life was itself religious, and the religious life was itself social. People had altars in their houses and feasted in the temple precincts, and with all allowance for the imperfection of the religious ideas of the times, admitting that the effect was to lower the ideal of religion as well as to lend a sanction to social life, there can be no doubt that to this close relationship much of the unity of ancient life was due.

To say this, however, is by no means to get to the root of the matter. This aspect of society had really its origin in one of the most deeply rooted customs of mankind. We need not admit with M. F. de Coulanges, that the whole fabric of ancient society was built upon the worship of the ancestral manes, or with Mr. H. Spencer, that the chief source of all religion is to be found in the funeral rites and the ceremonies and ideas which grew up around these, but there can no longer be any doubt as to the extent to which these customs, and the beliefs with which they were connected, permeated all ancient modes of thought. The Lares and Penates were in fact of more real importance in the religion of Rome than Jupiter or Minerva and the gods of the Republic. It was *pro aris et focis* that men fought and died, and the presiding genii of the altars were those of ancestors, often mythical enough, whose spirits still dwelt on the ancestral hearth. For the spirit of the dead still lingered near the place of sepulture of the Greek and Roman as about those of the ancient Kelt and pre-historic man, as he flits to-day round the burial homes of the Chinese. Periodically he returns, waits and watches till his surviving relatives come with their offerings of food and memorial prayers, takes the vacant seat at the banquet which they spread, and joins in their festivity at the anniversary feast. Just as the Hindoo is content to die if he leaves a representative to perform the obsequies and duties to the dead, so, though hardly to the same extent, was the undercurrent of thought in the mind of the Roman.

Hence when we leave out of sight the purely religious Collegia of the priests, which were rather the crafts and gilds of the priestly profession, to say that the Collegia were religious societies is to imply that they were burial societies and also social clubs. As we have seen in the case of Plato's school, they were generally established under the patronage of some god or hero, just as a mediæval gild took the name of a saint. *Cultores Dianæ*, etc., are the titles that constantly meet us in the inscriptions that remain. As members, they were bound together for certain purposes of social and common good, one of which was, as we learn from Cicero, the avoidance of lawsuits between brethren of the same society. The same object is aimed at in the ordinances of the Gilds of modern China, and was universal in the Gilds of later Europe. It is a very curious and interesting question indeed whether when St. Paul asks his Corinthian converts, "Does a brother go to law with brother," he is not so much propounding a principle totally opposed to all pagan practice, as appealing *a fortiori* to the members of the Christian Society not to lag behind the brethren of the heathen societies around, for we must remember that the Roman element was especially strong in the Corinth of that day. The ancient Gilds had indeed their periodical feasts in common, provided for by regular monthly payments or contributions, but the real festivals of the societies were the burial feasts and anniversaries of which the "wake" is a degenerate modern representative. We cannot do better than give the curious example of this which has been brought to light by modern discoveries in the neighbourhood of Rome. The inscription reads as follows:—"The place or field which lies on the Appian Way between the second and third milestones . . . on the estate of Julia Monime and other partners, on which there is erected a Schola under a portico, consecrated to Silvanus and the members of that brotherhood, has been conveyed, free of incumbrance, to the curator and the whole body of members of that brotherhood, for a nominal price by Julia Monime and her partners . . . . that the members may be free to assemble at that place to offer sacrifice, to eat, and to make their banquets, so long as that brotherhood endures." (15) So elaborate were provisions such as these that we have cases in which rugs, carpets, and festal robes were permanently kept for these strange anniversary feasts, with a costly statue of the founder at the head of the banquet, and a solemn injunction added that "all are to remain till the amount contributed has been finished."

In order to put before the reader a complete example of the organisation of these societies, as a basis for future comparison, we now give a translation of the deed of foundation (16) of one formed in the reign of Hadrian at Lanuvium in Italy, and found

(15) Orelli Henzen, No. 4917, quoted by O. B. Brown, *From Schola to Cathedral*, p. 18.
(16) Mommsen *De Collegiis et Sodaliciis Romanorum, Appendix.*

in 1816 inscribed upon the interior of the temple of Antinous. It should be compared with the deed of foundation of the Gild of St. John the Baptist, of Kingston-upon-Hull, of the year A.D. 1357, or with the account of the Anglo-Saxon Gilds, in subsequent chapters of this present work.

INSCRIPTION AT LANUVIUM.

(a) In the Consulship of L. Ciconius Commodus and Sextus Vetulenus Civica Pompeianus, on the 9th of June.

In the municipal town of Lanuvium, in the temple of Antinous, L. Cæsennius Rufus, thrice (b) *Dictator* and Patron of the town, ordered a meeting to be held, at which meeting he promised, through L. Pompeius . . . the (c) *President of the Gild* of the worshippers of Diana and Antinous, that of his liberality he would grant them annually (d) *the proceeds* of 15000 sesterces, *i.e.*, 400 sesterces on the 13th of August, the Festival of Diana, and 400 sesterces on the 27th of November, (e) the *Festival of Antinous*, and he ordered that the rules drawn up by the members should be inscribed on the interior of the portico of the temple of Antinous in the following words:—In the consulship of M. Antonius Hiberus and P. Mummius Sisenna, on the first of January, the Gild and Benefit Society of Diana and Antinous was formed under the patronage of L. Cæsennius Rufus (the son of L. Cæsennius Quirinus) thrice Dictator and also (f) *Patron* of the town, in accordance with the following decree of the Senate of Rome:—

License is hereby given to the following persons to hold meetings and assemblies, and to form a Gild. Those who wish to make a monthly contribution for funeral expenses are hereby permitted to meet once in each month for the business of the Gild, that is to contribute to a fund for the burial of their dead, but meetings more than once a month under pretence of transacting the business of the Gild are strictly forbidden.

Happiness, prosperity and good health to the Emperor Cæsar Trajanus Hadrianus Augustus, and to our princes of the whole house of Augustus, and to our Gild; and let us do our very best to pay them due honour on their decease. We all of us, therefore, by contributing right well, should work together with one mind, that the society may reach a good old age. If you wish (g) for admission into this Gild, first read through our rules, and then become a member, so that you may not afterwards have cause of complaint, or leave to your heir occasion for dispute.

(a) *i.e.*, A.D. 133. L. Ciconius Commodus was adopted by Hadrian, A.D. 130, under the name of L. Ælius Verus Cæsar.

(b) Cicero pro Mil § 10 mentions a Dictator of Lanuvium, a title possibly continued in that town to the time of Hadrian, though long obsolete in Rome.

(c) QQ.—Quinquennalem, usual name for president of a society or county town.

(d) The legal rate of interest fixed by Justinian was ½ per cent. per month, which would produce 900 sesterces as interest of 15000 sesterces. Allowing 100 for management, this would give 800 per annum. The more usual rate under the Emperors was 12 per cent.

(e) Antinous, favourite of Hadrian, drowned in the Nile, A.D. 122. Natalis dies may be the anniversary either of his birth or death, or of the day in which his statue was set up in this particular temple.

(f) *i.e.*, Consul-General at Rome for the interests of the town.

(g) Novos = Novus.

THE RULES OF THE GILD.

It was resolved unanimously that everyone wishing for admission into this Gild should contribute, as an entrance fee, 100 sesterces and a jar of good wine, and also pay 5 asses a month.

Also that if any member should not have paid his contributions month by month continuously up to his decease, no payment be made at his death, even though he may have assigned by will the money due at his decease.

Also that if any member of our Gild die with his contributions fully paid up, there shall be paid on his account 400 sesterces from the common chest, from which sum shall be deducted as a fee for attendance at his funeral (*h*) one sesterce [a head ?], to be distributed among the members present at the funeral pile. The procession shall follow on foot.

(*h*) ? May H S / N be an error for H S *L* N., *i.e.* 50 sesterces. It appears, however, from the next clause, that the fee for attendance was one sesterce a head.

Also that if any member die beyond the 20th milestone from the town, and his death be duly reported, three members chosen from our body shall proceed to the place to take charge of his funeral, and shall render a full and true account to the members of the Gild, and if any fraud be discovered they shall be fined fourfold. As a fee (for attendance at the funeral) they shall receive one sesterce apiece, and in addition, as journey money there and back, 20 sesterces. But if the death take place beyond the 20th milestone, and notice cannot possibly be given, then whoever may have undertaken the funeral shall be entitled, on producing a document to that effect attested by the seals of seven Roman citizens, and after proving his case (to the satisfaction of the Gild), to have the funeral money paid to him in accordance with the rules of the Gild, with the deduction of all loans and the amount distributed among the members on the occasion of a funeral, provided that he have previously given a guarantee that no further claim be made upon the Gild.

Let all fraud be far from our Gild, and let no claim be made upon the Gild by any former master or mistress of a freedman, or by any master or mistress of a slave, or by any creditor, but only by the person named in the will as the heir. If any member die intestate the arrangements for his funeral shall be left to the discretion of the president and the members.

It was also resolved that if any slave shall have deceased, being a member of this Gild, and his body be wrongfully kept from burial by his master or mistress, and no (*i*) *will* be forthcoming, then his effigy shall be buried with funeral honours. If anyone shall have committed

(*i*) A slave could not make a legal testamentum, but could leave documents (tabellæ) disposing of his peculium—*i.e.*, all property he could legally possess apart from his master's control.

suicide no payment shall be made at his death. If any slave, a member of this Gild, receive his freedom he shall contribute a jar of good wine.

If any member be Master for his year, according to the order of the Roll, for the purpose of providing a feast, and fail to perform the duties of his office, he shall pay to the public chest 30 sesterces, and his successor shall provide the feast on his behalf, and he shall repay him by providing the feast in his successor's turn.

THE ORDER OF THE FEASTS.

Feasts shall be held on the 8th of March, the birthday of Cæsennius, the father (of our founder); on the 27th of November, the Festival of Antinous; on the 13th of August, the Festival of Diana and our Gild; on the 20th of August, the birthday of Cæsennius Silvanus, the brother of our founder; on the birthday of Cornelia Procula, his mother; on the 14th of December, the birthday of L. Cæsennius Rufus, the patron of the town.

The Masters of the feasts appointed in the order of the Roll shall make the following provision for each mess of four members. For every mess up to the full number of the members of the Gild, they shall provide a jar of wine, and loaves of (j) *bread to the value of 2 asses*, four Sardian fish, table linen, hot water and attendance.

(j) Possibly "2 loaves of white bread."

It was also resolved that any member appointed President of the Gild shall be exempt from the levies due during his term of office, and shall have a double share in all distributions. The secretary and (k) *messenger* shall also be exempt from their levies, and in every distribution shall receive a share and a half.

(k) Perhaps porter, or beadle.

Any member who shall have served in the office of President faithfully and well, shall receive as an honorarium a share and a half of all distributions among the members, that others may be encouraged to follow his example.

If any member have any complaint or appeal to make, let him bring it forward at a regular meeting, so that on our festival days we may feast in peace and merriment.

If anyone change his seat at table through ill-feeling, he shall be fined 4 sesterces; if he speak insultingly to another member, or cause a disturbance, he shall be fined 12 sesterces; but if he speak insultingly or disrespectfully to the President during a feast the fine shall be 20 sesterces.

It was also resolved that on every festival day during his term of office the President shall make offerings of frankincense and wine, and perform all the other duties of his office in a white robe; and on the Festivals of Diana and Antinous he shall before the feast provide oil in the public bath for the use of the Gild.

The regulations shewing the community of men of wealth, freedmen and slaves, in the same society, the picture of harmonious social entertainment, have no detracting features, and point to the humanising effect such institutions must have had upon pagan society. They shew that the statement of Uhlhorn that it was only in Christian times that the beneficial character of these institutions was introduced must be recorded with some modification. What is true is that this charitable element was more strongly developed under Christian influences.

It will be remarked that the above constitute the rules of a purely religious Gild; there is nothing of the element of craft in them. Nor is it possible to give the exact ordinances of such a Gild, for we have none remaining to us. But it is certain that there was no essential difference between them. Add the purely technical element, and the above will serve as a type of the Collegia of the crafts. Our loss of these technical ordinances, from an industrial and economical point of view, cannot be too much deplored, but the principle of association is the same.

We can well understand the relationship of the Gilds to the Government of the day. Every Government must necessarily guard carefully the right of association. That only the King can make a Corporation is an old maxim of English law, and the despotism of the Cæsars had still more need for jealousy of the right of combination among its subjects. Hence we find the same rigorous attempts to put down the adulterine or unauthorised Gilds. Charlemagne was equally jealous of the Gilds in his day. Especially Trajan is noted as being rigorous in his prohibition. But the same result followed in ancient as in mediæval times. The tendency was too ingrained to disappear at the fiat of any Government, and the prohibition soon gave way to the wiser policy of state recognition and regulation which marked the reign of Alexander Severus. In these vicissitudes, however, as we have seen, the purely religious or burial Gild had a more even

course. Its functions, if genuine, could in no case be injurious to the realm. To bury Cæsar's friends was meritorious, while to bury his enemies was still more commendable. Hence the exception which was made to the rule in their favour, an exception which proved of momentous importance to the growing church of the Christian faith. Meanwhile, whatever the difficulties that may have lain in their path, the Gilds of the workmen continued not only at Rome but wherever the Roman civilisation had penetrated. As early as the reign of Claudius we have an inscription showing the existence of a Collegium Fabrorum or Craft Gild of the smiths in Britain, left undissolved by Augustus as "*legitima et antiqua*," and as our means of information become more diffuse under the later Emperors, their number rivalled that to be found in the cities of mediæval Europe. Upwards of nearly eighty of these trade societies are mentioned in the inscriptions. Masons and carpenters, soldiers and sailors, bakers and cooks, corn merchants and wine merchants, hunters and fishermen, goldsmiths and blacksmiths, dealers in drugs and carders in wool, boatmen and divers, doctors and bankers, scribes and musicians, all had their Gilds, and these must have formed an element in the social and even political life of the time of far greater importance than has been recognised in the standard histories of the times ([17]). If, however, we cannot reproduce verbatim their ordinances, we can say with tolerable certainty what was the manner in which they conducted their business. Each Gild had its lodge room called a *schola*, a name still surviving in Italy for the same thing. This was a small building of greater length than breadth, and with an apsidal termination like that of the traditional Christian Church, where sat the president for the time being of the Gild ([18]). There were also the *arca* or strong chest for the contributions and valuables, the regular meetings, the common oath, the ordinances, and the feasts. The analogy between this institution of 1600

(17) *Roma Sotterranea*, Northcote and Brownlow, p. 49.

(18) In Mr. Young's *Annals of the Barber Surgeons*, 1890, p. 185, is a plan of the Livery Hall of the Company, which is exactly similar to the plans of *Scholæ* in Imperial Rome.—See *From Schola to Cathedral*, by C. G. Brown, where several of these plans are given.

years ago and an Oddfellows Hall of to-day will at once suggest itself.

We will now turn to the kindred institutions which, *pari passu*, and doubtless not without mutual influence, grew up in the Eastern provinces under the Imperial rule in the realm of that larger Hellenism which resulted from the conquests of Alexander and his successors, and follow its course till we see it merged in the course of development of Western Europe.

Over those favoured lands, now silent and blighted beneath the sway of Islam, at the period of the Antonines was spread a busy and pleasure-loving people, covering the valleys with gardens and cities, and producing a state of material prosperity which has never been equalled in those regions before or since. Antioch, with its colonnaded street 4½ miles in length, cool and sheltered by day, and artificially lighted at night, with flowing water in every street; Tyre, with its still famous looms; Alexandria, then greater than now, with its rectangular streets like a modern American city; were but the chief examples of the general civilisation of the Imperial time. "Wherever," says Mommsen, "even a corner of the country is now opened out, then the first and most powerful feeling is that of astonishment, one might almost say of shame, at the contrast of the wretched and pitiful present with the happiness of the past Roman age." In such a condition of peaceful prosperity, trade and industry attained a very high level of importance. At Hierapolis, a merchant caused it to be inscribed on his tomb that he had sailed 72 times round Cape Malea to Italy. At one little town in the Rough Cilicia, Corycus, "the Christians were wont, contrary to the usual custom, to append regularly in their tomb inscriptions the station in life. On the epitaphs there were found by Langlois and Duchesne, a *notarius*, a wine dealer, two oil dealers, a green-grocer, a fruit dealer, two retail dealers, five goldsmiths, one of whom is also a presbyter; four coppersmiths, two instrument makers, five potters, one of whom is ἐργοδότης and the other a presbyter, a clothes dealer, two linen dealers, three weavers, a worker in wool, two shoemakers, a skinner, a mariner, a midwife, and a joint tomb of "the highly reputable money changers." (10) Such was the division of trades even in a small country town. That these several trades had their Gilds we know from many examples. At Ephesus was the "Gild of the Wool Weavers," the earliest also of the mediæval Craft Gilds of Europe.

If we ask now the extent of this commerce the answer may probably be given that in some respects it compares favourably with that of the present day. This was certainly the case with regard to the great overland trade routes from Eastern and Central Asia. This region is one of the most interesting in the world. Now where Mongolian and Thibetan live in pastoral ignorance or isolated superstition, were formerly flourishing towns, the seat of powerful kingdoms when the successors of Alexander established themselves there. Macedonian merchants penetrated to Sera in Eastern China. The trade from India came over the Indus and the passes of Afghanistan, and part passed over the Euphrates to Syria, part along the Oxus to the Caspian, thence to the Euxine and the West. Now the Oxus flows no more into the Caspian, the ancient routes are deserted, and the Russian railroad is crossing their tracks. In the time of the Empire raw silk came regularly from China by way of the Caspian Sea, and so to Syria to be worked up in the looms of Tyre and Berytus; vast stores came by the Euphrates routes from Central Asia, where Persia and Babylonia were still the seats of considerable industry; leather and skin goods, spices, and slaves were brought in large quantities to Antioch and Apamœa. Through Egypt passed a regular trade in the wares of India, the direct route across the Indian Ocean by the Monsoon having been discovered by Hippalus in the reign of Nero, and Roman gold coins became naturalised in India. In the Chinese Annals of the date A.D. 166, it is recorded that an embassy from Autun of Ta Tsin (Great Rome) landed at Tonking, and thence journeying by the land route arrived at the Emperor's seat at Wang: probably, Mommsen thinks, it may have been some venturous sea captain of the time of the Antonines. This vast traffic passed from the Levant along

(10) Mommsen, *Roman Provinces*, I., p. 859, Note. This was in 5th or 6th century.

the shore of the Mediterranean to Italy, Northern Africa, Gaul, Spain, and Britain. The intercourse between regions so distant as Syria and Britain was probably in some respects easier than it was a century ago. Plutarch speaks of a conversation he had at Athens with a Greek teacher of languages from Tarsus returning home from Britain. But it is to our purpose to note the peculiar means by which the traffic with which we are concerned was carried on. The caravan traffic was carried on by fixed companies of merchants who travelled under their *συνοδιαρχης* or caravan leaders, men of considerable standing, whose monuments are still to be seen at Palmyra, reminding us strangely of a monument in Holy Trinity Church, Hull, to certain of the merchant adventurers of a much later date. At Palmyra also was a notable Gild of workers in gold and silver (20). If we trace this commerce farther westwards across the Mediterranean we find the same system prevailing; the merchants largely took their wares—they did not sit at home and send them as they do now. Homer tells us how ubiquitous was the Phœnician trader of his day, and the Syrian Greek-speaking merchant of the Imperial period was his descendant. The ship captains in Syria formed not only a prominent and respected class, but also an organised body. Thus we find under Augustus at Aradus a *προβουλος των ναυαρχησαντῶν*, which can only answer to "President of the Shipmasters' Gild." At the most frequented ports they had "factories," which were, it appears, much more than mere warehouses and depots. The "Totius Orbis Descriptio" says, "They serve in the first instance for religious ends, *i.e.*, for the worship of the Syrian gods in a foreign place, and for this purpose a contribution was levied on all the mariners, which was employed for the expenses of the place of meeting." In the later period of the Empire, Syrian merchants, chiefly Apamœan, are found settled not merely in all Italy, but in all the larger emporia of the West: at Malaca in Spain, and above all in Gaul and Germany; at Bordeaux, Lyons, and Paris; at Orleans and Treves. They are found in these Gallic towns after the Frankish

(20) See Mommsen's *Roman Provinces*, II., pp. 99 and 130, *et seq.*

conquest, and Salvianus and Gregory of Tours both speak of them, and show that they retained their national customs and organisations. Here then at length we find the Roman cities of Gaul, and probably also of Britain, with their Collegia and Sodalicia, brought into close contact with the trade associations of the Syrians, representing the Greek and Phœnician tendencies of the commercial East; and this in full force while the Anglo-Saxon conquest was in progress in Britain. Cities like London and York cannot have been strange to these ubiquitous traders.

The importance of these facts will be at once perceived by the reader. The Trades' Gilds were doubtless sufficiently identical as to amalgamate, or to be hardly distinguishable. But the factory of the Phœnicians or Apamœan merchants "serving also," as the "Totius Orbis Descriptio" says, "for the worship of Syrian gods in a strange place," is an organisation of a distinct though kindred type. Its analogy is to be found in the Hanse or Merchant Gild in its most marked form as the settlement of compatriot merchants in a foreign place. Such in later days was the Teutonic Hanse of London or the earlier London Hanse of the Flemish cities. Such were the great Hanseatic settlements in Novgorod and Wisby and Bergen, and such with every probability was the settlement of the "Men of the Emperor" privileged to trade by the laws of Athelstan. It is not intended to be asserted that these were the lineal descendants of the more ancient form of the Merchant Gild, but it is important to point out the contact of the two.

We have now traced the ancient form of the Gild from the earliest evidence in the 5th century B.C. up to the period of the dissolution of the Roman imperial government, and the foundation of the kingdoms of mediæval Europe; that is for an uninterrupted course of 1000 years. We have seen how strong was their hold wherever man had attained to such a level of civilisation as allowed of their existence. We have yet to take up the broken and tangled threads of their history, and to trace the earliest forms in which similar institutions appear in the cities of the Middle Ages.

CHAPTER III.

THE ORIGIN AND EARLIEST FORMS OF THE ENGLISH GILD.

THE question as to the origin and earliest forms of the Gild in England cannot be dismissed as one of slight or wholly secondary importance. Viewed either from a historical or an economic standpoint, many questions present themselves which are vital to the clear understanding of the social, municipal, and economic growth of the people. The part they played in maintaining social order; the elements belonging to them which are now interwoven with the municipal and mercantile institutions of England; the completeness with which they embraced the early trade and handicraft of the country; all forbid us from dismissing their ancient history as unimportant because it is undoubtedly obscure. The most recent exponent of this view is Mr. Ashley in his valuable instalment of "Economic History." After his account of the rise of the Merchant and Craft Gilds into prominence in the period succeeding the Norman Conquest, Mr. Ashley concludes as follows:—"When the place of the young manufactures of the 12th century in the development of mediæval society is thus conceived, the discussion as to a possible Roman origin of the Gild loses much of its interest." From the point of view of a continuous development of the fully-formed Trades Gild from that date, whether "merchant" or "craft," this may be a justifiable statement of the case; but from the higher standpoint of an enquiry into economic history in its complete evolution, the task of distinguishing the threads of historical continuity which come down from earlier civilisations in the creations of mediæval Europe, as seen in the 13th century Gild, by no means lacks interest or importance.

Whence came the mould in which these institutions from Berwick to Dover were cast? Was it an indigenous product from the conditions of old English life, or was it partly a survival from the men of that more ancient world between which and the England of the Angevins the great gulf of Anglo-Saxon and Danish conquests yawns as an impassable chasm? It may seem a bold deed even yet to suggest that any detraction must be made from the well-rounded conclusions which have been drawn by those who have described, with such ingenuity and distinguished learning, the method of the foundation of the English nation and English institutions from the purely Teutonic race which overran the island during the 5th, 6th, and 7th centuries. It has become a shibboleth of patriotism to accept as a matter of indisputable fact the practical annihilation of the Roman colonists and the indigenous Belgic or Lloegrian and Keltic population, and to depict the growth of the nation in greatness as the gradual rehabilitation of the Anglo-Saxon genius after successive waves of conquest. It is true there have been rebellions. Carlyle's classic phrase (21) does not altogether comport with Mr. Freeman's eloquent pages. Bede's faithful lines shew anything but a healthy and vigorous national life. The corruption of Imperial Rome, if it were sufficient to account for national extinction, was equalled on a small scale by that of Anglo-Saxon society after only two centuries of existence. We can remember no parallel example in history shewing as complete a supersession and extinction of a populous nation by maritime invasion as that which is believed to have occurred in this country. The course of English history has been singularly different from that which has taken place in the Gothic and Teutonic lands from which the Angles, Jutes, and Saxons came.

It would indeed lead us far beyond our present subject to view this subject in its widest bearings. In one particular, however, it falls directly in our path, and it is essential to state

(21) "Pot-bellied equanimity."

what evidence exists of the indigenous Teutonic origin of the Gild, or of its derivation from elsewhere.

First as to the word itself. It seems to be probably English, though common also to the Frankish kingdom of the 8th century. The great Dictionary has not yet pronounced upon it. But there is evidence sufficient to enable us to trace it with reasonable certainty. It is derived from the Anglo-Saxon *gyldan*, to pay, and also, to worship, and the societies which took the name were so called on account of the regular payments which distinguished them. Mr. Walford quotes Bishop Smithies, of 1843, as his authority for the etymology. It can, however, be traced back continuously from ancient times. Blackstone gives the same origin (22). In an important case connected with the city of London, in 1609, it was held—"Gildan is a Saxon word, and signifies *solvere*, *i.e.*, that all of such fraternity shall be subject to pay scot and lot, and therefore at this day such part of the country which is contributory among themselves to pay common charges is called 'the Guildable,' and if there be any special liberty, it is called the franchise." It is true the law courts are not conclusive authorities on matters of etymology, but the decision is conclusive as to the traditional connection still current between the "Guildable" and the Gild. The identification of the payment with "scot" is also interesting, "scot" or "scot-ale" from an early period being the common contribution of burgesses for the purposes of municipal life, and originally, it is thought, the common contribution for liquor which we have seen formed the payment of the Roman Collegium, and appears as one of the main objects of the earliest English Gilds. Walford discards this derivation, and asserts as his opinion that it had [illegible] significance, viz., "a body of men associated together under oath for a common purpose." He, however, does not further explain his meaning, and gives no corroborative facts, so that it is impossible to pursue the question further. The editor of "Early English Gilds" also says "it is a mistake to connect the word with the German *geld*, payment. The real derivation is to be found in

(22) Blackstone, I., 478 Note.

Welsh *wyl*, Breton *goel*, *gouil*, a feast, holiday." He also quotes the Dutch *gulde*, a feast, also a gild or corporation. Here, again, in the absence of any literary facts supporting this etymology, it is impossible to accept it. There is no evidence that the essential features of the Anglo-Saxon Gild were Keltic; indeed, the absence of this peculiar form of association in purely Keltic quarters is a remarkable fact, and that Anglo-Saxons should under such circumstances have adopted a purely British name for such an institution is *prima facie* unlikely. In Anglo-Saxon the word was spelt either *gyld*, *geld*, or *gild*, and signified both a payment, or compensation, and a fraternity. Bosworth also gives "a payment to God, an offeriug, service, or sacrifice," and Gross corroborates this (23). The Dane Geld is familiar to all readers of English history. It is evident how fully the several meanings of the word embraced different aspects of the Gild. It is, however, in the Carlovingian Capitulary of 779 that the first mention of Gilds occurs, and the connection shows a certain prevalence of them already in the Frankish kingdom (24). The names used in Anglo-Saxon records are not only *congeldo*, *gegyldan*, but oftener *geferscipe*, *gegyldscipe*, or gildship, and *convivium* and *potatio* occur as almost synonymous.

Before giving a short account of the various facts relating to Anglo-Saxon Gilds which have come down to us, a few words are necessary on the general question of the character of the social and municipal organisation of England during the period from the 7th to the 11th centuries. We regard the population during this period as far less homogeneous than is often believed. Apart from the considerations briefly mentioned already, and without denying that in some particulars Mr. Coote (25) may have over-estimated the value of some of his deductions from the scanty records of the time, it seems to us that he has shewn clearly enough the existence of a strong Romanised element persisting in the country throughout the period of Anglo-Saxon

(23) Gross, *Gilda Mercatoria*, 1883, p. 10.

(24) Ibid, p. 9.

(25) *Romans in Britain—passim.*

conquest. Not only has he done this, but he has also shown in detail the close analogy between the imperial provincial system and many parts of the Anglo-Saxon social organisation which have been regarded as purely Teutonic. The early history of the manor, an institution which lies at the root of the national landed system, has also received new light in the same direction from the work of Mr. Seebohm on the Anglo-Saxon village community. The fuller elucidation of this view is to be awaited with great interest. In the meanwhile what is here put forth is merely that no inherent impossibility can be charged against a historical or traditional continuity in the case of the forms of mutual association which attained so strong a development in the mature stage of both the Imperial and English societies.

Not only is this the case, but analogy seems to place the burden of proof upon the other side. One of the most pregnant facts shewn by the labors of Sir Henry Maine, and other investigators in the same sphere, is acknowledged to be the steady persistence of popular social customs through many centuries while successive empires have nominally directed the destinies of the people. No truth has been more widely relied upon in tracing back old English customs to the vague fundamental traditions of the Teutonic peoples. In the ancient system of the Mark, in the Comitatus of Tacitus, have been found the original forms of manor and feudal service. Yet the gap between Tacitus and the Laws of Ine is greater than that between the Roman and Anglo-Saxon worlds. We can at least claim that equal weight shall be allowed to the same principles in respect to the organisation which the masterly genius of Roman colonisation had impressed upon this country during the centuries of its settled rule. The Collegia and Sodalicia were the forms in which the innate tendency to social organisation found refuge during the despotic peace of the Roman world. In the dissolution of the higher organisation of the State, men would cling all the more strongly to the lowlier bond of fellowship. Thus they were still brethren, if but in misfortune. When all else failed, they could meet at their saddened feast, and still do the last honor to the shade of the departed. Christianity, as De Rossi has shewn, altered the heathen complexion of the Collegia, but in no way abolished them. The old phrase in which the chronicles described the taking of a city, "The town was taken by an assault, and the inhabitants put to the sword," is understood to be received as a formula of speech. Cases are to be found in which cities underwent this operation more than once in a century, and appeared shortly afterwards with a considerable population and but slightly diminished prosperity. In A.D. 406, the Alans, Suevians, Vandals, and Burgundians overran Gaul from north to south, yet, as Thierry shows, in 437 Amiens was still a considerable town. Treves was sacked eight times in sixty-eight years, yet never lost its continuity of city life. That London, Lincoln, York, Winchester, Exeter, Canterbury, and the other well-known Roman towns remained is admitted, and there seems no reason to doubt that many others of less note remained also. The "hominum infinita multitudo (26)" which Cæsar saw in Britain were, according to Strabo (27), especially a commercial people. London was "a city famous in a high degree for the resort of merchants and for traffic." Ptolemy enumerates fifty-six of the towns of Britain (28), of which a large proportion remain to the present. Gildas, indeed, tells us with Keltic hyperbole that in his day (6th century) they were "deserted and *destroyed*," but so long afterwards as the 10th century we find Ethelweard observing that the buildings, "mirabili ingenio," were to be seen in his own day.

There can be no doubt that the decay and degeneration and bloodshed must have been of a most lamentable description. The old order was changed; but the study of the remains of Keltic literature of the earliest Anglo-Saxon period, whatever may be the difficulties which beset their interpretation, reveals unmistakable evidence of the continuance of the older population, and the persistence of many elements of Roman civilisation.

(26) Bell, *Gall.*, V., 12.
Strabo, Lib. IV.
Kemble, *Saxons in Britain*, II. 26

The works of Gildas show an acquaintance with the writings of Rufinus, Eusebius, the Epistles of Jerome, the Ecclesiastical History of Sulpicius Severus, and bear many traces of contemporary elements of Roman custom. The *Gododin* of Aneurin, who was probably his son, is classic in its main conception (29). Catterick, the old Roman town on the Swale, was still British in 603 (30). According to Henry of Huntingdon (31), the Britons in war "more Romanorum, acies distincte admoverent." The poem just mentioned seems to show the existence of wine taverns with fixed prices (32).

In the Druidic and Bardic classes also it is probable that an element of conservation existed to a much greater extent than has been admitted. Their old hostility to Roman conquest did not prevent them from assimilating the newer elements of Christian or semi-Christian civilisation. Baptism takes an honored place in the poems of Taliesin. We find striking instances of famous bards exercising also the functions of the Christian ministry along with many of their old traditional customs (33). According to the Triads, "On the coming of the Saxons," the Coritani, who had settled on the banks of the Humber, "united with them, and incorporating themselves with that people, they deprived the Lloegrians of their government, by wrong and oppression . . . All the Lloegrians became one people with the Saxons," and retained their land (34).

The Anglo-Saxons at the period of their conquest were alike unfitted and disinclined for city life; but there is no reason to attribute to them the folly, in their settled design of permanent conquest, of destroying such obvious sources of revenue and utility as were available in the resources of the towns. The singular ferocity with which they are supposed to have continuously exterminated the British race during the century and a half of their progressive conquest exceeds anything which can be put down to the credit of the Teutonic race in other lands.

(29) *Gododin*, Stephens and Powell, p. 13.
(30) Ibid, p. 80.
(31) *Hist. Ang.*, , 691.
(32) *Gododin*, p. 136.
(33) *Gododin*, p. 361.
(34) Ibid, p. 197.

Coming now to the first appearance of the Anglo-Saxon Gild, we find the following :—

Gegyldan in the laws of Ini and Alfred.
Gilds of London in time of Athelstan.
Cnihten-Gilds at London, Canterbury, and Winchester.
A Gild at Exeter.
Gild of Thanes of Cambridge.
A Gild at Woodbury.
Orcy's Gild at Abbotsbury.
A Gild of Clerks at Canterbury.
A Gildhall at Dover.

In Edgar's Ecclesiastical Laws (959-975), Gilds are spoken of in general. In the "Laws of Henry I.," dating from after the Conquest, but embodying earlier traditions, Gilds are also mentioned. Of these the following are the most noticeable points :—

1. The Gilds of the Laws of Ine and Alfred.

The earliest laws of all the barbaric nations which overran Europe are largely occupied with regulating the adjustment of compensation for injury. It was so with the laws of the Franks and Goths; it was so with those of the Anglo-Saxons. The most ancient of which we have remains are those of Æthelbearht, Wihtred, and Llothære ([35]). These make no mention of the Gild brethren, or gegyldas. It is the *mæga*, the kin, or clan, which is responsible. In the law of King Ine (688-725) the gegylda are twice mentioned ([36]). In both cases the man who slew a thief had to shew that he was really such, and not a *gegylda*, or associate. The meaning of the phrase in these passages by themselves is, as Gross ([37]) concludes, not clear. Further significance, whatever it may be worth, can only be read into it by the light gathered from later sources.

When we come to the laws of Alfred, of 890, we read (cap. 27), "If a man, kinless of paternal relatives, fight and slay a man, and then if he have maternal relatives, let them pay a third of

(35) V. Thorpe, *Ancient History and Institutions*.
(36) Ibid, sect. 16 and 21.
(37) *Gilda Mercatoria*, 1883, p. 92.

the *wer*, his gild brethren a third part, for a third let him flee. If he have no maternal relatives, let his gild brethren pay half; for half let him flee [38]." The reader should observe the significance of this law. In it the Gild is utilised as one of the fundamental organisations of society. It is taken as a matter of course that a man belongs to a Gild, whatever its form may have been. The Gild brethren both received and paid the *wer*, or compensation. In the earlier state of society the kin is the unit of such responsibility as was acknowledged; 150 years later, the Gild does not replace it, but is super-imposed upon it. This is quite a distinct process from the growth of a Craft Gild from a hereditary calling. It is an artificial association, utilised for purposes of social order, supplementing the imperfect and constantly shifting basis of the kin. To judge of its nature we must go to two sources of information. We must, firstly, enquire what other knowledge we have of the primitive organisation of Anglo-Saxon society for purposes of police; and we must, secondly, see if we can find any connection between this organisation and the earliest gild ordinances of a more general character. The first we shall find in the institution of the "tithing" and "hundred;" the second in the ordinance of the London Gilds in the time of Athelstan.

The ordinance of Edgar (959-975), regulating the organisation of police, bases it upon the hundred and the tithing as existing institutions, with the hundred man and the tithing man as executive officers. We take it as certain that the tithing, or the tenmannetæl of York, and the hundred, were *originally* divisions of men, and not of land. Thus the tithing men of Edgar's ordinance would be in a position similar to Alfred's *gegyldan* 70 years before. Edgar states that justice was to be done, as it was formerly by the enactment of Edmund, *i.e.*, A.D. 943. The presumption is very strong that so universal an institution as the Gilds of Alfred's law appear to have been, cannot have disappeared, and given place to the tithing and hundred of

(38) *Select Charters*, p. 65.

Edgar, but must be a development of the same under a different name.

Let us now turn to the ordinances of the London Frith Gilds in the "Judicia Civitatis Londoniæ" in the time of Athelstan, *i.e.*, midway between Alfred and Edgar. "This is the ordinance which the bishops and reeves belonging to London have ordained, and with weds confirmed, among our 'frith gegildas,' as well eorlish as ceorlish, in addition to the dooms which were fixed at Greatanlea, and at Exeter, and at Thunresfeld (39)." In this preamble are several most notable statements. It shews an agreement come to between bishops and reeves, and the numerous semi-private associations, for mutual protection and insurance, for the better preservation of order, and especial security against theft. This purpose had been served hitherto by the gegyldas of Alfred's law. Now, in accordance with the decree of Athelstan's Witan (Sect. x.), it was determined to consolidate this ruder system, in London as elsewhere, and to substitute a more uniform organization. Then follow minute directions as to the taking and punishment of thieves. The responsibility of the Kin and the lord both appear alongside of the gildship, and the institution of *frith-borh* or peace-bond or security is referred to. Stubbs observes that this expression was characteristic of the South of England. This, however, seems to be an accidental fact in the mentions which have survived, as we find the same word "borrowes" surviving in the Drapers' Gild at Newcastle as late as the 16th century (40).

So far we have noted the police function of these gilds. But the essential points of the Gild proper are all there. There were the common payments (Sec. 2); there was the bond of fellowship or "sodalitas," confirmed with "weds" or oaths. Also, "We have ordained . . . That we gather to us, once in every month, if we can and have leisure, the 'hynden men' [hundred-men ?], and those who direct the tithings, as with 'bytt-filling,'

(39) Thorpe, *Ancient Laws and Institutions*, I., p. 229.

(40) Mer. & St., p. 1126. The name of an apprentice and his "borrowes," or sureties, were to be enrolled.

as else it may concern us and know what of our agreement has been executed, and let these XII men have their refection together, and feed themselves according as they may deem themselves worthy, and deal the remains of the meat for the love of God." (Sect. 8, 1.) "And we have also ordained respecting every man who has given his 'wed' in our gildships, if he should die, that each gild brother shall give a 'gesufel' loaf for his soul, and sing a fifty, or get it sung within xxx. day." (Sect. 8, 6.)

There is one point which we have reserved till the last, namely, the connection of these Gilds with the tithings. It is to be found in Section 2: "That we count always ten men together, and the chief should direct the nine in each of those duties which we have all ordained,"—and these tithings constituted the hundreds. Here is the "Ten-manne-tæl" declared to be a universal institution of the Gilds in the most important ordinance between Alfred and Edgar. But here also is a curious mark of the Roman Collegia, as Mr. Coote has shewn from the highest authority. "Collegia divisa erant in decurias et centurias." The curious arrangement of the headman being the tenth was also Roman ([41]). Thus in these ordinances the fundamental forms of the tithing and hundred are interwoven with those of the Gild.

Dr. Gross will not allow the "Judicia Civitatis Londoniæ" to refer properly speaking to a true Gild. His chief reason is that a Gild is before all a voluntary association, the result of an impulse from below, and not, as in this case, from above. But this is in the first place to prejudge the question, and in the second to ignore the true relations of things at this period. That these regulations affecting the police of London must in any case have had the countenance of those in authority is plain, but the exact separation of a private corporation from public action is a conception which was foreign to such a state of society, and is indeed modern. The position seems clear. As we often find to be the case, the authorities made use of existing institutions, and regulated and enforced their customs. Apart from this Dr.

(41) Coote, *Romans in Britain*, p. [illegible].

Gross recognises the presence of the most characteristic Gild ordinances.

The other remains of Anglo-Saxon Gilds need not detain us long. Certain points however are essential to our subject. At Cambridge was the Gild of the Thegns or Knights. Its ordinances shew:—

> An oath of initiation.
> Burial by the Gild and provision to fetch the body from a distance (42) and a funeral feast.
> A reeve or warden.
> Contribution to the Wergild.
> Rules against abusive language and violence.
> The common fine a sextarium of honey.

At Exeter was a famous Gild of which the rules survive. They enact:—

> Meetings thrice a year.
> Each gild brother to bring 2 sesters of malt, and each "cniht" one sester and a sceat of honey, and say masses for the living and the dead.
> At the death of a brother each man six masses and each man five pence.
> At a houseburning each man one penny.
> If anyone misgreet another, thirty pence.

In order to give the reader an example of the foundation and rules of an Anglo-Saxon Gild, we give below the deed of foundation of Orcy's Gild at Abbotsbury as given in Kemble (43). It should be compared with that of the Roman Collegium on page 27 and that of the Hull Gild subsequently.

ORDINANCES OF ORCY'S GILD AT ABBOTSBURY.

> This writing witnesseth that Orcy hath granted the Gildhall at Abbotsbury, and the site thereof, to the honor of God and St. Peter, and for a property to the Gild, both during his life and after his life, for a lasting commemoration of himself and his consort. Let him that would set it aside, answer it to God in the great day of judgment.
>
> Now these are the covenants which Orcy and the Gildmen of Abbotsbury have ordained, to the honor of God, the worship of St. Peter, and the help of their own souls:—

(42) See rules of the Roman Collegium, p. 27.

(43) Kemble, Vol. I., p. 511; *Cod. Dipl.* 942.

1.
Scale of Contributions

Firstly: Three days before St. Peter's Mass, from each gild brother one penny, or one penny-worth of wax—look which the minister most needeth; and on the Mass eve, from every two gild brothers one bread loaf, well sifted and well raised, towards our common alms; and five weeks before Peter's Mass, let each gild brother contribute one gild sester full of clean wheat, and let this be paid within two days, on forfeiture of the entrance, which is three sesters of wheat. And let the wood be paid within three days after the corn-contribution, from every full gild brother one load of wood, and from those who are not full brothers, two; or let him pay one gild sester of corn. And let him that undertaketh a charge, and performeth it not accordingly, be mulcted in the amount of his entrance; and be there no remission.

2.
If one brother misgreet another.

And if one brother misgreet another within the Gild, in hostile temper, let him atone for it to all the fellowship with the amount of his entrance, and after that to him whom he misgreeted, as they two may arrange. And if he will not bend to compensation let him lose our fellowship and every other advantage of the Gild.

3.
Introducing guests.

And let him that introduceth more guests than he ought, without leave of the stewards and the caterers, forfeit his entrance.

4.
When a brother dies, a levy of 1d.

When sick or dead at a distance to be fetched.

All to be called, and to go to the funeral and pray for his soul.

And if any of our fellowship should pass away from us, let each brother contribute a penny over the corpse for the soul's hele, or pay . . . . brothers; and if any of us should be afflicted with sickness within sixty . . . . we are to find fifteen men who shall fetch him, and if he be dead, thirty, and they shall bring him to the place which he desired to go to while he lived. And if he die in this present place, let the steward have warning to what place the corpse is to go; and let the steward warn the brethren, the greatest number that he can ride or send to, that they shall come thither, and worthily accompany the corpse and bear it to the minster, and earnestly pray there for his soul.

It is rightly ordained a gildship if we do thus, and well-fitting it is both toward God and man, for we know not which of us shall first depart.

Now we have faith, through God's assistance, that the aforesaid ordinance, if we rightly maintain it, shall be to the benefit of us all. Let us earnestly from the bottom of our heart beseech Almighty God, etc.

In Milner's "History of Winchester" it is stated that a Merchant Gild was founded in that city in the reign of Ethelwolf, A.D. 856. The statement is taken from Trussell's MSS., which date from the 16th or 17th century, and contain much that is undoubtedly erroneous. It is also stated in the public Chronological Kalendar of Events in the history of the town, which was constructed in the 18th century. The fact is by no means improbable when we consider the importance of the city as the capital of Wessex and the early existence of a Merchant Gild after the Conquest, but I have not been able to find that the assertion rests upon any adequate evidence to be accepted as historical.

According to Stow, the Saddlers' Gild of London was founded in Anglo-Saxon times. In a charter of Edgar's reign we find three "geferscipas" or fraternities mentioned as existing at Canterbury. Stubbs thinks one of these may be the Priests' Gild, which is recorded in Domesday as possessing land; another the "Ceapmanne Gild" or Merchant Gild; and the third a Cnihten Gild, though the actual evidence we possess of these particulars dates from the time of Archbishop Anselm. An imperfect Canterbury charter of the reign of Ethelberht (860-866) is attested by Athelstan and the Corporation or Gild of burgesses, and Ethelhelm and the Gild of Knights. It is given in Kemble, *C.D.* 11, p. 83. Stubbs adds, "If this be genuine it is the earliest extant instance of such a gild in England." In the Book of Winchester, compiled under Henry I., there is also mention of a *Chenictehalla*, "where the cnihts used to drink their gild, and had it in free tenure from King Edward" (44) To Canterbury and Winchester must be added the Cnihten Gild of London, as to which Stow gives a most circumstantial account of knights holding a 14th century tournament in the time of King Edgar. Notwithstanding this, however, the fact of its having transferred the "Portsoken-ward" to the Church of the Holy Trinity in 1115 may be taken as a proof of its Anglo-Saxon origin and influential position (45).

These I think are all the contemporary mentions of Anglo-Saxon Gilds which have come down to us. They are referred to

(44) Gross, p. 23.

(45) On the relation of these to the Gilda Mercatoria see below p. 59

at length to show the wide extension of the institution. There is strong presumptive evidence of the existence of many others which appear as settled institutions almost immediately after the Conquest, but those given above are known from testimony which is contemporary or nearly so. We are now in a position to sum up the result of this evidence. In those cases where the ordinances remain, the central principles of the Gild are seen to be:—

1. Fellowship confirmed by an oath or promise.
2. Regular contributions.
3. Special care for the funeral rites of a member and commemoration by masses for his soul.
4. Periodical feasts and drinkings.
5. Rules for preserving courtesy and order.
6. The application of the fellowship or association to the most pressing need of the society of the day, whether mutual insurance against theft or fire, facilitation of trade, or, in an imperfectly organised society, for purposes of police.

The first five we take to be of the essence of the Gild. They can be traced in the associations of Rome from the early days of the Monarchy to the later days of the Empire in Greece, Asia Minor, and in Roman Gaul. They re-appear in the mediæval Gilds of England and the Continent of Europe. The last feature shews the secret of the stubborn persistence of the form of association. It was capable of being applied to all the varied purposes of the modern corporation.

What now was the relationship of the Anglo-Saxon Gild to the ancient Collegia and Sodalicia? Was the former an indigenous product? Was it a survival through native channels? Or was it imported from the Continent of Europe? We need now hardly hesitate in answering the first question in the negative. It would otherwise be impossible to account for the practical identity of the details of the ancient and modern forms. The notion that it was a Scandinavian product falls entirely to the ground. In the exhaustive work of M. Du Chaillu the Gild is nowhere mentioned. The distinguished author, in answer to an enquiry, confirms this fact, and states that the Scandinavian Gild belongs to a later period. In itself we grant that the supposition of a native

Romano-British survival during a submergence of three centuries can be nothing but a hypothesis, though not by any means impossible. Before answering, however, either of the two latter questions, we must cast a glance at the Continent, with which, from the time of Ethelbert and Offa, at any rate, this country was in frequent communication. It is known that in France the old Roman provincial life was much more continuous than in this country. According to Levasseur (46), "the cities preserved their Roman population, and even a portion of their ancient civil and political institutions." In the 5th century the History of the Hermit Apuleius, who lived at Cirneez, mentions the consul or chief of the locksmiths (47). The bakers are mentioned in the ordinances of Dagobert, 630. A last will and testament exists at Paris (48), about 700, drawn up according to pure Roman law (49). A capitulary of Charlemagne decrees that the corporation of the bakers shall be maintained in full efficiency in the provinces; and an edict of 864 mentions the Gild of the goldsmiths (50). Till the 10th century a legal distinction existed between Franks and Romans (51). It would be possible, according to Lacroix and Seré (vol. III., p. 30), to find traces of the Goldsmiths' Gild among the Gauls ever since the Roman occupation (52).

There is, however, another field of study which has hitherto attracted no attention from the writers on this subject, but which promises a very interesting contribution to its solution. Although there was certainly more continuity in Latin Europe from the Roman to mediæval times than in England, yet everywhere there is a break which it is hard for the historian to bridge over. There was, however, one city where the Hellenised Roman life lived on unbroken till the very close of the Middle Ages, and which, when that life was at length broken, scattered over

(46) *Histoire des Classes Ouvrières*, Vol. I., p. 122.

(47) Lacroix, *Le M. Age*, vol. I., p. 123.

(48) *Testamentum Erminethendis.*

(49) Thierry, p. 810.

(50) Ouin Lacroix, *Anc. Corp d'Arts, and M.*, p. 2.

(51) Thierry, *R. D. M.*, p. 95.

(52) For a useful summary of these facts see Gould's *History of Freemasonry*, p. 180.

Europe the remains and the tradition of classical literature and art. While Constantinople stood, the Roman Empire still was. Has it anything to tell of the old Collegia of Rome? When the great Sultan Mourad III. made his expedition against the Persians, in 1635, no less than 600 of the corporations, numbering 200,000 men, defiled before him, all the craftsmen in festal attire, and carrying curious and richly-ornamented emblems of their crafts. The procession lasted three days ([53]). Unfortunately, we have hardly any available sources of information as to the earlier period. It is known, however, that 35 such corporations existed in the times of the Byzantine Emperors. After the conquest, in the prosperous times of the Khalifat, they increased greatly. At the present day at Constantinople they number no less than 275. They also are to be found under the same name —Esnaifs—in Servia and Bulgaria, where their existence has also been continuous from the Middle Ages. Their constitution at Constantinople is as follows. The members are divided into three categories—masters (*ousta*), workmen (*kalfa*), and apprentices (*tchirak*). Each Esnaif has a council (*londja*), composed of the superintendent (*kehaya*), named by the Prefecture; the president (*yighidbachi*), elected by the general assembly of the craft, excepting the apprentices; and a certain number of the masters and workmen. There are also a treasurer, chamberlain, and secretary. The seal of the corporation is divided into four parts, of which one is kept by the *kehaya*, and the three others by three councillors respectively. All differences between members are dealt with by the council, from whose decision there is no appeal. The revenues are still derived in part from ancient endowments (though these have in very many cases been alienated), from monthly contributions, and from fines on admission. They grant aid in sickness and death, and assist members in setting up a trade. Formerly, when funds were more plentiful, they built churches and endowed schools. They, too, have their patron saints, and here comes in what is to Western ideas the oddest part of the interesting picture. The Christian saints are

(53) Walker, *Eastern Life and Scenery*.

little thought of under Mussulman rule. These crafts go back to earlier times. The patron of the bakers is Adam. The tailors, builders and sawyers are dedicated to the same. Eve watches over the washer-women, Nimrod over the smiths, Cain over the grave-diggers, Noah over the carpenters, Elijah over the furriers; Abel is the patron of the herdsmen, and Enoch of the makers of copper ornamental boxes. As is fitting, the bakers are the most numerous, though the butchers are the most wealthy. The great number of the corporations arises from the fact that every shade of difference in work gives rise to a separate Esnaif. Since the wars of 1877-8 they have much decayed in prosperity, and are said now to be in course of disappearance ([54]). If we change the saints and the language, we have, in fact, a description which would serve as well for London in the 14th century.

Bluntschli, in his "Theory of the State," traces the Crafts Gild in the Middle Ages from the cities of Lombardy as their earliest seat, to the cities of Southern France, and thence to England and Germany. What traces of this connection exist we do not know, but it is evident that from Amalfi and Ravenna, Venice and Genoa, constant intercourse with Constantinople was carried on during the centuries which in our history are so dark. The Esnaifs of Constantinople are not only similar, but identical in detail with the English mediæval Crafts Gilds, and this identity forbids the hypothesis of an independent origin. Although we at present lack the evidence which can enable us to compare the Esnaif with the Byzantine Collegia, we know enough to conclude with some confidence as to the latter being simply the descendant of the Roman Collegia and the ancestor of the Esnaif. Hence across the Channel and in the Frankish provinces, with which London, at any rate, and probably Winchester and York, were at nearly all times in communication, the ancient forms of association flourished during the ages as to which our English records are silent, and between France and the Roman world were there channels of continuity both indigenous and foreign.

(54) For these particulars see an article in the *Levant Herald*, 29th April, 1890, unsigned, but which I am informed is by M. R. A. Oöys.

Mr. Coote has shewn the analogy of the merchant of Athelstan's time, who by faring thrice over sea attained to thegn-right, with a Roman ordinance of Claudius. The Ceapmanne took his name through the Latin *caupo*. Trade and industry in Britain was never idle. From the dialogue in Turner's "Anglo-Saxons," we learn that "skins, silks, costly gems and gold, garments, pigments, wine, oil, ivory, and brass, copper and tin, silver, glass, and such like," were common merchandise. It is true that no trade can flourish in disorganisation and bloodshed, but in the York of the time of Alcuin, in the London and Winchester of the 9th century, there must have been no small traffic, judged by the standard of those times, and where there were city trades there would be early forms of the trade gilds. Kemble thinks that in every town there were quarters inhabited by workmen following the same trade, just as we find them in later days. Lingard independently arrives at the same conclusion, and this is a strong presumption of their association after the manner of the times. In Winchester in the 11th century we find the Scowertene-street, Olwarene-street, Flescmangere-street, Schyldwortene-street, Tannere-street, and Cypping, *i.e.*, Shoemakers', Mercers', Butchers', Shield-makers', and Tanners' Streets, and Market, respectively. In Eadward's time we read of the "aurifaber," "brandwirchte" (sword-maker), "savonarius" (soap dealer), "herengarius" (the seller of herrings), and "5 moneyers (55)."

The intercourse of the Eastern counties with the Baltic, which was never entirely absent from a period even previous to the dissolution of the Roman Empire, was by no means, as many writers have too much taken for granted, confined to the devastation of barbarians. Du Chaillu shews that from at least the beginning of the Christian era, Roman, Byzantine, and Kufic coins are successively found in numbers which must denote a very considerable intercourse with the seats of ancient civilisation. The chief seat of this trade in the earliest period, if we may trust the tradition of the Baltic, was Winetha, on the Oder; when this disappeared it was certainly the island of Gothland,

(55) *Historic Winchester*, p. 89.

with its great emporium of Wisby. "Zeeland and Fyen are especially rich in Roman objects, and shew the existence of great intercourse with the Roman provinces, while Gothland is particularly rich in coins." The following table ([56]) shews to what a great extent this is true:—

Summary of Roman and Byzantine Coins Found.

Mainland	57
Scania	617
Öland	196
Gotland	3182
	4162
Of gold	236
" silver ...	3907
" copper ...	39

12	before Augustus.
3918	Augustus—A. Severus. B.C. 29 to A.D. 235.
24	A. Severus to Theodosius. 235 to 395.
226	Theodosius to Anastasius. 395 to 518.
2	After Anastasius. 518 to 850.

But it is more germane to our present object to note the actual evidence of the commerce with England. Accordingly we find that the coins of Ethelred which have been found there actually exceed in number those which have been found in England itself, and there is evidence that they were not so much Danegeld as the produce of trade. In Egil's Saga (70) we are told "Arinbjorn gave Egil as Yule gift a gown of silk embroidered with gold, and set with gold buttons all the way down the front. He had this made to fit Egil. Arinbjorn also gave him a new cut suit of clothes *of many-colored English cloth* ([57])." These indications are sufficient to show that trade was by no means idle even in those days along the lines where now it is so brisk, and we cannot doubt that in England the great lines of Roman roads, the harbours and rivers of the land, and the great estuary of the Humber by no means least, were the channels of considerable traffic after the fashion of those days.

There is a very curious phrase in the Custumal, or ordinances of the well-known Gild of Preston, which does not seem to have attracted sufficient attention. It is the last of the document, and reads—"This is the law of Preston in Amundrenesse, which

(56) *Viking Age*, Vol. II., p. 556.

(57) Du Chaillu, Vol. II., p. [illegible].

they have from the Breton law." Now the writing is said by the editors, Messrs. Dobson and Harland, to be of the 13th century, and the Gild itself was chartered by Henry II. between 1175 and 1185. It is well known that these charters can never be taken as conclusive evidence of the actual origination of a town or gild, but as often as not confirm previously-existing customs or institutions. Now, considering the neighbourhood of the Keltic kingdom of Strathclyde, it is at least a possibility, which the foregoing considerations render more plausible, that we have here an actual survival from the Britain of the Roman occupation. In France the Roman law still lingered as late as the 14th century, and Lancashire was British long after Yorkshire was a settled Anglo-Saxon kingdom. More we cannot say, but the appearance of such a clause in a document written by a 13th century hand in a record of such a character seems at least to afford an indication of curious value in a field where we have so little certain knowledge.

Where direct evidence is so scanty, no conclusion can be drawn. But the facts above given seem to point to a lingering survival of the ancient traditional form of association. Intercourse with France, the influence of the Church, and the example of the monastic fraternities, brought England into contact with the forms of association which elsewhere never lost altogether the tradition of the universally-established Collegia from East and West, and when the inner constitution of the English Gilds is revealed, with their claim to immemorial tradition, we find them practically identical with the associations of Roman Imperial days.

CHAPTER IV.

GILDS AFTER THE CONQUEST.—THE ENGLISH BOROUGHS.

WITH the advent of William of Normandy commenced a new era in the life of England. His was the last of the waves of conquest which changed the current of English history. Kelts, Belgæ, Romans, Saxons, Angles, Jutes, and Danes had succeeded each other in their onslaughts, and had found a resting-place. After William there came no more. The consolidation of the people began. In England, at least, provincial home rule was at an end. Barons never succeeded in elevating their robber castles into the seats of independent rule, as they did in Germany and France. Despite times of bitter intestine struggle, the King's central rule in the main held good, and with the stern maintenance of the King's peace the national life became continuous. There was henceforth no break in the social institutions of the land, none of those successive degradations of the classes of the people by the super-imposition of a conquering caste, which make the early social history of England so hard to decipher. At this period, therefore, we begin to note those forms of municipal organisation whose completion belongs to a later age. The records which we possess of this period mark a new departure. The great and unique survey of the realm known as the Domesday Book affords us a basis for the study of English life which is wanting alike in previous centuries of our own history and in the history of other lands. By the survival of the great rolls of the Exchequer, giving the sources of revenue from 31 Henry I., we have a priceless mine of information. Shortly afterwards the Royal Charters begin, and with these, so far as they go, we have a sure and reliable foundation for an early knowledge of English towns. It is true that the Domesday Survey is incomplete. The part of Yorkshire in which Hull is now situated is included, although the book shews only the villages now included in the borough. In all, upwards of eighty towns are known to have existed at the time of the survey, 1086.

We have now to take up the history of Gilds where we left it at the close of the Anglo-Saxon dominion. There were, as we have seen, in English towns Gilds of a religious and social character, whose ordinances have come down to us. There were also, under whatever name, probably the remains of the old universally-established Frith Gilds of the time of Alfred and Athelstan, disorganised and changed by the Danish troubles and the introduction of the Danish element of population, but still closely intertwined with the organisation of the hundred and the tithing, and in the case of London, at least, having for a time shown a capacity to form the basis of a municipal association, taking upon itself the duties of police and mutual insurance, as well as being a bond of religious union. Of the Craft Gild proper we have no contemporary evidence. It is true some of the later Gilds traced their origin to Anglo-Saxon times; such, for example, was the Saddlers' Gild of London, according to Stow. The most reliable historians of the period, moreover, consider it highly probable, as we have seen, that such organisations did actually exist in most Anglo-Saxon towns of sufficient size, and there was no reason to doubt that such was the case. The early appearance of payments from weavers' gilds in the rolls of the Exchequer seems to be almost conclusive that they were already established institutions ([58]).

The class of gild, however, which claims our attention in the period we are now considering was of a somewhat different kind, and is characteristic of the 12th and 13th centuries

(58) See p. 64, on *Anglo-Saxon Craft Gilds.*

to a degree to which no other kind of gild can lay claim ([59]). This was the Merchant Gild, "Gilda Mercatoria," or Céapmannes Gild ([60]). An institution closely connected with this, and often identical with it, was the Hanse. The earliest record of the Céapmannes Gild is in the time of Anselm (1093-1109), in the town of Canterbury, where we read of "Cnihtan on Cantwareberig of Ceapmanne Gilde." There is hardly a doubt that this Gild dated from Anglo-Saxon times (see p. 49), though in the absence of details we cannot compare its constitution with that of the Gilda Mercatoria of thirty years later. It is here that Dr. Gross finds the most probable link between the old Gilds and the institution we are now considering. It is certain that in London, Winchester, and Canterbury were old Cnihten Gilds, and while the case of London is peculiar, as affording no trace of a Gilda Mercatoria, in both of the two other cities as the former drops out of sight the latter makes its appearance. In Wycombe also, as late as Henry III., the Gildhall bore the name "Knaveshorn," *i.e.*, Cnihtenhorn. The special connection of the Cnihten with trade appears at Canterbury in the passage above quoted, and in Athelstan's law, but the cases are few on which to form a very wide induction ([61]). It will perhaps be safer to find the cause of the wide prevalence which the Gilda Mercatoria attained during this period in the altered circumstances of the realm, and the capacity for general application which we have noted in the gild system, than in the previous existence of any one specialised form of the gild.

(59) As the proof sheets of this chapter were passing through my hands, the fuller work of Dr. Gross, in English, on the Gild Merchant was issued from the Clarendon Press. In it the author has laid all students of English history under a deep obligation, both by his publication of hitherto inaccessible documents of essential interest, and by his commentary upon them. After a careful study of the work, I have added a few notes, and been enabled to correct in one or two details statements in the text, but beyond this have not found it necessary to alter the account already written. It is right to add that this is largely due to a study of the work of the same author published at Göttingen in 1883. In only a few minor points have I ventured to differ from his conclusions. In referring to the two books, the date has been quoted to distinguish between the earlier and later volumes.

(60) Other forms of the name are "Gilda Mercatorum," "G. Mercanda," "Geld Merchants," or "Chepyng Gild."—Gross, 1890, p. 84.

(61) See Gross, *Gilda Mercatoria*, 1883, p. 98. In his later work Dr. Gross does not repeat this view of the case.

The early years of oppression which succeeded the Conquest had no sooner passed away than, with closer intercourse with the Continent and a stronger Government, trade revived, and the town life of England began anew. The Gild was the form which this influence naturally took. In the 12th and 13th centuries the Gilda Mercatoria became a marked characteristic of English towns. Dr. Gross gives a list of 162 towns in England, Wales and Ireland (*Gild Merchant*, 1890, p. 6), in which its existence is proved. His opening words deserve to be quoted:—"There are," he writes, "in history certain phenomena which appear as central points at which many other institutions intersect in their manifold development. Such a phenomenon is the Gilda Mercatoria, in whose history not only the development of Gilds, but those of trade and industry, the rise of municipality, the formation of the ideas of the Corporation and citizenship, as well as many other weighty questions, are interwoven in the closest degree" (*Gilda Mercatoria*, 1883, p. 1). Yet there is no part of our history which has been left in greater obscurity. The curious case given by Kyd ([62]) might be a type of the decision of our historians. The Mayor of Winchester accused a certain Wilks of having carried on a trade in the town without being a member of the Gild Merchant. "The Court was moved in arrest of judgment, and the judges observed that when in ancient times the King granted to the inhabitants of a villa or borough to have Gildam Mercatoriam, they were by that incorporated, *but what it signified in this declaration nobody knew*." This was in the 18th century.

We shall first describe briefly the position of the English borough at this period, and give a short summary of the constitution of the contemporary French commune as essential to a right understanding of the course of English development. We shall then discuss the origin and constitution of the Gilda Mercatoria, and its connection with the municipal constitutions, and give examples in the case of certain boroughs which may be deemed typical.

(62) *Law of Corporations*, Vol. I., p. 64.

THE ENGLISH BOROUGH IN THE 12TH CENTURY.

Of the English borough as it emerges in the 12th century no exact general account can be given. From Domesday we discern clearly the existence of the "burghwara," "burgenses," or "burgesses," as the essential constituents in town life; but the relation of these to the rest of the inhabitants is by no means clear. The qualification was the possession of a "burgage," or land and tenement, and this also tended in some cases to be hereditary. On the burgesses fell the responsibility for the King's taxes. In the ordinary town, wherever any kind of unity prevailed, and the town was not composed of the distinct, and even jealous and hostile jurisdiction of separate lords, the membership of the Town Assembly (Portmannemote, or Court Leet), the payment of scot, or town talliages, and bearing lot, or common burdens, constituted the bond of unity. The organisation was analagous to that of the hundred in the counties, and the *prepositus*, or *wic*, or *port-reeve*, and the bailiffs, were the chief officers; but in the older cities there was also the remnant of a burgher aristocracy, and a patrician element. In York, Lincoln, Cambridge, and Derby, we find the twelve law-men, or thegns, in some position of superiority; but of any struggle between an old and a new class, such as occurred abroad, we have no record. There was certainly an unfree element in the towns, probably of a very composite character, though we know little of it, and freedom was an essential for burgess-ship. In the ancient city of Lincoln, in the reign of John, when the fullers and dyers of Lincoln complained of the seizure of cloth by the aldermen and reeves, claiming the right of dying as they pleased, as free citizens of Lincoln, the aldermen and reeves declare that the craftsmen "have no law or fellowship with free citizens," ("non habent legem nec communiam cum liberis civibus.") And this has been taken as indicating a generally servile status of the artizan class. But before accepting this view two remarks are necessary. The Domesday Survey shews Lincoln as bearing traces of a more strongly aristocratic element in constitution than was the case elsewhere. As we have seen, twelve "lage-manni" (law-men) and a few others held the jurisdiction. It is possible it was a remnant either of Danish conquest or of a still more ancient state of things. But secondly, it is evident that in the opinion of the craftsmen the rights and privileges of the aldermen and reeves were a usurpation. They claimed the right of free citizens, and we cannot now say how far they may have had ancient custom on their side. As early as 5 Henry II. we find the weavers of the same city regularly recognised by the King, and paying their annual fine to the Exchequer. The Gild was evidently at that time a fixed institution, and it is difficult to believe that men thus licensed were of servile condition. Nor was fulling more servile than weaving, if we may judge by the case of Winchester, where in the same year the fullers and weavers each pay their fine (63). In connection with this question should be considered also the law so often quoted as to manumission by a year and a day's undisturbed residence in a town. This was a common privilege granted in the charters of the period; but if it was really acted upon, which does not seem to be doubted by historians, it is impossible to picture the free citizenship which was thus attained as the membership of a close or aristocratic community. It was too cheap. The gulf which was thus bridged over cannot have been very broad or deep. It is noticeable that the condition was also sometimes added that he should have held land for the year and a day. The peculiar term was also that of prescription for evidence of possession generally, and the possession of a tenement which would be the pledge of his burgess-ship was not such a serious matter, if we may believe the provision of the Preston Custumal, where forty days was allowed for its erection, and its frontage was twelve feet. Probably it was often only of light wooden construction (64). There is moreover in the earliest lists of names that survive in town records strong evidence of the

(63) See *Gild Merchant*, 1890, p. 108. Dr. Gross shows that weavers, fullers and dyers elsewhere were commonly enrolled in the registers of the Merchant Gilds.

(64) Dobson and Harland, p. 75

source whence the burgesses took their rise. Thus in Beverley we find that the great majority took their surname from some other place, either town or village, in the East Riding, shewing the place of their birth or origin, though they were then full burgesses of the town; and the same occurs elsewhere (65).

Whatever might be said to be the exact nature of the bond which held the townsmen together, so far as it is possible to generalise in what was probably a great variety of circumstances, it is only in a limited guise that they could be said to constitute a municipality. In some cases they were simply part of the demesne of the King or of some great lord, and subject to his jurisdiction. In others they were still in very much the same position as the "hundred" in the county or shire, and thus under the government of the sheriff, to whom they paid their taxes. In others they had already, in the Confessor's days, succeeded in paying direct to the King, in a fixed amount, the farm of the town ("firma burgi"), which freed them from the extortions of intermediate officers, and had their own pleas, and other rights; but there was nowhere the well-marked municipal organisation which we find two centuries later on. With the chartering of the boroughs in the 12th century the course becomes more plain. They gained, not all at once, but in varying proportions, independent jurisdiction within their boundaries, freedom from toll, the firma burgi, market right, the right to choose their officers, and the gilda mercatoria (66). It is at this period that the peculiar institution known as the Gilda Mercatoria appears on the scene. Let us now mark the position of the French towns in the same period.

(65) The fuller discussion of this point may be found under the consideration of the "Customs of Preston."

(66) Gross, 1883, page 58.

CHAPTER V.

THE INFLUENCE OF THE FRENCH COMMUNE UPON ENGLISH TOWNS.

IN his review of the development of the English towns, Dr. Stubbs remarks that its full history can only be understood by taking into consideration the contemporary history of the Continent. The justice of this remark is evident, whether we seek to trace their origin in the separate elements of the municipality, or to take a wider view of the ideas which governed the minds of those early English kings and barons who granted the first charters to English towns. The Communa, the Mayor, the Echevins (or Scabini), the Fraternity, the Association of Merchants, are names which can only be understood by reference to their Continental connection, while the differences between the English and French forms are as important to be noted as their points of resemblance. On the other hand, it must not be forgotten that our early monarchs were rulers of towns in Normandy, Anjou, and other parts of France, as well as of London and Winchester and York. They were in some instances, indeed, more French than English, and the earlier development of the French Communes, and their well-marked history, must necessarily have had a decided influence in framing the policy they adopted towards the rising English towns. Nor was this the case only under the Plantagenet or Angevin Kings, whose French domain was as extensive as their English one. Even before the Conquest the Duchy of Normandy was the most thoroughly organised and centralised of the provincial governments of France, and the ducal control of the Communes was more real and consistent than elsewhere (67). With Rouen as the model, communal government was largely granted, but it was never allowed to grow into the semi-independent form which it assumed under the more feeble and capricious rule of the Capetian Kings. The political astuteness of the Normans saw and utilised its value for purposes of frontier defence, while they checked its tendency to serve as a focus of disorder. John and Henry II., whose charters to English towns are a marked feature of their home policy, extended the principle, as circumstances permitted, to the rest of the lands under the Norman and Anglo-Angevin sceptre. Thus Rouen served as the model for Poitou, Poitiers, Niort, Cognac, Angoulème, St. Jean d'Angeli, La Rochelle, Les Iles d'Oleron, de Ré, and Bayonne. Soissons, copied by Dijon in 1183, thence served as a prototype to a considerable part of the Duchy of Burgundy. The reason was plain. The constitution thus granted interfered the least with the prerogative of the lord, and thus was able to gain recognition where a more autonomous type would have failed.

These facts will serve to shew the necessity of a short account of the progress of the principles of association which were prevalent in France at the time when the Gilda Mercatoria and the Crafts Gilds were bearing their fruit in the sphere of English town life. It is the more necessary to trace the outlines afresh as the pictures presented mostly to English readers have serious deficiencies. Since the great works of Thierry and Guizot, historical study has made much progress in France, and the constitutions of the French towns in their earlier period have been placed in the light of more exact knowledge and criticism.

We have already alluded to the more continuous existence of Gallic as compared with British towns across the dark period between the Roman Empire and mediæval France. It is true that the precise nature of this continuity may easily be exaggerated. While it is true that incidental notices shew the continuous existence of the cities themselves, like Arles, Amiens, and Orleans, and of the existence in them of corporations and associations of

(67) Luchaire, page 120.

trades and merchants from the time of the Romano-Gallic collegia till the rise of the mediæval commune proper in the 11th century ([68]), it is also true, as M. Luchaire says, that "One must resign oneself to state a fact against which one can do nothing, the absence of documents relating to the municipal constitution during 400 years, from the 7th to the 11th centuries. According to all appearance, this enormous hiatus will never be bridged over [page 11]." While it is a fact that the names such as Cives, Quæstores, Prætores, Forum, Curia, Senatus, Libertas Romana, remained, that Roman law to a great extent persisted, it is still unproved that the things which they represented were continuous over the centuries that had passed. Thus much critical accuracy compels us to state. On the other hand, it may be taken as proved that if not the persistence of institutions, at least that of manners and customs, is placed beyond doubt ([69]). And this is all that we require. The point at which an institution passes into one of another age may be difficult to mark; the presence of essential attributes is sufficient to prove the survival of the principle, commingled though it may be with the elements of the institutions of the ages through which it has passed. The universal prevalence of associations or collegia in the Gallo-Roman world is proved to abundance by Latin epigraphy ([70]). The existence of the principle which we have marked as essential in the earliest known forms of the mediæval Gild points to a presumption of identity of manners, custom, and tradition, which alone is sufficient to account for the phenomenon, and which is distinct from a spontaneous or religious growth. As in England, so in France, the chief Gild, that of the merchants, *changeurs*, etc., was the association which in many towns prepared the way for a more advanced form of municipal government, and took the foremost position in the administration. There is more evidence than in England of the co-existence of corporations of trades, and of the religious confraternities, but they had apparently but

(68) See the evidence well summarised in Gould's *History of Freemasonry*, page 181

(69) Luchaire, page 13.

(70) See Dr. Hatch, *Bampton Lectures*, p. 26, *et seq.*

little part in the initiation of a new order of things. At St. Omer, the Merchant Gild and its "gild-halla" is identical with the Commune. At Rouen the "Marchants de l'eau" preceded the Commune. At Paris "the Merchants of the Seine" for centuries were confused with the municipality; so the Gild of Cambrai, the Charities of Arras, Douai and Valenciennes, and the Amitiés of Lille.

And this brings into clearer view a fact which casts a strong side light upon one of the darkest questions respecting our English towns at the period of the Gilda Mercatoria. Hitherto historians have taken somewhat too hastily for granted the democratic origin and early constitution of the Communes of France and the towns of England. More exact research in respect, at least, to the former, shews the evidence upon which this view was based as deficient. These merchants de l'eau, drapièrs, and changeurs, were the aristocracy of commerce. To them was due, and not to a purely servile or democratic movement, the chief part in the establishment of the Commune. The statement is not absolute, but generally it is correct. The Commune was largely the adaptation and consolidation of previously existing elements, and what these elements were it seems now impossible exactly to determine. Even the Mayor, especially a mark of the communal regime, can be traced back to a previously existing office, and the heads of the trade corporations, as we find them in the 13th and 14th centuries, had the title of "Maires de Bannières." The same title of Mayor is to be found in the English Fraternity of the Staplers. It is hence easier to understand how in the 12th century, the period of the true Commune, we find the administration generally in the hands of a more or less aristocratic body of the citizens. The entry of the corporations of trades into the governing body, which occurred in France in the 13th and 14th centuries, and which had its analogy in England in London nearly at the same time, and in some provincial towns somewhat later, was, in its beginning, the assertion of popular rights as against this municipal

oligarchy, an assertion which was destined itself to develope into an oligarchy as onerous and aristocratic as that which it displaced. But in the earliest accounts which we possess, the free popular election of Mayor and Council, and the regular general assembly of citizens, have hardly a place. A few examples will make this plain. At Rouen, and to a varying extent in those communes founded upon its model, the government was in the hands of one hundred "pairs," or peers. These elected yearly from themselves twenty-four "jurés," or sworn men, and these were divided into two bodies—twelve échevins and twelve councillors—these committees, as we should now say, meeting, the one weekly, the other fortnightly; but the Mayor was chosen, not by any of these bodies, but by the seigneur or lord out of three men chosen by the peers. At Poitiers the hundred peers were brethren of the Fraternity of St. Hilary, who constituted the corps de ville, or "corporation," and only in the 13th century was this extended to all burgesses. At Beauvais, the charter of Philip Augustus, in 1182, had instituted a council of thirteen peers. A decree of 1282 shews that these thirteen were then elected by twenty-two corporations of trades and mysteries; but one of them, the corporation of merchants, elected seven, and thus had the majority. At Amiens, in 1299, were twenty-four echevins, of whom twelve were elected by the heads of corporations or Maires de Bannières, and these elected the remaining twelve. At Tournai, the charter of Philip Augustus, in 1187, shewed thirty jurés, but these were co-optative, and filled up vacancies ([71]).

A few words of explanation as to the relative positions of these several classes will serve to bring into greater clearness the relationship to English boroughs. Properly speaking, the jurés ("jurati") were those who took the solemn oath of the Commune ("sacramentum," or "juramentum Communie"). In some Communes, as at Amiens, Rouen, and Senlis, the term had a general signification, and included the collective members of the Commune, but by no means always. At Noyon, for example, it

(71) Luchaire, page 165.

meant only the magistracy, the "jurati" *par excellence* [72]. Yet in the book of the burgesses of Noyon, at the beginning of the 14th century, we have a very interesting account of the oath sworn on the entrance into the Commune. The applicant swore that he did not seek entrance to defraud anyone, on account of debt, or of illness of himself or his wife, or because he was of servile condition. That he was born of legitimate marriage; that he would be "prud'homme," and loyal to each member of the commonalty; not consort with strangers against the burgesses; that he would obey the Mayor, and pay his share of the debts of the town. Nothing could better bring home to the reader the closeness of the Communal ties. The different clauses seem to refer to the following:—The applicant swore that he did not seek entrance in order to defraud anyone. This probably refers to the rights of his lord, and shews the limitation of the clause often inserted in charters and stated in Glanville, that a residence of a year and a day in a town sufficed to secure freedom. It seems to have been much too broadly insisted upon by historians. At Abbeville the Count of Wonthieu had three years' right of reclamation; in some other places it was interdicted altogether. At Sens, as Stubbs shews [73], it was inserted in the charter of 1180, but on the re-establishment of the Commune by Philip Augustus, the right was withdrawn [74]. In some places in England seven years were required. The clause in the book of Noyon shews how dangerous was the exercise of the practice. The oath that he was in good health may refer to leprosy, or, as Luchaire thinks, to the right of funeral obsequies which a member of the Commune possessed, probably as a relic of the Gild. He swore that he was of free condition, not only for the reason given for the first clause, but because very early in the commercial movement the membership was recognised as one of privileged or free grades of society. The same clause is conspicuous in the early annals of London. The date of this oath

(72) Compare the oaths of the municipal officers in London, down to the beadle, in Thorpe,

(73) *Constitutional History*, I., 421, note.

(74) Luchaire, page 70. *et seq.*

must, of course, be remembered, but as early as 1129 Louis VI. enfranchises certain peasants, and adds, "They can now enter into the clergy, the army, or *the Commune.*" Further, he swore fidelity to each member of the Commune (as in gilds), to obey the Mayor, and pay his share of the debts of the town. Nor was this all. The clause engaging that he was not in debt hints, M. Luchaire thinks, at a collective liability for the debts of the members.

The Commune thus constituted entered, when legally recognised, into the feudal society of which it was a member. It had its seigneur; it was subject to the three-fold call, upon his being made prisoner, upon the marriage of his eldest daughter, and the knighthood of his eldest son. If a prominent one, it had even smaller communes, as it were, holding fiefs under it, and was the *chef de sens.* It was represented by the Mayor. The bell and the seal were its tokens of corporative existence, and when Laon was suppressed by Philip of Valois, in 1331, the bell and the seal were solemnly demolished.

It will readily be seen how the Commune thus constituted differed from an English borough. The difference arose from many causes. The want of a settled royal authority in its early stages, and its despotic character when established, the greater power of the feudal system, both lay and ecclesiastic, as well as the character of the people, contributed to its more rapid and complete development in France. As its more warlike character was necessitated by its constant struggle for existence, so it was pushed to greater excesses, and excited the hostility of the nobility, and especially of the great ecclesiastic fees. Mercilessly exploited by the crown, torn by internal anarchy and financial difficulties, the end of the 13th century saw the Commune everywhere in decadence at a time when the English boroughs were rising to greater power and influence. The influence of the Commune was probably on the whole not great upon English towns. The close acquaintance of its early kings with the communal propagànda of their French dominions is probably one secret of the careful and limited clauses of the

charters which they granted to their English subjects, and is well exemplified in the short and grudging grant of the Conqueror to the great town of London, whose communal rights, if they may be called such, were only fully recognised more than a century afterwards. The same names occur; the "mayor" soon became common in English cities, but either they or their royal masters had learned the lesson which events across the Channel had taught men, and were content with mercantile privileges and a limited amount of local jurisdiction.

As a matter of fact, the English borough in its early stages occupied in some particulars more the position of the privileged town, with which, even more than with the communes properly so called, rested the future development of the town life and the *tiers état* of France. Such were Lorris, whose privileges served as the model for 83 towns in Orleannis, Berri and Gâtinais, and Beaumont, which set the example to more than 500 in Champagne and Lorraine, in France and Belgium. These privileges, chiefly commercial and administrative, fostered the progress of the people, and did not excite the jealousy of the suzerain, while they slowly and surely developed the energy and well-being of the people, till the day came when it could once more claim its due share in the destinies of the land.

CHAPTER VI.

APPEARANCE OF THE GILDA MERCATORIA.

SUCH then was the English town, and such the foreign influences, when the Gilda Mercatoria took its rise. Was it a new creation formed to meet fresh circumstances, or did it mark merely the development of an institution already existing? We shall best satisfy the enquiry by tracing in outline the history of the Gilda Mercatoria in four of the towns which present special points of interest, and then summing up the general features which marked its character. It will be seen that what calls for a special consideration of this class of gild apart from others is its authoritative position, and the peculiar relations which obtained between it and the municipal constitution of the boroughs. Of the examples next considered, Beverley has one of the most ancient of the charters ([75]). Winchester is the ancient capital of the south, and served as a model for many of the other towns and cities in that part of the land. Southampton presents us, if we except the case of Berwick, with the only copy of contemporary merchant gild ordinances which survive, and Preston is the only English Merchant Gild which itself still lives in the 19th century.

THE HANSE OF BEVERLEY.

Beverley dates its Hanse from the charter of Thurstan, Archbishop of York, who was the lord of the town some year in the reign of Henry I. ([76]). "The men of Beverley are to have their Hanshus, as the men of York have theirs." This seems to imply that the Hanse or Gild was then first formed on the model of

(75) Gross, *Gild Merchant*, 1890, page 5, gives the Charter granted by Robert Fitz-Harmon to Burford, 1087-1107, as the earliest extant mention.

(76) *Select Charters*, page 100.

that of York. Whether this were really so, or whether it was in consequence of this charter established in a more public and authoritative position than it had hitherto occupied, will be considered later. The Hanse appears in the other documents of the borough a little later as the Gilda Mercatoria. According to Poulson, whose history of the town is very painstaking and minute, the identification of the Gild with the governing body of the town was rapid and complete. Twelve burgesses were elected annually as governors, who conducted the affairs of the municipality, and the Burgess Roll of the town was practically identical with that of the Gild. These twelve governors remind one of the twelve port-men whose election is recorded in the Ipswich Domesday Book. But these were chosen as distinct from the Gild, the alderman and four good and tried men of which were separately elected, and the rolls of burgesses and gildsmen were kept distinct (77). In the absence of a Beverley Domesday Book we cannot say how far anything answering to this took place there. It must be remembered that Beverley was a town in which the Abbots and the Archbishops of York held extensive rights, and anything like a strong independent municipal organisation would be looked upon with great jealousy. This may account for the greater influence of the gild form of organisation than was the case in places which had more natural unity.

Now as late as A.D. 1420 we find the following entry in the annual accounts of these governors :—" Paid to the Gild of S. John Baptist for rent of the Gildhall, 20s." In the year 1388 were ordered the returns from all over England of the Gilds of every kind, which Mr. Toulmin Smith found in the Record Office, and from which his invaluable collection in the volume of the Early English Text Society on Gilds was made. Among the few returns remaining of Gilds of Crafts is one from Beverley. It is entitled " The great Gild of St. John of the Hanshus," and when we come to look at the ordinances we find simply a copy of Thurstan's Charter, then over two hundred years old; for

(77) Gross, 1890, page 43.

the charter simply grants to the burgesses a hanshus. The entry in the town accounts shews us that the governors really did not own the Hanshus or Gildhall at all, but paid a rent to the Gild of St. John of Beverley for it, as long as 300 years afterwards. On the other hand, the return shews us the merchant "Gild of St. John of the Hanshus" sending up a copy of a town's charter as the account of its origin. It is not easy to reconcile these statements, and to trace the actual relationship between the Gild of St. John of Beverley and the Gilda Mercatoria. It is evident that the most probable explanation is that there was originally a Gild of St. John of Beverley which embraced nearly the whole of the burgesses. Either this itself was a gild of a strongly mercantile character, or it was the religious gild which was attached to a gild of that kind, and embraced the same membership. This gild then became the subject of express grant to the burgesses in general as a hanse-house with trade privileges, and from it grew the municipal organisation. But the original religious or social element of the gild was not thereby extinguished. It maintained its existence for funeral and social purposes, and was recognised by the governors as the real owner of the Gildhall, while the latter was by payment of a rent generally used as the Town Hall of the borough. The only other explanation would require us to believe that the twelve governors were not really officials of the Merchant Gild at all, and that the entries shewing the payment of rent for the Gildhall shew the town authorities who had risen into power on an independent basis using the Gildhall as a Town Hall, and paying a rent to the Gild which by that time had reached a state of decrepitude and unimportance. Poulson however states positively that this was not the case, and that the twelve governors or keepers were originally twelve officials of the Gild, and the return in 1389 confirms this. It has however its analogy elsewhere. In Lancaster twelve men took a similar position in the Gild ([78]). A small inner council of the same number does not appear to have been uncommon elsewhere. The more usual

(78) Early English Text Society, xxxviii.

officials of the Gild proper were one or two aldermen, two or four wardens, and sometimes stewards in addition; also a dean, decenner, or beadle and clerk (79).

The "Liber Custumarum" exhibits the Gild of Beverley (80) in a somewhat exclusive and unworthy character, in company with Marlborough and Winchester. About the 13th or 14th centuries it was laid down that before admission to the Merchant Gild an artizan must abjure his craft (81). When this arose, or how long it lasted, we cannot tell. In 1344 we find one Stephen of Otley, a tailor, admitted, and paying his 40s. entrance fee, and apparently remaining a tailor still. In 1366 we have a detailed list of ten trades whose boxes made regular payments to the town treasury; and in 1466 the list of persons paying scot and lot is composed almost entirely of craftsmen, recorded by their crafts (82). In 1488 we find the governors had become a somewhat close corporation of thirty-six, and six fresh burgesses were ordered to be chosen annually. In 1 Elizabeth a charter was obtained confirmatory of the Gilda Mercatoria and other liberties. In 1560 appear the last rules of the twelve governors, "with the assent, consent, and agreement of the twenty-four assistant councillors of the said town and commonalty;" and in 15 Elizabeth the first charter of incorporation creates "one body politic and corporate by the name of the Mayor, Governor, and Burgesses" of Beverley (83). The twelve governors became twelve aldermen. In the rules of the Corporation of 1576 (84) the following two are found, both identical with those of a gild proper:—

1. No one is to abuse the governors on pain of 40s.

(79) Early English Text Society, xxxviii., and Ashley, *Merchant Gild*.

(80) 60 B.O., 1.

(81) A similar provision is found in the Leges Burgorum of Scotland, in 12th century. —Gross, 1890, page 218.

(82) Poulson, pp. 118, 180, and 212.

(83) In spite of this apparent first appearance of a Mayor, in the ordinances relating to the weavers above quoted from the London records, and certainly dating from the 13th or 14th century, we find the same official mentioned. It was probably a title attributed by custom to the chief magistrate of the borough.

(84) Poulson, pp. 254, 314, 317, 321, and 323.

2. At the burial of the mayor, or any of the governors, the rest of the governors, and others the head burgesses, at the mayor's appointment, shall go with him to the church and said buryill.

The above outline shews us the mode of growth of this ancient and important borough, and the important part played by the Gilda Mercatoria. Not having its freedom direct from the King, and having to face the jealous privileges of powerful lords, the Gild served as a centre of unity first for its trading and manufacturing interests, and thence for the town itself. The amalgamation is imperceptible, probably on account of the same citizens being at once members of the Gild and burgesses of the town. Only in the 16th century does the Mayor authoritatively crown the edifice, and then the old gild officers sat in the seat of honor with the title of aldermen.

Let us now turn to the ancient capital of Wessex, even then claiming equality in honor with London.

Winchester.

We have already alluded to the uncertain tradition that Winchester had a Merchant Gild as early as 856 (see page 48). It is certain, however, that when the Survey of Henry was made, between the years 1107 and 1119, several gilds were already in existence. The surveyors record one "Chenicte-halla," near the East Gate, and another near the West Gate; and of both it is said the "Chenictes," or cnihts, had free tenure from the days of King Edward. There was also a "Hanta-chevesle," the nature of which seems doubtful; but it seems to be admitted the first part of the word is another form of the "Hansa," and it probably means a Hanse-house as at Beverley. "The men of the three Gilds paid xxxvs." The three Gilds, Dean Kitchen thinks, were the Gild Merchant, the Knights' Gild, and the Palmers' or Pilgrims' house of call ([85]). Anselm writes to a Winchester monk warning him against the habit of "maximo imbibendo" to be found in these Gilds, just as Hincmar had written four

(85) *Winchester*, p. 73.

centuries before. A "gemot-hus" is mentioned as existing in Winchester in a royal grant to the Abbey of Hyde in 901.

Now it appears from the rolls of the Exchequer that in 2 Henry II., Godfrey and Wulfwine pay the ferm of the "Chapmanshall" of the city of Winchester. In 17 Henry II. the sheriff of Hants pays the ferm of the same. So also in the 27th and 33rd of the same king, and in the 8th and 9th of Richard I. But in the first year of John the citizens of Winchester paid the ferm of the said "Chapmanshall" (86). It is a probable interpretation of these facts that Godfrey and Wulfwine were the representatives of the Chapman or Merchant's Gild, which was thus of prominent importance, but still a semi-private institution. Its growing authority is perhaps indicated by the Sheriff of Hants next farming the tax till the 9th of Richard I. Then in the first year of King John the citizens themselves pay the ferm direct to the King. The Chapmanshall was by that time an affair of public and municipal concern.

With this evidence before us as to the existence of these several gilds it is impossible to say whether we are to identify the subsequent Gilda Mercatoria with any one in particular of the pre-existing gilds, or to attribute it to an amalgamation of more than one. What is certain is that a gild at this period attained such a position as to appropriate to itself the title of the Gild of the city. As in York the earliest direct proof of its existence comes to us from the charter of another town. As early as 1103 Hawise, Countess of Gloucester, granted to her burgesses of Petersfield to have a Merchant Gild with its privileges like the citizens of Winchester. Thus the Winchester Gild was a well-known and established institution at the very beginning of the 12th century, and in all likelihood was in its earlier form in existence before the Conquest (see page 54).

The earliest extant charter is that of Henry II., and it is granted to confirm the liberties and customs which were possessed under the first Henry. It is remarkable too that the

(86) Madox, *Exchequer*, I., p. 339.

charter is given, not, as was usual, to the citizens or burgesses simply, but to "my citizens of Winchester of the Gild of Merchants" ([87]). In the fuller charter of Richard I., A.D. 1190, the same terms are used. This form of charter should be compared with the one to Reading ([88]), which runs as follows: "That all the burgesses of Reading who are in the Merchant Gild in Reading may be for ever free from," etc. The heading of the charter, is "Charter to the Merchant Gild at Reading." Dr. Gross's opinion is probably correct, namely, that such a form of grant was due to the existence of a powerful overlord, who in this case was the Abbot. In point of fact, however, the charter to the Gild was regarded as a charter to the town. The "Warden" of the Gild became the "Mayor" of the town. Yet in the time of Henry VI., when a former Mayor of the town thought he would like to have a mace carried before him, the Abbot objected. The Mayor appealed to the crown, but he was told that it was contrary to the franchise and liberties of our church and monastery; that he was only Keeper of the Gild at Reading, admitted by the Abbot, and might only have "two tipped staffs" carried before him as a badge of office ([89]).

The three forms of grant, of a Merchant Gild to a town, of liberties to the gildsmen, and of a charter to the burgesses who are of the Gild, shew how closely the Gilda Mercatoria of the period was associated with the freedom of a borough. They may not quite justify Blackstone's statement where he tells us, "It is held that if the King grants to a set of men to have Gildam Mercatoriam, ... this is alone sufficient to incorporate and establish them for ever" ([90]). But they shew that a Gilda Mercatoria was one of the most prominent marks of a "liber burgus" or free borough. Whatever was the distinction in particular cases between the town and the Gild, the privileges of the latter were so important a part of the constitution of a free town as practically to outweigh its other liberties. Notwith-

(87) *Select Charters*, p. 165.

(88) See *Liber Custumarum*, p. 671.

(89) *Reliquary*, July, 1880, p. 144.

(90) Blackstone, I., p. 473.

standing the position of the Gild in the charters, it does not seem in the case of Winchester to have been really identical with the government of the town. The position of the city with regard to its powerful bishops must, as in the case of Beverley, be borne in mind. The jealousy of the ecclesiastic lords would no doubt more easily brook a Gilda Mercatoria than an independent city chamber. Still we read of a mayor as early as King John. In 1269, however, in a great Borough Mote, we find two bailiffs mentioned but no mayor. This seems to confirm our conclusion in the case of Beverley. The "Mayor" or *Major* was a kind of "Elder," like the "Alderman" of a much earlier time, long before his definite allocation to the post of formal chief magistrate of a borough. The Governor of the Merchants of the Staple was a "Mayor," like the "Maires de Bannieres" of the contemporary French Gilds (see pages 67 and 68). In the "Customs of Winchester" in the 14th century we find a mayor, 2 bailiffs and 24 sworn men, and the curious phrase occurs "Major et ejus dusiperi," *i.e.*, the Mayor and his peers, meaning the bailiffs. The peers also remind us of the French Commune. The formal acknowledgment of the office does not appear before 1587, when the charter of Elizabeth states that the city had long been governed by a mayor and two bailiffs (91).

The merchants of Winchester enjoyed great fame and prosperity. Its great fair of St. Giles was said to be second only to that of Beaucaire in Languedoc, and Henry II. made purchases there for his Queen. During its continuance the shops in the city and for seven leagues round, including Southampton, were closed, and the Mayor gave up the key of the city gates to the Bishop's deputy. The manufacture of Winchester cloth, and especially of men's caps, was famous from times before the Conquest. Its measure was the measure of the kingdom—the Winchester bushel only ceased to be the standard in the time of George IV. Its mints existed from Anglo-Saxon times and lasted till the end of the reign of Henry III., when the last of the five minthouses was

(91) Milner, App. II., p. 208.

changed to the Cloth House or Draperie ([92]). Its merchants, as we read in the articles of the Lorraine merchants ([93]), had the right of preemption of wine after the merchants of London. In 1273 we read of the citizens meeting again to choose the mayor, bailiffs, and the 24 ([94]). But the next century saw its decay, and after a brief term of prosperity under Edward III., as a trading city it seems never to have revived. According to Milner the removal of the Staple to Calais was a fatal blow. In 1450 houses were tenantless and the manufactures idle.

Let us now turn back for a moment and observe the subsequent traces of the Gild. It is remarkable that notwithstanding the close connection of the Gild with the burgesses, this later evidence shows that the two were nevertheless distinct. Their approximation must have been followed by a divergence, probably dating from the decay of the commercial activity of the city. As the trade diminished membership of the Gild became less of a privilege and more of a burden. In the 15th century at some time, we are told, all merchants were given liberty to buy and sell and work here without toll or custom, probably a measure eloquent of the failure of the gild influence, while the city government took its own course. But the measure, whatever it was, was temporary only. From 1660-70 the assessments of merchants, not members of the Gild, varied from 3s. 6d. to 6d., and a certain Mr. Hobbs paid a fine of £5 for a license to live in the city ([95]). In 1705 Prince George of Denmark, on his visit with Queen Anne, was made a citizen freeman and a member of the Gild of Merchants ([96]). In 1728 the last permission to trade was granted, William Clarke being ordered to pay one guinea into the city coffers for carrying on the trade of a barber (p. 346). Writing in 1798, Milner says (II., p. 192), "At the junction of this with the High Street on the east side stands the Hall of the Guild of the Merchants of

(92) *Historic Winchester*, p. 126.

(93) *Liber Custumarum*, xxxvii. Possibly this may refer only to the men of the Bishop.

(94) *Historic Winchester*, p. 129.

(95) *Historic Winchester*, p. 324.

(96) Ibid, p. 342.

Winchester, which guild or society is the most ancient institution of that nature that does exist or is known to have existed in the kingdom. . . . It is now vulgarly called the Town Hall. The final abolition of the Gilda Mercatoria was by the Municipal Reform Act. In 1832 the number of freemen belonging to the Merchant Gild, who elected the Parliament men, had sunk to sixty-seven (97).

PRESTON.

Preston is quoted as the only Merchant Gild which still survives in the country, and is therefore of very great interest.

When, however, we come to examine carefully the "Guild" as it is now held in the town every twentieth year, and the documents which relate to it, we shall at once discover a peculiarity which has not been prominent in the other cases we have considered. The name has here really a different meaning from what it had at Beverley and Winchester. It is here not properly a society; it is a celebration or meeting which takes place at certain recurring periods. We shall see presently how far this can be held to be the original meaning of the Gild at Preston; meanwhile it is important to ask how far this subsidiary meaning could reasonably be supposed to attach to the word when used elsewhere.

The sense is certainly ancient. In the ordinances of the weavers of London, 28 Edward I., Article III., we read, the "four proved men ought to hold one gild each year in the Church of St. Nicholas Acon, the Day of St. Edmund, to which gild ought to come all those of the craft, and who does not come let him be amerced at 3 pence at such gild." But in Article XVI. of the same ordinances, we find "gild" used in the common sense of society (98). Again, in the ordinances of Worcester, 1467, Article VIII. directs "That the acts of this gild and of the other gilds precedent should be enacted and engrossed," etc. (99), the

(97) Kitchen, *Winchester*, p. 164.

(98) *Liber Custumarum*, pp. 123 and 540.

(99) Early English Text Society, *Gilds*, page 376.

meaning being evidently that attached to the Preston "Guild" of the present day. At Preston itself the usage dates at least from the 2nd Edward III. (1328), where it is found in the regulations entitled the "First Guild Merchant at Preston." "Also the same Mayor, etc., have ordered that it shall be lawful to the said Mayor, etc., to set a Guild Merchant every twenty years."

The actual records of these celebrations from the 14th century are imperfect; but, with some variation which may have resulted from the disturbed state of the country at certain periods, and from other causes, the series of "Guilds" has been fairly continuous to the present day. The last "Guild" was held in 1882, and was the occasion of much picturesque pageantry illustrative of the ancient trades and customs of the borough. The origin of this peculiar phase of the Gild will appear as we trace the outlines of its history, and will afford a valuable insight into the essential nature of these institutions.

The charter of Preston from Henry II. is undated, but internal evidence shews it to have been given between the years 1175-1185 (100). It is short, and grants to the burgesses of Preston "all the same liberties and free customs which I have given to my burgesses of Newcastle-under-Lyne." This charter is extant, and reads—"That our town of Newcastle-under-Lyne be a free borough, and that the burgesses of that borough have Gilda Mercatoria in the said borough, with all liberties and free customs to such Guild Merchant in any way belonging: and that they may pass through all our dominions with their merchandise, buying, selling, and trafficking well and in peace, freely, justly, and honourably," etc. The date is 1173. It will be seen that this grant of a gild merchant differs not at all from the typical one to other towns. The subsequent charters, of which there were several, shed no additional light upon the point which we are endeavouring to illustrate. There is, however, in the archives of the borough a very ancient document in the handwriting of the 13th century, which is endorsed "The Liberties of Preston,"

(100) Dobson and Harland, page 9.

and which is an invaluable exponent of the constitution of the town at the end of the 12th or beginning of the 13th centuries. It is really what is generally known as a "custumal," or body of ancient customs by which the municipal proceedings were regulated. We have in an abbreviated form the "customs" of several towns as Chester and Lincoln in Domesday itself, and shortly afterwards those of Newcastle (101). None, however, are more full of interest than the one we are at present considering.

The first clause reads, "That they shall have Gild Mercatory with Hanse and other customs and liberties belonging to such Gild." This is the grant, evidently much prized, which we find in the charter of Henry II. The only addition is that of the words, "with Hanse," on which we shall offer some explanation presently. The next clause is, "So that no one who is not of that Gild shall make any merchandise in the said town unless with the will of the burgesses." This provision goes to the root of the Gild, and it will be most convenient to consider it along with some of the other clauses.

2. If any nativus dwell anywhere in the same town and hold any land, and be in the forenamed Gild and Hanse, and pay lot and scot with the same burgesses for one year and one day, then he shall not be reclaimed by his lord, but shall remain free in the same town.

4. If anyone wish to be made a burgess he shall come into court and give to the Reeve (*præposito*) 12d., and shall take his burgage from the Pretors, afterwards he shall give to the Pretors' servant one penny, that he may certify him to have been made a burgess in court.

5. Also when any burgess shall receive his burgage, and it shall be a void place, the Reeve shall admit him so that he shall erect his burgage within forty days upon a forfeiture; but if he does not erect it, he shall be in mercy 12d.

15. No one can be a burgess unless he have a burgage of 12 feet in front.

27. A stranger may not participate in any merchandise with the burgesses of our town.

28. Also when any burgess shall be desirous to sell his burgage, his next of kin is to buy that burgage of him before any other, and when it shall be sold and he hath not another burgage, when the other shall be seised he shall give 4d. from the issue, but if he hath another burgage he shall give nothing.

9. A burgess shall be bound to come to no more than three portmotes yearly.

(101) *Select Charters*, pp. 87 and 110.

16. If a burgese shall sell for more than the assise he shall be in mercy 12d. and he who bought in nothing, the burgesses of the Court aforesaid shall have fuel, fire, and water to make judgment.

19. If a burgess wound another, and they shall be willing to agree amicably, friends appointed between them may require for every hidden cut the breadth of a thumb 4d., and for every open or visible wound 8d., and whoever is wounded may prove what he has lost by the wound, and the other shall pay him, and in like manner what the wounded has paid to the surgeon for healing the wound he shall repay, and the arms shall be brought to him and he shall swear upon his arms that he has been wounded, and such things have been done to him, so that if his friends consent and approve, he may take what is offered to him.

21. If a burgess marry his daughter or grand-daughter to anyone he may marry her without the license of anyone.

44. It is the custom of the borough that no burgess ought to be taken for an accusation by the lord or by the Reeve if he have sufficient pledges.

The whole 47 clauses into which the "Custumal" is divided by the translation are of extreme interest [102]. Those given above will serve our purpose.

Now the first thing that will strike the careful reader of these clauses is the evidence they bear of a very high antiquity. By clauses 1 and 2 it will be seen that the Gilda Mercatoria occupied a position of authority, and aimed at including the whole of the burgesses engaged in trade. In clause 19 we find the old Teutonic regulation of "wergild" or money compensation for violence, just as we find it in the laws of Ine and Alfred, or the laws of the Franks and Goths; and in clause 44 we find the institution of mutual security or "frith borh' just as we find it in the ancient tithings. The connection of this form of borough, based upon the Gilda Mercatoria, with the Anglo-Saxon form of the Gild will at once occur to the reader. The gegyldan or gild-brethren of Alfred's law are those who stand security as here, while the "wer-gild" as paid at Preston recalls the amalgamated "frith gild" of London in Athelstan's time, or the simpler entity of the hundred or wapentake. Clauses 16 and 44 show the old Saxon custom of trial by ordeal of fire and water alongside the Norman one of trial by battle, and both reveal a primitive and

102 See Dobson and Harland, p. 75.

semi-civilised condition of society. Clauses 21 and 44 as well as others shew the burgesses still only partially freed from some of the vexatious exactions of the feudal lord, which teach us that the grant that Preston was to be a free borough was by no means an unmeaning concession.

The Preston Gild affords us a clear insight into the peculiar position of the Gilda Mercatoria as one of the chief foundations of the borough liberties. Impelled by the necessities of defence and mutual support, by the instinct of trade, and perhaps with the examples before them of the ancient cities of the land, and also probably acquainted with the rumours of the more advanced and vigorous life of the communes and towns of the Continent, our forefathers sought to consolidate the loose bonds of the unprotected manor and hundred into a more independent and self-sufficing unity. The portmanne mote or court leet or common assembly, the reeve or bailiffs, constituted a step towards such a body politic, but they were still subject to the services to the lord, or to the exactions of the sheriff. The numerous tolls and payments which the charters specify with such exactness, passage, pontage, stallage, lastage, alnage, and many others, rendered lucrative traffic almost impossible and never secure. The several jurisdictions within the limits of a single county hampered communication and made justice uncertain. In this predicament the gild system of association supplied a principle of independent and regulated fellowship which was familiar and traditional. The charter of the king or lord legalised this institution, and elevated it into one of public authority. The mercatorial element gave a license to members of this association to trade, and gave the traders a status and assured position in the shire and kingdom.

We have seen in the cases of Beverley and Winchester indications of the continued separation of the Gild and the town, even in cases where the two organisations were so closely identified as to seem to be merged. But it is nevertheless true that in other cases the amalgamation was practically complete. The custumal of the borough, as in the case of Preston, was practically the list of ordinances of the Gild, so the essential features of the latter were lost in the municipal element which in process of time it moulded to itself, and only in casual features does the true gild survive.

It will illustrate the fundamental character of our borough system if we examine those clauses of the Preston Custumal which we have placed first in the extracts given above. The grant of the gild in the charter was to the burgesses; they were the grantees. What then were the qualifications for possessing this freedom? Great care is requisite here to distinguish between the different stages of the borough. If we turn to the case of London in the 13th or 14th centuries we at once have indications of a more exclusive body of burgesses than we find in Preston at the end of the 12th. No one, we learn from of old, was made apprentice, nor admitted into the liberty of the city unless he were known to be of free condition; or if, after he was made free, it became known that he was of servile condition, he lost the liberty of the city, which happened in the case of Thomas the Bedel, etc., who in the time of the mayoralty of John Blount lost their freedom because it was discovered that they held land in villeinage of the Bishop of London ([103]); or again, in 2 Richard II. no one whose father was a "nativus" was to hold office ([104]). It is plain that here we have a condition of things far less liberal than that which was the case under the Customs of Preston. There a "nativus" remaining unclaimed a year and a day, holding land and being in scot and lot, was free in the town (clause 2). We can see why this was so. The acquisition of fresh burgesses was still a desideratum. By clause 4 any suitable man wishing to be a burgess could come into court and pay 12d., and receive a "burgage." This burgage was probably a "void place," and he was to erect his burgage or tenement within forty days (clause 5), and it was to be twelve feet in front (clause 16). This was a very different state of things from that of London, where houses began

(103) *Liber Albus*, page 33.
(104) Ibid, page 452.

to be built of three storeys, and affairs were complicated by people possessing these several storeys as separate freeholds (105). Nevertheless, the principle was firmly held that the right to trade, though not to work, was a monopoly of the Gild, and the gildsman who was not a burgess was probably a rare exception. "No one who is not of the Gild shall carry on any merchandise in the said town unless with the will of the burgesses." And the same rule might be easily shewn to be universal elsewhere. It was so in London as in Preston. "No merchant who is not of the liberty of the city shall sell by retail any wine or other merchandise within the city or the suburbs (106)." Nor should we hastily condemn the principle which dictated this rule in the times during which it prevailed. It must be judged by the circumstances which gave it birth. The law of settlement with which it is connected is a necessity of early states of civilisation. The times were not ripe for what would then have been a species of cosmopolitanism; and our forefathers might well have argued, it may be in defiance of Adam Smith, but with a strong *prima facie* ground of right, that the prosperity of the country rested upon the growth of self-sufficing and prosperous patriotic municipalities, and that these must be allowed to protect their own autonomy by their own means.

There was a two-fold object in these measures of exclusion. The first was the preservation of the borough rights as against strangers; or, as they were known in those days, even if they came from the next county, as against foreigners; and the second object was the preservation of the same rights as against bondmen.

The borough was not to be a mere arena for traffic, like the site for a fair; it was to be a fixed and permanent seat of trade and habitation. Hence the regular trading privilege was for the holder of the borough burgage tenement, a man who was resident, who was in his place at the town assembly (or court leet), who took his share of the responsibility, and who paid his taxes. There were regular fairs for the merchant stranger, and to the

(105) Ibid.

(106) Charter of 5 Henry III., *Liber Custumarum*, page 812.

great fairs of the country, such as Winchester, St. Botolph's at Boston, or Stourbridge, men could come, and did come from all parts of the kingdom, and even from abroad, and traffic in peace. They paid their stallage and their tolls; and there was the "Court of Piepoudre" to settle the disputes that inevitably arose. The amount of trade which was thus transacted must have been great. Thus the great herring fair at Yarmouth, which lasted thirty days, was the resort of merchants not only from all parts of England, but from Flanders, France, Germany, and even Italy. In Whitaker's Almanack for 1890 are the dates of upwards of 1,475 fairs still held in various towns of England, most of them the relics of mediæval times. Thus the exclusive trading policy of the boroughs was largely counteracted by the great carnivals of barter which came round once or twice in the year, while the keys of the permanent trade were firmly kept by the burgesses of the town.

The second object of the measure of exclusion was the preservation of the burgess-right against those of servile condition.

Here again we must look at the matter from the point of view of a contemporary. The existence of a semi-free population was a fact which dated from time immemorial. Though not free, they were by no means slaves. If the villein could not marry his daughter without the consent of his lord, neither could the baron without the consent of the King. Their lot was in many respects as prosperous, compared with the rest of the population, as the artizan class of the present day. Even in London we find that when the alderman summoned the "wardmote," after receiving the warrant he was to instruct his "bedel" to summon all householders ("viros domos tenentes"), and also all men worthy for hire ("servientes mercenarios") of his ward to assemble at a certain day and hour. "After they have been summoned the bedel shall have the names of these inscribed on a roll, viz., those of the free men of the city resident in the ward by themselves, and of the serving-men ("famulorum mercenariorum") by themselves." The names were then to be called, and the absentees fined (107). They were recognised as part of the population, although they were not free. To have abolished the settled grades of society in the nascent boroughs would have been to have thrown them out of harmony with the nation of which they formed so small a part. For we must bear in mind that the very existence of free boroughs was not yet a fact accepted without question. They were in the 12th century an insignificant power in the land. Their independence of the baronial power was only won by degrees, and granted with suspicion. Nor could they have been ignorant of the course of affairs on the continent of Europe. There too often the primitive assertion of communal independence had been quenched in violence and bloodshed. Here the early consolidation of the royal supremacy over the power of the barons co-operated with the more gradual assertion of municipal rights to secure a slower but more certain and permanent development. All these elements must be considered when we try to estimate at their true value the exclusion on the one hand of the stranger, and on the other of the villein, from the full privilege of trade in these early ages. The process of amelioration was meanwhile never stationary, and when the great visitation of the plague in 1349 had revolutionised all the economic and industrial relations of society, and had paved the way for the religious propaganda of Wickliffe and his poor priests, and the uprising of the populace in 1380, the old conditions of villeinage were shaken to their foundations.

Such then were the principles and tendencies which ruled the policy of the Gilda Mercatoria in the times of their foundation in the 12th century, and were the sources of their power for the two centuries which followed, and which we find so well exemplified in the case of the early Custumal at Preston. The next comprehensive view we gain is after the lapse of two hundred years, and will afford us a clear understanding of the development of the character of the Gild from a fixed municipal organisation into that of a periodic celebration, which it has now borne for so many centuries. This document is entitled "The

(107) *Liber Albus*, page 87, 1358-58. Manner of holding a wardmote.

Ordinance of the first Gild Merchant of Preston ([108])," held "on the Monday next after the Feast of St. John Baptist," 1328, St. John the Baptist being apparently the patron saint of the Gild. They are the ordinances of a "Mayor-court," "by assent and consent of the same mayor, bailiffs, and burgesses, with the whole commonalty, for the profit and welfare of the said town, to all manner of burgesses in our Gild Merchant, to have and to use, them and their successors (clause 1)." They then ordain that it shall be lawful "to set a Gild Merchant at every twenty years, or earlier if they have need, to confirm the charters that belong to our franchise (clause 2)." And the fees "shall go wholly to the Mayor at the renewing of the Gild and refreshing of the town (clause 3)." Then follow the rules of procedure, which enact that "no burgess's son shall be admitted to the full privileges of freedom unless he has purchased his freedom at our Mayor's Court, as his father did before; no burgess shall hold office unless" his name be "in the Gild Merchant last made before," "for the King gives the freedom to the burgesses which are in the Gild, and to none others (clauses 4 and 5)." Dr. Kuerdon's account states further that the accounts were made up and published, the rolls of burgesses were read over, and absentees fined. The town clerk then entered on the records a declaration that "This court of election was one of the three grand portmotes, formerly in use within this our borough of Preston during the Saxon era, at which all burgesses under a penalty were then bound to appear." It will be unnecessary to trace the history further, for at this stage already all the essential features are present which have continued till the present day. By this time (1328) the work of the Gild proper was accomplished, and the independent borough, with its customs and privileges, was established upon a firm basis, having completed the incorporation into its organisation of the ancient Gild.

There were two objects in the peculiar celebration every twenty years. The first was "the renewing of the gild," the establishment of a fixed festival with pageantry and feasting, when all

(108) Dobson and Harland, page 11.

came together as in the gild assembly, when each stood in his place at the Gildhall, answered to his name, and swore faithfulness and brotherhood. The second was the more strict limitation of the higher offices of the borough, enhancing their dignity and shewing the extent of the honor which they conferred. There was exclusive privilege, it is true, but it is easy to see also that there was the groundwork of a sturdy patriotism and a local solidarity which would prove alike a bulwark against the Scots and a stronghold of constitutional freedom.

Southampton.

We come now to consider the Merchant Gild of Southampton, in many respects the most interesting of any whose records remain. The attention which we have already given to the Gilda Mercatoria elsewhere will enable us to appreciate the fulness of information here on several points which otherwise must rest upon conjecture.

Southampton can claim a very high antiquity. Although the site of the town has shifted, there is every reason to believe that from the early Roman Clausentum there has been a chequered, though to some extent continuous, town life down to the present day. As is too often the case, the gap between the Roman occupation and the early Anglo-Saxon settlement is too wide to justify assertion. We may state with certainty that what was the Roman town had sunk low when it re-appears as the Hamtun; there were none of the lasting monuments of old Rome which stood at Lincoln and Exeter and York, but whether as a tun or a vill it continued as a place where men congregated and dwelt. The first charter shews us the town at the beginning of the 12th century. Henry II. grants that his "men of Hanton shall have and hold their Gild, and all their liberties and customs by land and by sea, in as good, peaceable, just, free, quiet, and honorable a manner as they had the same better, more freely and quietly, in the time of King Henry, his grandfather. Richard I. confirmed these privilodges in greater detail, and John gave still fuller municipal autonomy by granting to the burgesses the farm of the town for the heavy sum of £200 per annum. We can thus take the reign of Henry I., or the same period as Thurstan's charter to Beverley, as the earliest date at which the Merchant Gild of Southampton can be shown to have existed. It cannot be asserted that it actually originated then, for the words of Henry II.'s charter merely shew the peaceable existence in the reign of the first Henry and may well mean that it had already been long a prominent feature of the town.

The ordinances of this Gild, which have been described as the only ones of the kind remaining (Ashley), are contained in a very curious quarto volume on vellum, bound in oak covers, of which we give an illustration on the opposite page. The date of the compilation seems to be about A.D. 1300. It is written in Norman French ([109]). It must suffice to give here a short summary of those ordinances which chiefly illustrate the general history of the Gilda Mercatoria.

The officers were an alderman, a seneschal, a chaplain, 4 echevins or scabini (to keep the goods of the Gild), and an usher (Ord. 1). The alderman was chief of the town (Ord. 53). Though not called "Mayor" in the ordinances, it appears from independent evidence that there was a mayor in 1217, and from 1237 to 1249, when the burgesses obtained a grant from the king that they might not have a mayor any more. In 1270, however, he reappears, and has continued in existence to the present day. From Ord. 53 and subsequent usage it appears that the alderman of the Gild and the mayor when in existence were the same person. The Gild was to be held twice in the year, on the Sunday next after St. John Baptist's day and the Sunday next after Hilary (1). This throws an interesting light on the custom at Preston. The Gild was both a society (or collegium) and a periodical celebration. The connection with St. John Baptist curiously recalls the Preston Gild, and the chaplain, gild priest, or mayor's priest, who continued to exist till 1543, shews one of the essential features of the true Gild. (A more usual dedication

(109) The full text may be seen in the *Archæological Journal*, Vol. xvi., 1859, pp. 283-296; and an English translation in Davies' *History of Southampton*, pp. 139-151.

was to the Holy Trinity.) The biennial meeting has the same character, and justifies the interpretation we have given of the later 20 years period at Preston. During the meetings payments were made by the members, gifts of wine and candles were brought to the alderman and officers, and "2 cesters of ale" to the lepers, to the sick, and the Friars Minor (Ord. 1, 3, 4,). As in the Roman gild at Lanuvium or the social gilds of Anglo-Saxon and mediæval times, a sick member was visited, and wine and bread and cooked food were brought by two gildsmen (Ord. 6). "When a gildsman dies, those who are of the Gild busy themselves, likewise all who are of the Gild and in the town shall be at the service of the dead, and gildsmen shall carry the body and bring it to the place of burial. The ward to which he belonged shall find a man to watch with the body the night that the dead shall be in the house. At the vigil and mass there shall burn 4 wax tapers of the Gild, each taper of 2 pounds or more, till the body be buried (Ord. 7)." "If a gildsman be in prison in any place in England during a time of peace, the alderman, with the seneschal and one of the echevins, shall go at the cost of the Gild to purchase his deliverance (Ord. 11)." Ordinances 12 to 16 forbid reviling, striking, or speaking evil. In case of contention arising between burgesses in the town, those between whom contention and strife have arisen shall be sent for, and he who has committed the offence shall be obliged quickly to make amends before the prudehommes, so that good peace and unity may be kept among the prudehommes of the town; and if anyone be refractory and will not be ruled, he shall be dealt with according to the ordinances of the town (Ord. 56), just as in Rome according to Cicero, in the Chinese gilds of to-day and among the early Christians if they followed the directions of St. Paul.

It is easy to see that in the foregoing ordinances we have the special characteristics of the gild principle of association as already set forth on p. 50. The evidence thus afforded is of peculiar value. Almost universal as was the Gilda Mercatoria in English towns of the 12th century, the ordinances and forms of the gild proper were often at so early a period merged in the municipal organisation that they have practically come down to us in many cases in the form of the custumals of the borough, rather than in that of the ordinances of the gild. At Ipswich and many other places originally it was otherwise, and the gild ordinances were recorded in a separate book. It is thus not strictly correct to refer to those ordinances of Southampton as the only ones which are extant. The "Custumal of Preston" is a similar document. Traces are to be found in the usages of Winchester. The distinction is really to be found in the degree in which the character of the ancient principle of association is either merged in the ordinances of the borough of whose trade it had been the custodian, or is assumed independently, as universally familiar to the townsmen of the time.

If now we study the remaining rules of the Southampton book, they will be seen to be of interest in two directions. Firstly, they shew the application and development of the spirit of exclusion and protection, of which we have already spoken in the case of Preston. This may be classed as the universal or generic character of the Trades' Gild as distinct from the Gild in general, and the ordinances in which it appears may probably be placed next in order after those which have already been quoted as constituting the most ancient parts of the book. Ordinance 19 enacts that "No one shall buy anything (in the town of Suthamtone) to sell again in the same town except he be a gildsman, or of the franchise; and if anyone do so, and be attainted thereof, all that he has so bought shall be forfeited to the King. And no one shall be quit of custom unless he have made it clear that he is of the Gild or of the franchise, and this from year to year." Again (21)—"No one shall be partner . . with any person who is not of the Gild." The gildsman, if present, was to have the first offer of all goods from a stranger (23).

Ord. 24 is curious. "Any one of the Gild Merchant shall share in all merchandise which another gildsman or any other person shall buy, if he comes and demands part, and is on the spot when the merchandise is bought, so that he satisfy the seller, and give security for his own part." It may be compared with a similar rule in the amalgamated Gild ordinances of Berwick (A.D. 1284)—"Whoever buys a lot of herrings shall share them at cost price with the neighbours present at the buying. Anyone not present and wanting some shall pay to the buyer 12d. for profit (110)," and with the Hull Coopers' Gild (see index). The customs shew clearly the strong influence of the principle of fraternity, and should be read in the light of what has been already said in the case of Preston.

There is no trace of the old rule admitting fugitives of servile status by residence of a year and a day, as at Preston; and at the date of the ordinances the membership had already become hereditary. Primogeniture was the rule, and the eldest son took his father's seat without payment, the younger sons being admitted on payment of ten shillings. No husband by reason of his wife had a right to admittance, nor could anyone sell or give to another the right of membership (9 and 10). These ordinances betray a later stage in development than the early Preston Custumal, and may mean either that they were added later than those which relate to the essence of the Gild, or that the town at a comparatively early period arrived at a condition of self-sufficiency. The ancient and typical conditions of membership were residency, enrolment in the town assembly, and payment of scot and lot; but the boroughs in almost every case were so early invaded by tendencies which required a more fixed and substantial basis for admission to full burgesship, that we have no exact records shewing the undoubted and complete prevalency of the more democratic municipality. Inhabitants as such had a recognised status, and somewhat fluctuating and undefined privileges; but as in this case, the full burgesship became at a very early period limited to those who fulfilled more stringent conditions. If the early typical constitution of residency for a year, and enrolment and ratepaying be accepted as having had an actual historical existence (as argued by Merewether and Stephens), the present constitution of an English borough since 1835 probably can be shewn, nevertheless, to be the period during

(110) Ordinance 87, Early English Text Society, page 345.

which it has prevailed in its greatest and most universal purity.

There is still a second class of ordinances of very great interest. The interest, however, only partially falls within the proper sphere of this study. In these the Gild appears as the controlling body of the town. The alderman, or mayor, assisted by twelve "prudehommes," reminding us of Beverley, not only ruled, but governed. The various trades of the town were strictly supervised. The assise of bread and ale was kept month by month. The markets for fish and poultry were governed by four chosen prudehommes. The King's peace was guarded, very much as by the municipal organisation of to-day.

It is a common belief that these ancient boroughs were altogether careless of sanitary laws. On the contrary, nothing is more common than rules such as these:—"No butcher or cook shall throw into the streets any filth or other matter, whereby the town or the street may become more dirty, filthy, or corrupt," on penalty of 12d. (42). Again:—"No one shall have any pigs going about in the streets, or have before his door or in the street muck or dung beyond two nights. And if anyone has, let whoever will take it away," on penalty of a fine. The difficulty of pigs was one which we find also in the city of London. There, however, it was complicated by the introduction of the religious question, for the "pigs of St. Anthony," which wore a bell, were privileged, and the citizens were not slow to take advantage of this to evade the vigilance of the aldermen by investing their pigs with an ecclesiastical character. In Southampton the court leet was obliged sometimes to fly at high game. A presentment of 1530 runs—"Mr. Maire keepeth a sowe in his backsyde, whiche is brought in and oute contrary to the ordinance of the town. Wherefore be yt comanded to hym and all other that they kepe no hoges within the towne to the anoynance of theire neighbours upon payne that every of them that so kepe any swyne to forfyte for every xv daies he shall so offend xxd." "The Proffesto of God's house" in 1559 was presented for neglect of sanitary laws. Muck heaps are recorded as standing before even church doors, and again in 1576 "There is a greate heape of soyle and roobidge befor Mr. Mayor his garden in the Easte Street." One alderman even went so far as to assert the liberty of the subject, but was quickly suppressed. He of Portswood was presented for "haveing severall loades of dunge within Rockstone Gate wch hee is pleased to calle his priveledge, but we amerce him ijs. vjd." (111) Similar regulations may be seen in the Gild ordinances of Berwick (112), where the penalty was 8s.

From the foregoing quotations the outlines of the Gilda Mercatoria may be fairly well filled in wherever the institution itself can be shewn to have existed. The case of the Scotch town of Berwick, indeed, is simply analogous. A comparison of these rules with those of Southampton will shew that there were but few differences other than those necessarily involved in the local ones. Both were, in fact, Gilda Mercatoria.

Summary of the Evidence respecting Gilda Mercatoria.

It will now not be difficult with these examples before us and by referring more briefly to the evidence from other towns to define generally the construction and functions of the Gilda Mercatoria. Its close identification with the government of the town was incidental, and not essential to its idea, which was in its initiation that of an association of men for mercantile purposes. But the central idea of the whole, in accordance with the spirit of the times, was the monopoly of the regular trade privileges of the place. No private gild could accomplish this without either a direct establishment by charter of king or lord or an overwhelming exercise of local influence, and the latter, where it existed, must necessarily have attained in such a state of society to an authoritative position in the town. Hence we find the clear statement in the charters "that no one who was not of the Gild should carry on any merchandise with them in city or burg or vill or socage." Moreover their monoply was not only at this period a trade in gross or by wholesale; it is stated expressly to be also by retail, which constitutes a clear distinction between

(111) Davies, page 123.
(112) Early English Text Society, page 341.

this kind of Merchant Gild and that which we find in the 15th century and thenceforward (see later). The enforcement and maintenance of this privilege necessitated an exercise of authority, and where the Gild existed, the carrying out of its ordinances by the Gild constituted a part of the jurisdiction of the town. Dr. Gross seems to lay down too absolutely the statement that with the exercise of this power, even in mercantile cases, the Merchant Gild had no proper jurisdiction, but that this was entirely the work of the borough courts. Such a distinction would be contrary to all analogy of the trading customs of the times, and would place the Gilda Mercatoria in a worse position than the lower Gilds of the Crafts. Even the Gilds of the Weavers had their courts, and could distrain the loom of a recalcitrant member (see index). The Fraternity of the Stapelers were entrusted with the exercise of mercantile jurisdiction in the staple towns. The "lex mercatoria" was different from the ordinary law of the court leet, and the Mayor was bidden lend his aid in carrying out its provisions. Each craft when chartered by the Crown, or licensed by the Mayor, occupied a position of delegated authority by which its ordinances became enforceable with the aid of the municipality. The barber surgeons of London could put offenders in ward. The tailors at Exeter could put a man in the stocks, and even in the 16th century we find the Hull Merchants' Company having the right of imprisonment for refusal to obey its ordinances. It would be strange if the great Gild of all, which took its place beside the town chamber, had no sort of parallel jurisdiction. And the ordinances of the Gilds at both Southampton and Berwick, as well as the customs of Preston, shew us plainly that they were of the nature of bye-laws which were enforceable. What the ecclesiastical courts were on a great scale the mercatorial were on a smaller one, and the same parallel may be traced in the gradual development from the time when the bishop or archdeacon sat along with the alderman or the sheriff, through the times when the church overshadowed the lay jurisdiction, to the later period when it almost lost its separate existence in the exercise of the supreme power by the State.

On the other hand, Dr. Gross has confirmed the opinion insisted upon by Merewether and Stephens ([113]), that the Gild and town were not identical. The Gild could and did include non-residents and those who were not burgesses, even women. At Shrewsbury such members were entered in a separate list. At Lincoln the charter of Henry II. established a Gild of "men of the city and other merchants ([114])." But it is doubtful if much importance is to be attached to this fact. The grant of the Gild was to the burgesses, or even the grant of a free town was to the men of the Gild, which latter case would seem *ipso facto* to constitute the gildsman a burgess. The entrance of the men of a neighbouring ecclesiastic fee, as at Derby ([115]), of monks and Templars, seems to mark the approach to municipal unity which was such a desideratum in the cases where independent jurisdictions prevailed. The converse was also true. The burgess need not necessarily be of the Gild. So it will have been observed was the case at Southampton, where the distinction was drawn between the Gild and the franchise; and Gross notes also Edmundsbury, Newcastle, Reading, Lynn, Shrewsbury, Marlborough and Derby as presenting the same phenomenon. But here again the rule was for the two qualifications in ordinary circumstances to go together. No burgess was to trade without being a gildsman "unless by the will of the burgesses." This implied a fine, which we know to have been generally a heavy one, if the burgesses were to be induced to consent to an exception. The custom was afterwards universal that no craft should be exercised without apprenticeship, followed by freedom of the town and craft; and the rule of the great Gild was but the expression of the general custom of trade. The exceptions probably arose, as at Derby, from attempts by the gildsmen to stretch the privileges to an oppressive extent, and to hedge round

(113) *History of Municipal Institutions.*

(114) Gross, 1883, page 57.

(115) Gross, 1883, page 57.

the conditions of membership for purposes of exclusion, a process which can be traced in both the Crafts' Gilds of the 14th century and the Merchant Companies of the 16th.

The privileges, moreover, were not limited to the locality where they had their domicile. Freedom from toll throughout the realm was often expressly laid down in the charters, and Dr. Gross thinks was a universal condition of the royal grants. It must, indeed, have been a privilege of great value. There are, however, many points in this custom which are obscure. The merchant generally from ancient times had a peculiar privilege to come and go in peace, and this was confirmed by Magna Charta. If the right to come and go toll free in the 13th century rested upon the terms of the charter of each obscure town, by what means could the privilege be made available to the merchant? What evidence could he carry with him which would be a passport through the tolls of different towns and lordships? If it required a "Placita de quo warranto" to find out the privileges of a town, how were the separate privileges of nigh two hundred towns to be known to all the rest? And what was to prevent any merchant from asserting a right based upon the liberties of some unknown or supposititious Gild (116)? It does not appear to have been noticed how closely the typical wording of this clause in the charters follows the formula in the deed of manumission ordinarily granted in the case of a villein. Take the following example. William de Sproteburgh, knight, in manumitting one John, says (A.D. 1470)—"Concedo autem eidem Johanni, cum tota sequela sua procreata et procreanda plenam licentiam eundi habitandi et redeundi super feodum meum ubicunque prout decet hominem liberæ conditionis et fidelis sine perturbatione mei vel hœredum meorum (117)." Thus the free passage of the merchant gildsman was simply analogous to that of the free man over the fee. The licenses for travel which

(116) Dr. Gross thinks that it is with reference to this privilege that copies of the charters in other towns were entered in the archives of various boroughs, as London, Southampton, Yarmouth, and Bristol. This may have been one of the causes. But there may well have been others, and it would appear that these entries were not general, nor would they suffice.—See *Gild Merchant*, 1890, page 44.

(117) De la Pryme's *Diary*, page 172.

were enacted by Richard II., so far as they were enforced, belonged to a period two centuries later (118). There is no doubt the clause in the charters, when it occurs, grants an important privilege, but as to its actual extent and the means of its exercise there seems certainly need for more light before we can form a very exact and clear idea of its worth.

Another point which has been somewhat passed by is the curious element of communism which appears to have been an essential part of the gild system.

Nowhere does the difference between ancient and modern conceptions of trade come out more strongly than in the kind of common partnership which in the gilds mitigated and interfered with the freedom of competition. The system of corporate monopoly and privilege was not limited to the right to carry on a trade or craft which we have already noticed. It also extended to common participation in the merchandise itself. In the scarcity of detailed merchant gild ordinances, the evidence of this, which was a matter left to the bye-laws of the gild, and did not appear in the charters themselves, has not come down to us with any fulness, but in those of the two towns which we possess, —Berwick and Southampton—it is clear (see p. 94). The brethren shared in common purchases of goods, either to the exclusion of or in preference to outsiders. The curious "town bargains" of Liverpool, Dublin, and Plymouth, by which cargoes were actually bought by the municipality to be shared by the burgesses, constitute a further development of the same principle (119). In Hull we find a similar custom strongly developed in the Coopers' Gild, and in force down to the beginning of the 18th century. How far this extended it is difficult to ascertain, but the right of pre-emption at any rate was very widely spread if not universal, and prevailed as a settled right of a town with commercial rights in the Hanse Towns (120). That it was abused, and that it excited opposition which was sometimes suc-

(118) See *La Vie Nomade*, page 250, English edition.

(119) See Gross, *Gild Merchant*, 1890, I., p. 135.

(120) Marquardt.

cessful, we know from the case of Derby, the Gild of which town was in 4 Edward III. accused of having exercised this right of pre-emption on all goods, and suffered in consequence ([121]). There is no doubt, however, that both this custom and the right of sharing in purchases were prevalent, and this feature of the Gild thus revealed connects it with the closer union of the Gild of a much greater antiquity on the one hand, and affords a point of contact with the more modern commercial company on the other.

So much has been written on the question whether the Gild Merchant was a private mercantile association, or identical with the borough constitution, that it is perhaps advisable to state once more our conclusion. The former was the view of Merewether and Stephens, the latter of Thompson and Brady. The truth seems to have been that at its most flourishing period, in the 12th century, generally it was neither; that, as a matter of fact, in its earliest stage it was in many cases simply an important mercantile association; in others, as at Ipswich, it was formally established by public authority, but that in either case, at the period of the early charters, it took the semi-independent position of a department of the borough administration dealing with trade. It did this without losing its gild character, and many of the peculiar features of the Gild were incorporated into the framework of the borough by its means. In the 13th century in some cases, especially under mesne lords, but more generally in the 14th century, borough and Gild Merchant became largely identical ([122]). Meanwhile the Craft Gilds increased in number and importance, and assumed greater control of their special departments of trade, in some cases, as London, York, Newcastle, Durham, Carlisle, Morpeth, Dublin, Kilkenny, Drogheda, and to some extent at Beverley, becoming an integral part of the municipal constitution ([123]). The struggle which has been assumed to have taken place between Gild Merchant and Craft Gilds is,

(121) Gross, 1881, p. 61.

(122) See Gross, *Gild Merchant*, 1890, p. 76.

(123) Gross, *Gild Merchant*, 1890, page 111.

so far as England is concerned, a mere myth. It prevailed in Scotland and on the Continent, but not in this country. After this period the importance of the Gild Merchant declines. In many cases it was practically absorbed into the wider town constitution. In others it survived as, rather than was transformed into, a religious social Gild. Here again in Scotland the course was different. Out of sixty-six towns having Gilda Mercatoria in the past, in forty-three they still survive ([124]).

There is still one feature of the Gilda Mercatoria which demands attention. This was the peculiar institution so often connected with it known as the Hanse, as to which no satisfactory explanation has yet been given by historians. The following account does not claim to supply the want, though it may serve to bring out more clearly the few features of it which are still distinguishable.

Many writers state broadly that the two terms were synonymous ([125]). There can be no doubt as to their being so closely connected in many cases as to have been identified with each other, but a more careful consideration of the evidence will shew that, at any rate originally, there was a distinction, and that in fact the distinctive meaning was not entirely lost in after times. The word appears first in in the Gothic version of the New Testament by Ulphilas in the 4th century, and it is there used to denote the band or company of men who came with Judas into the Garden of Gethsemane. The Anglo-Saxon form was Hós, which bore the same meaning and occurs in the Lay of Beowulf for a group of maidens ([126]). It will thus be seen that the idea was that of association. In the case of the Gild the fundamental idea was also that of association, but specially for payment or worship. Now the very case which Mr. Ashley quotes seems to clearly show the distinction. It is as follows :— "Si aliquis nativus alicujus in civitate manserit, et terram in eo tenuerit, et fuerit *in gilda et hansa et scot et lot* cum eisdem

(124) Gross, *Gild Merchant*, 1890, page 208.

(125) Mr. Ashley, *Economic History*, takes this view.

(126) Bosworth, *Anglo-Saxon Dict.*, S—V.

civibus nostris per unum annum et unum diem, deinceps non possit repeti a domino suo sed in eadem civitate liber permaneat." The fugitive bondman was to be in gild and hanse and in scot and lot for a year and a day, holding land there, and then to be free. Giving full weight to the tendency of legal writers to accumulate words which are almost synonymous, it is carrying this consideration too far to hold that they all meant the same thing. The exact distinction is very difficult to draw, owing to the fact that whatever it originally was, it very early practically ceased to exist in common usage, but this does not justify us in assuming that there was no such distinction at all. Dr. Gross ([127]) gives a list of 45 towns where the charters granted a "hanse," and after quoting many examples of the use of the word he concludes that "when a charter granted to a town gilda mercatoria 'cum hansâ' or 'hansis' it doubtless meant the Gilda Mercatoria with the right to exact money requisitions or prestations from the brethren as well as from non-gildsmen trading in the town." There can be no doubt that the word is used, as he shows, for a money tax. But it would seem that we should hardly be justified in limiting the meaning to the extent above quoted. When Thurstan granted to the men of Beverley to have their Hanshus, it is evident that such a limitation would not hold. As appears from the later charters and returns, it was the grant of a gild with its hall and accompanying privileges. Take next the charter of John to York, A.D. 1200. It runs: "Know that we have conceded to our citizens of York all their liberties and laws and customs and their Merchant Gild and their hanses in England and Normandy." Bearing in mind the early examples of the Hanse of London, the Flemish Hanse, and the Continental usage of the word, it seems most probable that in this charter John granted the right to have "factories" or settlements on the gild basis in other parts of his kingdom, for York was, as William of Malmesbury shews, a port with a great foreign trade. So late as the 18th century the members of the "old Hans" at York are said by Drake to have been held in

(127). *Gild Merchant*, 1890, p. 192.

special honor. From these considerations we do not seem warranted to deny to the English "Hanse" its primary proper meaning of a mercantile association. That it points to the prevalence of settlements of foreign merchants in the earliest period of trade, or to the special body of non-resident members of the Gild Merchant, are possible conjectures.

To conclude our account of the Gilda Mercatoria. From the foregoing examples a fairly clear outline can be traced of its most characteristic forms. Local variations were numerous; but on the whole these varied examples have strongly marked features in common. They shew the commercial complexion of an early English town. In the Gildhall met regularly all the principal burghers, and not only "drank their gild" but "sua statuta tractent." There they drew closer the bonds which held them together as townsmen by great tankards of ale and wine, by the exercise of their discipline, and the collection of their tribute to the King. There the Court of the Gild sat monthly or quarterly, received reports from its officials, admitted members, fined unlicensed traders, and dealt with the emergencies of the time. There stood the great chest with its three locks, under which were kept the precious charter of their liberties, the common hoard, and the possessions of the Gild. At the head sat the Alderman, "ye yldeste man of tham heape," as he was termed at Canterbury ([128]), supported by the council of twelve, or the four eskevyns, the ancients, and the younger brethren of the Gild. There they cherished the warmth of local patriotism, and trained men in fellow feeling and the discipline of free discussion and concerted action. When a gild brother died the great lights burned round the bier, the pall of the gild covered him, and the prayers of the survivors followed him in their faith to the dark realm whither he had gone to the company of the departed.

(128) Gross, 1883, page 46.

Chapter VII.

Religious or Social Gilds.

THERE is no part of the study of ancient Gilds which surpasses in interest that of the religious or social Gilds. Of their origin and early history we have spoken elsewhere, and the interest attaching to them does not flag until we come to the great catastrophe which befell them at the Reformation. No attempt to understand or depict the English social life or thought of the period from the 10th to the 16th century can be true to its original in which these institutions do not play a large part. Their objects are described in the ordinances of the Gild at Exeter before the Conquest, "for the love of God and for our souls' need, both in regard to our health of life here and to the after life which we desire for ourselves by God's doom," and such they remained until the end. Their number throughout the country was very great. In Norfolk, the most densely populated county of England, Taylor is said to have counted no less than 909, and in Lyme Regis alone 75 (130), though it is hard to believe that some exaggeration has not crept in here. The volume of the Early English Text Society has placed a collection of their ordinances from all parts of England within the reach of every reader, and of these hardly a single one is not worthy of careful study. They were not limited to men or women, or to a single class. Good behaviour was strictly enforced. As at Stratford, they paid their contributions, brought great tankards of ale, prayed over them, gave to the poor, and sisters and brothers drank them in pious mirth. Yet "if any man be of good state and use him to lye long in bed, and at rising of his bed will not

(129) W. Rye, *History of Norfolk*, page 44.

work, but wyn [waste] his sustenance, and keep his house and go to the tavern, to the wine, to the ale, to wrestling, to schetynge [violence], and in this manner falleth poor, and left his chattels in default for succour and trust to be holpen by this fraternity, that man shall never have good nor help of companie neither in this life nor at his death, but shall be put off for evermore of the companie (130)." At Lincoln in 1350 "They would rather not have people like mayors or bailiffs among them," "being founded by people of the common and middling sort;" "at any rate if they be admitted they shall keep their proper place, and not thrust themselves too forward." At Ludlow, "If anyone wishes, as is common, to keep night watches with the dead, this will be allowed on the condition that he does not call up ghosts (131)." In the Hull Gild of St. John Baptist, "Yf a brother despyse the monyshying of charity, yat he be put out of ye Gilde, yat he noght als a rotten schepe to infect alle ye floke."

As an instance of the importance which a purely religious and social gild might assume, as well as to give an insight into their working, it will be interesting to give an outline of the great Gild of St. George in the city of Norwich. From the return given on page 16 of the work just named, it appears that the Gild was begun in 1385, that is, only three years before the writ was issued for the returns. Its object was largely religious, in honor of the glorious martyr St. George. Every brother and sister was to hallow evermore the day of St. George, the service of both the evensong and mass, and to pray for the sisters and brethren of the fraternity, and for all true men that travail in the King's viage. They were to offer a "candel brennande" in the Cathedral Church of the Holy Trinity, to be at the chandelers at the pryme of the day, to pay a halfpenny each at the mass, and if absent to pay a lb. of wax. From the returns made in 1389, we find that on the day after St. George's Day the members were to come to the Church by pryme and sing a mass of requiem for all

(130) Gild of St. Anne, Church of St. Lawrence, Jewry, London.

(131) In Iceland, if we may believe the Sagas, more effectual means were adopted to this end, one shade who persisted in revisiting this sublunary sphere being stopped by summary process of law.

Christian souls. All were to come to dirge and mass "when a brother or syster dyeth," to offer a farthing, and give a farthing for the soul of the dead, and a penny to the mass, to provide two candles of 6lbs. of wax. When any brother or sister fell into poverty a levy was made of a farthing a week. The poor brother received 8d. a week. What was left was taken to provide the image of St. George. At the time of the return the sum in hand was 40s. (132)

The Norwich Gild soon attained a prominent place in the institutions of the city. In 1416 Henry V. granted to it a charter of incorporation (133) by the name of the aldermen, masters, brethren and sisters of the Fraternity and Gild of St. George in Norwich, with power to choose officers, to make ordinances, to clothe themselves in one livery, to hold a yearly feast, have a common seal, and to sue and be sued; to maintain a chaplain, and to purchase land of the value of £10 per annum in mortmain. Then follows a clause which had important consequences. The Prior, Mayor, Sheriffs, and Aldermen of the Gild were to have power to expel or remove all members for misbehaviour. The position of the city worthies shews the public importance of the Gild at the time, but it is added that because of this clause, it was looked upon at the time of the statute of Edward VI. as an existing public corporation, and was exempted from the spoliation which befell most of its contemporaries. This is the more noteworthy as it does not appear to have had any particular connection with trade. By virtue of the power to make bye-laws its ordinances were accommodated to the Reformation changes, and the name

(132) The Norwich folk were wide in their sympathies. In the Gild of St. Christopher, begun the previous year, the members were to pray for Holy Church, the peace of the land, Pope, cardinals, Patriarch of Jerusalem, Holy Land and Cross, archbishops, bishops, especially him of Norwich, parsons, priests, and all orders of the Church; for the King, Queen, dukes, earls, barons, and "bachelers of ye londe"; for knights, squires, citizens and burgesses, franklyns, all true tillers and men of craft, widows, maidens, wives, and all the commonalty and Christian people; for all true shipmen and true pilgrims; for the fruit of the land and of the sea, and "ye wedering;" for all men in false belief; for our fathers' souls and mothers', brethren and sisters, and for all the brethren and sisters of this Gild, and for all Christian souls. Amen. And this prayer was to be said whenever the aldermen and the brethren came together.—[See the Gild of St. George in Hull (chapter xv. of this work), founded in 1499, possibly not without reference to this great Gild of Norwich, thoug its objects were commercial.]

(133) Blomefield, iv., 347.

Company used instead of Gild. This however, is in anticipation. In 1451 arose a great dispute with the city, and by the mediation of Judge Yelverton it was agreed that the Mayor, the day after his discharge from the mayoralty, should be chosen alderman of the Gild, and the common council was taken into the council of the Gild.

The great event of the year was the procession. In 1471 every alderman was to send a priest with a cope, and was himself to wear a scarlet gown; commoners also were to wear gowns. Later we read of crimson velvet, and hoods of sanguine and red. The image of St. George, the dragon, and Margaret, the lady of the Gild, were carried with great pomp till 1549. Then we read of an inventory and sale of these superstitious articles, and in 1550 the Gild granted their temporals to the house of poor people called God's house, in Holme-street. Curiously enough, while St. George and Lady Margaret were abolished, the dragon survived, for in 1558 there was ordered to be no George or Margaret, "but the dragon to come in and shew himself, as in former years." In 1471 the members numbered 217, and in 1450, 264. The feasts were held in the great hall of the palace. In 1704 the Company presented to the Mayor a new sword of state; and in 1731 all their possessions were delivered to the city if the city would pay off their debts, which then amounted to £236 15s. 1d. In 1731 a feast on the day he was sworn was substituted by the Mayor for the ancient procession and gild breakfast. This, be it remembered, was one only of the gilds of Norwich, although the most important. The Craft Gilds also had their pageants, and no small influence in city affairs ([134]).

Such was but one of these gilds, although one of the most striking. It well illustrates the important part which they played in individual life. Below will be found other typical examples from Kingston-upon-Hull. There are few towns in England in which similar institutions did not exist. While on the one hand the typical form changed hardly at all during the

(134) Their importance may be judged from the fact that in the Statute 5 Elizabeth, c. 4, regulating the affairs of Trades Gilds, by section 33 Norw and London were alone excepted, being allowed to retain their old customs.

lapse of centuries, for the Gild of Imperial Rome, of Anglo-Saxon times, and of the 15th century are almost identical in constitution, on the other hand the benevolent and social purposes to which it was applied embraced almost all the elements of social life. The help of the poor and sick (especially of members), the burial of the dead, insurance against theft and loss and shipwreck, the care of pilgrims, the education of children, the maintenance of roads, the building of bridges, are some of the objects which they took in hand. With the increase in the practice of masses for the dead, and the establishment of obits and chantries, there is no doubt that their foundation was largely encouraged by the clergy, and in many cases took an almost purely ecclesiastical aspect; but their convivial and benevolent purposes still remained, and might well have been preserved without their superstitious adjuncts.

For a fuller account of a purely religious gild the reader is referred to the chapter on the Corpus Christi Gild, following.

Chapter VIII.

The Religious Gilds of Kingston-upon-Hull.

RECORDS of six Gilds of this class existing in Hull in ancient times still remain, and are of very considerable interest. These are—

The Gild of the Holy Trinity.
The Gild of St. John Baptist.
The Gild of Corpus Christi.
The Gild of the Blessed Virgin Mary.
The Gild of St. Barbara.
The Gild of St. Clare.

Of the last we know nothing except the name (135) and the fact that it was probably not in existence in 1389. St. Barbara's Gild also probably took its rise at some period posterior to that date, as its returns are not among the returns now at the Record Office, and made in that year. It must, however, have been of no small influence, if we may judge from the fact that it possessed a hall in Salthouse-lane with a large chapel adjoining it in the 16th century; but its ordinances and all details respecting it seem to have disappeared.

The Gild of St. John the Baptist.

The late Mr. Toulmin Smith observed that the three returns of Gilds sent up from Hull in response to the King's writ in 1388 differed from all others at the Record Office in that they were copies of the original deeds of foundation, instead of being merely descriptive accounts of their ordinances. In none, however, of the three cases (including this and the two following gilds) does he give us the full text of the return. Below is a translation

135) See Sheahan, page 431.

from the Latin of the original of the ordinances of this Gild, now at the Record Office in London. In it we have the typical legal document in which our forefathers founded a Gild for themselves and their successors for ever.

RETURN OF ST. JOHN BAPTIST'S GILD.

In the name of God, Amen. . . . . 7th day Calends April, year . . . was founded a certain Fraternity or Gild at Kingston-upon-Hull, in these words . . . . . (We) . . . . . John de Tharlestorp and Matilda his wife, Thomas Yowngth, Alan Calver, Alice his wife, John de B . . . and his wife, Stephen Inglis, Robert de Wakefield, Margaret his wife, Robert de Wawyne, Thomas de Asseburgh, Joanna his wife, William, domestic tailor to the Lord William de la Pole, Matilda his wife, John de Newland, Isabella his wife, John de Feyfelay, Avice his wife. John Wade, and John de Hayton, with our unanimous assent and consent on the day of foundation aforementioned, have ordained, founded, and decreed a certain Gild in honor of St. John Baptist in Kingston aforesaid, to be held annually on the Feast of the Nativity. To maintain the said Gild well and faithfully, and for its perpetual sustenance, we the above-named, for us and our successors, freely and of our good will have given and granted, and by this present deed have confirmed, each has given, granted, and by this present deed confirmed for payment to the Gild aforesaid, a payment of two shillings of silver of the goods and chattels of us and our successors every year, at four times of the year by equal portions, that is to say, at the Feast of St. Michael the Archangel, 6d.; and at the Feast of the Nativity of our Lord, 6d.; and at the Feast of Easter, 6d.; and at the Feast of St. John Baptist, 6d., etc.; the said payment of two shillings to be had and held freely and well, quietly and in peace by law and custom, without gainsaying of us or our successors in perpetuity.

And if it should happen that the aforesaid payment to the Gild of two shillings in silver in part or in whole, should be eight days in arrears at any term, we will and grant for us and our successors, and each one wills and grants individually, that the President, called the Alderman of the Gild, shall have right with the aid of the town to take and levy the aforesaid debt double without gainsaying, unless it be by special grace of the fraternity.

We wish and ordain, that if any man and his wife enter into the aforesaid Gild, with the assent of the whole fraternity, they shall pay two shillings of silver every year conjointly for their whole life, the one who lives the longer paying the same.

Also, if a man sole without a wife, or a woman sole without a husband, brother, or sister, shall enter into the said Gild, we will that each of them shall pay two shillings singly. And if it should happen that any brother or sister afterwards should be married, let the said Gild be content with the two shillings of silver every year for himself and his wife, so that in sustentation of the aforesaid Gild from the husband and his wife, the one of them who lives longest is to pay two shillings every year. And so from a man alone, and from a woman alone, as above said let it be levied.

Moreover, it is ordained and granted, for us and our successors, that whenever any one of the aforesaid Gild shall become surety for anyone in the Society for any debt of goods and chattels to the aforesaid Gild on a certain day, on which assigned day the principal debtor shall fail in payment of the said debt, and has not to pay the said debt by his surety without going to law, it is to be entirely and immediately levied. And if ever the President, called the Alderman, seeking payment of any debt of the aforesaid Gild, should find debtors of this kind, or their successors, rebellious by word or deed, or resisting wrongfully, we, the assembly of this Fraternity, by virtue of this our deed, for the contempt done us in the name of the said Gild, will that for the sustentation of the same, the said debt is to be taken and levied from the rebellious and resisting double without relaxation.

We will and grant for us and our successors, that whoever of the said Fraternity shall be elected to the office of Alderman, the same Alderman, with the aid of his Fraternity, shall elect and take to themselves two discreet men from the whole assembly of the said Gild, we, the aforesaid, submitting ourselves and all our successors to the aforesaid Alderman and the two men when they shall be sworn in the presence of us and our successors, and that we will hold to whatever the said Alderman and the two men in future shall cause to be done for the good of the Gild in the name of us and our successors.

Also, if any defrauder of the said Fraternity resist the Alderman when he seeks payment, or touching the profit of the said Gild, or otherwise withstand him in the exercise of his office, so that it be fairly proved, we will that for the aid of the said Gild, by the officers deputed for the purpose, shall be levied 2 lb. of wax.

We have provided and firmly agreed that we all and singular of us, as well men as women, being in the said Fraternity, shall be summoned to the Feast of the Nativity of St. John Baptist, both to the offerings and carrying the lights of our Gild, as is the manner of the like, none withdrawing and excusing themselves under the penalty of one pound of wax, in aid of the said Gild, from each thus absenting himself, except for reasonable and excusable cause, to be paid on morrow of said Gild.

Also we will, for us and our successors, that if any brother or sister of ours, whoever they may be, is openly rebellious or contemptuous whenever and wherever the said Fraternity are gathered together, so that it can be proved by the major part of the community, we and our successors decree that there shall be taken from him for his transgressions done, for the sustentation of the aforesaid Gild, by those then in office, 1 lb. of wax.

Also, if it should happen that any man or woman of the said Gild shall be infirm, bowed, blind, deaf, dumb, maimed, languishing with perpetual or temporary infirmity, either in youth or age, so that they have not wherewith to live: it is ordained and granted to each of them for charity, and for the souls of those in the Gild, of our own goods and chattels as long as they continue, each brother and sister by the officer for the time being, weekly one halfpenny of silver. Similarly let him take and receive one from a man sole and woman sole for their sustentation.

Also, from the goods and chattels of the said Gild, 5s. of silver at the Festival of St. Martin in winter for one garment, to have and hold the said halfpennies and 5s. of silver, for the whole of their lives every week as is above said, freely, well, and in peace, of law and custom, without gainsaying of us and our successors. And if it shall happen of those thus poor and infirm that at any time they be in such case that of their goods and chattels, through the weakness aforesaid, the payment of two shillings of silver in aid of the said Gild they cannot pay as above said every year, then we will and ordain that from the said halfpennies and 5s. thus to be received by them a deduction be made every year of the amount, so that the said payment of two shillings of silver be by no means withdrawn or relaxed.

Also, it is ordained that whenever any brother or sister of the said Fraternity shall depart from this world, we will, under penalty of 1 lb. of wax, to be paid to the said Gild, that all, both brothers and sisters of the said Society, without excuse of any kind, shall be present and come to the burial of the dead.

Also, when the obit of the said brothers and sisters shall happen to be, that they shall be present under penalty of ½ lb. of wax, unless by reasonable cause as aforesaid.

Also, we will and ordain that when any man shall marry any sister of the said Gild, and afterwards wishes to enter into the aforesaid Gild, by no means shall he enter for less than 6s. and 8d., to be paid to the said Gild on his entrance, unless by special grace of the aforesaid Fraternity. And if anyone else, brother or sister, shall come into the said Gild, he shall not enter for less than 13s. of silver and 4d., to be paid at his entrance, unless by grace aforesaid.

Also, it is ordained and granted that if any brother or sister of the aforesaid Fraternity shall take or receive any apprentice, that from the aforesaid apprentice shall be taken of the aforesaid Gild, at his first entrance, or his master for him, 12d. of silver and 1 lb. of wax, to be paid without any gainsaying.

Moreover, whenever any one, brother or sister, shall happen to come into the said Gild by the unanimous assent and consent of us and our successors, that at the entrance and reception of this brother or sister, without gainsaying, all the articles of this our deed shall be read distinctly and openly in their presence, so that should it happen by any means that those brothers or sisters should confess to any transgression towards the Alderman or community gathered together in a certain place as above said, afterwards that they may not say that there was imposed upon them a greater penalty than right, to which they have given their assent of their own accord on the first day of their entry, and moreover sworn to observe faithfully.

To keep all these articles faithfully, we, the aforenamed, for us and for example to our successors, have each bodily taken an oath on the Holy Evangelists. And for the better secure observation of this in totality and perpetuity, we have separately put our seals to this deed in witness to the foregoing.

Witnesses to this:

William Transale, then Mayor of Kingston-upon-Hull.
Nicholas de la More, } then Bailiffs of the same.
William Bate, }
Gilbert de Birkyn.
Walter de Bosc . . . .
John de Barton.
John de Lambard, of the same, and others.

Given on the day and year aforesaid.

[*Added in another hand.*]

Also ordained and granted that if any brother or sister of the said Fraternity shall take or receive any apprentice, that the said apprentice shall be holden and bound to the aforesaid Gild on his first entrance, or his master for him, to pay 12d. of silver and 1 lb. of wax without any gainsaying.

And the brothers of the said Gild have in hand 20 lbs. for the sustentation of the said Gild, and many goods or possessions. They neither have congregations, nor make conventicles, nor give any liveries.

After some considerable lapse of time, how long we cannot tell, for the dates of both are gone, but probably not less than 150 years, we have the following ordinances of the same gild, this time in English, and English of a somewhat remarkable kind. They are given in Tickell's History without any indication of the quarter whence they were derived. By comparison, however, it is plain that the author copied them from De la Pryme's MS., but so inaccurately that mistakes occur literally in every line. De la Pryme's entry begins as follows—"And another there was (which I do not find returned) called St. John Baptist's Gild, near unto ye Low Church, which at ye Dissolution came into ye hands of ——— Thurscross, who gave ye same unto ye Company of Merchant Taylors, which being very much alterd from what it was before, is now called ye Merchant Taylors Hall, where they meet to concert matters about their Trade, ye rules of which old gild they now preserve, a coppy of which I have here added." Thus it appears that De la Pryme copied them from the original, which had been preserved in the old Hall of the Gild. The ordinances are greatly changed from those of earlier date. The alderman remains; the two men of discretion had become two chamberlains; and "eight of the discreetest men" are added as assistants; the entrance fee remains 6s. 8d., and the yearly 2s. also remains; but the payments for widow and widower are changed. The solemn legal phrase of the rebellious brother becomes now a "rotten schepe," and the penalty is raised to 6 lbs. of wax. They keep a priest of their own, "who is an abill man," to say their prayers for them. The signatures numbered 220, of whom seven were clergy. Thus it is evident the Gild had flourished greatly in the interval.

The Orders and Rules of the Gild or Fraternity of St. John ye Baptist, in Kingston-upon-Hull.

In ye nam of ye Bliesid Trinite, Fadir, and Son, and Holi Goste, and in wyrschipp of Saynt John Baptist ye holi martir, in whoso Lovyng and Wirschipp we er gedird at yis time. Be yt knawen to alle men, yat yis charter sall here or see, yat ye bredurs and sistirs in alle articles followyng has made our vow and stately set our purpos, and be our faith bounden us with wyll and with dede serely for to kepe and trewly at our power to fulfill yaim, yat is at say:—

First Articlo es, yat ye Alderman what som eur he sall be, be new chosen on Saynt John Baptyst Day at Midsomor, and also two chamberlayns, and when yai are chosen yat yai have to yaim 8 of yo discretist men of all ye Gyld chosen be alle yo Gyld, whylk 8 may giff to yo alderman and chamberlaynes help, favour, and councel for ye Gilde profete als often als nede es; wo wyll also and we ordan, yat all brethirs and sistirs of ye Gild hald firm and stapill what somever ye alderman ye two chamberlaynes and yo 8 chosen do or ordan, for ye profete of ye Gild, and uphaldying of yo Gild.

Also we wyll we ordan and we graunte, be our fre and willfull wyll, in yis present charter for us and for our successours, yat ylk brothur and sister of yo Gild shall pay at his incomoyng sex schillyngs and 8d. of monay of ye Kings of Inglond to ye foresayd Gild to be maintend and withouten end to be sustende; and also ylk brothur of yo aforesayd Gild sall pay for him, and for his wyff, a yeroly rent of 2s. of yair gudes and yair cattalles, at fouer termes for to be taken, yat is atte say, at ye festis of Saint Mychael, atte yo Nativity of Saint John a Baptist to have and to hold yee aforesaid yerely rent of 2s. to ye aforesayd Gilde, well and in Pees be right and be custom withouten gaynsayng of us withouten end.

If any man sole withouten wiff, or woman withouten hosband, after ye dede of ayther dwel still in ye Gild, he shall pay 18d. and she 12d. at ye fower termes beforesaid. And if it happen yat yis yerely rent for to be behynde unpayd half or hale be a hall yere and he will noght pay, or refuse to ye Gilde, yat even forthwith he be put out of ye Gilde.

Also yf yar be any brothur or sistir whilk yat stufes agaynes ye alderman and his chaumbirlaynes and ye 8 chosen or gaynsays ye ordinaunce of ye alderman or his chaumbirlaynes, and yf he despyse yair monyshying of charite, yat he be putt out of ye Gilde, yat he noght als a rotten schepe infect alle ye floke.

Also we will and we ordain, yat there sall no brothur nor sistir be recevyed into yo Gild, wythowten assent of ye alderman, ye 2 chaumbirlaynes, and ye 8 chosen.

Also we ordain and we decree, that all brothirs and sisteres be personolly yerely at dirige in yo vigill of ye nativite of St. John Baptyst, and at messe on ye day for to offyr and for to pray for yo brethren and sisters saules yat ar passed of ye worlde, hav and in mynd yat it is medefull and nedefull to pray for saules, yat yai may be assoiled of sinnes, under paine of 1 pound wax to be raysed on yo morne of alle so absent withouten reasonabill excusacion.

We wyl also, and wee ordan, yat brothurs and sisteres be noght all onely at yo dirige and messe general yerely, but at all dirigies and messis of all brothir and sisteres yat dies out of ye Gild, under payn of one pound wax for to be taken and truly payd, but yf yai may reasonabilly excuse yaim.

We wyll also yat yer be 2 serges birnand at dirige and messe about ilk brothir and sistir body yat passes out of yo Gilde at ye first day 7 day.

Also wee will and wee ordan, yat alle things yat are necessary to the Gylde profet, yat es at say, in torches, or serges, or other necessarie whilk, yat longe to yo honesto wirschipp or solace of ye Gild, be ordand be yo alderman, 2 chaumbirlaynes, and ye 8 chosen.

Wee ordain, also, for us and our successourors, yat we have a prieste yat be ane abill man, and honest of conversation, for to pray for us and for our brethur and sisteres yat er passid of ye worlde, and for all christen sauls, in ye chapel of ye Trinite of Kyngston-upon-Hull, whilk preste sall take yerely till his salery of yo gudes of yo Gyld als mykill als we and he may acorde, we will also yat ye same preste be dayly in ye Quere at divine service when it is dun with note, but yf ye alderman, ye chamberlaynes, and ye 8 chosen, think it be other way to do.

Also, if any Brothur or Sistir fall in sekeness, not abil, or into poverte, be ye hondo of God: We will yat he be relieved with 8d. in ye weeke, or else aftir discrecion of ye alderman and hys council, and at Martynmesse, a coate, and a hode, be way of Almons in wirschipp of God and Saynt John Baptyst, als lang alse yo Brotherhode es in power.

Also we ordan, yat ye alderman and his chamberlaynes gyff yair rekkenyng on yo nativito day of Saynt John Baptyst, or on ye morne aftir, of allo ye gudes and cattles yat longes to ye Gild peny or penyworth, and yat he mako deliverannco of ye gudo within 8 days, nnder payne of a hundred schillynges.

Also wo will yat what things sall bo don or ordand for ye profite and honeste of ye Gild be yo alderman and his chaumberlaynes and his conncel, yat als ye most parte of allo ye Brethir assents so sallo men halde it ferme and stabill.

We will and wo ordan, also yat what man es chosen be yc Brethir of ye aforesayd Gild to be yair alderman, yat ho refnse noght yat office nndir ye payn of a nobill, to be payd unto ye profit of ye Gyld; and yai yat ar chosen for to bo chamberlaynes on ye same wise refuso noght yai office under the payno of 40d. for to bo paied of him yat will noght resayve his office when he es chosen.

Also wo ordan, and wo wyll, yat yo alderman, and yo chamberlaynes, yerely when yai recavye ye gndes and yo cattell of yo Gyld of St. John, bo bonnden in ano obligation unto three men chosen of yo same Gyld, to delyver agayn unto yo Gyld atto yo yere ende with a clene rekennyng alle yo gndes yat yai resayve of yo Gyld.

Then follows yo names of the Brethren and Sisters of ye sayd Gild, to the numb. of 220, of which 7 are clergymen :—

Dom. Johannes Woodhouse Capellanius.
Dom. Jo. Dalton Capellanius.
Dom. Will. Smyth Capell.
Dom. Will. Sharp Capell.
Dom. Alanus Hewet Capell.
Thos. Bywell Vicarius.
Dom. Will. Swattok Capell, &c. (136)

The Hall of the Gild stood in Low Church Alley, close to St. Mary's Church, and I have elsewhere given reasons for believing that the Gild was closely connected with the craft of the tailors (137).

Along with the other gilds of Hull, the property of the Gild of St. John Baptist at the Dissolution came into private hands, and soon afterwards the Hall was given by Luke Thurcross to the "merchant tailors," in whose hands it remained till the end of the last century, when it seems to have been used as the "Leaden Hall," and was only demolished in 1863-4. From a drawing

(136) De la Pryme adds—"There are fragments of 12 seals yet hanging at ye charter; but that which is rather strange is that it has no date." Tickell ends as follows—"There are fragments of twelve seals yet hanging at the charter; but what is rather singular it has no date."

(137) An interesting light is thrown by these ordinances upon the legal status of the gilds in general.

preserved by E. S. Wilson, Esq., it seems to have been at the latter time a plain upper room, with no ornaments or architectural pretension. De la Pryme tells us, however, that it had been "very much altered," and probably its last stage gave no reliable indication of what it was in the flourishing days of St. John the Baptist's Gild.

Chapter IX.

. The Corpus Christi Gild.

THE Corpus Christi Gilds as we know them in the 15th century occupied a unique position among kindred institutions. The ordinances of the Hull Gild are remarkable as shewing that in their earlier forms they differed hardly at all from the other Gilds of the time. The peculiarly religious and processional characteristics are absent, and the ordinary funereal and benevolent provisions take their place.

The Register of the Corpus Christi Gild ([138]) of York contains very full and interesting documents shewing the nature of that fraternity in the 15th and 16th centuries. The first point which strikes the reader who compares these with the Hull ordinances is that the later York Gild was founded in 1408 "by chaplains and other worthy parsons both secular and regular," and "to the praise and honour of the most sacred body of our Lord Jesus Christ." This religious character appears throughout, like that in the celebrations on the Continent at the present day. In a sermon prefixed to the Register of the Corpus Christi Gild at York, we have clearly laid down the purely religious objects sought to be attained by its formation, and the manner in which these were connected with the current teaching as to the Holy Sacrament and the unity of the Church. After dilating on the text, "Hoc est Corpus meum," the preacher continues—"Wherefore dearly beloved, when our fraternity is established in veneration of that precious sacrament, we shall be peacefully gathered together in the unity of the faith of the Church, as it were a homogeneous part of the mystical body of Christ in

(138) Published by the Surtees Society, 1871.

prayers, vows, and almsgiving, and the unity and concord of the fraternity is rooted in charity, which is one in root and sevenfold in the performance of works of pity, as the body of Christ is one under the forms of bread and wine, nevertheless the same body appears under those forms; a sevenfold miracle, as appears figuratively from the one book sealed with seven seals (139)." The ordinances which are given in accordance with the seven rules of charity, enjoin that the government of the Gild is to be in the hands of six chaplains as masters or keepers, who are to be chosen yearly on the Sunday within the octave of the festival of Corpus Christi; all members are to be present at the mass on the same Sunday, and to pay 2d., when there shall be said also an obit with note for all deceased members. On Corpus Christi Day all the chaplains are to go in procession in surplices, and two at least of the masters with white wands to order the procession. Ten lights are to be borne before the sacrament. The other rules relate entirely to the religious observances of the members. The Gild in 1458 received a charter of incorporation from the King, and in the year 1477 a fuller set of ordinances was drawn up and sanctioned by the Archbishop (140). In these the master and six keepers, twelve chaplains, and the parochial clergy in York who are members, appear as the electoral body, and the two senior keepers in the procession having white wands are to attend diligently upon the shrine; the other four keepers also with white wands are to regulate the procession. In the following year the ancient Hospital of St. Thomas transferred their house and possessions to the Gild, the governing body being increased by the addition of "twoyne sadde and discrete persons temporell." The number of members who joined the Gild was extraordinary, upwards of 16,850 names being recorded in the register extending from 1408 to 1546. The annual procession was an affair of great magnificence. The shrine is exactly described in the inventory made in 1546 by Arch. Holgate—"The said shryne is all gilte, having 6 ymages gylded,

(139) *Corpus Christi Gild*, page 4.

(140) See *Corpus Christi Gild*, pp. viii. and 260.

with an image of the birthe of our Lord, of mother of perle, sylver and gylt, and 33 small ymages ennamyled standyng aboute same, and a tablett of golde; 2 golde rynges, one with a safure, and the other with a perle, and 8 other litle ymages, and a great tablett of golde havyng in yt the ymage of our Lady, of mother of perle, which shryne conteyneth in length 3 quarters of a yerd and a nayle, and in brede a quarter di. and more, and in height di. yerd, over and besides the steple stondyng upon the same; estemyng the same shryne, besides the said steple, to be worthe above £120 ,, 0 ,, 0." "The steple with the wedercock" was estimated at £40 14s. 6d.; "the sylver bell within the steple at 11s. 8d.; Juells of golde £10 0s. 6d.; Juells all gylte £30 16s. 6d.; Juells parcell gylte £3 0s. 0d.; Juells of sylver £5 15s. 0d.," making a total of £210 18s. 2d. In the inventory of the possessions of the Gild appears also the large bowl called Archbishop Scrope's Indulgence Cup, valued then at 40s., and now preserved in the vestry of York Minster. It bears the inscription—" + Recharde archebeschope Scrope grantes on to all tho that drinkis of this cope XL^ti dayis to pardon. Robert Gubsun. Beschape Musin grantes in same form afore saide XL^ti dayis to pardun. Robert Strensall." The inventory adds that the indulgence was for those "penitents and confessed who drank soberly with moderation and not to excess nor *ad libitum*, and with a pure mind." It was given by Agnes Wyman, widow of Henry Wyman, who died in 1411, to the fraternity of Corpus Christi, and on the dissolution of that Gild seems to have passed into the hands of the Cordwainers' Company of York, the last governor of which, Henry Hornby, placed it in the hands of the Dean and Chapter (141).

On the dissolution of the Gild in 1547, the old hospital reasserted its existence, and managed to retain possession of the property, and it is curious to find them in 1551-2 having recourse to the same expedient which saved the great Gild of St. George at Norwich (see p. 108)—" If yt wolde pleas my lorde maier and his

(141) See *Corpus Christi Gild*, page 291; and *Proceedings of Archæological Institute*, 1846, by R. Davies, F.S.A.

brether aldermen of the citie of Yorke to be brether with us in the same hospitall, that wolde bee the rediest waie to upholde the saide house and mayntane the poore folkes." The Lord Mayor and aldermen consented, and in 1552 we find the then mayor master. But in 1575-6 John Mawhe and other citizens of London obtained a grant of the lands, and finally in 1582 conveyed them to Recorder and Alderman Askwith and Town Clerk as trustees for the Mayor and commonalty for the hospital (142).

Of any similar celebrations at Hull we have no record. The Gild there must, however, have been of considerable importance. It had a handsome and spacious building in Monkgate (now Blackfriar-gate), near the Augustinian Friary, and had ten tenements belonging to it. There is also extant in the Town Hall the deed of conveyance of certain premises in Whitefriargate by William Drax and John Drax to Robert Houll, alderman, and Randulph Langton, Thomas Dalton, and William Goode, brethren of the Gild in 17 Henry VII. The copy of the deed of foundation is in the Record Office. The following is an abstract of it (143) :— It was founded on Thursday, 31st May, A.D. 1358, by 43 persons, 18 of whom were women, and the rest men. The founders charge their estates with 10s. yearly for five years, afterwards with 1½d. a week, and the latter is the scale for each new comer. Sureties were to be liable, and in case of resistance or arrears the dues are doubled. The officers are an alderman, eleven chamberlains, and eight discreet men, as in the later ordinances of St. John Baptist's Gild. All meet on Corpus Christi Day. If any brother or sister is in need 20s. is granted on loan. If he cannot repay it is extended for one year. If at the end of the third year he cannot repay, it is released to him. 14d. is given weekly to the infirm, and the subscriptions are to be carefully deducted from the dole. Members are to come to the burial of a deceased brother or sister, but at this date no mention is made of the offerings or masses, which in a gild which generally was

(142) For the mystery plays connected with the celebration see *York Mystery Plays*, by L. T. Smith.

(143) See *Early English Gilds*, page 160

closely connected with the priesthood is remarkable. The ordinances are to be read to new comers. Among the witnesses the Mayor and bailiffs stand first.

There is a postscript to the effect that none of the money belonging to the Gild shall be risked in trading beyond sea, and this, together with the higher scale of payments, seems to point to their being connected with the merchants of the town. Finally it is added now that 3lbs. of silver shall be the entrance fine unless the entrance is by patrimony ([144]), which points to the inference that membership had come to be thought much of.

The Gild of the Blessed Virgin Mary.

This Gild seems to have been unknown to our local historians. Its ordinances, dating from 23rd July, 1357, are to be seen in full in Mr. T. Smith's collection, p. 155. The following is a summary. 22 founders' names are given—10 men and 12 women. The founders' charge their estates with 2s. 2d. a year, paid quarterly, and arrears were to be distrained for. The officers were an alderman, steward, and two helpmen. In case of poverty 10s. was granted by way of loan; if not paid in three years to be released. Whoever is afflicted shall have help during life; and a pilgrim to the Holy Land shall be released from all payment.

All were to meet on Assumption Day to make offerings on penalty of one pound of wax, and the same on the burial of a member.

Ill-behaviour was strictly punished, and every quarrel was to be settled by the alderman.

If the wife of any brother dies in her husband's lifetime, and he marries again, "as is natural and customary," the second wife shall be admitted without any payment.

These ordinances are to be read to every new comer, and each one is to take an oath.

The seals are put to the deed, and that of the Dean of Herthill is added to attest these.

The Gild had in hand in 1389, £19.

(144) See *Early English Gilds*, page 160.

We have no further record of the Gild till the year 1463, when their book of accounts now in the possession of the Corporation of this town begins. It constitutes a folio in old calf neatly written and extending to the time of the Reformation. No rules are given, these, along with the minutes of the Gild, in all probability having been recorded in a companion volume which has been lost. The title is "The Gilde of St. Marie the Virgin in the Chapel St. Trinity." The officers appear as one alderman and two stewards (senescallores). There are regular entries of rentals received for tenements and other property, amounting in 1463 to £3 9s. The stock had increased to £200. Its chaplain, a priest of the table, received 100s. a year and fees in addition. Among the payments in 1483 are the following: 5s. 2d. for wax, 14d. to the bellman and others for carrying round the rood on Crossdays. In the following year we find, paid for wine, 4s.; for freight of wine [1 pipe], 2s. 9d.; for stowage of the same, 2d.; for bread, 5s. The social and religious elements were thus well blended, though it would appear that the latter tended to predominate. Among the stock were, 1 old hair [cover] for the altar, one new ditto, some old altar clothes of plain cloth, one old green frontal, two twill alter clothes, two plain towells, 1 twill towell, a damask frontal with flowers of gold, a vestment of cloth of gold, a mass book, a chalice, two images of St. Katherine and one of St. Margaret, and a spruce chest bound with iron. Of the fate of these things at the time of the Reformation we have no knowledge. It is much to be desired that this old book could be reprinted in its entirety.

Chapter X.

The Gild of the Holy Trinity.

A PECULIAR interest attaches to this ancient Gild. While the history of its kindred associations in Hull, like that of the vast majority of similar Gilds throughout England, ends with the reign of Edward VI., the Trinity Gild remains in altered form to the present day. After more than 500 years of chequered but honorable history, it is still closely linked with the prosperity and well-being of the maritime population; and having by its public position and usefulness escaped the envy of the spoilers, endowed by the benevolence of its members with no small part of the spoils of the confiscated monastic foundations, it has restored their revenues to avenues of public utility and benevolence. Below are the constitutions or the deed of foundation of the Gild in 1369. It will be noticed that the document contains no special reference to seamen. This, as we have seen, is no proof that it was not really from the first closely connected with that occupation. It was, moreover, anciently known as the Shipmans' Gild [145].

It is remarkable that no return from this Gild is now to be found among those at the Record Office. It is possible that it may have shared the fate of others and been destroyed. A full account of its subsequent career would be a valuable contribution to local history, and it is much to be desired that it may be written. What we can do here is simply to put down the chief events which stand out in its history, and then to enumerate the principal works of charity, education, and usefulness in which it is engaged at the present day.

(145) See Hadley, p. 807; and *Centenary of the Trinity House Navigation School*, by E. S. Wilson.

In 1443 King Henry VI. granted the members important privileges, which it appears from a return still existing cost the fraternity the sum of £30 12s. 1d. This was the first of the royal grants of which the Gild boasts. In 1456 a priest was appointed to say mass daily and yearly for ever, and about the same time a chapel was erected, the "masters and rectors of ships" putting upon record at that time their firm belief that "as the body cannot live without food, etc., no more can the soul which is the principal part of the body." But the exercise of religion was shewn in a more practical way, and the next year an almshouse was founded for the relief of poor and infirm seamen from the dues called lowage and stowage, the money being paid to the Alderman of the Fraternity of the Trinity of the said town of Hull on behoof, etc., of the charitable work. This seems to have been the first of the seven hospitals which the Corporation now maintains in addition to large numbers of out-door pensioners. An ordinance which had decreed that no one unless a member and inhabitant and freeman should be a pilot was confirmed in 1512 and again in 1546.

The next year, 1547, Henry VIII., at the time engaged in his nefarious designs upon gilds, chantries, schools, and colleges, recognised the usefulness of the Gild of the Trinity, incorporated the Gild, and confirmed with fresh privileges the charter of Henry VI., a course which was followed by Elizabeth and the first Charles. In the latter reign, in 1637, occurred a terrible visitation of the Plague, and the Gild sacrificed its revenues without stint in alleviating the distress which raged in the town. In the same reign also, in 1631, Thomas Ferries, once Alderman of the Gild, gave to it the old estate of Whitefriars, and nine years later, Thomas Seale, master and mariner, did the same with all his residuary goods and chattels. Then came Lord Fairfax, and took pawn on 2000 oz. of its plate.

At the Restoration, Charles II. granted a special charter, testifying that the Gild "had much tended to the furtherance of navigation, the increase of shipping, and the well-breeding of seamen in the town and port of Hull." It obtained, in consequence, "a new grant of 12 elder brethren and 6 assistants, the rest to be younger brethren by the name of the Guild or brotherhood of masters and pilots, seamen of the Trinity House of Kingston-upon-Hull." And the first elder brethren were nominated by the King, doubtless good and loyal burgesses. They were to have power to purchase land to the amount of £300 per annum, and to have various dues relating to seamen and shipping, and the Gild was to be aided and assisted by the mayor of the town. Under this charter, subject to recent legislation and other royal grants, the Gild still acts.

Its subsequent history does not come within our purpose. Suffice it to say that it now maintains, in addition to its chaplain, the benevolent work already mentioned, a large and most efficient navigation school more than 100 years old, and constituting one of the best in the kingdom. It affords facilities, also, for the further study of navigation to adults, and maintains a most useful benevolent society for mariners, for aid in sickness and old age. In its public capacity it maintains a lifeboat, sees to the lighting and buoying of the river, and when called for, its brethren are to pilot Her Majesty's ships of war when the nation claims their services. It will thus be seen how beneficial these ancient gilds might have become, if they had been everywhere developed with a view to public utility.

CONSTITUTIONS ORDAINED IN 1369.

In the Name of God, Amen. On the fourth day of the month of June, in the year of our Lord, 1369, was begun a certain Fraternity, called the Guild of Holy Trinity of Kingston-upon-Hull, in these words:—

Know all men present and to come, that we, Robt. Marshall, Alderman, Wm. Scott, John de Wormeley and my wife, Hugo de Hughtoft and my wife, Rich. Ward and my wife, Thos. de Chestre and my wife, Simon Sergeant and my wife, William Say and my wife, John de Blacktoft and my wife, Henry de Hullbank and my wife, John de Wolfreton and my wife, Thos. de Hodelston and my wife, Adam Forbesco and my wife, Thomas de Swanland and my wife, Emma, formerly the wife of Thomas Taverner, Robert Taverner and my wife, John de Wrawby Cachman and my wife, John Lebster Cachman and my wife, Elena Car, Johanna Baxter, Robert Scope, Robert de Flynston and my wife, John Rudd, Catherine Racy, Christina Kyng, William Dunegeton and my wife, William de

Driffield and my wife, Simon Cutt, Robert de Cunescliffe and my wife, Richard Seagle and my wife, Hugo Sergestan and my wife, Margaret, formerly the wife of Martin Coke, Thomas de Sitheray and my wife, Robert Wing and my wife, with one assent and consent, have ordained, founded, and appointed, the aforesaid Guild to the honour of the Holy Trinity, to be held yearly at Kingston-upon-Hull, on the day of the Holy Trinity, and to the maintaining and perpetually supporting of the aforesaid Guild well and faithfully, We, the aforenamed, for ourselves and our successors, of our own free and good will have given and granted, and by this present writing have confirmed, and each of us severally hath given and granted to the aforesaid Guild, a certain revenue of Two Shillings of Silver, to be paid out of our goods and chattels, and of our successors, at four times of the year, that is to say, at the Feast of the Nativity of the Blessed John the Baptist, Saint Michael, the Nativity of our Lord, and Easter, by equal portions to have and to hold the aforesaid yearly revenue of 2s. to the aforesaid Guild, well and peaceably according to law and custom, without the contradiction of us, or our successors for ever. And if it shall happen that the said revenue of two shillings shall at any of the times in part, or in the whole, be in arrear by any of us, or of our successors (which God forbid), we will and grant, for us and our successors, and each of us willeth and granteth, that from that time it may be lawful for the aforesaid Aldermen for the time being, with the assistance of the Fraternity, to take and levy in double the aforesaid sum without any contradiction, unless it be by the special favour of the said Fraternity.

Moreover, it is ordained, That when any of the Fraternity of the aforesaid Guild, shall become surety for any one of the said Society, for the goods and chattels of the said Guild, until a certain day, at which day, the principal debtor fails in payment of the said debt, or hath not wherewithal to pay the aforesaid debt, it shall, without plea or delay, be forthwith levied of such surety. And if the aforesaid Aldermen in demanding any debt of the aforesaid Guild, shall find such debtors, or their sureties, rebellious or refractory without cause, in word or deed, then by virtue of this our writing, double the aforesaid debt, for the contempt done to us, shall be taken and levied of such rebellious or refractory person without abatement, for supporting the said Guild. And we will and grant, for us and our successors, that when any of the said Fraternity into the office of Alderman shall be chosen, the same Alderman with the assistance of the aforesaid Fraternity, shall choose two Constables and four other sufficient and discreet men, who shall be sworn in the presence of the whole Fraternity, to hold authentic and agreeable, whatsoever shall be done or ordained, for the benefit of the said Guild, in our and our successors names. And if any person defraud the said Fraternity, or be rebellious towards the aforesaid Alderman, Constables, and Elect, in demand of the revenues or profits touching our said Guild, which may be well proved, We will that two pounds of wax be taken and levied of him, in aid of the aforesaid Guild, by the aforesaid Constables and Elect.

And that no one be received into this our Fraternity without the will and assent of the Alderman, Constables, and four Elect aforesaid. And if any one shall enter this Fraternity, upon his entrance, upon the Holy Evangelists of God, and by his faith, shall be obliged faithfully to pay his yearly sum, and to his utmost power to maintain and support the aforesaid Guild.

Moreover, We order and strictly enjoin that all of us be present in the Church of the Holy Trinity, in Hull, on the day of the Holy Trinity, as well at the Offertory, as to carry the Candle of our Guild (as the custom is), not absenting or excusing ourselves, under the penalty of one pound of wax, to be paid to the said Guild the next day, in aid of the same Guild by each so absent without a reasonable cause. And whensoever any of the Brothers or Sisters of the said Guild shall die, the funeral shall be celebrated in the town of Kingston, and all the Brothers and Sisters shall be present at the Placebo dirge, and at Mass, making offerings there for the soul of the deceased, every one under the penalty of one pound of wax for the aid aforesaid, unless they have a reasonable excuse; and four tapers of the goods of the said Guild shall be burning, and thirty masses for the soul of the same deceased shall be celebrated immediately after the burial, or at least within the first week. And if a child of the said Brothers and Sisters shall die, two tapers shall be burning, and the Brothers and Sisters shall offer at mass. Also, if any Brother or Sister of the said Guild be rebellious whensover it shall happen that the said Fraternity are met together, which can be proved by the major part of the said Fraternity, immediately one pound of wax shall be levied of such rebellious person for the support of the said Guild.

And if any discord shall arise among the Brothers or Sisters aforesaid, it is our will, that by the Alderman and Brothers aforesaid, concord be restored. And if any shall be rebellious or behave contrary to reason and concord, two pounds of wax shall be immediately levied of him for the use of the said Guild. And if he be a second or third time rebellious and contumelious, he shall immediately be ejected out of the said Fraternity without recovery, unless by the favour of the Alderman and others of the said Guild.

And if any of the Brothers or Sisters of the said Guild languishing in a perpetual infirmity, so that they have not of their own to support themselves with, We ordain that such infirm man or woman shall take every week of the goods of the said Guild eightpence; and at the Feast of Saint Martin, in winter, one tunic and a little cap; and in case the goods of the said Guild shall not be sufficient for this (which God forbid), then there shall be a collection among the Brothers and Sisters of the said Guild to support the said infirm man or woman. It is also our will, and we ordain, that when it shall happen, that any one shall come into this our Guild, at his entrance and reception, all the articles of this our writing, shall be read openly and distinctly before him; lest our constitutions and ordinances aforesaid should hereafter be contradicted or changed by any of the Brothers or Sisters of the said Gnild. And faithfnlly to hold, and firmly to snpport all and singular these things. We, the aforenamcd Brothers, for us and the example of onr sncceseors, have taken onr corporal oaths npon the Holy Evangelists of God.

In witness whereof we have alternately put onr seals to this our present writing. These being witnesses: Robert de Selby, then Mayor of Kingston-npon-Hnll; William de Cane and William de Bnbwith, Bailiffs of the said town; Thomas de Sancton, Peter de Grimsby, Henry de Selby, William de Snaynton, John Lambert, and others.

Given at Kingston-npon-Hnll, tho 12th day of the month of December, in the year of onr Lord abovo said.

Andrew Davy and Johanna his wife.
William Best and Alicia his wife.
Thomas Bellerwell and Johanna his wife.
William Power and his wife.

Afterwards received into the Fraternity aforesaid, that is to say: William Wymonk and Jnlian, his wife, Robert Brise and Alicia his wife, Richard de Walton and his wife, Richard Dnndale and his wife, Robert de Weighton and his wife, Robert Bowes and Anna his wife, William de Lepton and Constance his wife, Richard Wilberry and Johanna his wife, Thomas de Hornsea and his wife, Roger Bassett, Alicia Bower, John de Swanland and his wife, John Page and Katherine his wifo, Robert Stolfyn and his wife, Thomas de Walton and his wife, John Campion and his wife, John Lilio and his wife, John Baker and his wife, John Ravon and Agnes my wife, William de Meton Bocher and Anna my wife, John de Clee and Alice my wife, Peter Barker and Margaret his wife, Robert Guerdson and Johanna his wife.

Chapter XI.

The Minstrels' Gild and Feste du Pin.

IN the book of ancient London ordinances known as the "Liber Custumarum" occurs a curious account of the Brotherhood of the Pin, introduced, it is supposed, from France about the end of the 13th or beginning of the 14th century. This was a Gild of minstrels [146], regulated by strict rules of procedure, and whose chief minstrel was known as the "Prince." The editor adds that "no other evidence of such a fraternity having ever existed in England is, it is believed, known to exist."

It is therefore of peculiar interest to note the Gild of the Minstrels, which appears to have been of indigenous growth, and to have had its centre for the North of England at Beverley. The claim to descent from the time of Athelstan must, of course, be taken with qualification. Athelstan in the old records of Beverley is a kind of eponymous hero. At the same time the peculiar relations between the minstrels and the baronial halls, as well as the town's minstrels, refer to customs which undoubtedly are very ancient, and we know that among no class would tradition linger so long as among those whose trade it was to preserve it. Whether we have here really a relic of the Celtic bards can only be a matter of conjecture. The form of the fraternity is simply analogous to that of any other craft, though the fact of its being an organisation which embraced the whole of the brotherhood from the Trent to the Tweed is a peculiarity which marks it as unique. Among the French craftsmen generally such widespread fraternities were common, and attained to a very remarkable development, but England affords hardly a trace

(146) See the Ordinances, *Liber Custumarum*, page 216.

of such a tendency. Nor does this Gild shew any signs of foreign extraction.

There are, however, remains of several other Gilds of Minstrels in existence. In the 15th century we find the King complaining (147) that "uncultured peasants and workmen of different trades in our kingdom of England have passed themselves off as minstrels: some have worn our livery, which we did not grant to them;" so he orders them to resuscitate the old Gild of Minstrels. It was attached to St. Paul's Cathedral on its religious side, and had a marshall and two wardens. Whether it was lineally connected with the Feste du Pin does not appear. The society was restored again in the 17th century, and expired in 1679.

The ordinances of a Gild of Minstrels at York officially recorded in 1561 still exist (148), and of another in Canterbury in 1526 (149). None of these, however, seem to have had any connection with the Beverley Gild.

Philip Stubbes (150) in the 16th century tells us that "Every towne, citie and countrey is full of these minstrelles to pype up a dance to the deuill, but of dyuines so few there be as they maye hardly be seene."

Though long extinct, the Beverley Gild has left a peculiarly interesting memorial of its existence behind it. In St. Mary's Church is a pillar on the north-east part of the nave with the statuettes of four minstrels in stone on the capital; underneath is a scroll with these words—"Thys pyllor made the maynstrels;" and on the back, "Orate pro animabus histeriorum." The date of the architecture is abont 1524. The figures are clad in short coats, painted blue, with red stockings, yellow girdles and stocks. The instruments they bear are a crowth, a guitar, a treble and bass flute, a side drum and tabor; doubtless true representations of the brethren who stood in the "Castels" on

(147) Patent Roll of Edward IV., pt. I., m. 17, and Rymer, April 24th, 1469.

(148) *York Plays*, Oxford, 1885, pp. xxxviii. Note, 125 Note.

(149) W. Welfitt's *Extracts from Canterbury Records.*—[Lucy T. Smith's Note in *A Wayfaring Life*, page 202.]

(150) *Anatomy of Abuses*, pp. 171, 172.

Corpus Christi Day and made music, as Olliver says, "in complete and harmonious concert (151)."

THE ORDER OF THE FAMOUS COMPANY OR FRATERNITY OF MINSTRELS IN BEVERLEY.

Whereas it is and hathe been a very annciente custome ante of the memorie of dyvers aiges of men heretofore contynnally frequented from the tyme of King Athelstone, of famons memorie, sometyme a notable Kynge of Englande, as may appeare by olde bookes of antiquities. That all or the most part of the mynstrell playing of any musicall instruments, and therby occupying there honest lyving. inhabytyng dwelling or servyng any man or woman of honour, and worshype of any citie or towne corporate or otherwise, between the rivers of Trent and Tweed, have accustomed yerely to resort unto this towne and borough of Beverley, at the Rogation Days; and then and there to chose yerely one Alderman of the Mynstrells, with stewards and deputies, authorized to take names, and receive customable duties of the brethren of the said Mynstrells' Fraternitie; and the Alderman to correcte, amend, execute, and continue all such laudable ordynances and statutes as they have hitherto ever used for the honestee and profit of their science and art musicall, to be only exercised to the honour of God, and to the comfort of man.

Therefore, William Pridsay, Robert Thompson, Christopher Farer, Richarde Craven, William Sands, William Yong, Robert Sparrowe, Robert Haryson, Henry Powre, Alexander Guy, and William Farley, the governors of the said town, A.D., 1555, by virtue of the ancient charters granted to this same towne of Beverley, by the noble kyngs of this realme of Englande, and successyvly confirmed the same under their brode seall from the tyme of the abovenamed King Athelstone, hitherto and now last of all confirmed in most ample manner by the gracious goodness of our most virtuous sovereign Lord and Ladye Kynge Phylip and Queen Marie, do grant unto the said brotherhood of mynstrells the renewing of all godly and goodley orders concerning the said science, of late partly omitted to be revyved in as large and ample a maner and form as they have been hitherto at any tyme used, and so to be continued at the said place and tyme yearly for ever, in manner as followeth:—

Imprimis.—It is ordained and statuted for ever, to be kept by the assent and consent of all the brethren of the Fraternity of Mynstrells, —That all the brethren within that science shall come at the comandment of the Alderman or his stewards, to what place within Beverley as he shall assign them, and there to chose the Alderman and stewards, and to keep the hour to them assynged in payne of every offence xijd.

Also if there be any brother that will not come in or being comed will depart without licence, before the new Alderman and yearers be chosen, and other honest orders there to be taken, for the profit and

(151) *Hist. Beverley*, page 168.

comodity of tbe said scyence and hrotherhood, shall bave for bis fyne ij*s.* iiij*d.* withont forgyvness.

Also it is ordyned and statnted hy the Alderman of the Mynstrells, with tho hole assent and consent of all the hrethren of the same, tbat wben tho new Alderman is chosen, that then he shall have two honrs respite for to provide him two honest men, inbabiters and hurgesses within tbe towne of Beverloy, to be his snerties for tbe saveguard of the stock which then shall he delivered unto him by the old Alderman, and of the performance of all his other dnties according to this present original, which sureties shall be bounden in donhle valne of the said stock, and if no such snreties are found, then that eleccyon to he voyd, and anotber Alderman to he chosen.

Also the Alderman shall make eleccyon of two able men for the guilde to fill, and himselfe to he tbird, and of tbem three all the fellowship sball chuse for that year, to fill the said offys; also the Alderman with bis stewards shall set two ahle men on the eleccyon to these two that occupie, and of these fower tbe Alderman sball chose one for the sterwerd, and tbe fellowship sball one for that year.

Also an ordynance made by tbe assent of all the brethren, with the Alderman of the Mynstralls, that tbere shall no man heen any offys for the said fraternity to the tyme that he have paid his dne, and be full brother npon payn of vj*s.* viij*d.*, paid to the Alderman.

Also it is ordayned and statuted by the Alderman of the Mynstralls, witb the hole assent and consent of tbo Mynstralls themselves; that no Alderman shall take in any new brethren unless be bo mynstrell to some man of hononr and worship, or waite of some town corporate, or other ancient towne, or else of some honesty and conyng, as shall be thongbt laudable and pleasant to the hearers there or elsewbere, npon pain of vj*s.* viij*d.*

Furthermore it is ordayned hy the Alderman and his hrethren, tbat if there be any made hrother already, not being able as aforesaid, or has been so ahle, and now declinetb from the same for lack of bonest usage, tbat tben tho Alderman and hrethren and officers sball thom expell from their brotberhood; as Alderman and officers will make answer to the Kyng's officcrs wben tbey speak of vagabonds and valiant beggars.

And if any person or persons so deprived shew himself obstynate, and stands in contencyon arrogantly, that then the kyng's officers be sent for to carry tbe offender or offenders to tbe gaile, and there to remain nntil he be reconcyled to honest order, and for his obstynacy to forfeitt as tbo Alderman and his bretbren shall think meate and convenient in that behalfe.

It is ordeyned also tbat mynstrells to men of worship, waits, conyng men, and able men, being honestly esteemed, and within tbe liberties of the hrotherhood of Beverley, shall come in and be brotbers in the said brotberbood at the next Rogaison Days; after admonition and warning be given to them, npon payn of xx*s.*, except

they can show lawful cause to the Alderman and his brethren they being thereof examined.

Also it is ordeyned by the Alderman and his brethren, that no brother shall have but one apprentice at one time, upon payne of vj*s.* viij*d.*, and he be presented to the Alderman in one year and one day to be enrolled and made full brother, upon payn of vj*s.* viij*d.*

Also it is ordeyned by the Alderman and his brethren, that no mynstrall shall teach his own son or any other for a particular sume of money, but he shall present him as is abovesaid, upon payn of vj*s.* viij*d.* It is ordered also that no mynstrall shall take any apprentice to teach or any other, as is abovesaid, except the same mynstrall be able and approved by the Alderman and his brethren, upon payn of xx*s.*

Also it is ordeyned that when the Alderman and his brethren are settlin accompts, that then none of the other brethren shall come but as they are called, upon payn of ij*s.*, that is to witt, the steward xvj*d.*, for the negligence, and the offender, viijd.

Further it is ordeyned that no mynstrall, being a foreigner or a stranger, shall remain upon faires and feates within the said liberty longer then one fortnight to pass and repass, to be there masters and friends, and so to depart of the said liberties, upon payn of xij*d.*, every tyme they be taken, they being once thereof admonished and warned.

It is ordeyned also that no shepherd or husbandman, or husbandman's man, or man of other occupation playing upon pipe or other instrument, shall sue any wedding, or other thing that appertaineth to the said science, except it be within the parish wherein he dwelleth, upon payn of vj*s.* viij*d.*

Also it is ordeyned that no mynstrell shall play at any wedding or alderman's feasts within this town of Beverley (the liberties of the Cross Days and all other fair days excepted) unless he be a burgess sworne upon scote and lote within the same, upon payn of iij*s.* iiij*d.*

Also if there be any man that is no brother that taketh a brother's castle from him, he shall pay xij*d.* to the Guilde.

And also it is ordeyned that none shall play in a castle except he be a brother, upon payn of xij*d.*

Also it is ordeyned that all manner of forfits aforesaid shall be divided into three pts., that is to say—one part to the comon place of Beverley, the second part to the Brotherhood of the Mynstralls, and the third part to the stewards or the officers which the straine is made or the forfeit paid, and within the town of Beverley, the half to the common places.

Also it is ordayned by the Alderman and his brethren that if there be any old or honest brother syke or at Male East by the visitation of God within the said liberties, being destitute of help and succour and fen friends, then the Alderman, being thereof admonished, shall, at the discretion of himself and four of the brethren, relieve and succour the brother so being visited with some parcel of money, with all Godly customs that have been used heretofore, as nigh as ability may sue or attaine.

Also an ordnance made by the assent and consent of all the brethren, with the Alderman of the same fraternity, that no man be made brother with the occupation of the mynstralls without he be a a mynstrall and able.

Also if there be any brother that dispraise his Alderman and stewards, and will not do at the command of them at that time, that is to say, that when he or they will not come at the prime Gild or ony other thing which shall be at the welfare of the said, they shall pay ij*s*. vj*d*.

And also an order made by the assent of all the aforesaid brethren, that the Alderman shall receive of every mynstrall that stands in the castles upon Cross Monday, without he be brother to the said fraternity, then to pay xij*d*. to his contribute and to the welfare of the said fraternity of our Lady of the Read Arke in Beverley.

And it is ordeyned by the Alderman and his brethren that every officer of the said science, authorized by several letters under the common seal of the fraternity, shall yearly make a true account of all the receipts of him or them, or any of them, takes of any brother or other mynstrall, upon such payment as shall be thoughte mete by the Alderman and his brethren, in case any fault can be proved in him or them so receiving any customs.

Also it is ordeyned by the Alderman and his brethren that if any brother of the said science or other do receive or gader any money of any brother or other of that science, having no authority so to do by lawful letter seal[d] as is premised, then it shall be lawful to punish such an untrue offender, and so proceed according as the law shall permit, or to cause him to make a true account of all such untrue and unlawfully taken receipts.

Also it is ordeyned and statuted by the Alderman and his brethren for ever to be kept, That the said brotherhood of minstralls of their own grace and good will shall pay and give unto the governors of the corporate of Beverley, and to the comonalty of the same, xx*s*. as often as they shall have to renew the confirmation of the great charter, for there lawful aid in maintaining the said fraternity of mynstralls, as hath been the custom heretofore.

Also it is ordeyned that every brother of the said fraternity shall pay to the Alderman for his brotherhood ij*s*. within two years of his entry, upon payne of iij*s*. iiij*d*. [152]

(152) Oliver's *History and Antiquities of Beverley*, pp. 557-559.

CHAPTER XII.

THE HULL TRADING COMPANIES.

"THE history of a commercial city," says Prof. Freeman, "is sure to be the history of its commercial companies (153)." Nearly three centuries before this Lord Bacon had written, "I confess I did ever think that trading in companies is most agreeable to the English nature, which wanteth that same general vein of a republic which runneth in the Dutch, and which serves them instead of a company (154)." The truth of Prof. Freeman's remark becomes the more evident as we look more closely into the records of English trade. Our historians have hardly recognised the extent to which it is true. They have treated of commerce rather from the modern point of view of individualism, without sufficiently realising how subtilely the pervading atmosphere of present modes of thought colors their interpretation of ancient facts. Whether with Lord Bacon we are to attribute the fact to the peculiar temperament of the Anglo-Saxon race, or to the closer communal tie of the Netherland cities which gave to their municipal bodies more the features of great mercantile corporations, the power and extension of our early mercantile companies is inextricably bound up with the history of commerce. The history of Kingston-upon-Hull is a remarkable instance of this. The local historians have dwelt upon the ancient commerce of the town, but its mercantile companies have hardly gained mention. Yet it will be seen that although the barest outlines of the constitution of some of them can now be recovered, enough remains to shew that it was formerly the seat

(153) *Historic Cities, Bristol*, Introduction.
(154) Anderson, ii., 232.

of numerous busy and influential societies, and that these practically conducted and monopolised the trade of the town. The ordinances of the Company of St. George remain, and are given below. But here were also branches of the Fellowship of the Merchants of the Staple, of the great Corporation of the Merchant Adventurers, of the Eastland Company, and of the Merchants of the Steelyard or the Hanseatics. The monuments of the members of these societies still remain in the old Parish Church; their charitable foundations still bear fruit; while still more it may be said that if we wish to see their true monuments we must look around at the mighty structure of trade and industry of which they laid the foundations.

It is in the seaports of the realm that we must look for the best examples of that mercantile spirit which is characteristic of English trade. In London, York, Hull, Bristol, and Exeter are the old merchants seen at their best. The "great aventure" necessary to send cargoes beyond sea fostered the spirit of enterprise; the closer intercourse with the greater seats of foreign commerce inspired them with more liberal and wider ideas than the cities of the interior.

The earliest condition of trade was necessarily not unlike that which prevails in a New World store, where the distinction between retail and wholesale is lost, alike in fact and prestige. Yet from a very early time there had existed a distinction between the merchants in the modern English sense and the smaller traders. Athough the term "merchant" or "mercator" seems always to have carried with it a tradition of the more dignified kind of traffic, yet the early distinction was by no means clear. "Tradendo" and "mercator" were confused. We have seen that in the Gilda Mercatoria of the 12th and 13th centuries, the right of selling by retail was one of the privileges of the burgess and gildsman, and the distinction was rather between the burgess and gildsman on the one hand, and the stranger and unfree man on the other, than between the retail and wholesale dealer (see p. 97). The same distinction prevailed also strongly in the city of London. In the language of Edward I., the traders who attended public fairs were merchants, and we may compare the Scotch use of the word at the present day. Yet the distinction very early prevailed. By 37 Edward III., merchants were forbidden to deal in more than one kind of merchandise, though this part of the statute had to be repealed the following year. The provision in the same statute relating to crafts continued in force till the 5th year of Elizabeth (155).

The reign from which the ordinances of the earliest Hull Merchants' Gild date is remarkable for the royal change in the title of the Tailors' Company to that of the Merchant Tailors', and in that of the Brotherhood of St. Thomas to the more pretentious term Merchant Adventurers. In Beawes' "Lex Mercatoria" we find it laid down, "None therefore in Great Britain can properly be styled merchants but such as export her native products and manufactures, or those of her colonies, to foreign climes, or import the commodities of different countries into these kingdoms (156)."

The early history of the word is curious. In the time of Cicero, the merchant (mercator) was a trader of higher grade than the mere negotiatores. Among the latter, but not the former, were the muliones, fullones, fascinatores, textores, etc. But the difference consisted in another respect in this, the merchant was one who had his domicile at Rome; but who for the sake of exporting or importing goods, made excursions into the provinces. The negotiator on the other hand was one who was indeed a Roman citizen, but fixed the seat of his fortune in the provinces, and rarely returned to the city, unless for the purposes of registration. According to Justinian, negotiatores were those who "ergasterio officinæ aut tabernæ præsunt," and by the title "mercator" were excluded "campsores, seu nummularii, argentarii, trapesitæ, et collybistæ." It is probable that here we have the origin of the aristocratic tinge which from the dawn of the Middle Ages clung to the term "mercatores" on the Continent,

(155) Anderson 1., 348.
(156) Mortimer, p. 81.

where, for example in Cologne and the Rhine towns, it was often synonymous with burgenses.

In the Hanse Towns, in the 16th century, the distinction was strictly defined. The status of a merchant was to be gained by free men, by apprenticeship, and matriculation—generally through the mercantile Collegia or Gilds, though without the exercise of merchandise it was not complete. "Matricula probat, mercatura facit mercatorem," and poverty was held to imply cessation from commerce. The merchant was one who did not deal "minumatim," or as the French say, "en d'etail," but in quantity. And a scholastic foundation was given to the distinction in the fact that the artisan changes the form of a thing, but the merchant does not. So the Senate of Lubeck, in 1607, decreed, "That no one of the citizens who was a merchant (kaufschlagen), should carry on a handicraft, nor should anyone in service or handicraft be a merchant, under penalty of 5 marks of silver, excepting such victuals and material as they wanted for their own houses or trades." The clergy were forbidden to be merchants, but not to exercise a handicraft; though in England the traders under the color of the clergy often constituted a great difficulty in the jurisdiction of the towns. It is curious to find the Hanseatics attributing the estimation of trade in England in part to the law of primogeniture, which excluded the younger nobles from the aristocracy (157).

As a matter of fact the merchants never lacked recognition in this country from the Anglo-Saxon time, when the man who fared thrice over the sea became thegn-worthy. In 1290, and in Magna Charta, freedom was granted him to go and come in peace (158). The founder of the free port of Hull called a great representative assembly of merchants, both English and foreign, from 42 towns, in 1303, for their consent was needed to replenish the treasury by fresh taxes upon wool (159), and at this time the sub-estate of the merchants was something very like a fourth estate of the realm.

(157) For authorities on many of these points, see Marquardt, Lib. 1., vii.
(158) Art. 41-42.
(159) Stubbs, 11. p. 200.

In tracing the history of the Associations of Merchants in this country, as in the case of the other forms of association which we have considered, no small light can be brought to bear upon the subject by reference to the kindred associations elsewhere, and especially in those towns with which Hull and the other towns of the East Coast were in frequent contact. In Wisby, Rostock, Lubeck, and Hamburg were from a very ancient date Collegia or Societies of Merchants in which the principle of association was carried to a much greater extent than in England. The account given by Marquardi of the origin of these societies is full of interest. After referring to the College of Merchants mentioned by Livy, he goes on to shew the existence of similar societies in the island of Rhodes. The Emperor Antoninus committed to it the adjudication of naval matters, and called it the Mistress of the Seas. At the decline of Rhodes, a little before Charlemagne, the supremacy passed to Oleron for the countries west of the Rhine, and to Winetha and Wisby for the Baltic and the parts of Europe to the eastward; and the Collegium of Merchants established itself especially at Wisby, and thence spread to Lubeck, whose College became the most famous, and the court of appeal for the others. Hamburg, Rostock, and Dantzic had also powerful societies. These, he tells us, were the great companies or fellowships, for these Collegia were nothing else than fraternities, and the members are brothers. The three great Collegia of Lubeck were the Collegia Familiorum Antiquorum, founded about 1379, whose patron was St. Olaf; the Kaufleute Compagnie, founded in 1495; and the Schonenfahrer Schütting, the most numerous and powerful, founded in the infancy of the State. These all had their ordinances, rules to preserve morals, peace, and trade, a certain jurisdiction, feasts, and a peculiar ornate and solemn manner of conducting funerals with places of their own in the churches, thus possessing the true gild features.

But there was also a sort of association which seems to have closely resembled a monastic establishment, but in a purely commercial character. The members dwelt together, and obeyed a kind of rule or discipline as members of the same brotherhood or collegium. The apprenticeship answered to the noviciate, and the matriculation of the merchant closely resembled that of the student. The old Roman rule held good that three were requisite to constitute a Collegium, and a federation of "families" or Collegia constituted a university. Such when transplanted to foreign ports were the Colony at Bergen and the Merchants of the Steelyard in London. It is interesting to observe the same ideas of association prevalent in the different spheres of the church, the university, and commerce.

These commercial companies of the Baltic were then ancient, highly privileged, and flourishing institutions, and were in frequent communication with the English ports on the Eastern Coast. There is, in fact, no line of demarcation to be drawn either here or abroad between the ancient companies of the 14th and 15th centuries on the one hand, and the new companies which sprang into being in the 16th century at the impulse of the discovery of the passage of the Cape, of the New World and the White Sea, on the other. After the Companies of the Merchant Adventurers, the Eastland Company, the Spanish Company, and others, there followed the East India Companies of England, Holland, and France. Thus we can see in the latter the ancient form of association taking to itself by the force of circumstances the responsibilities of government to an extent to which its previous history affords no parallel. No longer shaping the constitution of cities, it assumed the rule of empire, and the 250 millions of Hindostan to-day owe the foundation of their more than Roman peace to what was originally nothing but a great English Gild. To the same origin, more remotely, Africa, East and West and South, and Borneo, seem to be likely to owe the foundations of their civilisation (160).

(160) See Marquardt, Lib. III., *passim*.

CHAPTER XIII.

THE MERCHANTS OF THE STAPLE.

THE Staple was one of the standard institutions of English commerce for at least four centuries. The circumstances which gave rise to it are these. In the first place there was the manifest advantage of a fixed and stated mart. Just as a fair was the mediæval method of promoting internal trade and exchange, so the establishment of certain definite ports where the regular materials of export and import might be brought was a great convenience, and was considered a necessity of commerce. To this must be added the exigencies of the Exchequer. The export and import duties could only be collected with any certainty if certain ports were fixed through which all trade must pass. Hence the origin of the word. "The English word staple," says Anderson, "is in the civil law Latin of those times termed Stabile Emporium, *i.e.*, a fixed port or mart for the importing of merchandise. From whence came the word staple as used all over Europe (161)."

In the highly-developed mercantile law of the Hanse Towns, the staple-right acquired a more exact meaning, and was strictly defined from the "jus emporii." The "jus stapuli" was defined as of the nature of a continuous fair, with right to trade between stranger and stranger; whereas the "jus emporii" gave the privileges of trade with strangers to the burghers of the port (162). It does not appear, however, that these niceties were recognised in this country. The custom was very ancient, and

(161) Anderson, I., 315.—(Marquardt traces its origin to the French word "Estable," through its meaning from the Latin "Stapulum," or the old Saxon word "Stapeln.")

(162) Marq., Lib. II., c. IV.

has its analogy, if not its origin, in the fixed marts on the Rhine in Roman times.

The institution of the Staple has been sufficiently noticed by historians; but it has not been clearly stated that the organisation of the trade, thus forced through these definite channels, was in the hands of a great Gild or Fraternity, named the "Mayor, Constables, and Fellowship of the Merchants of the Staple of England (163)." The exact date of the origin of this Gild is uncertain, but is thought to have been about the year 1248, when John, Duke of Brabant, gave important privileges to the society, which was then and long afterwards known also as the Brotherhood of St. Thomas Becket (164). Writing of the year 1314, Gerard Malynes, in 1623, says, "that there are records in the Pipe Rolls shewing it was a Corporation at that time (165)." In addition to the Staple towns in this country, the custom was also to fix a foreign mart, as the exclusive port where the seat of the foreign trade was to be held, and whence the merchandise might be distributed. The important position of the Gild is well shewn by the fact that this port was to be appointed by the Mayor and commonalty of the Merchants of the Staple. This was fixed in 1312 at Antwerp, as the chief port for the import of English wool (166). Eight years afterwards, in 1320, the Staple ports in this country were Weymouth, Southampton, Boston, Yarmouth, Hull, Lynn, Ipswich, and Newcastle. At this time we find both Louis X. and Philip V. of France endeavoring to fix the Staple at St. Omer, but without success, though it seems to have been tried for a short time. Shortly afterwards we find it at Bruges. Then followed one of the curious attempts to force the development of the home cloth manufacture, by arbitrarily prohibiting all exports of the raw material. In 1328, Edward III. orders that all Staples both at home and abroad should cease, with the mercantile result of a disaster to commerce, and a re-establishment of the Staples

(163) The occurrence of the "Mayor" as the head of the Gild is contrary to English custom, but is very common in France, see p. 67

(164) Anderson, I., 216.

(165) Ibid, 291.

166) Anderson I., 281.

shortly afterwards. The nation was then growing rapidly in population and trade, and from the "Fœdera" (V. 273), we learn that in 1341, the Staple for English wool, woolfels, leather, and tin was re-established at Bruges, the king directing "the Mayor, Constables, and Community of the Merchants of the Staple of England to govern the trade thither, and to impose taxes and tallages."

In 1353 the Statute of the Staple names Westminster, Canterbury, Chichester, Exeter, Winchester, Bristol, York, Norwich, Newcastle, and Hull as the Staple ports for England; and Dublin, Cork, Waterford, and Drogheda for Ireland. All goods were to be brought there and exported by merchant strangers only, and the King's subjects were to take an oath not to hold any staple beyond sea, but the attempt again failed, and four years afterwards denizens as well as foreigners were allowed to export. About this time (1362) we gain an insight into the organisation of the society. By 36 Edward III., c. 7—Six persons were to sit as judges in every Staple town, *i.e.*, four aliens, two of Germany, two Lombardy, and two English; and in all cases where the strangers had complaints, to name two of their number, who were to sit with the Mayor and constables of each of the respective Staple towns, who by another act of the same year were appointed to be annually elected by the body of the merchants, as well foreigners as English; and although the Mayor of each Staple was a distinct officer or magistrate from the Mayor, bailiff, etc., of the town itself, the latter were to give needful assistance to the Staplers, who were hereby made a distinct corporation or body politic, with a corporate seal, and were to sit and hold courts of law-merchant for determining all mercantile affairs, and punish offenders—with distinct prisons [107].

This period seems to have been that of the greatest prosperity of the company. The trade of the country was now sufficiently advanced to export its own manufactures, as well as the raw materials in which the Staplers dealt; and the new Brotherhood of St. Thomas Becket, afterwards known as the Merchant

(107) Anderson, I., 348.

Adventurers, came into being to appropriate the new departure to itself. The Continental Staple was removed to Calais; and while we find the list of English towns constantly varied, the town of Hull is always to be found in it. On one occasion we find King Edward III. giving a license to a Hull ship to take to Prussia (which was beyond the ordinary limits of the Baltic trade) four pipes of Rhenish wine, provided they brought back bowstaves ([168]).

Many interesting details of the trade of the port at this time are given by Frost ([169]), to which the reader is referred who may wish to pursue the subject further. From the time of the rise of the Merchant Adventurers, the Staplers begun to lose the pre-eminence they had enjoyed; but it would be a mistake to attach too much importance to their relative decline. In 1458, Malynes states, on the authority of an entry in the Exchequer, that the Company paid to the crown for the farm of the customs of the staple ware of England £68,000, and as late as the 3rd year of Elizabeth a new charter was granted them, confirming all the privileges which they possessed the year before the taking of Calais; and again in the reign of James I. The Staple had then been removed to Bruges. It is noticeable, also, that in the charters granted to the Merchant Adventurers the privileges of the Mayor, Constables, and Fellowship of the Staplers are always reserved ([170]). Such is the outline of the history of the powerful Gild which regulated the mediæval commerce of England, and had one of its chief branches in Hull. Beyond the names of some of its members it has left no trace. Even in London they seem never to have had a hall, though the Inn of Chancery, and the Wool Staple, at the end of Canon or Channel Row, bore their name ([171]). So late as the 18th century the Corporation still continued, and meetings were held, though its trade and importance were no more.

(168) Anderson I., 362.

(169) *Early Notices of Hull.*

(170) They were privileged also by 51 Henry III., 12 Edward II., 14 Richard II., 11 Henry IV., 9 Henry V.

(171) Anderson, I., 292.

CHAPTER XIV.

THE MERCHANT ADVENTURERS.

THE old symbol of the Merchant Adventurers is still to be seen on the seal of the Exchange of Kingston-upon-Hull. Some of the most worthy names in her roll of citizens bear the title. Yet the great brotherhood to which they belonged, and which did so much to found that commerce with the Baltic and North Sea, not only of Hull, but of England, never yet has had its story told to the world. Our local historians dismiss it with a line or two. Lingard tells us it was founded by Queen Mary ([172]). It is time that at least something of its origin and constitution should be told.

Like the Merchants of the Staple, they originally had the name of the Brotherhood of St. Thomas of Canterbury; and in the earliest notices there seems some confusion between the two societies. This seems to have arisen from the fact that both were offshoots from the Gild of the Mercers, whose patron saint was the same, for St. Thomas' father was himself of the craft ([173]). Their rise marks the period when the trade developed into something like a wholesale commerce with foreign lands. As already noticed, according to Wheeler, the secretary of the society in 1601, they received important privileges from Louis, Count of Flanders, in 1358, in return for fixing their factory, or Staple, at Bruges ([174]). It does not appear, however, that this was the date of their origin. This is stated at 1296, when they had their Staple at Antwerp; the authenticity of this, however,

(172) *Hist.*, v., 262.
(173) Herbert.
(174) Anderson, I., 312.

is not without question, though they appear at this port in 1313. Their merchandise was almost entirely manufactured cloth.

In 1406 Henry IV. granted them their first charter as the Brotherhood of St. Thomas Becket. As yet, anyone might trade with them by paying the "haunce," or freedom fine ([175]). Twenty-four years afterwards, Henry IV. confirms their privileges.

In 1444 they removed from Middleburgh on account of its unhealthiness, and went to Antwerp again, where, and at Bergen op Zoom, they remained, excepting for a short time in the reign of Henry VIII. at Calais and Middleburgh. In 1497 great outcries arose from Adventurers of other parts of England, of the abuse of their privileges by the Brotherhood of St. Thomas. Their fine had formerly been an old noble (6/8); then they had made it 100 shillings Flemish, and then £40. Possibly the old rhyme was still told ([176]) :—

For foure things oure noble sheweth thome,
King, schip and schwerd, and power of the See.

Now, the fine was fixed at £6 13s. 4d. At this time there were great doings among the mariners of the Hull Street, or High Street, and at Southend. One John Taverner, of Hull, got a royal license to carry wool, tin, lambswool, hides, or any other merchandise, the property of English or foreign merchants, and carry them to Italy on paying alien's duty. This was, probably, one of the dispensations granted by our kings from time to time "non obstante" any privilege of Staplers and Adventurers, which brought in great gain to the royal purse, and were a great thorn in the side of the regular chartered companies ([177]). John Taverner, however, built one of the biggest ships of the period to make good use of his license, and realised a very large fortune thereby ([178]). Up to this time the Society had been entitled simply the Brotherhood of St. Thomas, although the term Merchant Adventurers is found previously in common use. Now, in 1505, Henry VII. granted them a

(175) Malynes.
(176) Marquardi, V., 7.
(177) Anderson.
(178) Lindsay, *History of Commerce*, p. 445

charter by the name of the Fellowship of the Merchant Adventurers of England, with further exclusive privileges; eight years later, Henry VIII. confirmed this by another. From this time their commerce rapidly extended.

It was the period of the Renaissance and the Reformation; of the discovery of the New World; of the discovery of the Archangel route to Russia, by Willoughby and Chancellor, whereby the old monopoly of the Hanse Towns was broken. Wheeler claimed that in 1550 the Merchant Adventurers employed in Antwerp alone 20,000 persons, and in the Netherlands 30,000 besides. Sir Thomas Gresham, himself a mercer, saw the greatness of the opportunity in the East, for in early days the Baltic was the East, and the Mediterranean the West (179). By the charter of the 6th year of Elizabeth, the Merchant Adventurers first received the full power of an English Corporation, with a common seal and succession, and power to exercise government in all parts of England (180).

It will best give the reader an insight into the objects and constitution of this Corporation, if we transcribe the account given by the secretary on the occasion already referred to (181).

> The Company consists of a great number of wealthy merchants of divers great cities and maritime towns in England—London, York, Norwich, Exeter, Ipswich, Newcastle, Hull, etc. These of old times linked themselves together for the exercise of merchandise by trading in cloth, kersies, . . . whereby they brought great wealth to their respective places of residence. Their limits are the towns and ports lying between the River Somme and along all coasts of Netherland and Germany within the German Sea: not into all at once at each man's pleasure, but into one or two towns at most within the said bounds, which they commonly call the Mart Town or Towns, because there only they stapled their commodities and put them to sale, and thence only they brought such foreign wares as England wanted, and which were brought from far by divers nations flocking thither to buy and sell as at a fair. The Merchant Adventurers do annually export at least 60,000 white cloths, worth at least £600,000, and of coloured cloths of all sorts—kersies, bayes, cottons, northern dozens, and other coarse cloths; 40,000 cloths more worth £400,000 more, in all £1,000,000 sterling, besides what goes to the Netherlands from Eng-

(179) Anderson, I., 868.
(180) Anderson, II., 115.
(181) Anderson, II., 202.

> land of woolfels, lead, tin, saffron, coney skins, leather, tallow, alabaster, corn, beer, etc. And our Company imported of the Dutch and Rhenish merchants Rhenish wines, fustians, copper, steel, hemp, onion seed, iron and copper wire, latten, kettles, pans, linen, harness, saltpetre, gunpowder, and all things made at Noremburg [such as toys, small iron-ware, etc.]; of the Italians, all sorts of silks, velvets, cloth of gold, etc.; of the Easterlings, naval stores, furs, soap, ashes, etc.; of the Portuguese spices and drugs.

With the Spanish and French they

> [The Staplers of Antwerp] had not much to do, by reason that our merchants have had a great trade direct to France [the Exeter Merchant Adventurers had privileges for the French trade] and Spain, and so serve England directly from thence with the commodities of those two countries. Of the Netherlands they buy all kinds of manufactures—tapestry, buckrams, white thread, incle, linen cambrics, lawn, madder, etc. Philip the Good, Duke of Burgundy, and Sovereign of Netherlands, the founder of the Order of the Golden Fleece, gave the Fleece for the badge of that Order in consideration of the great revenue accruing to him from the tolls and customs of our wool and woollen cloth."

The reader's curiosity may be roused by the quantity of "white cloths" spoken of in this extract. These were simply undyed. At that time the English were able to export large quantities of cloth, which competed well with the towns on the Continent, but had lost their skill in dyeing. The attempt made by James I. to introduce this art is a curious instance of the ideas prevalent at the time. One, Cockayne tried to introduce the industry into England, having learned its secrets abroad. King James took the matter up, prohibited the exportation of the white cloth, and seized the charter of the Merchant Adventurers. This was in 1608. The result was the Netherlands in retaliation prohibited on their part the importation of the dyed cloths, which at the same time proved insufficient for the home demand. The result may be imagined. In 1615, Cockayne's patent was annulled, and the Merchant Adventurers were re-established. This was the occasion of the saying of Lord Bacon, quoted on p. 138, and he added, "I dare not advise to adventure the great trade of the kingdom, which hath been so long under government, in a free and loose trade." At this time the members of this Company numbered upwards of 4,000 (182).

We must now go back a little, to take up the story of the society in the momentous times of Elizabeth. The fierce struggle of the Low Countries with Spain, and the continual warfare between the latter and this country, deeply affected the merchants who hitherto had kept their Staple at Antwerp or Bruges. In 1568, Alva seized their merchandise at Antwerp, to the value of £100,000, and Elizabeth replied with heavy retaliation on the Spanish shipping; but it was impossible to keep the Staple any longer at Antwerp. The jealous hostility of the Hanse Towns prevented an entrance at first into any of its great towns. They still hoped to keep their monopoly to themselves. The port of Embden, however, was open to the English merchants, and there they fixed their factory. Hamburg soon saw the mistake it had made. Embden began to flourish exceedingly under the new impetus; Staden also for a time had the new trade. In spite of the hostility of the Hanseatic League, Hamburg then took the step of independently inviting them thither, and the invitation was accepted, only to be revoked in 1597 under political influences. For some time the Staple is unsettled—at one time they settle at Dort: Bruges invites them again, only to be informed that until religious freedom is granted, and taxation reduced, it is impossible. Finally in 1651 we find them at Hamburg, where they remained until their work in the trade of the world had to give place to the great wave of modern commerce. Their trade in the 17th century must have been very valuable. In 1643 the Parliament settles their admission fines at £100 for a Londoner and £50 for a merchant at one of the outports—such as the port of Hull, and for this they paid the handsome sum of £30,000. This was double that fixed by King Charles nine years before, it being expressly provided that no shopkeeper, unless he gave up his shop, was to be admitted. The same monarch in 1632 made a curious use of the dispensing power which was so much

(182) Anderson, II., 282.

contested by his subjects. Queen Elizabeth in 1564 had prohibited the members from marrying foreign wives. King Charles now, in favor of four persons named, dispenses with this prohibition, "provided they did not keep their wives anywhere out of England." If we may believe our early authorities, the Hull men were specially addicted to marrying more than once (see p. 124), and this relaxation may have been specially welcome.

A glimpse of the Hamburg Factory is afforded by Wm. Lee, who gives a "Studie within the English House at Hambrough, Jan. 24, 1620." "The Sweet Singer of the Songs of Zion set for God's deere ones who sitt here by the brookes of this world's Babel," dedicates successive portions to John Powell, Thomas Barker, Michaelmas Backhouse, William Christmas, Isaac Lee, Walter Pell, William Walcot, Edward Meede, John Greenwell, John Stampe, and George Franklyn, "Assistants of the most worthy Companie of Merchant Adventurers residing at Hambrough, and one Christmas, a deacon of the English Church there ([183])." The establishment would correspond very nearly with the "Hanses" of the merchants of York spoken of in the charter of Stephen to York (see p. 104). In 1661 the Company was called upon to defend itself in Parliament against the complaint of the merchants of Exeter. Their reply was as follows ([184]):

> The Company do not pretend to be the only Merchant Adventurers, yet count as their honour that they are no Company of one city, town, or burgh, but a national corporation, and dispersed all over the kingdom; that they all meet together in their marts abroad, where their consultations are for the interest of the whole kingdom in the clothing trade, and where a majority of the freemen and traders present governs in all matters; yet nothing concluded in that chief mart town beyond sea but by the concurrence of that other court which resides in the Netherlands, and of this here in London. And this court at London maintains a correspondence all along with all other their distinct marts, as of York, Hull, and Newcastle; and Exeter had once one of the most considerable courts in it, though now there be only one member there . . . Any freeman may ship his goods directly abroad from the next port, as from York, Hull, Beverley, Leeds, Newcastle, Hartlepool, Stockton, Norwich, Yarmouth,

(183) *Notes and Queries*, 4th S. ix., 81.

184) Anderson, II. 407.

Lynn, Ipswich, Colchester, and all other ports of England where they have members . . . They carefully inspect true making of cloth, and prevent exporting of wool and fuller's earth.

THE EASTLAND COMPANY.

The "Eastland" of our forefathers answered to what we call the Baltic Provinces to-day. The traveller Wolfstan related to Alfred the Great an account of a land bordering on what we now call the Baltic Sea, called "Est-land," a large tract of country having many towns, with a king in each. It produced a great quantity of honey, and had abundance of fish, the rich men drinking mares' milk, but the poor men mead. Adam of Bremen in the 11th century speaks of them as piratical, and Canute IV. of Denmark in 1030, with 760 ships, invaded their country and forced some of them to embrace Christianity. About this date Dorpat is said to have been founded by Yaroslaf I., Grand Duke of Novgorod. In 1158 the crew of a Bremen trading vessel, wrecked near the mouth of the Dvina, established trading relations with the country. In the 13th century Bishop Albert founded the Military Brethren of the Order of the Sword, and in 1237 the Knights of the Teutonic Order were summoned to their aid in the conversion of the country after the fashion of the conversion of those days. The ancient towns of this land contain many curious and interesting relics of the old trading companies. At Riga is the Schwartzhaupter Haus, erected about A.D. 1200, a brotherhood of unmarried merchants called Blackheads, from their patron saint, St. Mauritius, with a very rich collection of ancient plate, mostly of Hanseatic origin.

The Livonian constitution had four estates :—(1) Composed of half merchants and half lawyers, four burgomasters, and sixteen councillors, having supreme power; (2) the greater Gild of Merchants and men of learning, for whom a bench of Aldermen and Mayor acted as committee of the whole, the members being either full citizens eligible to office, or only brothers with votes; (3) the lesser Gild or Corporation of Artisans; (4) the Honorable Blackheads.

Esthonia remained subject to the Danes till 1347, when they sold it to the Livonian Knights for 19,000 marks. From the Knights it passed in 1561 to the Swedes, who held possession till it was annexed by Peter the Great.

Among the commercial companies which shared the trade of Hull in the 16th and 17th centuries we find occasional mention of the Eastland Company. There are, however, none of its records now extant in the archives of the Corporation. Chartered in 1579 to trade to all places in the Sound excepting Narva, it appears to have carried on an extensive trade until the ports of Norway were thrown open to other competitors. Its central organisation was jealously maintained in London, though branches, or "residences" as they were called, existed at the chief places of trade. In the archives of the Merchant Company of York are several of the old records of the York Residence which would well repay careful study. The Book of Acts and the Court Book, both dating from the early part of the 17th century, still remain, and contain frequent references to correspondence and dealings with the Hull merchants of the time. The meeting hall was upon Ouse Bridge, the chief official being the Deputy, whose appointment by the head court in London was a source of great contention between the local and central bodies. The number of members was, apparently, however, not large; and they were also in most cases brethren of the Merchants' Company; but the trade they carried on was comparatively large, and their influence considerable. They secured a renewal of this charter from Charles II. From the document printed on a later page, it appears that in 1619 they numbered a dozen out of 160 merchants of the town of Hull, and the references to them in the report of John Ramsden, in 1622, seems to shew they were regarded with some jealousy by the majority.

Chapter XV.

The Merchants' Gild of St. George.

THE earliest independent society of Hull merchants of which we have any record, is the Gild of St. George, of which the ordinances are given below, dating from the last year of the 15th century. Its constitution marks the transition period to which it belongs. On the one hand, it is a mediæval Gild, pure and simple. Its first ordinance is for the maintenance of a priest to say mass daily. It is the Gild of the Craft of the Merchants, who are seen to be clearly differentiated from the other trades of the time, and who have no other means of getting a livelihood. On the other hand, it occupies a position plainly superior to the other crafts. Though not chartered by the Crown, it is established by the Mayor and Aldermen, at the Guildhall, "for the liberty and freedom of the merchants inhabiting in the said town," "for ever to endure." The privileges granted to it are almost as extensive as those conferred by charter of the crown, though lacking, of course, the grant of a corporation proper.

No one was to carry on the trade of a merchant, but such as were duly apprenticed, and had been made free of the Company. At the same time, though thus established and supported by authority, it was no more a mere branch of the town chamber than the succeeding company, chartered by Elizabeth, or than any of the crafts gilds of the town. It was an organised estate, so to speak, of the inhabitants, which was regulated and invested with the control of its own concerns; and inasmuch as these were closely interwoven with the well-being of the whole town, were subject to special license from the Mayor. Merchant strangers were forbidden to open a shop or a booth, except on market days, and hawkers from house to house were prohibited, both measures intended to preserve the privileges of the settled population, who were in scot and lot with the town. Thus it will be seen that the customs which marked the establishment of a Gilda Mercatoria are to a great extent here re-enacted. But the difference is equally marked. The Gilda Mercatoria where it existed included practically all regular traders and all burgesses. Now we find all these traders free of the town, but also free of the gilds of their several trades respectively, and the Merchants' Gild containing only those who lived by "grete aventour." The distinction is typical of the course of development in English towns from the 13th to the 16th centuries.

The history of this Company is obscure. De la Pryme seems to have been unaware of its existence. We have none of its records, and the document which relates to the establishment of a Merchant Company in the 9th year of Elizabeth does not mention it. There are indeed notes of later amendments on the composition itself, and if we may judge by the handwriting they seem to indicate that the Gild continued to exist well into the 16th century. It is not improbable that though a trade gild, and thus not directly coming under the Statute of Dissolution, its strongly religious character, the maintenance of the priest, the lights and masses, rendered its continuance impossible if they did not cause its suppression.

Articles and Ordinances of the Merchant Gild of Kingston-upon-Hull, 1499.

In the name of God, Amen. The xxiiij day of the moneth of August, In the yere of oure Lorde god mcccclxxxxix, And in the yere of the Reign of our Sufferaign Lorde Kyng henry the vijth, effter the Conqnest of England the xvth. In the Gelde hall of Kyngeston nppon Hull, Robert Houll* than beyng mair, and all hys brethern Aldermen of the same town then gadered and assembled principally for the lawde, honour, and Worshipp of all myghty god and of the holy martyr Seynt George. And than for the liberte and Freedom of the Merchaunts Inhabitauntts within the sayd towne, hath ordeyned, enacted, and established for ever to endure, all poynts and Articles

* Met elsewhere as "Howle," "Howll," probably the name we know as "Howell." He had been Chamberlain of Hull in 1486.

under written, and every of theym from this tym Furth inviolably to be observed, fulfilled, and kepte withoute brech or contradicc'on:—

1\. First that every yere uppon the thursday next followyng the Fest of the holy martyr Seynt George, which shalbe named and called their elecc'on day, the sayd Merchaunts assembled in the place accustumed, with the Advice, consent, and assent of the mair for the tyme beyng. And the more parte of the brethern of the sayd gilde than being present, shall chose oon of theym whome it shall to theym apere and seme most expedient to be Alderman, and two of the sayd brethern to be Stewards, which shall bere name and be called the Alderman and the Stewards of Seynt George gyld, which Alderman and stewards so by theym chosyn diligently and yerely shall endevour theym to gader of every man merchaunt of the same town and brother of the sayd gild xiid., withoute that nowe in the begyninge every brother shall towarde a stock frely gyff iiis. iiijd., with the which contynowelly an able and vertouus preste and oon of the priests of the table shall be founden dayly to say or cause to be sayd at the Altar of Seynt John Baptist and of Seynt George, bytwixt v and vi of the clokke in the mornyng, a masse called the morning mass, with other observances as the prests ther called the priests of the table be accustumed to syng and to say as the mater' ffest cause and tyme shall conveniently aske and requyre.

Every year to elect one Alderman and two Stewards.

3\. Item it is ordeyned, inacted, and estableshed by the sayd mair and Aldermen That where as here to fore the sayd merchaunts havying non other science, cunnyng, ne crafftt wherwith to get their lyvyng, bot oonly by the way and the meanes of bying and sellyng, and by grete aventour, hath gretly been hyndered and prejudicially wronged, and yitt be by men of dyvers occupaccions and of crafftt, and as by tailyours, shomakers, and other which presumptouonsly hath taken uppon theym to by and to sell as merchaunts, and in their howses, shoppes, and wyndowes opynly haff showed much ware and merchaundises of dyvers kyndes which never wase apprentises to merchandise, ne yitt fynars ne contributores to their grete charges contrary to right and good consteaunce. In consideraccion wheroff it is now ordeyned that fro this day furth no man of crafftt inhabitaunt within this town, burges, or other nether by ne sell any manner ware or merchaundise bot such as aperteyneth to the occupacon and crafftt whereto he wasse bounden as apprentice, and that he make non opyn showe utwards ne inwards, nether in pryve ne in aperte, of any manner ware bot of such as is before rehersed, uppon the payn of forfeatour

Every man to keep his craft, to which he was apprenticed, and not presume to be a merchant.

of xx*s*., the oon half to be disposed to ye mayntenaunce, sustenac'on and upholdyng of the sayd gylde of Seynt George, and the other half to chamb'r of the forsayde town of Kyngeston uppon Hull, as offten as he shalbe founden gylte and theroff convicted. Provided allway that if ther be any man within the sayd town, inhabit'unt, burgess, or other which intendith to by and to sell and to occupie as a merchaunt, it shalbe lefull for hym or theym to cum to the place accustomed of the day of theyr eleccon, or at any other tyme, and than and ther by the advice, assent, and consent of the mair and aldermen of Kyngeston uppon Hull byforsaid, for tyme being, and also of Alderman and Stewards of the sayd gylde, make fyne for a resonable sume of money bytwen theym appoynted, whych doon he or they so making fyne shall and may lawfully occupie and by and sell and shewe as a merchaunt, the premisses noght withstandyng.

3.

Marked in margin "voyd," in an Elizabethan hand.

Item it is ordeyned and agreed that every man of crafftt within this town, Inhabitaunt, burges, or other which hath any manner ware or merchundise in his howse, shoppe, or wyndowe opynly shewed other than which to hys crafftt apperteyneth, shall bytween the day of makyng of thes presents, ordinaunces, and the fest of the purificaccion of oure lady, take in all such ware and make sale of the same, and nevyr effter to shew it ne non other unto tyme that he haff made fyne as is before sayd uppon payn of xx*s*. as offten as he theroff shalbe convicted, which xx*s*. shalbe disposed and devyded in manner and forme by fore specifyed.

4.

No man to colour another's goods, or be a "broggor," *i.e.*, broker.

Item it is inacted and ordeyned that non inhabitaunt within this town, burges, or other, covour no straunge man goodes under hys nor in his name, but such as he his own propre goodes, uppon payn of xx*s*. as offten as he therein shalbe founden defectyffe, which shalbe devyded in manner and forme before reherced. And also whate inhabitaunt within this towne that taketh uppon hym to be as broggor (*a*) between straunger and straunger cummyng to this town to by any manner ware or merchaundise shall in lyke wise forfeite xx*s*. as often as he theroff shalbe convicted, which xx*s*. shalbe devyded in manner and forme byfore reherced.

(*a*) Broker. One of the town's officials in olden days was the Brogger, or Broker, whose duty was to deal with the goods of "strangers," "aliens," or "foreigners."

5.

Merchant strangers and hawkers forbidden.

Item it is inacted, established, and ordeyned that no merchaunt straunger other than which within this town be inhabitaunt shall nether oppyn shopp, sett stall, ne buthe, bot of the market day, and in the markete place during the space and tyme of the said m'kete. And who that goth in the town ahowte fro howse to howse in hawkıng with his merchanndise shall forfeat and lose iii*s*. iiij*d*. as offten as he so shalbe founden and therwith

(b) MS. worn away. takyn or the [rof con (b)] victed, which iiis. iiid. shalbe devyded as byfore rahereed and sayde.

6\. Item it is fynally inacted, estableshed, ordeyned, and aggreed that every merchaunt inhabitaunt within this town shalbe brother of the sayd Gylde of Seynt George, And yerely therto do his dewtye as a brother uppon payn of iiis. iiijd. yerely, to be ordered and disposed as is byfore sayd, All way provided that if any merchaunt within this town allege povertie, through the which he may noght be contribitour and do his dewty to the forsayd Gylde of Saynt George as a brother of the same, Iff it evidently may be founden and proved by the Mair and Aldermen, his brothern, And also by the Alderman and the Stewards of the sayd gyld of Saynt George for the tyme beyng That the sayd povertie so alleged is trewe and withoute Feynyng colourable, then that brother so being in povertie shall noght incuor and ryme in any penalte of this present Article, the p'misses ever noght withstanding. Geven at Kyngeston uppon Hull befor-sayd, under seale of the office of the Mairalte ther, the day, moneth, and yere in the begyning of these presentes recited, specifyed, and rehereed.

Every merchant to be a member of the Gylde unless in poverty.

The Merchants' Company of 9th Elizabeth.

The next record which we possess is one which I have not found in the Town Archives, but which was copied by De la Pryme, and is here given from his MS. (185).

It will be observed that his heading is "The Incorporation of Merchant Adventurers." It is evident, however, from the document itself, that it refers to the Hull Merchants' Company, and not to the Merchant Adventurers proper. While on the one hand the provisions are very like those of the Gild of St. George, it is now a "Company," and not a "Gild," the latter name being avoided for obvious reasons.

"The Incorporation of Merchant Adventurers.

"The first record that I meet with of them is the following grant of one of the Mayors of this town for their incorporation in the 9th year of Queen Elizabeth, in the following words:—

"To all Christian people to whom the present writing shall

(185) In the possession of E. S. Wilson, Esq., F.S.A., to whom I am indebted for permission to copy it.

come, John Thornton, Mayor of Kingston-upon-Hull, and the Burgesses of the town send greeting in our Lord God everlasting. Know ye that we, the aforesaid Mayor and Burgesses, with one full assent and consent for the better preferment and advancement of the commonweal of the said town of Kingston-upon-Hull, and for divers other good and reasonable causes and considerations, as at this present time specially moving at the special and earnest request of the Company of Merchants inhabiting within the same town, do (as much as within us lys) give, license, and grant to the said Company that they and their successors forever hereafter shall be a fellowship of themselves, incorporated by the name of a Master, fellowship, and assistants of the Company of Merchants inhabiting in Kingston-upon-Hull, and that it shall be lawful for them and their successors yearly the Wednesday next ensuing the day of the election of the Mayor of Kingston-upon-Hull to elect and choose amongst themselves one sober and discreet man to be the Master of that Company for one whole year next following, and also the same day yearly to choose 6 of the same Company to be Assistants to the said Master, which said Master and Assistants shall be sworn to do and execute their offices, and only in and by all things thereunto appertaining; and furder, we the said Mayor and Burgesses for us and our successors (as much as in us lys) do give license unto the said Master, Assistants, and Fellowship of Merchants inhabiting within Kingston-upon-Hull, that it shall be lawful for them and their successors to ordain and make amongst themselves all such acts and ordinances as shall be meet, convenient, and requisite for the maintenance of ye said Company and fellowship, so as ye same acts and ordinances do touch none but such onely as be of that Company, and be not contrary to any of the Queen's Majesty's laws or statutes, or contrariant, prejudicial, or hurtful to the charters, liberties, priviledges, and commonwealth of the said town of Kingston-upon-Hull, nor to the liberties or freedoms of the fellowships of the Merchant Adventurers and of the Staple, or of either of them. The said Master, Fellowship, and Assistants of the said Company yielding and paying for and in consideration of the premises unto the said Mayor and Burgesses and their successors for the use of the Town Chamber the sum of 40s. of good and lawful money of England, at the feasts of St. Martin Bishop in winter, and Pentecost, commonly called Whit Sunday, by equal portions. In witness whereof we the said Mayor and Burgesses have fixed our common seal, etc. Dated Kingston-upon-Hull, 30 July, 9 year of the reign of our Sovereign Lady Elizabeth."

CHAPTER XVI.

THE GOVERNOR, ASSISTANTS, AND SOCIETY OF MERCHANTS.

FROM the charter from the Mayor was not a great step to the final act by which the Hull merchants succeeded in gaining a charter of incorporation from the crown. The Mayor's charter is indeed a notable example of the kind of incorporation which a Mayor could give. The term itself, indeed, is not used as it is in the Tailors' composition, quoted later, though by the unobservant the grant "that the said company and their successors forever hereafter shall be a fellowship of themselves, incorporated by the name of a Master, Fellowship, and Assistants," might easily be taken for an actual grant of incorporation proper. As a matter of fact, however, it fell short of it in every essential particular. They were not yet a body politic and corporate; they could not sue or be sued, save as represented by the Warden in his personal capacity, or as trustee, or hold lands; their power, moreover, was simply that delegated to them from the Mayor for the time being. Hence it came about that the merchants aimed at something higher, and ten years later, in the 19th year of the same Queen, they succeeded in obtaining the formal charter from the crown which is given below.

The preamble states that owing to the great ravages of the Humber on the dykes and walls of the town, and losses by pirates, as well as by the expenses incurred in supporting the crown against rebellion, the burgesses were reduced to great straits, and could not extricate themselves without royal aid. There was doubtless no small truth in all this. From early times the defence of the town and low-lying country around against floods was one of the greatest difficulties of the inhabitants. The Chronicle of the Abbey of Meaux contains grievous accounts of the ruin thus wrought. In 1527 the cellars and lower parts of the town were all under water, and great damage done. In 1571 a still higher tide occurred, and the effect was even more disastrous. In 1622 the yearly cost of the embankments and other expenses were put down at £1,000 (186). Possibly this liability to floods, and the swampy state of the country round which must have accompanied it, contributed also to cause the epidemics which also desolated the town. In 1550, and again in 1576 were terrible visitations of the Plague. The pirates were also dread realities. They hovered about the mouth of the Humber, and pounced upon unlucky vessels from among the shipping of Hull, Grimsby, and York. The charter of the York Merchant Adventurers, granted about this time, is more explicit on this head than the one granted to Hull (187), and in the same year in which the Hull charter was granted a great capture was effected, and after trial six pirates were hung in chains at various parts of the coast.

Nor was the Queen's allusion to the loyalty of the inhabitants without good cause. The last of the risings of the old Roman Catholic party took place in 1569, and its leaders had been foiled in an attempt to seize Hull as a port for the entry of foreign aid. But on the other hand, the picture of desolation drawn by the charter must not be taken too literally. Notwithstanding that the Queen granted the charter, as she asserts, "of her own free will," there are extant among the papers of the Company several sheets containing the draft of the grant for which the merchants petitioned, and drawn up by themselves, and they were, no doubt, careful not to under-estimate the grounds of their application. We know from other sources that at this time trade, on the whole, was prosperous, and that the town was in fact shewing signs of considerable development.

(186) See Hadley, 1622.

(187) See the original in the possession of the York Merchant Company.

Below we give a translation of the charter, now in the possession of the Corporation of the town. The best commentary on its provisions is the subsequent history of the Company itself.

CHARTER OF MERCHANT COMPANY.

Elizabeth, by grace of God, Queen of England, France, and Ireland, defender of faith, to all to whom these present may come, greeting. Since our town of Kingston-upon-Hull, and the port of the said town, by the fury of the waters of the Humber, which is an arm of the sea, inundating and breaking over the walls and dykes there erected for defence, has come to such decay and desolation that the Mayor and Burgesses of our aforesaid town, from their resources cannot repair such desolation of the said town and its port, nor provide a fitting remedy, unless quickly succoured by us, and having regard to the good, willing, and useful services and aids shown by the Mayor and Burgesses of the said town, their labors, expense, and great burdens undertaken for us and our progenitors, and especially for us in the rebellion in northern parts; and also for the labor, burthens, and heavy expenses which they sustained in respect to the safety, guardianship, and defence of the aforesaid port, and our castle and fortifications, and do still sustain, and wishing therefore to deal graciously with them, by what means soever they may best remove the detriment of the said town and harbor, and repel the fury and inundation of the sea. Of our special grace and of certain knowledge, and our own free will, we grant and give license for us our heirs and successors to the Mayor and Burgesses of our town of Kingston-upon-Hull aforesaid, and their successors forever, that no stranger or man unfree of the liberty of the said town [*extraneus neque forinsecus a libertate ville*] may buy from another stranger or man unfree of the liberty of the said town, or sell to any stranger or man unfree of the liberty of the said town, within that town, any merchandise, or any other thing whatever, except alone in the time of market and fairs, fixed to be held within the said town, salt and victuals alone excepted, under penalty of the forfeiture of his goods thus bought or sold against the order aforesaid, to be converted to the use of the Mayor and Burgesses of the said town and their successors. And that they and their successors from time to time, by their officers or any of them, may make seizure without account rendered, paid, or made to any other to us and our successors.

But further, of our rich favor and certain knowledge, and freewill, we grant and give full power and authority, and by these present grant for us our heirs and successors to our loved and faithful lieges and our Burgesses, merchants of our said town of Kingston-upon-Hull, and by these present will and ordain and constitute and declare for our heirs and successors that the same lieges, our Burgesses, being merchants of the said town, are and shall be of themselves one body corporate and politic of itself in thing, deed and name, and one perpetual and corporate community of the Governor, Assistant, and

Charter of Elizabeth to the Hull Merchants' Company.

Society of Merchants inhabiting in the town of Kingston-upon-Hull, and by these present we erect, ordain, decree, constitute, and establish there a body corporate and politic in perpetuity in reality and to the full in all and by all, for us our heirs and successors, by the name of Governor, Assistants, and Society of Merchants inhabiting in the town of Kingston-upon-Hull. And that the same Governor, Assistants, and Society of Merchants inhabiting in the town of Kingston-upon-Hull and their successors, have a perpetual succession, and that they and their successors forever shall be called, taken, and formed by the name of the Governor, Assistants, and Society of Merchants inhabitors in the town of Kingston-upon-Hull, and by the same name they shall be empowered to implead and be impleaded, and to answer and be answered, to defend and be defended, to petition, to affirm and prosecute before any court of justice, or other officer or minister of us, our heirs and successors, and by any persons in any court and place whatever, in all and singular matters, disputes, actions, demands, and causes whatsoever. And it is decreed that they may have a common seal for their affairs and business.

And further of our rich grace we will and by these present for us our heirs and successors, grant to the aforesaid Governor, Assistants, and Society of Merchants inhabiting in the town of Kingston-upon-Hull and their successors, that the said Governor, Assistants, and Society and their successors, from time to time may make, ordain, and establish for the salutary government and better rule of the said Society, ordinances, rules, provisions, and statutes, convenient to the laws and custom of our kingdom, as often as may seem to them convenient. And that they and their successors, for the better government of the said Society, may have and make with impunity, without molestation, without disquiet of our heirs and successors, a hall or house of counsel and congregation freely and honestly, and there may make statutes, rules, and reasonable ordinances, according to the laws of our realm; according to their discretion, for the use of the said Society, and for other lawful causes, which they may please. And they may be able and be empowered from time to time to reform those laws, ordinances, and statutes, and change them to better, according to their own wise discretion, whenever and howsoever shall seem to them to be expedient. And that the same Governors, Assistants, and successors, or the major part of them, annually or otherwise, at which other time or times shall seem best to them, according to the ordinances thus made or to be made of themselves, may elect and make their Governor and six Assistants of the Burgesses and Merchants aforesaid, to rule, govern, superintend the Society, and from time to time may elect into this Society, expel [*Expellere*, Charter of Charles II., *Appelere*] and remove from their Society whomsoever they will.

And moreover of our more ample grace we hav given and granted, and for our heirs and successors by these present we give and grant to the said Governor, Assistants, and Society of Merchants inhabiting in Kingstown-upon-Hull, and their successors, that they lawfully and with impunity be empowered to hold, receive, and obtain for themselves and their successors in perpetuity lands, tenements, and hereditaments which are not held of us immediately in chief or by military service, provided that such lands, tenements, and hereditaments then to be acquired, do not exceed the clear value of thirty pound per annum besides all burdens and drawbacks. And all and singular lands, tenements, and hereditaments aforesaid thus from time to time to be acquired, to alienate, let, and dispose as may seem to them expedient, the Statute of Mortmain, or any other act, statute, ordinance, provision, or restriction to the contrary notwithstanding.

And further from our rich special grace and from certain knowledge, and our free will, for the better sustentation and amelioration of the free men of the said society, and also for the better maintenance of the fleet and ships of this our realm of England according to the intention of a clause in an Act of Parliament made for maintaining our fleet at the Session of Parliament held in the fifth year of our reign, and for and in consideration that the said town of Kingston-upon-Hull, and the inhabitants and Burgesses of the same town, by the commerce, and merchandise, and industry, labor, and skill of the merchants aforesaid, are maintained, supported, and sustained, And also in consideration of the great poverty and destitution of the said merchants by many misfortunes of sea and pirates happened to them, We, in consideration of the great poverty, desolation, and ruin happened to the said merchants, and having regard to their fidelity and faithful services at their expense and heavy burdens constantly exhibited towards us, and other things considered, we of our special grace and of certain knowledge, and our free will, for us, our heirs and successors, grant and give license to the said Governor, Assistants, and Society, and their successors, that no Burgess or inhabitant within the town of Kingston-upon-Hull aforesaid who is not nor wishes to be free or a member of the Corporation or Society of the said Governor, Assistants, and Society aforesaid, shall carry on merchandise nor trade with any merchandise or goods to be brought or carried from parts across the sea, or shall exercise any commerce in the town or harbor aforesaid to or towards parts across the sea or the Kingdom of Scotland, or from foreign parts or the said Kingdom of Scotland to or towards the said town or harbour, nor are to be admitted to any of the said liberties or privileges granted, held, exercised, or obtained by these present, or any one of them is to be admitted unless by the will and by the admission of the said Governor, Assistants, and Society, under penalty of forfeiture of all merchandise, goods, and things aforesaid, to be converted to the use of the Governor, Assistants, and Society aforesaid. Provided nevertheless always that if any person or any persons, Burgesses, being without a Burgage of Kingston-upon-Hull, or exercising without occupation any kind of business art beside commerce, should seek or desire, or has sought or desired admittance into the said incorporated Society by the name of

The interior of the Ante-room and Court-room of the York Merchants' Company, 1891.

the Governor, Assistants, and merchants inhabiting in the town of Kingstown-upon-Hull, and shall wish or has wished to renounce and cease their art, mistery, or occupation, and also shall wish or has wished to exercise and carry on the art or business of a merchant, and to observe, hold, and fulfil all and singular such acts and ordinances as are made or shall be established by the said Governor, Assistants, and Society from time to time, that then the said Governor, Assistants, and Society may enroll him into the said Society for and during the whole time that he shall exercise no other art, mistery, or occupation except merchandise. Provided also always that on pretext of this our concession covenants and treaties entered into and concluded between us and any princes whatever . . . shall in no way be restrained or infringed, nor in any part derogated from or diminished, but that the subjects of other princes from time to time may freely and quietly carry on their merchandise and business in our town aforesaid as in other towns and cities of this our realm, according to the form and tenor of the covenants, agreements, and treaties aforesaid, without any disturbance or molestation whatever, our grant aforesaid notwithstanding. So that the express mention of the real yearly value or certainty of the foregoing, or of the other gifts without grants made by us or our progenitors to the same Mayor or Burgesses before these times made by these present stands good, any other statute, act, ordinance, or permission thence made, published, or ordained without provision or any other thing, cause, or matter whatever notwithstanding. In testimony to this we have caused to be made our letters patent. Witness my own hand, 11th May, 19th year of our reign.

It will be of interest to compare this Charter with some of the provisions of the one granted in 33 Elizabeth to the Company of Merchant Adventurers at York, which had frequent intercourse with the Hull Company, and which, unlike the latter, which has been extinct for nearly two centuries, still exists, with its fine Hall, its three-locked chest, its records, and its memorials of its worthies, in the ancient city. The Hull company was, it will have been observed, in its origin purely a Society of Merchants. In York it was different. In 1430 Henry VI. had chartered the "men of the mistery of mercers." In the ordinances of the 16th and 17th centuries the brethren were the "Merchants, mercers, grocers, apothecaries, and ironmongers within the city of York." Yet the charter of Elizabeth shews that "when they fall into destitution they have no arts and handicrafts to fall back upon," being in fact the merchants and superior shopkeepers of the city. Though a distinct and independent society, the three members to be put up for election for Governor were, however, ordered to be free of the Merchant Adventurers of London; and these certainly took care to exclude shopkeepers. Entrance was by apprenticeship for seven years, or merchandise for ten years. The privileges granted to this Company are more explicit than those to the Hull one. Very extensive jurisdiction was given, including private causes, debts, offences, and rebates, and they could compel obedience by fines, forfeitures, penalties, imprisonments, and otherwise, the keeper of the gaol being expressly ordered to receive persons thus committed by the Governor. Even as late as the beginning of the present century the Company sought to put these privileges into operation ([188]).

Of the earlier history of the Hull Company we have few details. Under date 1619, the Lansdowne MSS. ([189]) in the British Museum gives us a glimpse of the position of the several Companies, which in the dearth of records is precious. Frost has referred to it, but as it is important in itself, and has been evidently misinterpreted in some particulars, we here print it *in extenso*:—

LANSDOWN MS., 162, FOL. 1.

19th Nov., 1619.

The question between Hull and the merchants Adventurers ([190]) Touching the free transportation of leade ([191]) from Hull by all merchants inhabitants of Hull to Germany and Lowe Countries.

Two points considerable, right and practise.

The Merchants Adventurers, a company in E. the 3. his time.

A charter to the Merchants Adventurers in 37 Eliz. for trading to those countries, with prohibition to all other men not to trade there . . . . . .
and hath bene alwaies common to all men.

(188) I am indebted to Joseph Wilkinson, Esq., the Secretary of this ancient Company, for the inspection of the very interesting documents enabling me to give this summary. It is much to be wished that the history of this Company could be given to the world.

(189) Lansdowne MSS., 162, vol. 1.

(190) The question was really, it would appear, between the Merchants' Company of Hull and the Merchant Adventurers' Company, which had its chief seats in Hamburg and London, but to which many of the Hull merchants belonged.

(191) Hull was the port from which the lead of the Peak district was obliged to be shipped for many centuries.

Exterior of the Hall of the York Merchants' Company, 1891.

From a drawing kindly lent by Jas. Wilkinson, Esq., York.

The imposition npon leade is xx*s*. to the kinge uppon every kentall from the subject, and xxv*s*. from the stranger, by certificate of Sir Jo. ——ostenholme, the like from the customers of Hull.

Hull the common port to Hull and York.

Somersetshire leade is transported from Bristoll, but he Peake leade from Hull.

A corporation of the marchants of Hull granted in 19 Eliz.

27 E. 3. Staple. Leade, Woll, Wolfels, Leather and Tin — the five Staple commodities of this kingdom. All these commodities must be carried to the Staple townes to be weighed (192).

Anno, 1556, the Merchants Adventurers stinted amongst themselves the transporting of leade, touching every man's quantity respectively.

The Marchants Adventurers have to deale with cloth, with which those of Hull will not meddle (193).

The towne of Hull payeth to the kinge yerely custome—6000 lib. at least. Which they cannot continue if the leade should bee taken from them.

27 E. 3 The marchants of the Staple interveninnt pro interesse suo.

28 Eliz. stat. or charter. They of Hull are in proportion but a dozen of 160 that make this question; for the rest of the Hull marchants are 9 partes to one, and are Marchants Adventurers (194).

The transportation of leade into Germany and the Lowe Countries in the port of London is . . . and law, practise, and charters.

20 H. 7. Leade never carried from Hull to the Lowe Countries till Ann. 1587.

What was the end of the dispute we cannot tell. In 1622, according to Hadley, an able and interesting report was drawn up by John Ramsden, Mayor of Hull (195), shewing the causes

(192) See p. 144 for the Company of Merchants of the Staple.

(193) This has been interpreted to mean that the Company of Merchant Adventurers did not deal with cloth in Hull. The meaning evidently is that the Hull Merchants' Company did not deal with it. The book of the Company shews that 50 years later this was not the case, and the statement is inconsistent with our information of three years later.

(194) This term here seems to be used in the general sense of merchants trading beyond sea, and not simply members of the great company of that name.

(195) De la Pryme records in his MS. history (*Diary*, p. 286), under date 1637, "In this year, 7th Dec., died Mr. John Ramsden, merchant and Mayor of this town, of the plague, who was a pious, learned, and ingenious man, and was carried by visited people into St. Trinity's Church, and there buried in the Chancel, under a great marble stone with a long inscription thereon. And Mr. Andrew Marvel ventured to give his corpse a Christian burial, and there was preached a most excellent funeral sermon to the mournful auditors, which was afterwards printed." This sermon, in MSS., is now in the possession of E. S. Wilson, Esq., to whom I am indebted for an inspection of it.

of the decay of trade, and suggesting remedies, and from this we gather a pretty fair idea of the kind of commerce which was carried on in the town at the time. From this source it appears that there had been an active export of "northern kerseys, northern cloths and dossons into the Eastland" (that is, the Baltic), and into Germany and Holland, and also into France in return for wine. We might fancy we were reading a trade report of to-day when it is stated that this export had been much injured by "the people of Dantzic and Prussia and Silesia" putting on heavy duties and manufacturing goods themselves. The trade in lead was endangered from two sources. The Low Countries were importing it from Poland, and the men of Bawtry had set up a beam, thereby interfering with the old Staple right of Hull. This was an old grievance. In 1596 a petition was sent up to London against the Bawtry lead beam, and a practice of sending the lead by river crafts to Hull, and thence to London, thus escaping the weigh-house. As a result the Star Chamber ordered that Hull should have all its old privileges [196]. From the above it appears that the Bawtry people carried on their beam notwithstanding.

At home in the cloth trade we are told that "A set of young adventurers had lately set up at Leeds and other places amongst the clothiers, who at little or no charges buy and engross as they please, to the great hurt of the merchants and inhabitants of this town." A very interesting statement [197] occurs next as to the fishery and whaling at this early date:—

> When we had used the weighouse and the coast of Lappia, we did usually set forth 700 great ships annually [these figures cannot be accepted as reliable], that brought home 200,000 fish, besides 100,000 ling every year out of Holland; 200 or 300 lasts of herrings from Malstrand, besides the Yarmouth men that brought the North Sea fish and herrings, all which fish was brought and sold in this port yearly for money, but now it is no more than $\frac{1}{18}$ of the amount. We can give you, however, no reason for the same, except it be the poverty of our husbandmen, which for want of money are forced to live on cheese and butter, and the over great husbandry of our

(196) Hadley, page 99.

(197) Ibid.

gentry that keep no fish days . . . The summer trade in fish, being ruined by the King of Denmark and the wardhouse; . . . we did seek to revive again by searching and finding out the land called Greenland, where we were the first that found that country, and gave the first hazard of any Englishman to kill the whale, which we hoped would retrieve our fortune; but the Russia Company of London do so exceedingly disturb us therein. Another special cause of decay we humbly suppose to be the strict restraint thereof by the Company of Merchant Adventurers and the Eastland Company of London, who abridge and monopolise the whole trade of these countries into their own hands, though many of them are of small ability, and hinder often those that are better able.

Bearing upon this condemnation it is curious to note the subsequent connection of the family with the same Company. In 1660 William Ramsden was Mayor of Hull. At York, William Ramsden, late apprentice with Mr. William Ramsden, was admitted to the freedom of the Fellowship of Eastland Merchants residing in the city of York, 25th Dec., 1650. George Ramsden, son of William Ramsden, late Alderman, deceased, the like, 16th Dec., 1661 (198).

The following remedies were suggested :—

That export of raw material be forbidden.

That duties be taken off cloth and lead.

That the merchants dwelling in all Corporations in this Kingdom which have exercised the trade of merchants beyond sea by the adventuring of English commodities for the space of seven years may be admitted into all companies of merchants according as the State shall think fit, whereby the trade of the land will be better carried on, and that a penalty may be imposed upon any that shall trade not being qualified as heretofore, and that no merchant be compelled to adventure with any of the Companies in joint stock (199).

That the subjects of all the ports of this kingdom may not be detained from killing the whale or seahorse in Greenland or elsewhere, and that the fishing trade in Newfoundland and Virginia and other places may be freely exercised by all His Majesty's subjects.

Importation of dressed flax, hemp, tow, or linen yarn to be prohibited.

That the immoderate use of tobacco be restrained and regulated . . . and the excess of apparel . . . be moderated (200).

(198) Skaife's MS. Collections, quoted in De la Pryme's *Diary*, Appendix.

(199) Hadley, 117.

(200) Hadley, pp. 113-116.

The recommendations as to corporations shews us the extent to which reforming public opinion went at the time. That trade should be carried on by companies or gilds was accepted as a matter of course, and the compulsion to become free of them was logically enforced. But the evils of exclusiveness were to be remedied by recognising the right of all exercising the trade of a merchant to enter the Company, and this without exorbitant entrance fees.

Chapter XVII.

The Hull Merchants' Company.

(Continued)

FROM 1647, however, our information is ample, as the new "Court Book," or book of minutes of proceedings of the Hull Merchants' Company from that date, is still extant and complete up to the collapse of the Corporation in 1706. From this we learn that the old Court Book had extended to 1645. On the 1st November, 1647, an entry occurs ordering two new books to be bought, one a Court Book (this one) and the other for the Companies' Acts, and the cost, apparently of the two, was 13/4. The second, Book of Acts or Ordinances, is lost. The York Company, however, still has its Book of Acts complete, and from it we can conclude that the lost book of the Hull Company contained a long list of ordinances and bye-laws, and also copies of wills, deeds, and other documents of interest and importance. The attendance at burials of all members was one of the rules which was ever strictly enforced. The list of members remains complete in the Court Book still extant. From it we learn that the first meeting was held the 8th June, 1577, the date of the charter being the 11th May. Alderman John Thornton was then elected the first Governor. In that year 39 members signed the roll. The book extends to about 300 pages, and is well and neatly kept. We must confine ourselves to giving those portions which enable us to comprehend the inner working of the Company, and to trace its history, noticing incidentally some entries of more general interest.

The courts or meetings might be either general or ordinary,

the "general" courts being the yearly assemblies for the election of officers, and the more important business; the monthly or quarterly courts being for the ordinary transaction of business. They were held in the Merchants' Hall, which was in the upper storey of the old Grammar School on Church Side. The appearance must have been similar to that at York, whose venerable Company still exists at the fine old hall in Fossgate. At one end of the old oak-timbered hall sat the Governor and the Deputy, and six Assistants sat around, while the brethren filled the benches in the body of the hall. There stood the old iron-bound chest with its three locks, each kept by separate officers, and containing the stock of money, as well as the documents of the Company. From an entry dated 24th January, 1647-8, it appears that the cellars belonging to the merchants had formerly been used as an Exchange; but whether these were the cellars under the Grammar School, or in the High Street, does not appear. In York are fine cellars under the hall, which may well have been used for a similar purpose.

The work of the Court consisted largely of admitting new members. A candidate having served his apprenticeship, and become a burgess of the town, was admitted a member on payment of "the usuall ducty" of 6s. 8d.; the old term of apprenticeship required was eight years. In 1649 this order was repealed, and seven years substituted, "for that the lawes and statutes of this lande doth not require any to be bounde for above seaven years." Notwithstanding this, however, towards the end of the century, the eight years apprenticeship is found again prevalent. It is curious, also, to find that at the later period only occur the entries of admission by patrimony. The 6th August, 1677, we find that "whereas Joseph Snaith had had his freedom entered by patrimonie, the Court objected, and it was ordered that his freedom should stand only as a personall capacity." In spite of these entries admission by patrimony shortly afterwards occur without any qualification being mentioned. But besides the regular "upsetts" there were fines, varying very much in amount, when a member was

Plate now in the possession of the Hull Corporation, formerly the property of the Merchants Company.

The gift of Mr. Robert Derier
to the Marchātz Hall, 1649.

The guift of Israel Popple
to the Marchants Hall, 1648.

The gift of Mr. Robert Derier
Marchant to the Marchants Hall, 1649.

The Guift of Israel Popple
to the Maerchants Hall, 1648.

The gift of Mr. Robert Derier
to the Marchants Hall, 1649.

The guift of Israel Popple
to the Marchants Hall, 1648.

admitted, in proportion to the trade he had carried on before desiring his freedom. John Peckett, in 1647, pays 6s. 8d.; but Ed. Thompson pays in the same year £3 6s. 8d. for admission, according to the Company's order of 1612, and £3 6s. 8d. for trading as before. In some cases the amount of fine went up to £20. Another curious custom appears which explains to some extent the great wealth of these old companies in plate. Several instances occur in which merchants who had been refractory, and refused to join the Company, were at length compelled or induced to desire their freedom. The Court then fixed a fine proportionate to their defiance, and pieces of plate were then offered in payment of part or the whole. Thus, on 5th June, 1648, Mr. Israel Popple brings in £3 6s. 8d. and three silver bowls in lieu of the £6; on August 4th, 1650, Mr. Ambrose Metcalfe gave a silver salt to the Company's use, according to the Court's former order. It is a curious proof of the oblivion into which this comparatively recent Company has fallen, that the six pieces of Corporation plate figured in the illustration have never before been identified as originally belonging to this Company. The inscriptions, according exactly with the minutes of the Court Book, place the fact beyond all doubt.

The enforcement of the clauses of the Company's charter, requiring all traders to obtain their freedom, seems to have been a matter requiring constant attention. Another regular source of the Company's income was the imposition of a duty upon goods. From an entry dated 1647, we learn that a duty of 1d. per lb. (*i.e.*, pound sterling) had been imposed on all goods bought of unfreemen, and it is now declared to be intended for goods brought into this port by alien strangers only; and strange merchants bringing goods were to sell them at the Exchange, which doubtless facilitated the assessment of the duty. At this period some of the old ordinances had already fallen into disuse, for it is ordered that "noe breach of acts in the said oulde book shall have anie penaltyes paide until they be openly read in courte, except such as are mentioned in this booke." The impositions, however, and certain fines for non-attendance and disobedience, were regularly insisted upon. In 1670, the imposition was 2s. trade imposition and 4d. per £100, and in 1699 a final attempt was made to recuperate the treasury by laying a duty of 2s. 6d. per cent. on all goods of Englishmen, and 5s. on all goods of alien strangers. At the same time fines were imposed upon shipmasters for selling to chapmen at low prices, and it would appear also for acting as merchants in any way. Nor was any brother allowed to be joint partner with a stranger (1659). At the same time heavy bounties were given, as we learn from an order of 13th January, 1663-4, to shipmasters for "foording ([201])," £20 to the master and £10 to the mate, and also a bounty [which is illegible] to the common seamen. A matter which occupied constant attention was the attendance of the brethren at the Exchange, and the orders under this head are exceedingly curious. It must be premised that the Exchange was entirely under the government of the Company. It was the rule in 1647 that every brother should be at the Exchange daily "at foure of the clocke betwixt Michaelmas and Lady Day, and at five of the clocke betwixt Lady Day and Michaelmas, unless he be lett by sickness or other extraordinary occasion." This order, however, seems to have gone too far, and later in the same year it was changed to an order to appear once in three days, and this "on paine of 6d.," which was, if necessary, to be levied by distress; and the next court every brother was bidden subscribe his name in a book when he went. He was to be there "at the begining of the bell ringing," and to further induce the brethren. "Masters of ships" were desired to "hang up a bagg a week before their sailing, that merchants may putt their letters therein, and soe the masters to take the same away the night before they intend to saile." On the arrival of a ship the bag was brought to the Exchange to be opened. From an entry of 17th October, 1666, it appears that the Company claimed free carriage of letters within the realm: "Whereas by Act of Parliament wee are allowed postage, a coppy of accounts of a sheet of paper per covert, paying

(201) I have been unable to find an explanation of this word.

1.

8.

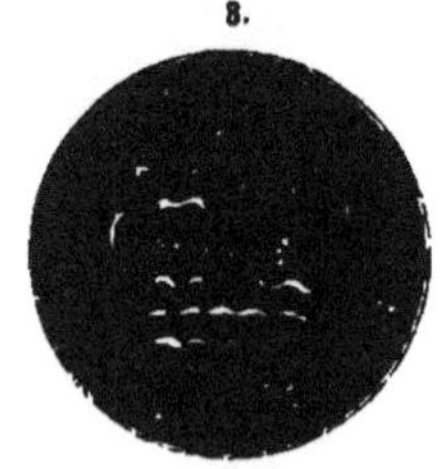

2.

1. Matrix of the Seal of the Hull Merchants' Company.

2. Impression of the same.

3. The Seal of the Hull Court of the Merchant Adventurers of England.

nothing for the same, yet if coppy of accounts of far less quantity of paper bo enclosed wee pay double, though it be opened in tho presence of the postmaster here." Thus it appears that postal grievances are of more ancient date than we are apt to imagine.

In 1674, we find the hour of meeting at the Exchange was from 11 to 12, and the bell was to ring for half-a-quarter of an hour, so that no one could have any excuse. At the same time George Dickinson was engaged at £4 yearly to post up daily, at 11, a list of merchandise entered as to the port of Hull inward or outward at the Custom House there. Still these numerous attractions were found inadequate, and we find numerous entries ordering, remonstrating, and threatening the brethren to be more regular in their attendance.

There is still remaining in the custody of the town a fine seal about six inches in length, of ivory, tipped with a matrix of silver. Its history is curious. The charter, as has been seen, authorised the Company to have a corporate seal; but it would appear that only in 1647 was one actually ordered, it being thought likely to be useful to write abroad about the Company's affairs. Accordingly, "after debate, it was agreed that the same should bee a shipp and three crowns or four, as the workman should advise to be best." The "workman," however, does not seem to have thought fit to alter the ancient arms of the borough by adding a fourth crown, and accordingly on the 17th of April, 1648, the seal was delivered and used.

The stirring political events of the time are treated with admirable philosophy. The courts were quietly occupied with their usual business throughout. On the 4th August, 1650, Mr. Ambrose Metcalfe duly presents his silver salt for the Company's use, and it is ordered "that with all convenient speed, the arms of the Commonwealth and the Merchants' arms be got made and put up in the hall," which was accordingly done. Three years afterwards, in accordance with an Act of Parliament, a new oath was ordered for the Governor, which was as follows:—

"You shall sware that you shall be true and faithfull to the Commonwealth of England, as it is now established, without a King or House of Lords, and you shall well and truely execute the office of a Governor of the Society of Merchants within the town of Kingston-upon-Hull, whereunto you are now chosen, to the best of your skill, power, and knowledge, so helpe you God." This lasted till 6th August, 1660, when it is quietly agreed "That the new oath in this book be abrogated, and the old oath in the old book be administered." At the same time the "late Parliament of England's armes, now hanging in the Merchants' Hall," were taken down, and John Smeadley was employed "to draw the King's arms upon the same table, and hang them up again," which he hesitated to do until he was informed "what satisfaccion he should have" for the job.

A much more important matter at this time was the renewal of the charter by King Charles. The Governor was instructed to write to Col. Anthony Gilby (the member for the borough) on the matter, and shortly afterwards a committee was chosen to treat with the Colonel, Mr. Andrew Marvell, and Mr. William Lister, the Recorder. The special object of the Company was to put an end to the difficulty under which they had hitherto labored of having their charter included in that of the town, and so in the keeping of the Mayor and Aldermen, who refused to deliver it up. This they succeeded in effecting by getting an "Exemplification" or authorised copy, made out and handed to their own keeping, and on 23rd November, 1661, it was ordered "That fifty poundes of good and lawful money of England be given out of this Company's stock to His Majesty;" and the 8th January following, £5 was sent to Mr. Wm. Lister for his fee in the same business.

The members for the borough were accustomed to write to the Company on the commercial proposals before Parliament, and desire their opinion, and their efforts were well rewarded by their constituents. It 1664, it was proposed to put a duty "on forraine iron," and also to impose duties to pay the debts of the Merchant Adventurers. Both were vigorously opposed, Col.

Charter of Charles 2nd to the Hull Merchants' Company.

Gilby being informed that as to the iron "there hath been formerly brought sufficient reasons against it, and that ye Company could produce 1000 voyces for one against that offer, and that His Majesty's Ambassador now coming to treate with ye Crowne of Sweden, it were very unreasonable to lay an imposition upon that commodity to exasperate that Crowne against us;" and a 40 gallon cask of ale was forthwith sent to Col. Gilby.

It is curious to find the following entry in view of more modern controversies.

> January, 1698-9.
>
> That an answer be writt to S. Wm. St. Quintin to his letter about the passing a Bill for making the Rivers Aire and Calder navigable, that it is the opinion of this Court and Company, and in generall of all tradesmen in this town, that passing such a Bill will be injurious to this town, and may in time ruine the trade hereof, and to request him to engage all his friends and himself to oppose the passing the said Bill.

In the same year we find De la Pryme, in his diary (p. 184), setting down as follows:—

> Several projectors have been exceedingly busy this last Sessions of Parliament to have had the Rivers Ayre and Calder navigable, and there has been the greatest lugging and pulling on both sides, the one to effect, the other to hinder the same, that ever was known, and thousands of petitions have been sent up *pro* and *con* about the same, but the Parliament has broke up before the Bill was three times read. There is huge papers in print of reasons both for and against it, but those on the latter are farr the strongest, tho' some of the latter are weak enough.

The internal history of the Company is chiefly a record of the varying success with which they succeeded in enforcing the monopoly with which their original charter had endowed them. Before the commencement of the Court Book, which is now extant, there had evidently been a gradual relaxation in the strictness with which it was maintained. An entry appears in 1647 stating that the ordinance in the old book had decreed first a fine of 3s. 4d. for refusing to appear, and in default the recalcitrant merchant was to be imprisoned. This is now repealed and a fine of 5s. substituted. But the real strife arose about the determination of the Company to allow no trade unless by their own freemen. Many examples of this occur in the court minutes: it will suffice to give a typical instance. Mr. Francis Dewicke seems to have been a considerable merchant of the town, and, as was not an unusual practice then, and is one not unknown now, being inclined to be troublesome, he was elected an assistant. The honour however was not appreciated by the recipient. On the 6th March, 1647-8, it was reported that he would not come, and on being expostulated with, this was "his badd answere"—"That for his place of assistant there was noe need of him, and for his payment of impositions at so much a lb. the Governor might stay for his answere; neither did he value what the Court might doe, for hee believed that he had 8 or 10 that would join with him, meaning in affronting the court with some other uncivill language besides." The Court thereupon fined him 40s., which he refused to pay. On the 1st May a warrant was issued to distrain on his goods for the 40s. fine, and a fortnight afterwards, he being still refractory, another 10s. was added, which he also did not pay. Accordingly in November he was solemnly disfranchised. This was only a step to further action. In January a warrant was issued to seize his goods for trading, not being free of the Company; and in March a pack of cloth of Mr. Dewicke's was reported as seized and now lying at the woolhouse. It was ordered to be sold, but the keeper of the said woolhouse was first promised an indemnity against all legal consequences upon the part of Dewicke; nor was this needless, for in September we find him in prison in consequence, and the Court of the Company undertake his defence at its own cost, and Mr. Dewicke's cloth is again ordered to be sold. It is not clear how far this was done, for the same order is several times repeated, and the next month a deputation waits upon Mr. Dewicke to see if he will come and conform.

Again after the lapse of three years the same Mr. Dewicke, who now appears as an Alderman, is again ordered to come and take his freedom, and his goods are ordered again to be seized, with what result is again left in obscurity. On the whole it would seem that he succeeded in his defiance, though other men during the same period were less successful.

It is probable that this was a case which had much to do with the events which followed. At the end of 1664 the Company got news of trouble brewing against them in London, although of its exact nature they could for some time get no information. A Mr. Man, however, was dispatched thither, and a committee appointed to draw up his instructions. From these it appears that proceedings had been instituted by the Hull Trinity House, touching the privileges of the Company, and Mr. Man was directed diligently to keep watch, and by some means or other, if possible, to get a copy of the indictment. Letters were sent at the same time to Lord Monck and Lord Belasize. On the 20th December, Mr. Lister informed the Governor "That ye Trinity House Masters desired a meeting (but the time they could not fix, for that severall of their chiefest members were weake and lame) to be betwixt them and this Society, to compose if it might be the present differences." The infirmity of the said elder brethren seems to have been of a diplomatic kind, for "weake and lame" though they were, they displayed no small astuteness and energy. We next find the Company writing to Mr. Man, and instructing him not to consent to any abridgement of the charter as to seizure and restraint of trade, and Mr. Thomas Johnson and Mr. Hall were further to be sent to his assistance. On the 3rd of January, the Governors (Mr. Crowle and Mr. Johnson) met the Trinity House Masters, but without result, and they write again to the Duke of Albemarle. But on the 25th of the same month, the infirm elder brethren say clearly that "Nothing would satisfy them but to injoy their demands aforesaid, and that this Company's charter and power therein expressed might cease; and that this Company might confirm it under their seale, and that they should not at any time hereafter sue for a new charter." Upon this the Court was thoroughly frightened. Orders were given to Mr. Wm. Foxley, Deputy Governor, to use the Company's stock and plate, and to defend the charter at all hazards, and a deputation sent to lay the whole matter before the Mayor. In April, however, the matter was decided, as appears by the following entry:—

2nd April, 1665.

The Worshipful Wm. Ramsden, Aldermn. and Governor, presiding.—The determination of His Majestie's Counsell, Jeffrey Palmer, the King's Attorney-Generall, Heneage Ffinch, the King's Solicitor-General, touching the clauses of this Societie's Charter for the exclusion of all persons of this towne from exercising of any merchandise by importation or exportacion, other than of such as be free of this Company, and for the forfeiture and seizure of all goods so exported or imported, shall not for ye future be put in execution against any of ye Corpn. of ye Trinity House, or any other inhabitants, seamen, or freemen of this towne, as by the instrument of determination more fully appeareth.

Thus the Trinity House triumphed. The Company of Merchants, however, took the matter quietly. The charter had not been revoked, and the fines and seizures for contempt and non-payment of trade impositions continued with apparently little difference. On February 11th, 1678-9, "Lemuel Kingdom, Esq., by recommendation from his Grace the Duke of Monmouth, Lord High Steward of this town and county, in order to be elected one of the representatives in the ensuing Parliament, came into this Court and desired his freedom, which was readily complied with," and next day Mr. Wm. Gee, without the ducal recommendation, did the same.

In May of the same year the Court again took courage, and it was ordered "That a warrant be made against the persons hereafter named, to seize their goods for their unfree trading." And again in 1690 the same order occurs. Probably the King's Council at this time were thought likely to be more favorable. Sir Wm. St. Quintin, who was then member, seems to have been a warm supporter, and was present at several of the courts that were held in the last decade of the century. In 1696 a copy of the charter was sent to him to advise upon, and this copy was delivered to the Attorney-General, who lost it, and the Secretary had to prepare another. This caused delay; but in November, 1697, the opinion of Sir Thomas Trevor, Attorney-General, was read, and this being apparently entirely favorable to the Company, it was forthwith resolved to put its provisions in force. At the same time Mr. Erasmus Darwin enrolls the indentures of his son, Wm. Darwin, for eight years, from the 1st of May, 1697. This was a branch of the family which has since earned a world-wide fame.

It was not to be expected that the Hull Merchants, any more than the old Pharoahs, should write down the record of their defeats. Possibly the traders of the town heard of the determination of the old Company, and went on their own way with a smile. At any rate, in the last year of the century: "Whereas the antient grandeur of this Corporation of Merchants is much of late decreased," the Court again determine to put in force the impositions.

Sir William Quintin appears as Governor in 1701, and in this, the last regular entry, Aldn. Hydes is the Deputy, Mr. Wm. Maister is among the Assistants; and among the brethren are Aldermen Wilkinson, Trippett, Grey, and Nettleton; Mark Kirkby, Wm. Crowle, Erasmus Darwin, Thomas Broadley, and John Thornton.

There is in the book a detached sheet giving the sequel. It reads as follows:—

1706—Thursday, 13th February.

Ordered that Aldn. Hydes, Ald. Trippett, and Ald. Thorold take care that the Plate and Books in the Merchants' Hall be removed to the Town Hall for their better security in regard of the Governors' absence, and that Courts there are very seldome kept.

At the Merchants' Hall, 22nd February, 1706.

Present—Ald. Hydes, Deputy-Governor.
Ald. Trippett.
Ald. Thorold.

Pursuant to the aforesaid order they tooke an account of the Plate, and removed it and the charter to the Towne Hall the same day. Also took notis of what repairè is needfull to be don at the said hall.

PLATE MARKT AS FOLLOWETH:—

One Ivory Seale, tipt with silver.
One Guilt Cup and Cover, gift of Aldn. Ramsden, his coat of armes.
Two flatt Wine Bowles, the gift of Mr. Rob. Berior.
Two Wine Bowles, the gift of Mr. Israel Popple.
One Beer Bowle, the gift of Mr. Rob. Berior.
One Beer Bowle, the gift of Mr. Israel Popple.
One Salt, the gift of Mr. A. M. Metcalf, A.M.
In Cash, Twelve Shillings and Sixpence. I say £0 12s. 6d.
The Charter belonging to the said hall in a Tin Box.
Februnary 27th, from Aldn. Hydes, Deputy-Governor, Two Merchants' Hall Acct. Books.
Six Small Keys.

CHAPTER XVIII.

THE FRATERNITIES OF THE CRAFTS.

INTRODUCTION.

FROM the great Merchants' Companies we pass to the smaller Companies or Fraternities of the several crafts.

The reader, however, must put aside the distinction which he is accustomed to draw between the various grades of handicraft, trade, and manufacture at the present day. The analogy between the Fraternity of 200 years ago and the Trades' Union of to-day, as between the shopkeepers of these different dates, must alike, for the present at least, be put out of mind, for both would tend to falsify rather than assist the realisation of the actual facts. The relations between rich and poor are perennial; but the organisation of society, either by legal and established rules, or by social custom and opinion, has changed, and the change has been more fundamental than is generally recognised. We are now speaking of the period which is included between the latter part of the 14th century and the latter part of the 18th, and incidentally of the 13th and 14th centuries. During that period the municipal organisation, though undergoing great changes in many details, was fundamentally the same in its main outlines. It possessed a certain organic unity, which from the 18th century up to the present day it has lacked. Now the commercial and industrial life of a town are generally independent of the municipal organisation proper. There are commercial companies, trade combinations, and unions. These are common interests, but the Corporation of the town is separate and distinct. On the one hand burgess-ship is no necessary qualification for trade, nor on the other hand is the trader in his trade answerable to Mayor or Alderman. Then the opposite was the fact.

Before a man could be a merchant, a trader, a shopkeeper, or artizan, he must be a burgess of the town. Before he was an apprentice he must shew that he was a native of the town, must be registered, and when he had completed his apprenticeship, must be enrolled a burgess before he "set up" on his own account as journeyman or master. Over every trade the Mayor stood as the source of authority, and the ultimate referee in cases of dispute or complaint. Even the companies which, like that of the Merchants' of Hull, had obtained a royal charter, were nevertheless, though in a minor degree, dependent upon him. Strangers wishing to become traders must first settle with him, and pay a fine more or less heavy; for the trade of the town was the right of the townsman and none other. This organisation, however, was in reality based upon a system which was analogous to that of the realm. Just as Lords, Churchmen, and Commons formed distinct "estates"—deliberated apart under one head, while the whole formed the Constitutional Government, so was it in each town by itself. Each trade had its gild, fraternity, society, or company.

The claim which has been advanced for independent origin or autonomy for these fraternities in every case cannot be substantiated. The most ancient, and many of the more recent, were so, but it was by no means universally true. In the most ancient cases which are known to us, as soon as the royal authority began to be supreme, we find royal licence required, and an annual fee paid to the Exchequer. Those who presumed to set up a gild without this authority were heavily fined. So it was under Henry II.

In the next stage we find the Crafts' Gilds divided into two sections. The most influential obtained by royal charter or letters patent direct authorisation from the crown; the rest came under the control of the rapidly developing municipal government of the day. Only so far as the Gilda Mercatoria had become merged in the latter was it the licensing or governing body of the Gilds of the Crafts during this period. In the 12th century it probably had more influence, but the materials for determining the relationship are lost, and it is probable that from the time of the differentiation of the separate crafts, the governing bodies of the towns exercised their authority over them.

During the period under consideration the mode of this control was the following. The craftsmen of a trade, when they became sufficiently numerous, formed themselves into a Fraternity on the same lines as the old gild system of the country. But for this to be effectual in its trade aspect, it must have two things: it must have the privilege of monopoly, and it must have the power of enforcing its regulations. Neither of these conditions could be realised without the co-operation of the Town's Chamber. On the other hand, many of the trade customs not only interfered very largely with the liberty of the subject, but also with the supply to the burgesses of necessary or convenient articles of manufacture or use. The members of the Fraternity, therefore, generally the "ancients" or elder brethren, submitted the chief of their proposed ordinances to "the Mayor and his brethren the Aldermen." When these had been modified and approved, they were engrossed upon a sheet of parchment called a "Composition," or later an "Indenture;" and the Mayor on the one hand, and the petitioners on the other, affixed their seals or signatures. These "grants and privileges," or "points," or "ordinances," were then endorsed with the municipal authority. The Warden and Searchers became not only officers of the Gild, but also in a sense municipal officials. The enforcement of fines could be carried on with legal authority. Refusal to obey was followed by suing by action of debt, or by distraint of goods and chattels, which in case of necessity was aided by the officers of the Mayor. In the earlier examples the original document seems to have passed into the hands of the Gild, and a copy was preserved in the town's archives. Later it was engrossed in the form of indentures. Two correlative documents were prepared, and when divided from each other, one half remained with the Company and the other with the town. In addition, however, to these compositions, each Gild preserved the power to make more detailed ordinances, which were recorded in its own "White Book," as in those of the Coopers' and Bricklayers' which are extant in the case of Hull. It was provided that these should not be opposed to the law of the realm or the town. And not only the composition, but also the ordinances in the book were inspected and approved by the Mayor. In each of the above cases some of the ordinances are endorsed "not allowed." This system was in force long before it was legalised and enforced by the statutes, and is to be found in the records of the City of London as early as the 13th century [202]. Later, in accordance with statutes [203] we have examples of endorsement by the Justices of Assize, as in the case of the Joiners and Carpenters of Worcester of 1723 and 1793 [204]. Similar examples are to be found in the MSS. of the Gilds of the city of York. This does not seem to have been actually enforced, for though we have the ordinances of the Hull Gilds from 1490 to 1723, there is no authorisation by any but the Mayor of the town.

There is, however, another case of which many examples may be quoted from the 14th to the 18th centuries. Here there is no evidence of any antecedent organisation of the trade itself. For the better government of the trade and the benefit of the town, the Mayor calls together the chief craftsmen, and after consultation, gives them a body of rules, appoints officers, and constitutes them a society. The Fraternity of Cobblers was alone in Hull in having its officers yearly appointed by the Mayor, and its fines for breach of rules given to the first informant; but in nearly all cases the half of the fines went to the Town's Chamber, and the other half to the stock of the Gild. The Bakers were to come

(202) See Riley, *Mem.* and *Liber Albus*, *passim.*

(203) 15 Henry VI., c. 6. 19 Henry VII., c. 7.

(204) *Early English Gilds*, p. 334.

weekly to the Mayor to receive the assise of bread; but in every case the craftsmen engaged, either expressly or by implication, to supply good workmanship and material, and at reasonable rates.

It will thus be seen that the system, so long as it worked, was one of great completeness and evident advantage to all concerned. Not only municipally, as now, but industrially and socially, the organisation of the town was complete. The several subordinate estates of the trades were each supreme in their own spheres. Each man had his place. Every article, from a 500 ton ship to a basket or a glove, every profession from that of a merchant to that of a dancing master, was under rule. Every member was answerable for the excellence of his work and for his honesty and behaviour. The completeness of the system is as remarkable as its antiquity. Both, nevertheless, have their explanation in the conditions of an earlier phase of civilisation. We have already noticed the necessity of a law of settlement as one of the first steps of civilisation. To keep order, every man must have his domicile, and must be subject to some responsible authority. The Romans had such a law. The Anglo-Saxon law treated a homeless man as an outcast and a criminal. The laws of the tithing and hundred, and of frank pledge and of family responsibility have this explanation. So in the towns every man must be in scot and lot. The organisation of the trades followed on the same lines. Every craftsman had his fixed status, and with it came his liberties as well as his responsibilities. Were the elements of society and the conditions of industry perfectly fixed and stable, some such system would be in many respects the ideal of their organisation. Its duration in this country for six centuries is a sufficient evidence of its utility. But when the organisation of society and the methods of industry change with an expansion as rapid and immense as they have done within the last century and a half, it is evident that the old system must break up. It would not be true to say that it possessed no capacity for expansion; had that been so it would not have lasted as long as it did; but its elasticity was altogether unequal to the strain which was put upon it. The Reformation implanted the seeds of these changes, but they took two centuries to develope. The great landmark of industrial change in this country is not the 16th but the 18th century. It was then the old system changed and the new era began in the full vigorous life of which we live.

It will be noticed that in what has been said above no reference has been made to the mutual relations of capital and labor, or employers and employed. And this omission has been intentional, for as a matter of fact the separation of the two classes into hostile camps has only a secondary place in the industrial records of the English towns of this period. The great industrial change which followed after the Black Death in 1349 was indeed one which altered materially the position of the unfree craftsmen, but its effect is hardly visible in the organisation of the crafts. Mr. Howell, in his work on "The Conflict of Labor and Capital [205]," traces back the modern trade union to the fraternities of journeymen, such as those which are met with among the masons and among the London tailors in the 15th century. There is no doubt a social and economic analogy, but these fraternities were not the crafts' gilds, nor have we any reason to believe that they were anything but exceptional during the period we are considering. Their position in this country is altogether different from that which they occupied on the continent of Europe. Generally speaking, in this country the journeyman simply had his place in the Craft Gild, and within its limits his position was on the whole a settled and fairly prosperous one. Every workman was, with a few exceptions, one who had served his seven years apprenticeship to the trade. He was then duly enrolled and had a fixed position and a share of whatever work there was. There is nothing in any one of these ordinances which puts any difficulty in the way of an apprentice or journeyman becoming a master and employer. The status of a master's son and that of any other apprentice was the same. There would be the natural advantages of

(205) 2nd Edition, 1890.

wealth and position, but no more. In the Company of Shipwrights we find a master workman distinguished from a yard-holder, but only with respect to the number of apprentices which each might take. Not, however, that it is intended to imply that the organisation of these Trade Gilds was, as has been sometimes held, of a purely democratic kind. In some it is laid down that no journeyman might vote at elections; in others that they were not to congregate and make disturbances. On the other hand we have an indication of the relative positions of the average journeyman and master in the fact that where the fine and contribution of each is laid down, the former is generally about one-half that of the latter. This account is true of the various grades within the circumscribed circle of the fraternities. It is when we look outside these limits that we see where the "unemployed" and the "laborer" was to be found. The door of apprenticeship was open only primarily to "those born and remaining in the town." The number of apprentices each master could keep was generally limited, and an interval of two or four years must elapse between the enrolment of each. An "unfree apprentice with an unfree master" in one case is to be admitted, but only at a heavy premium. The rules relating to alien workmen are very common and very strict. No workman was to be taken without being registered and approved by the Warden; a rule evidently intended as a check upon the importation of labor from outside the town. No workman having wife or children outside the town was to be engaged, and if he were suspected of being under contract of marriage in one composition he was to be dismissed. No work was to be taken to be done outside the town, and all goods and material brought in were under strict supervision. If literally carried out it is easy to see that rules like these would be seriously detrimental if not suicidal. They were, however, modified by two important exceptions. Strangers might always compound with the Mayor by payment of a fine or license, and thus the Town's Chamber had the power, when necessary, of lightening the conditions of immigration or conniving at evasion of the ordinances. It was where, as in the case of the Merchants' Company, which had independent rights of monopoly, the rules of exclusion were carried out solely from the point of view of a company without regard to the general welfare, that the attempt to put them in force provoked the fiercest resistance. The second exception was to be found in the freedom of trade allowed on market days, Tuesdays and Fridays in each week, and in the fair time. The importance in olden times of these occasions, which now have such a limited effect upon the general industry of a town, can hardly be overrated. Then the shackles of the craft rules were cast off, and much greater freedom of trade prevailed. At these times the men unfree of the fraternities brought their wares, and the inhabitants flocked to the sale of them.

So long as the traditional industries were sufficient to keep up the life of the town, and the foreign and external trade moved in its old channels with only gradual change, the old companies maintained their position. But when the population increased so that the number of the "aliens" exceeded that of the home-born men; when the methods of trade and its extent changed with an irresistible development, the waves of the flood raged round the fenced-in enclosures of the Gilds with an onset as sure as that which sapped the foundations of Ravenspurn, and buried it beneath the waters of the Humber. It was in vain that the defenders tried to meet the danger by drawing in more narrowly the boundaries and stopping the rills of leakage. The surrounding force was overwhelming and irresistible. The ordinances remained, but no one could enforce them. The brethren passed rules and imposed fines, but the rules were disregarded and the fines remained unpaid. Still they met yearly, elected their Warden and Searchers, ordered their dinner, and displayed their plate. At length the dinner was deserted, the silver tobacco pipe was unlit, and the punch bowl cold. What were they to do? In most cases they passed silently into oblivion; the remains of the plate passed into private hands; the books disappeared. In a few the surviving officials met, presented a faithful account of their stewardship, and solemnly bequeathed their records and the few remnants of their plate to the Town's Chamber. Then those men, having paid the last honors in true gild fashion to the brotherhood of so many generations of men, went forth with honest hearts, girded on the armour, and took the weapons of the new time, held their own, and won foremost places in the ranks of modern industry and commerce.

The Records of the Hull Crafts.

Such is a general summary of the history of the old fraternities of the towns. It remains to analyse briefly the documents which are presented in the following pages. The following is a list of them, and of the sources from which they are drawn.

1.—The "Compositions" of 15 trades, ranging from the year 1490 to 1714, all of which are in the archives of the Town Hall:—

The Weavers	3	Compositions of	1490, 1564, and 1673.
The Glovers	2	,,	1499 and 1598.
The Brewers	1	,,	1557. *
The Tailors	3	,,	1550, 1563, and 1680.
The Joiners	2	,,	1598 and 1620.
The Carpenters	1	,,	1598.
The Goldsmiths, Smiths, Pewterers, Plumbers, Glaziers, Painters, Cutlers, Musicians, Stationers, Bookbinders and Basketmakers	1	,,	1598.
The Bricklayers, Tilers, Wallers, Plasterers, and Pavers	1	,,	1598.
The Coopers	2	,,	1598 and 1624.
The Bakers	1	,,	1598.
The Cobblers	3	,,	1622, 1622, and 1680.
The Cordwainers and Shoemakers	3	,,	1624.
The Inholders	1	,,	1673.
The Shipwrights	1	,,	1682.
Barber Chirurgeons and Peruke-makers	1	,,	1714.

In all 26 compositions, representing 31 trades.

2.—The books of two trades, viz:—The Bricklayers' Book, extending from 1598 to 1743, now in the possession of the Hull

Subscription Library; the Coopers' Book, from 1681 to 1788, now in the possession of Mr. Councillor Fewster.

3.—Various incidental notices from the MSS. of De la Pryme, now in the possession of E. S. Wilson, Esq., F.S.A.; from the histories of Sheahan, Tickell, Hadley, and Gent; and from miscellaneous documents in the archives of the Town Hall.

The titles which these associations give themselves are Gilds, Companies, Brotherhoods, Fraternities, Societies, Fellowships, and Occupations. Two, the Weavers and Glovers, are from the reign of Henry VII. These present the features of the Pre-Reformation Gilds; keeping lights on special altars; paying fines in wax; and having "Aldermen" at their head. Alike in the Tailors' Composition of Edward VI., and the Brewers' of Philip and Mary, as well as in those which follow, these features are absent. The head of the fraternity becomes a Warden or Master, or Master Warden. The other features of the Gild remain. The annual elections are universal, except in the case of the Cobblers, in which the officials are nominated by the Mayor. The rules respecting order, silence, abusive language and reviling, are the traditional ones, almost verbatim. In some the quarterly meetings are held, when quarteridges are paid. The regular monthly meetings are generally implied. In some, annual payments of 12d., called "Brotherhood Twelve-pences," are the rule. Where the ordinances of the Gild itself are revealed, it is ordained that the secrets of the fraternity should be strictly kept. The usual organisation consisted of one Warden, two Searchers, and a Clerk. Among the Tailors of 1680 there were in addition twelve Assistants, including two Stewards. The Warden was to be chosen from among the elder brethren, and the Stewards from the younger. Among the Shipwrights of 1682 there were twelve Assistants appointed for life, four Auditors, and one Beadle appointed for life. The Tailors and the Coopers had also "ancients" or elder brethren, like those of the Trinity House at the present day. Bond was taken of the Warden and Searchers, ranging from small sums to as much as £50 or £40 in the case of the Shipwrights and Inholders. We have knowledge of two halls, those of the

Coopers and Tailors, and the Coopers' Book shows that the former was let at small rents to many other fraternities. The Inholders met at the "White Horse." All members must be burgesses, the term of apprenticeship was seven years, though in one case it was specified it was not to end till the age of 24, and "strangers" could only gain admittance by compounding with the Mayor and Company.

Most of the fraternities paid to the Town's Chamber an annual fine called "Composition Rent," varying from 3s. 4d. in the case of the Weavers of 1673 to 40s. in that of the Shipwrights of 1682. The "upsett" or fine for setting up business after apprenticeship, was generally 6s. 8d., which was either divided between the town and the fraternity, or went entirely to the town. In one case, that of the Tailors of 1680, it is 3s. 4d. Some of the details have been already noticed; for the others, including the various technical points, the reader is referred to the introduction to the several trades and to the printed documents.

Note on the Origin of Apprenticeship.

The origin and history of apprenticeship is one of curious interest. The mere fact of a lad becoming the pupil of a skilled workman for a definite time, in order to learn the secrets and dexterity of the trade, is one which follows from purely natural causes, and is universal. The custom seems to shade off indistinguishably into the transmission of a hereditary craft, and lends itself readily to the theory of Sir Henry Maine, as to adoption and artificial kinship. But the peculiar form of the custom which obtained in this country needs other considerations for its elucidation. The word itself is first found at the end of the 13th century. The endorsement of a writ in the Rolls of Parliament for 20 Edward I., reads, "De attornatis et apprenticiis," but it is not certain whether the endorsement is due to a later hand. Before this, however, in 1261, we find ordinances of the Lorimers against enticing away another's apprentice, and against having an apprentice for a less term than ten years [206]. In the 28 Edward I., we have a city ordinance as to the enrolment of apprentices and their presentation at the hustings [207]; and in the same year the term of seven years is laid down for the Weavers [208]. And this period, with a few exceptions, appears to have been universal. In the ordinances of Paris, given in Boileau's "Livre des Metiers [209]" of c. 1260, the period varies from two to twelve years, though seven is a usual term.

The rule as to presentation at the hustings or elsewhere to the Mayor, as in Hull, had for each chief object the prevention of any but those of free condition becoming apprenticed. Thus in 10 Richard II., no foreigner was to be enrolled, nor any to be received into the freedom of the city, unless he swore that he was a freeman and not a nativus [210]. So in 1405, when the statute required evidence that persons binding their children as apprentices had 20s. in land and rent, it was objected by the mayor, aldermen, and commonalty that ancient custom allowed all freemen to apprentice their children, and it was granted that the ancient customs should hold good [211]. These examples shew that the object in view was to prevent unfree men from thus gaining their freedom by what were regarded as surreptitious means. If we trace the matter still further back we find an analogy in some of the most ancient laws and customs of English society. Thus, in the laws of Alfred, section 11, we read that "If any person should buy a bondman, he shall serve for 6 years, and on the seventh he shall be free gratis." So in the "Leges Burgorum" of Scotland it is laid down that though a year and a day sufficed for freedom yet the person was not absolutely free for seven years. So also in the "Regiam Majestatem," section 14 and 15, it is stated if a bondman has dwelt and remained peaceably upon any man's land for seven years, not challenged as to his estate, he shall be free. This old custom appears in English law in the 16th century. By 32 Henry VIII., c. 2, if the lord

(206) *Liber Custumarum*, 78 and 536.
(207) Ibid, p. 96.
(208) Ibid, p. 548.
(209) Gould, *History of Freemasonry*, p. 189.
(210) Merewether and Stephens, p. 724.
(211) Ibid, 725

had not had seisin of his villein within six years he was freed from claim ([212]). That this was closely connected with the municipal custom appears from a case at Yarmouth in 1398, when a man was presented on the charge "That he holds apprentices and is not a burgess," evidently lest the town should be held liable for the act of any person taking as apprentice the villein of any lord. And similarly at Newcastle, where an apprentice and his "borowes" or sureties, were to be enrolled, lest, having served his seven years, he should be entitled to be treated as a freeman. As late as 1607 it was held that "If a man hath not seisin of a villein in gross within six years he shall be barred by 32 Henry VIII., of limitation *in nativo habendo*, for liberty is favored." Not till 1714, in the Act for the government of London, was it ordered that the part of the oath relating to taking an apprentice, '" if he be freeborn, that is to say, a bondsman's son," be omitted, as the distinction had ceased to exist.

An account of the laws and customs relating to apprenticeship would be very lengthy, and would lead us beyond our subject. Sometimes attempts were made to impose various premiums and property qualifications for admission to various trades, and caused much hardship. The Act of Elizabeth consolidated the ancient law, and was the basis of much of the subsequent enactments on the subject.

(212) See Merewether and Stephens, p. 813.

Chapter XIX.

The Company of Weavers.

THE Hull Weavers' ordinances remain for three several periods, separated each by about a century, viz.:—1490, 1564, and 1673. We are thus enabled to compare the usages of the craft at these intervals, corresponding with the social and industrial changes which had taken place. This, as in the case of the Glovers, is specially remarkable when we pass from the composition of 1490 to that of 1564. In the interval the great changes of the Reformation, and the accompanying suppression of the religious Gilds, had taken place, and we can see the exact nature of the changes which these revolutions effected in a purely craft organisation, without any accumulation of endowments such as might have excited the cupidity of the government. In common with all the ancient crafts, the Hull Weavers had a strongly marked religious element. The fines were paid in most cases half to the light of St. Peter and half to the Town's Chamber; in some others the fine was the old gild custom of 1lb. of wax. St. Peter would appear to have been the patron saint. The chief officer was an "Alderman," that is, in the old sense of the officer of a gild and not of an official of the town. In 1560 the fines are divided between the "Occupation" and the Town's Chamber, and the 1lb. of wax becomes 2s. The election day is fixed for the feast of St. Michael the Archangel, and the "Alderman" becomes a "Warden." No dissolution of the Gild took place, and the ordinances of 1564 are simply those of 1490, reproduced with some minor alterations required by the trade, and the addition of some interesting new rules. Possibly what ornaments belonged to the Gild at the shrine of St. Peter were seized, and if it had possessed endowments, or been the trustee of sums for obits or other religious uses, like the London companies, it would have been mulcted as those companies were. As it was, its lowliness allowed it to weather the storm with little change. And this must have been the lot of multitudes of similar gilds thoughout the country. In other respects the early document is instructive. It is simply a copy of the grant deposited in the Town Hall. The later "Composicions" are "Indentures" in the original meaning of this term; that is, the agreement was engrossed upon two sheets which were "indented" or cut in corresponding manner, one part becoming the property of the Company, while the other remained with the Town's Chamber.

In a "Composicion" given later the older plan is seen of an unmeaning scribble being traced across the dividing line and cut through the centre. This was the ancient device, which has now ceased to have any legal weight or significance. The ordinances of 1673 retain some of those of both earlier dates, and the same fundamental organisation is seen, but the changes in the century had been great, and the document is worth reproducing in its entirety.

The ordinance which is carefully preserved during the two centuries, that no journeyman could vote at elections, shews that the craft contained men of considerable wealth, and is unusual in the Hull ordinances.

The Weavers of Hull do not seem to have been in any way famous for the product of their looms like the men of Beverley, whose cloth was known far and wide throughout the kingdom. In the reign of Henry III., complaints were made of the Beverlonians that buyers purchased cloth by very long measure, and sold it at a very small one; and even from Whitby we hear of the insufficient length of the Beverley webs. In Magna Charta "dyed cloths, russets, and halbergets" are spoken of, and the breadth was fixed at two ells within the lists.

The ordinances of 1654, however, reveal wherein the Hull Weavers excelled. In the supplementary ordinances the rules of the trade relating to sail cloths are strictly laid down, the length, breadth, and weight were fixed, and they were to be "well skowred, thicked, milled, and fully dressed." Thus were made the sails which carried the men of Edward III. and Henry V. to France; which followed the great Armada round the British Isles; which served Cromwell's admirals; bore the tempests of the Arctic seas; served the commerce of the 17th and 18th centuries; and the wars of Marlborough and Napoleon (213).

It will be useful to supplement this account of the Hull Weavers with a short notice of the history of this ancient and most important of English trades.

Weavers' are amongst the earliest of Gilds alike on the Continent and in England. Under Henry I. they enjoyed "liberties and customs" of their own along with the Bakers. The second Henry by charter confirmed their privileges "so that no one, except by them, might introduce himself into the city of that craft and unless he be of their Gild, neither in Southwark nor in any other places pertaining to London (214).

In the same reign we find Weavers mentioned in the Pipe Rolls at Lincoln, Nottingham, Huntingdon, Winchester, York, and Oxford, as paying fines or license fees to the Exchequer. Fullers also have separate gilds, as at Winchester. In the efforts of London for municipal government, the jealousy displayed towards the Weavers' Gild is perhaps the best testimony to its influence, for no sooner had the city gained its communal status than it prevailed upon the King to cancel their charter, and undertook itself to pay the accustomed tax. This was in the first year of King John (215). But as we find in many other instances in the history of these organisations, the victory was short lived, the organisation was suspended rather than suppressed, and the Weavers' Gild soon after reasserted its existence. In the 14th year of Edward II., many interesting details come to

(213) See Shipwrights' Ordinances.

(214) *Liber Custumarum*, p. 33.

(215) Herbert, I., p. 26.

light respecting their organisation from a plea which was served upon the Gild to show by what warrant they exercised their customs. From this it appears that the craft yearly elected bailiffs, ministers, or assistants, who were sworn before the Lord Mayor. They held their own court every three weeks, and persons of the Gild were not to be impleaded of matter concerning the mystery but in these courts. They compelled all members to have good and honest instruments, and to pay proper wages. A refusal to pay the due share of the King's "ferme" or fine was followed by distraint of the loom. They were also charged with making ordinances that none were to work between Christmas and the Feast of the Purification, at night by candle light, or at other prescribed times. At this time the craft had decayed from 380 to 80 looms.

There is difficulty in determining the exact position of these early craftsmen. The ordinances and notices first given would seem to shew considerable independence and prosperity. The finding of the jury in the case last noted, was that "The Weavers were from the aforesaid time to buy and sell in London, freely and quietly, what belonged to their trade, like other freemen of the city." Yet if the ordinances given in the London "Liber Custumarum," and endorsed with the names of Marlbro', Beverley, and Winchester, are to be taken as actually in force, "No freeman might be attainted by a weaver or fuller, nor might one of the craft even bear witness. And if any one becomes so rich so as to wish to forsake his craft, let him forswear it, and all looms he shall remove from his house." If he went out of the city to traffic, all his goods might be seized and forfeited. We can hardly fix any period when the craftsmen of any licensed Gild were in such a bondage. In the building assise of London in 1212, the artizans were small landowners, and Fitz Stephen, in his description of the Trades of London speaks in glowing terms of their organised and flourishing condition. A century later, no one could take an apprentice unless he were free of the city, and even holding land in villeinage was counted a disqualification (216), yet the Weavers had long taken apprentices. It may be that we have the key to the difficulty in the ancient jealousy of the city authorities, or it may be that the Weavers in question were foreigners. We know there were such in London from very early times, and in the "Liber Albus" we find recorded that these were not only sworn Weavers of England, but Weavers of Flanders, and Weavers of Brabant (217). Some of these were in London long before the encouragement to their immigration by Edward III., and may well have been regarded with the jealousy which was to be found in similar cases at all periods up to the present day. Yet this hypothesis is only tenable as applied to foreign weavers in the provincial towns, for in London itself they were fully recognised as having gilds of their own.

It may be that the ordinances refer to the period when the craftsmen had become subordinate to the "pannarii" or drapers, who sold the cloth, and were in a position of dependency as artizans; but this seems to be contradicted by the mention of traffic and the evidence of their growing rich by their trade. In the third year of King John, David, a dyer of Carlisle, paid a fine to the King "that his messuage might be a burgage, and that he might have the same liberty as the other citizens of Carlisle," but we cannot argue from this bare fact to any disqualification of the craft. In the next year the men of Worcester pay for a licence to buy and sell dyed cloths, as they had been accustomed to do in the days of King Henry, and the men of Bedford, Norwich, Huntingdon, Northampton, Gloucester, Nottingham, Newcastle, Lincoln, Stamford, Grimsby, Barton, and Lafford, St. Albans, Boldack, Berchampstead, and Chesterfield do the same (218), testifying to the extent of the traffic. It would seem that, in the absence of direct evidence, we must leave the fact without satisfactory explanation. It is probable, indeed, that any general statement as to the status of handicraftsmen in the period from the 10th to the 13th century would be inaccurate. On the one

(216) *Liber Albus*, p. 86.
(217) P. 654.
218) Madox, Exchequer, page 160.

hand labor was not in itself servile. On the other hand there was undoubtedly in the towns a very considerable population of servile or semi-servile condition.

It is remarkable that generally speaking the Weavers' Gilds did not in this country attain to so prominent and influential a position as might have been expected, or as indeed they did on the Continent. They are not among the great Livery Companies of London. The reason of this was simply that the trade was one which early differentiated itself into the several economic divisions to which it gave rise. From it arose the Drapers, the Clothworkers, the Fullers, Dyers, Burrellers, Hurers (or Hatters), and to a great extent the Haberdashers; and both the Merchants of the Staple and the later Merchant Adventurers were dealers in the same material in its various forms. Of these the Fullers, Dyers, Burrellers, Hurers, and Weavers, or Tapeners, at the time we are speaking of, retained the artizan section of the trade, and we find traces of their being at times in circumstances which recall the "poor weaver" of three centuries later. Thus the fulling of cloth seems to have been done very largely by water mills, and some craftsmen had set up a similar machine for the fulling of the hures, or shaggy caps, from which the Hurers took their name. Whereupon the "Community of Hurers of the city of London, men of low degree and simple," make a "grievous complaint." They had, they say, been apprenticed to the trade, and know not how to do anything else by which to support themselves. The caps are not so good, and the said simple folk of the said trade are "so greatly impoverished that they are at the point of perishing." The Mayor makes enquiry, and orders that "the fulling of the hures in the mill shall cease, because such caps were falsely wrought and deceitfully, and not so profitable to the community." This was in the 14th century (219). The Burrellers were so called because of the burrels or measures of cloth. The Gilds of Fullers do not come much into notice except at the earliest period, although the art was carefully cherished. As late as 1639 we find King Charles, in the charter by which he

(219) Riley, page 408.

confirmed the privileges of the Merchant Adventurers, forbidding the export of tobacco-pipe clay, "which now," says the King, "is found to be of the same nature and use as fullers' earth."

The early prosperity of the weaving craft in the reigns of Henry II. and Richard I. suffered in the disturbed periods of John and Henry III., and then began the increased exports of wool to Flanders, whence it was re-imported in the form of cloth. The great impetus to the trade given by Edward III. was really a revival of its earlier prosperity, and from that period its course may be studied in the history of the Merchants of the Staple and the Merchant Adventurers. Defoe, in his "Plan of English Commerce," says that "Henry VII. set the manufacture of wool on foot in several parts of his country, as particularly at Wakefield, Leeds, and Halifax, in W. R. of Yorks. . . . he secretly procured a great many foreigners who were skilled in the manufacture to come over and instruct his own people here in their beginnings (220)." And this was in 1489, the same date as the first ordinance of the Hull Weavers, but it is not likely that it is more than a coincidence. The ordinances plainly relate to an organization of native workmen.

WEAVERS' COMPOSITION, 1490.

Ordinaciones facte tempore Laurentii Swattok, Major, ville de Kyngeston-super-Hull, Anno Regni Rege Henric Septum, quinto per arte textornm (*a*).

Be it knowen to all manner of men that this nnder wryten is the ordinannce of the crafte of Wevars by agrement made a mong them selff, ratifyed and conferred by Laurence Swattok, then Mayor of Kyngeston-uppon-Hnll, by forsaid, by consent and aggrement of all his brethern, aldermen there.

1\. *No one to take a felowe to work without consent of the Gild.*

Im primis there shall no man of that occupation take uppon him to take a ffelow to wyrk with hym ageynst the wyill and withonte consent of the maister and the ffelyshipp off that occupacion. And if any of theym attempte to do the contrary, and so ffownden by the rewlers and sercheres of that occupacion, than he or they that so offendys os offtyn os he or they so doth shall fforfeit vj*s*. viij*d*., the oon halff to the lyght of Seynt Peter, and the other halff to the Chambr of Kyngeston-nppon-Hull (*b*).

(*a*) This is not an indented agreement of two parts, but is the sole copy prepared and left in the hands of the Corporation for reference

(*b*) In ordinance of 1561, it is "half to the said occupation and half to the chamber, etc."

(220) Cunningham, *History of Commerce*, page 458.

2\.

No one to take office while owing anything.

Item, it is ordeyned and aggreyd by their hole assent and consent and aggrement, that there shall non of them take uppon hym to be alderman and maister of that ffelyshipp, nor shall bere any rewll at their eleccon day, if he awe any dewty to the lyght of Seynt Peter (*c*).

3\.

Letting his apprentice work for another.

Item, that there shall non of that occupacon late his apprentice to wyrk with any man, and if he wyrk wt any man ovyr and aboven the space of xiij days, he shall forfeit and pay to the said light of Seynt Peter, ijd., and to the towne and Chambe of Hull, ij*d*.

4\.

Slandering a brother.

Item, it is aggreyd and ordeyned by the maister and sayd ffelyshipp, that if any of theym make infamye or sklaunder of other, other wyse than may be proved and abydden by, he or they that therein trespassys or offendys, shall fyue (*d*) and make amendes, and stand to the award of the alderman and serchcors of the same occupacon for the tyme beynge (*e*).

5\.

Setting up a loom without apprenticeship.

[Inserted]. Item, that no man sett up a loome within hys howsse, bot if he have been prentyse VII. yere at that occupacon, under payne of *xli*. (*f*).

6\.

The serch before setting up.

Item, it is ordeyned and aggreyd that noon of that occupacon shall sett up wtin Kyneston-uppon-Hull, bot he shall first aggre wt alderman and sercheours of that occupacon for the serch, xij*d*. And they shall serch whoder his werkhowse be goode and able or no, and it be ffounden able, he then shall aggre wt the alderman for the tyme beyng, for his upsett, iij*s*. iiij*d*. (*g*). And if he worke in an other man's howsse and lome, he shall under the same forme pay——

7\.

If any come not at the Alderman's call, 2lb wax.

Item, it is ordeyned and aggreyd that if any of that occupacon, eyther maister or journeyman, com not to the Alderman for the tyme beyng when he is warned and sent fore, withowt a lefull and a resonable excuse, he that so offendys and trespassys, shall as offten as he so dose, to the lyght of Seynt Peter, 1lb. wax, and to the Chamber of Hull, 1lb. wax (*h*). And if the alderman for the tyme beyng be slawe and rechelesse in recoveryng and levying the sayd forfeit, he then shall content and pay the same of his Awn purse.

8\.

No journeyman to vote at elections.

Setting a journeyman to work.

Item, it is ordeyned that no journeyman shall at the eleccon day gyff any voyce to the chesyng of any Alderman or other officer. And if any maister of the sayd occupacon sett a journeyman of Warke a ffourthnyght and a day, he shall pay to the Alderman, to the behove

(*c*) 1564, "to the said occupation, and so throughout."
(*d*) 1564, "shall forfeite."
(*e*) 1564, xx*d*. to the occupation, xx*d* to the chamber.
(*f*) 1564, half to the occupation, half to the chamber.
(*g*) 1564, vi*s*. viij*d*. to the towne's chamber and vi*s*. viij*d*. to the occupation.
(*h*) 1564, to the said occupation, ii*s*., and to the towne's chamber, ii*s*.

of the said occupacon, ij*d*. And if he pay not the sayd ij*d*. in forme, be forme byfore written, he shall content and pay to the lyght of Seynt Peter, 1lb wax (*i*).

Item, it is aggreyd if any journeyman wyrkying wt any man in that occupacon, of malice make any talys contrarey to treuth to th' entent to make discorde and debate among any of the sayd occupacon, he that soo doth shall forfeit to the sayd light of Seynt Peter, iij*s*. iiij*d*., to the Chamber of Hull, iij*s*. iiij*d*. And to the Alderman of the sayd occupacon of Wevars for the tyme beyng, iii*s*. iiij*d*.

9. Arbitration by four men in case of default.

(*j*) Item, it is ordeyned that if any of that occupacon make any defawte, he shall abyde and stand to the awarde of iiij men of the same occupacon, chosen by the Alderman for tyme beyng, uppon payne of iiij*s*. iij*d*. to the light of Seynt Peter, and iij*s*. iiij*d*. to the Chamber of Hull.

10. Only two apprentices, and for seven years.

(*k*) Item, it is agreyd that non of that occupacon shall take and kepe bot ij apprentises. And he shall take ueth of bounden unto hym for lesse space then for VII. yeres, uppon peyn of xl*s*. to the light, And xl*s*. to the Chamber of Hull.

11. No alien to set up without licences. Penalty, 40s.

Item, it is ordeyned that non alian shall worke or sett up in this town wtoute licence of the mayr for tyme beyng, under payn of xl*s*., to be distrobuted in forme os is aforsaid, and in defaute of payment of any sayd forfets, the Alderman shall attempte accone of dett, and the defendaunt shall not wage hys lawe.

12. No women to work. Penalty, 40s.

Item, ther shall no woman worke in any warke concernyng this occupacon wtin the towne of Hull, uppon payn of xl*s*. to be devyded in forme by fore reherced.

13. Strange Servants to be appointed.

Item, is it ordeyned that no servaunte commyng fro an other town to this town shall presume to wyrke wt any man, bot he be proved and examend by the Serchears of the sayd occupacon. And it is ordeyned that the upsetters of that occupacon pay for their upsettyng in in the first yere, or the Alderman to pay it for them.

14. Division of the stock.

Item, it is aggreyd that the Alderman shall delyver xiij*s*. 4*d*. of the stokk to the Serchears. And the Alderman shall have the oyer (*l*) parte. And the residewe to go among the brethern of a sufficiaunt pawitt ond plege, as the Alderman wyll admytt. And in Witness that the premisses in every poynt And article shalbe observed and fulfylled, the seall of office of

(*i*) 1564, Instead of the above, it is, "ii*d*. to the said occupacion and ii*d*. to the chamber.

(*j*) Omitted in 1564.

(*k*) See below.

(*l*) 1564, "other."

mairaltie of Kyngeston uppon Hull by foresaid, herto is putt the xx day of ffebruary, the ffifft yere of or sufferayn lord Kiynge Henry the VIIth. [Fragment only of the seal left.]

WEAVERS' ORDINANCES OF 1564.

The earlier ordinances of this Composition are, with the exceptions noted in the text, identical with that of 1490. Those that follow are additional ones, together with some supplementary rules of about the same date, which form part of the same document.

10. To be loving, gentle, and friendlie one to another.

Item yt is ordeined yat if any of yat occupacion be at any debaite betwene one and another contrarie to good order, but to be one lovinge and gentle and friendlie one to an other. He that doithe the contrary shall pay to the same occupacion iij*s*. iiij*d*., and to the towne's chaimber of Kingston-upon-Hull iij*s*. iiij*d*.

11. Taking apprentices.

Item yt ys agreid yat every of one of yat occupacion shall take and kepe so many prentises as his poore (*a*) may extende, and yt he or they shall take none no lesse then for vij yeres, for he yat doith contrarye shall paie to the said occupacion xl*s*., and to the towne's chaimber xl*s*.

15. Dealing in "forryn" work.

Item there shall none of this occupacion carrie no woorke, forryn nor other, from this towne under the paine of vi*s*. viij*d*., th' one half to the town's chamber and th' other halfe to ye wardein.

16. Brethren not to sue each other out of this town.

Item yt is ordeyned and agreid yat no Brother of yat occupacion that and yf any of them fall at any contravers for any debte or any other trespas yat he shall not Sewe one an other into none other courte owte of this towne upon peyne of xl*s*., th'one halfe to the said occupacion and th' other halfe to the towne's chaimber.

18. 6s. 8d. to be paid to Town Chamber, and upsetts and due forfeitures.

Ffor the havinge, inyoinge, usinge of all and singuler ya premisses, John Spurriour, wardein of ye said occupacion, william nordarbye, and laurence Reyner, Searchers of the same, for them and there successours doe covenaunte, promisse, and graunte By these presentes, to and with the maior and Burgesses of Kingeston upon Hull, and there successors, well and trewlie to contente and paie, and cawse to be contented and paied to ye same maior and burgesses yerely, and by yere at the feaste of St. Michaell th' archaungell, unto th' use of ye towne's chaimber, not onlye the somme of vi*s*. viij*d*., but also all upsettes and other forfeiters whiche shalbe then by any meanes dewe to ye saime maior and burgesses, to th' use

(*a*) *Sic*—The later ordinances have it "as the law may allow.

afforesaid, by reason of ye premisses or any of them. In witnesse hereof the said Wardein and Searchers for them and there successors have to thos presentes putto there Seales, the xiiij[th] daie of September, in the sixte yere of ye Reigne of our Soveraigne Lady Elizabeth, by the grace of god of englande, ffraunce, and Irelande, Quene, defender of the ffaithe, etc. [The seals are gone.]

Endorsed in another hand:—

19. "Colouring" goods or dealing deceitfully, 6s. 8d.

Item it is also ordeyned and enacted by that if any of the said occupacion of weavers doe at any time or time or times, by any kinde of waies or meanes, colour or thinges falsely, deceiptfully, craftelye, or subtilly woorke, use, or handle any yeirne brought to them to be maide in cloithe, to the deceipte of the quene's majestie's subjectes, yat then every one of them so offendinge to forfeite for every suche offence *vis.* viijd., th' one halfe to the use of the said towne's chaimber and th' other halfe to th' use of the said occupacion.

20. Sail cloths to be according to Statutes 5 Edward VI., and 4 and 5 Philip and Mary.

Item it is ordeyned and enacted that every one of the said occupacion shall from thensfourthe at all time and tymes woorke there saile cloithes in Broade lenghts and weight accordinge to th' assise and Raite lymitted and appointed for northern cloithes by the Statutes maide in ye fifte yere of Edwarde ye Sixte and the fowerthe and fyfte of king Phillippe and quene Mary, viz., in lenght betwene xxiij and xxv yardes yerde and withe of the Rewle, and in Bredthe beinge thorowghe wette vi quarters and a half within ye liste thorowghe, and by all the whole cloithe at the leaste. And beinge well skowred, thicked, milled, and fully dresed shal weigh lxij[li] at the leaste upon peine to forfeite for every peace of cloithe otherwise wrought then ys afforesaid *xxs.*, th'one halfe to th'use of the said towne and th' other halfe to th' use of the said occupacion.

WEAVERS' ORDINANCES OF 25 CHARLES II.

A Composition indented dated the eleaventh day of September in the ffive and twentieth year of the reign of our Sovereign Lord Charles the second, by the Grace of God King of England, Scotland, Ffrance, and Ireland, Defender of the ffaith, etc., Annoq. Dni. 1673, Made Between the maior and Burgesses of the Town or Borough of Kingston upon Hull On the One Party And Thomas Ord, Samuel Rutter, Thomas Botcherby, George Smith, William Belgrave, Bartholomew Ord, Edward Beacock, William Ellison, William Norrey, and Richard Starr, of Kingston upon Hull, aforesaid, Weavers, on the other Party, Witnesseth that the said maior and Burgesses, for them and their successours (as much as in them is), Upon the desire and suit of the said Company, ffellowshipp, or Society of Weavers: And to the intent that their said Trade, Occupation, or Mistery may better flourish within the Town of Kingston upon Hull aforesaid, Have Given and Granted these Ordinances, Grants, and Clauses hereafter ensuing and following:—

1. To be one entire Company.

First, That all and every the severall Persons within the Town of Kingston upon Hull aforesaid, of the said Art, Occupation, and mistery, being free Burgesses of the said Town of Kingston upon Hull, shall from henceforth be but one intire Company, And Shalbe called by the name of the Company of Weavers, Which Company shall have amongst them one Warden and two Searchers, to be chosen yearly by the most Voices amongst themselves, without any Journey-man's Voice or Voices, Alwaies upon the Monday Before the ffeast of Snt Michaell th' Arch-Angell. And that Two shalbe of the Election for the Warden, whereof the One shalbe chosen, And Four of the Election for Searchers, whereof Two shalbe chosen. And the said Maior and Burgesses do Elect, Appoint, and nominate Thomas Ord for the ffirst Warden, and Samuel Rutter and Thomas Botcherby for the ffirst Two Searchers, Untill the said Eleccion day: And that the Warden and Searchers hereafter to be elected shall yearly the Morrow after the said election day be sworn upon the Holy Evangelists of God, before the Maior or his Lieftenant for the time being, ffor the true, just, and upright using and exerciseing of their Places, Roomes, and Offices ffor one whole year, or to such effect. And if either the Warden or Searchers, or any of them, shall happen within their year to change this life, or to Refuse their place, being Elected, Then others shalbe elected and chosen by the most Voices among the said Company in the stead and place of such Warden and Searchers, within Eight days following, to serve for the rest of the year, and the said Warden or Searcher to be likewise sworn: And if any Warden now appointed or hereafter to be elected, shall refuse to execute the said place, he shall forfeit for such Refusall Twenty shillings. And if any Searcher now appointed or hereafter to be elected shall refuse to execute the said place, he shall forfeit for every such Refusall Tenn Shillings:

One Warden and two Searchers to be chosen yearly, but no journeyman to vote.

To be sworn the morrow after the election.

A Warden refusing, 20s.; a Searcher, 10s.

2. Bond to be taken.

And moreover that the said Company of Weavers and their Brethren shall take Bond or Bonds of the said Warden and Searchers, or of any others from time to time ffor ever, in the name of the maior and Burgesses of Kingston upon Hull aforesaid, ffor the performance of any accompt, Debt, Damage, demand, or other thing or matter whatsoever, Which Bond or Bonds shall, notwithstanding, be To the only Use and Beneffit of the said

Company: And not to the Behoofe or Benefitt of the said Maior and Burgesses.

3. And also that the said Company of Weavers and their

None to be admitted but Burgesses.

Brethren shall not receive any Person or Persons whatsoever into the said Company Unlesse he be first a ffree Burgesse of the Town of Kingston upon Hull aforesaid.

4. And likewise that noe Person exerciseing the Trade of

None to set up unless apprenticed for seven years, and a Member and Burgess, on pain of £10 a week.

a Weaver not having served Seaven years as an Apprentice to the said Art or Occupation, and not free Burgesses as aforesaid, and free of their Company, shall keep any Shopp or sett up a Loom, Or work in his own or another man's Loom, or any other work about the said Trade within this Town, or the Liberty's thereof, upon Pain of Tenn Pounds, to be paid for every week he soe offends, and so after that rate for more or lesse time.

But a Widow may may carry on her husband's trade.

Provided That it shall be lawfull for the Widow of any Weaver (who at the time of his death was a free Burgesse of the said Town, and a free Brother of the said Company), to use and occupy the said Trade by herselfe, her Apprentices and Servants, So long as shee continues a Widow and observeth such Orders as are or shalbe made to be used amongst the Company of Weavers within this Town of Kingston upon Hull.

And further, that no Person or Persons being a

5. Weaver and not free of the said Town and Company,

No strange Weavers to come in.

and dwelling without this Town and Libertys thereof, shall come into this Town and the Libertys aforesaid, and receive or carry out of the same any yarn of any inhabitant of this Town: To the end to work the same into Cloth for the said Inhabitants, In Pain to forfeit for every such offence Six Shillings Eight Pence. Neither

Nor any yarn to be sent out of the town to be wrought.

any Inhabitant within this Town shall send or carry or cause to be carryed or sent out of the same or the Libertys thereof, any of the said Yarn to the end to be wrought into Cloth for him, her, or themselves: Neither shall any inhabitant aforesaid sett on work or imploy any Weaver not free of the said Town and Company, upon paine that the Owner of the foresaid yarn and Work, and the Imployer of such Unfreeman shall forfeit for every such offence: Three shillings ffour pence.

But if the Company will not work reasonably others may do it.

Provided Alwaies: That if the said Company of Weavers upon Complaint made to the maior of Kingston upon Hull, fr the Warden of the said Company for the time being, will not work well and at reasonable rates and in reasonable time: That then it shalbe lawfull for any Person or Persons inhabiting in this Town to carry or send any work out of the same: Notwithstanding this order.

6 And also, That the Warden and his Brethren shalbe loving, gentle, and ffriendly one to another: And That if any of the said ffelloweshipp or Company shall slander, revile, or abuse the said Warden or any of his Brethren by any opprobrious words or language, he or that offendes therein shall forfeit and pay the summ of Three shillings and fourpence, And if any of the said Brethren fall at Controversy for any Debt, Trespass, or other cause of Action, they shall not sue one another in any Court, but only in the Court of Record, held before the Maior and Sheriffe in this Town, on pain to forfeit for every such offence the summ of fforty shillings:

To be loving, gentle, and friendly.

7. And also, That if any of the said occupation or Company, come not to the Warden and Company at their Assembly and generale meeting, when he or they is or are warned and sent for, then he or they shall forfeit and pay for every such offence the Summ of four shillings.

4s. fine if they come not at the Warden's call.

8. And likewise that none of the said Trade or Mistery of Weavers shall sett up within the said Town of Kingston' upon Hull without notice thereof given to the said Warden and Searchers of the said Company for the time being. Neither shall any Brother of the said Company take any Journey-man to work Before the said Person or Persons so setting up or working as a Journey-man shall and doe first agree with the Warden and Searchers for the Search, and pay to them Twelve pence: who shall search whether his work, Work-house, and tooles be good and able, yea or noe: And if they be found able, then they shall agree with the Warden for the time being for his Upsett. The Person coming in to the said Trade by Apprenticeshipp to pay Two shillings: And the Person coming in ffine to pay Twenty shillings: To increase the Stock of the said Trade. And shall also pay to the said Town's Chamber of Kingston upon Hull aforesaid the sum of Tenn Shillings.

All workmen to be examined & approved, and their workshops and tools likewise.

9. And moreover that none of the said Company shall take upon him or them to be the Warden and Searchers of the said Company, nor shall bear any rule at the Election day: If he owe any debt to the said Company, and refuse to pay the same: and if the Warden be slow in recovering and levying the severall fforfeitures as well before as hereafter in and by these presents mentioned, to be sett and imposed for any offence, or which at any time hereafter may or shalbe sett and imposed, Then the said Warden to makè it good and content, and pay the same out of his own purse.

None to bear office while in debt to the Company.

If the Warden be slow in recovering debts, to pay them himself.

10. And likewise that every one of the said Occupacon shall or may keep so many Apprentices As the Statute alloweth, So as that he or they shall take none for lesse

To take as many apprentices as the Statute allows, and for seven years. time then Seaven years, under the Penalty mentioned in the Act of Parliament made in that Behalfe: And that there shall none of that Occupacon lett his Apprentice to work with any man: And if he work with any man over and above the space of ffourteen days he shall forfeit and pay ffour shillings:

11. Making tailes contrary to truth, 6s. 8d.

And further, That if any Journey man working with any man of the said Occupacion or Company, of malice make any Tailes Contrary to Truth, to the intent to make discord and debate among any of the said Occupation, then he shall forfeit for every such Offence the summ of Six shillings, eight pence: And if any Master of the said Occupacon sett a Journey man On work above a ffortnight and a day, he shall pay the summ of four pence.

12. Division of the stock.

And also That the Warden for the time being shall deliver Thirteen shillings four pence Of the Stock to the Searchers: And the Warden shall have the other Part or Residue thereof, or dispose of the same among the Brethren, on sufficient Bond with Suretys, as the Warden will admitt, or to him shall seem meet.

13. May make ordinances.

And furthermore, That the said Warden and Searchers for the time being, with the greater number of the said Company of Weavers, shall from time to time make any Laws, Ordinances, and Orders for good rule, order, and government to be kept and preserved amongst themselves, which Laws, Ordinances, and Orders shall bind the said Warden, Searchers, and the whole Company of Weavers: And sett down pains, penalties, and forfeitures for breach of such Laws, Orders, and Ordinances, Provided Alwaies That the same Laws, Orders, and Ordinances tend not to the hurt and harm of the Common Weal of this Town, at the Judgment of the Maior, for the time being and the greater number of his Brethren the Aldermen (if the same come in question).

14. Warden and Searchers may distrain.

And Lastly: That the said Warden and Searchers, or any of them, their, or any of their Deputy or Deputys, in their sicknesse or absence, upon Warrant from the said Maior, may Distrain the Goods and Chattels of any Offender or Offenders in the premisses, or any part thereof, ffor the ffines, fforfeitures, and Paines above sett, or to be sett, according to the true meaning hereof: And if any Person or Persons whatsoever shall resist them, or any of them, the said Warden and Searchers, or any and every of them, their, or any and every of their Deputy or Deputys shall be aided by the Officer or Officers of the said Maior: And all Distresses by them taken shalbe kept till satisfaction be made for the Offence with the Charges about taking such Distresses and the keeping of the same: And every such Officer aiding them shall have for his Pains ffour pence a time he doth so aid them.

In Consideration of all which premises, The said Warden and Searchers and Company of Weavers do for them and their Successours Grant and agree That the one halfe of all the ffines and fforfeitures above sett or to be sett By these or by any other Lawe or Orders hereafter to be made by the said Society or Company, and which shalbe levyed or received: Or the One halfe of so much of the same as shalbe taken shalbe paid to the said Maior and Burgesses and their Successours (Except the foresaid upsett to be paid to the Trade): And also That three shillings four pence yearly for this Composicion shall yearly be paid to the said Maior and Burgesses and their Successours for the Towns use at the Town's Auditt, without drift or delay.

Half fines to be paid to the Mayor.

Upsetts to the trade.

And 3s. 4d. for the Composition.

In Witness whereof To the One Part of this Composition Indented remaining with the said Warden, Searchers, and Company of Weavers, The said Maior and Burgesses have caused the common Seal of the said Town of Kingston upon Hull to be affixed: And to the other part of the same remaining with the said Maior and Burgesses: The said Warden, Searchers, and Elder Brethren of the said Company for themselves and the Residue of the said Society and Company of Weavers and their Successours Have putt to their hands and Seals the day and year first above written, 1673.

Tho. Ord (His mark) Saml. Rutter (His mark) Thos. Botcherbie.
George Smith (His mark) Willm. Belgrave (His mark)
William Marshall

[*Endorsed*]

Sealed and delivered by the within-named Thomas Ord, Samuel Rutter, Thos. Botcherby, George Smith, William Belgrave, and also by William Marshall, a Brother of the said Company, in the presence of

Chas. Vaux,
John Bewley.

CHAPTER XX.

THE CRAFT OF THE GLOVERS.

THE two bodies of ordinances of the Glovers which are given below are separated by an interval of just a century, and afford a useful instance of the course of development between the reigns of Henry VII. and Elizabeth. The earlier document has the same features as those which contain the ordinances of other gilds 150 years before. Beyond the fact that it states that it is that of the Craft of the Glovers, it gives us no insight into the trade itself. It is granted by the civic fathers gathered together "for the libertie of the Craft of the Glovers"; and this liberty was defined by very strict prohibition against alien-born men, whether apprentices or workmen. The chief officer was an Alderman, as in the case of the Weavers, and the election was in the hands of the masters of the craft. The two Searchers had power to see to the wages of the workmen, as well as to the quality of the work; and the fines, which are partly in wax and partly in money, are divided between "the comen wele of the town" on the one hand, and the light before the image of our Lady of Pity in Holy Trinity Church, or the craft, on the other.

Yet there is a singular element of brotherly-kindness in this legal deed. "It is ordeyned also that whate tyme it shall please Almighty God to call any of the brethren or systers fro this present lyffe to his mercy," they were to have the lights free even though they died in poverty or debt. "Also it is agreed that every brother and syster of ye same crafte be at every offering within the sayd town with every brother or syster as well at weddynges as at buryalles."

A hundred years later the Composition has entirely changed

its character. It must be borne in mind that the rules of the craft itself were probably as strictly laid down at the earlier period as at the later one, though they do not form part of the Composition agreed to by the Mayor. But in 1598 the document is simply business-like. The wax "for the image of oure Ladye of Pitie" is of course gone, and the trade customs come out into prominence. The Alderman has become a Warden; the gloves are seen to be of leather; and the trade was evidently a considerable one, though purchases by wholesale were forbidden. The influence of the craft is seen in the fact that they had succeeded in appropriating the whole fines in some cases to themselves, though London and Stamford mercers were privileged. The Wardens had power to distrain for non-payment of fines.

The industry was one which was shared by several trades. As we have seen, the Mercers of London and Stamford brought gloves here. Strype speaks of the haberdashers exposing for sale French and Spanish gloves in 1580 (221). Nevertheless the ordinances of the London Glovers are extant for the year 1349. At that time no one was to sell his wares by candlelight, "seeing that folk cannot have such good knowledge by candlelight as daylight whether the wares are made of good leather or bad, or whether they are well and lawfully or falsely made (222)."

ORDINANCES OF THE CRAFT OF THE GLOVERS, 1499.

The xth day of March, the yere of the Reign of Kyng Henry the viith, affter the Conquest of England the xiiij, the Maire and Aldermen of Kyngeston uppon Hull, in the Yeld hall ther gadered, for the libertie of the Crafftt of the glovers of the said towne hath graunted that all and syngler Glovers of the sayd towne fro this tym forward all and syngler liberties underwritten under seale of office of the mairaltie of the sayd town.

1\. Ffirst, that every yere be choayn the day of theire election an Alderman of oon of the sayd Crafftt, And than they shall chese two goode and trewe sercheors to serch, overse, and to examyn the sayd craffte, which effter theire eleccion shall cum to the Comyn Hall, and ther be sworn be fore the maire duly and truly to present all the forfetts and defawtts dam wt in the sayd crafftt. And if ther be any defaute don which the forsayd Alder-

Every year an Alderman to be chosen.

And two goode and trewe Sercheors to be sworn.

(221) Herbert, II., 534.

(222) Riley, M., page 247.

man and serchers can noght amend and reforme wthin theymselff, than they to present it to the Maire, he to determyn and correcte as he shall thynk best, and to punysh the trespassers after the qualite and the quantite of his trespasse for a resenable fyne, to be departed in two, the on halff theroff to warde the fyndyng of a light by for the Image of our lady of Pyte within the trinitie Church of Hull, and the other halff to the comyn wele of the sayd town.

Fines—one half towards the fyndyng of light before the Image of our lady of Pyte, and the other halfe to the Comyn wele of the said town.

2\. Item it is ordeyned that the forsayd Alderman and sercheours yerely be chosyn by maisters of the sayd crafft. And if any withdrawe him or absent hym fro the sayd eleccon effter he be warned withoute cause or excuse resonable, than shall he forfett to the sayd light a lb. of wax.

Alderman and Searchers to be chosen by masters of the craft.

3\. Also it is ordeyned that non of the sayd craffte withholde no salary fro his servaunt over a certeyn day of payment bytween theym appoynted, and he that so doth and wyll noght content the sayd dowtie effter that he be warned by the sercheours, shall forfett as offten as he so doth iij*s*. iiij*d*., to be devyded in manner and forme byforsayd.

None to withhold due payment of wages.

4\. And if any of the sayd Crafftt of Glovers make restistence agaynst the said sercheours or any of theym in executynge their officery, the ffirst tyme that he so offendith he shall pay to the sayd light a lb. wax, the second tym xx*d*., the third tyme iij*s*. iiij*d*., And the ffurth effter the discrecion of the Maire. And that no stranger Alyant born (*a*) sett upp in the sayd craffte as maister upon payne of xx*s*., all the sayd summes to be devyded in forme befor sayd.

Resisting the Searchers.

No stranger aloyant born to sett upp.

5\. Item it is ordeyned that no sercheour nor sercheours take non extortion of any manner of gedering other than he or they shall trewly accompt uppon. And he or they that doth the contrary, and of the same is convicted, shall pay xx*s*., to be devyded in by fore reherced.

No extortion by the Searchers.

6\. It is also ordeyned that every maister of the said crafftt shall yerely pay to warde the ffydinge of the sayd light viij*d*. And every hyred man iiij*d*.

Master to pay 8d., hired man 4d., towards the said light.

7\. Also it is ordeyned that no maister of the sayd crafftt take a prentice for less space than for vij yeres, and that by Indentur. And for every prentice so taken the sayd maister shall pay to the light xij*d*., And the sayd prentice so to be qwitt for the sayd vij yeres.

Masters to take apprentices for 7 years, and pay 12d.

8\. And that non of the sayd crafft take to prentice non Aliant born, ne to warkman uppon payn of xx*s*., to be devyded in manner and forme before specifyed.

None to take an apprentice or workman aliant-born.

(*a*) "Born" in original, abbreviated for "borne." The reader will observe how some of these contractions are the parents of modern spellings.

9. None to set up unless abled.

Item that non sett upp but he be abled by the Alderman and the searcheours. And he yat is abled and settes upp shall pay effter the custom of the town to the town iijs. iiijd., and iijs. iiijd to the crafft.

10. Any craftsman who shall brybe, purloyne, or stele above 7d., and persist, to be cast out utterly for ever.

It is ordeyned also that if any of the sayd crafftt bryhe, purloyne, or stele fro any person anythyng to the valour of vijd., or abovyn, and warned by the Alderman no more so to do, and will noght sece, he never effter to occupye the sayd crafftt within the sayd town, bot utterly for ever to be refused for any of the ffelyshipp.

11. Every brother and sister to come to every offering, as well at weddynges as at beryalles.

Also it is agreed that every brother and syster of ye same crafftt be at every offeryng within the sayd town with every brother or syster of the same crafftt as well at weddynges as at beryalles, uppon warning (*b*) gyffen to theym. And he that therein offendes shall pay for every defaute a lb. wax.

12. Brethren and sisters to have the lights at their decease, and if in poverty to have them freely.

It is ordeyned also that whate tyme it shall please allmighty god to call any of the brethern or systers fro this present lyffe to his mercy, if the sayd brother or syster happen to disceace within the sayd towne, than they shall haff the lyghtes before theym that longith to the same, and if it so fortune that they be in povertie, and hath no goodes the tyme of theyr dett, than they shall haff the sayde lyghtes of ffre coste, withoute any thyng payng for theym.

Provyded all way that nother Alderman, Sercheour, ne any other of the forsayd crafftt of Glovers, any thyng attempte ne do presume to attempte by vertue and strength of this privilage which shulde redunde to the derogacion of the comen wele, or he prejudiciall to the Comen lawe of the same towne of Kyngeston uppon Hull.

(Town's seal attached.)

[*Endorsed*]

Glovers Composicon, 14 Henry 7.

Composition of the Glovers' Company, 1598.

A composicon indented dated the one and twenty day of ffebruary in the one and forty yeare of the reigne of or soveraigne Lady Elizabeth, by the grace of god Quene of England, ffraunce, and Yreland, defender of the faithe, Etc. Betweye the Mair and Burgesses of Kingston upon Hull on th'one party, And John Caverd th'elder, William Ellis, John Dickonson, John Caverd younger, John Thirgill, × Pofer Horncastle, Oswald Raper, John Pickering, John Baxter, Richard Caverd, Hugh Russell, William Chapman, Edward Copley, Gilbert Hadley, and William Cordley, of Kingston upon Hull, aforesaide, glovers, on the other party, Witnessethe that the saide Maior and Burgesses for theim and their successores (as moche as in theim is), upon the desire and suto of the saide glovers, and to the intente

(*b*) In original "warnyng" (= warnnynge).

that the saide occupacon and traide may better flourishe within the towne of Kingston upon Hull aforesaide, Have geven and graunted and doo hereby geve and graunt theis ordenaunces, grauntes, and clauses hereafter ensewinge and following :—

1. Ffirst, the glovers within the towne of Kingston upon Hull shall from henceforthe have emongst theim one warden and two searcheres to be chosen yearly by most voyces emongst theimselves, upon the monday next after the firste day of the Nativity of St. John Baptist. And that twoe shalbe of eleccion for warden, whereof th'one shalbe chosen, and fower for searchers, whereof twoe shalbe chosen, which warden and searcheres shall yearly after the morowe after the saide eleccion day be sworne upon the wholy evangelist of god before the said Maior or his Lieutenaunte for the true and just using of their places and offices for one whole yeare, or to like effect. And if any of the saide officeres dye, then a newe shalbe chosen within tenne daies in the place or rowme of him so dyeing, to serve forthe the rest of the yeare, and to be sworne as a foresaide; and the said Maior and Burgesses doe appoint John Caverd yonnger for first warden, and John Thirgill and John Pickeringe for first searchers till the saide eleccion day. And if any warden appointed or to be elected refuse his place he shall forfaite xx*s.*, and if any searcher appointed or to be elected refuse his place he shall forfaite x*s.*

To have one Warden and two Searchers.

To be sworn on the the morrow.

A Warden refusing, 0s.; a Searcher, 10s.

2. Item that the saide company of glovers shall at their liberty take bonde or bondes of the saide warden and searchers or of any otheres from time to time in the name of the said Maior and Burgesses, for the performaunce of any accomptes, debts, or other thinges which, yet notwith-withstanding noe benefitt, shall thereby accreue to the saide Maior and Burgesses, but onely to the saide company of glovers.

Bond to be taken of Wardens & Searchers.

3. Item that they shall receive none into their fellowshipp as free of their company unles he be free Burges of Kingston upon Hull. And that no glover unles he be free Burges and free of their company shall kepe any shopp there upon paine of everie weeke v*s.*

None to be admitted but free burgesses.

And none but members to set up shop.

4. Item that no person or persons not free Burgesses of Kingston upon Hull and free of the saide company of glovers shall buy any maner of skinnes within this towne appe:teyning to the glovers trade but upon the tewisdaies and fridaies markitt daies, and in the open markitt, and that by hand and not by greate, upon paine of everie dosen the buyer to forfaite iiij*s.*, and so after that raite for more or lesse.

None but burgesses and members to buy skins appertaining to Glovers, except on Tuesdays and Fridays.

5. Item that all lether belonging to the glovers traide brought to this towne to be solde shalbe vewed by the

All lether of the

trade to be searched, and seized if not good, and Searcher to have 4d. per 100 skins.

saide searcheres of the saide company, and if the same be not merchannteable and good stuf, it shalbe seized and forfaited in whose handes soever the samo be, whether solde or unsolde, and if it be good the saide searchers shall have for the saide company for everie hundred vewing iiij*d*., and so after that raito for more or lesse.

6\.

None but members to deal.

Item that no person or persones shall bny any lether belonging to the glovers traide here or ells where to th' end to sell the same againe within this towne, unles he be free Burges and free of the said company of glovers, npon paine of everie hnndred the seller to forfait of a hundred iiij, and so after the raito for more or lesse.

7\.

No glover to set on any journeyman having wife or children out of the town.

Item that no glover shall sett any Jonrneyman on worrke having wife or children dwellinge withont this towne upon paine to forfaite everie weke xij*d*.

8\.

None to sell any such wares unless he have served 7 years.

The mercer selling London and Stamford wares excepted.

Item that no person or persones shall sell any waires within their howse belonging to the occnpacion of a glover unles he have beno seven yeares apprentise at the trade of a glover (the mercer selling London waires and Stamford waires excepted) upon paine of seiznre and forfaitnre of the saide waires (fayre and markittes excepted).

9\.

Power to make ordinances.

Item that the saide company of glovers and searcheres, or the most parte of theim for the time being, shall make any orderes from time to time for good government and rnle to be had amongst theimselves, or otherwise, concerning the Traide, soe the same tend not to the hnrt of the common weale of this towne at the Jndgment of the Maior and the most parte of the Aldermen his Bretheren, if the same come in question, nor against the lawes of this land, and to sett downe paines and forfaitnres for breache of soch orderes.

10\.

Power to distrain for fines.

Item that the saide warden and searcheres, or their sufficient depnty or depnties in their sicknes or absenc occnpyeng their rowmes, or any of theim, may distreyne the goodes or cattelles of any offenderes in the premisses, or any parcell thereof, for the fines, forfaitnres, and paines above sett or to be sett according to the trne meaning hereof, and if any resistannce be then they shalbe ayded by the officer or officeres of the saide Maior, and all distresses by theim taken shalbe kept till satisfaccion be made for the offenc, and everie soche officer ayding theim shall have iiij*d*. of theim for his paines therein taken.

Glovers do grant half of fines and 5s. yearly.

In consideraccion of all which premisses the saide glovers doe grannte to halfe of the saide fynes and fforfaitnres to the towne, and more v*s*. yearly for ever to be paied all at the townes anditt yearly, and they will take no apprentice withont the consent of Mr. Maior and the most of the Aldermen his Bretheren, bnt soche as are borne or [r]emaining within this towne, and that by there consent likewise if their be any soche sufficient to serve their turnes. In witnes whereof unto th' one p'te of this composiccion indented remaining in th' custody of the saide glovers, the saide Maior and Burgesses have affixed their common Seale, and to th' other parte hereof remaining in the custody of the saide Maior and Burgesses, the glovers aforesaide have sett their handes and scales, geven the day and yeare first above written, and in the yeare of our Lorde according to the computacion of England one thousand five hundred ninety and eight.

John Cavard, younger.	John Thirgill.
John Pickering.	John Caverd, senior.
Wllim. Ellis.	Oswould Raper.
Hew Russell.	Jno. Raper.
× Pofer Hornecasle.	Gilbert Hadley.
Edwardi Copley.	

[There have been other seals (now gone), but the places for the other signatures are blank.]

[The seals are attached in the usual manner by strips of parchment. Several of them are cut from an old indenture of apprenticeship by which one James undertakes to train one Thomas in "the occupacon of a gunmaker (gonmaker)" in Hull.]

[*Endorsed*]

Lect. sigillat et delivat in p'ri'e, Willm. Dowsone, Walter Cave, Mathew Brownell, Wm. Bower.]

CHAPTER XXI.

THE MYSTERIE OF BERBRUERS.

THE following is an inventory of the utensils of the brewhouse of Richard, a minor, son of Laurence le Long, situate in the Parish of St. Martin, Ludgate, in London, in January 25th, 1335.

Two leaden vessels.
One leaden cistern.
One tappetroghe (tap-trough) of lead.
One old chest.
One mash-fat (mash-vat), value 18d.
One rarying-fat (fining-vat), value 6d.
One heyr (?) for tuns, value 12d.
Three sets of handmills, value 4s.
One piece of lead, value 2d.
One tun.
One-half tun, value 6d.
One yel-fat (ale-vat), value 18d.
Two kemelynes (tubs for brewing), value 10d.
One clensing becche, value 4d.
One alegeste (gist or stand for small cask ?).

The said Richard possessed one brewhouse and three shops, probably the earliest mention extant of "tied houses." The nett yearly value of the whole was 40s. 2d. ([228]).

The year before the foundation of the free town Hull, Henry le Galeys, Mayor of the city of London, presents a writ of our lord the King to this effect:—"Forasmuch as we have heard that bakers, brewsters, and millers, do frequently misconduct themselves in their trades, and that misdoers by night going about the city aforesaid with swords and bucklers, and other arms, as well at the procuration of others as of their own

(228) Riley, p. 194.

malice, do beat and maltreat other persons, and are wont to perpetrate many other offences and enormities to no small damage and grievance of our faithful subjects," the Mayor and Sheriff were bidden to chastise all such bakers, brewsters, and misdoers with corporal punishment. This writ was dated 28th May, 26 Edward I. at York (224); at the same time the King was considering the humble prayer of the people of the vill of Hull, that he would grant them the liberties of a free town.

In 1345, we find that "whereas of old a certain conduit was built in the midst of the city of London, that so the rich and middling persons therein might have water for preparing their food and the poor for their drink," the brewers had well nigh taken possession of it. The Mayor and Aldermen thenceforward forbid the water of the chepe to the brewers. If any disobeyed, the tankard [a large pail holding about 3 gallons] or tyne in which he brought it was forfeited, and he was to be fined 40d. (225).

In Hull, among "the most antient laws, ordinances, and constitutions of ye town, which were according to custom proclaimed every year in ye Market Place (226)," were the following :—" That no Taverner, Brewster, nor Tippler keep any guests after coverfeu be rung, on pain of 4d." "That no one pesume to sell a pound of candles for more than one penny, or a gallon of ye best ale for more than ye same, or a gallon of small ale for more than a half-penny." Again in the ordinances of 18 Henry VI., "That all brewers shall sell their best ale for no more than 1d. a gallon, and their small ale for no more than ½d." In 1426, "That no vintner or aleseller sell any ale or wine unto any one before 11 o'clock on Sunday, unless to strangers, under penalty of 6s. 8d." It is interesting to find modern early and Sunday closing regulations thus anticipated.

The ordinances which follow contain several points of interest. People of various trades had taken to brewing beer, but this

(224) Riley, p. 86.
(225) Riley, p. 225.
(226) De la Pryme, MS.

was to cease, except for their own use. Only Mr. Mayor and his brethren the Aldermen might have a craftsman to assist them. This, however, seems to have been resented, and the words "every honest burgess who may desire it" were inserted. The two kinds made were "doble bere" and "merchaunte (or shipping) bere," and both were to be "lastyng and helthsome." For every tun of beer made, 2d. was paid to the town. There are no express ordinances as to searching. It is stipulated that the hired workmen must be those who have served the seven year apprenticeship.

The Hull ale was celebrated. The Merchant Company's Book shows that a cask of ale was a favorite present for sending to London to the members of Parliament, when engaged in special services on behalf of the Company, and the same practice was in vogue by the Mayor and Town's Chamber. The following ordinances shew the trade as it was in the time of Queen Mary.

To all trewe Xpian people unto whome this Composytion indented shall come:—

Robarte Dalton, Mayo[r] of Kingeston aponne Hulle, and his Bretheren the Aldermen, w[th] the Burgesses of the same, Greating in o[r] lord god everlasting, for somuche as th'occupacon or mysterie of the Berbouers w[th]in the same town of Kingeston apone Hull inhabitynge havynge greate charge and beinge contributorye in all assessementes, taxacons, and duties levyable w[th]in the same town or buroghe of Kingeston apone Hull, presentlye ys in greate Rnyne and decay, not onely by reason of th'onordynate and hyghe prices of all mauer of thinges to the sayed occupacon or Science appertenying. But also by reason that dyverse and sundry other persons having & occupying other good and sufficient trades to lyve appone, and also beyngo not experte in exhercysing of the sayed occupacon or mysterye of Berbrnyng nowe of late tyme have taken in hand to exhercyse, practyse, and use y[e] mysterye of berbrnying, by reason whereof the saied occupacon or felowshipp of berbruars w[ch] have ben apprentises to the occupacon or mysterye aforesaied, and broughte npp in tho same, having non other traid of lyving, and beyng fre burgessez of the same town, cane gete noo sufficient lyvinge as here'tofor they have hadd, by reason that their occnpying y[s] taken away from them,

The Mysterie is in greate ruyne and decay.

Men of other trades have taken to berbruying.

and the King and queens Subjects therby muche worse served and the commen welthe hydred, For reformacon wherof, and to revyve the same commen welthe in this behalf, and soo to be governed, ordered, and kept contynnally according to the king and queens highnes Lawes and statutes, Know ye us the sayed Mayor and Burgesses by one assente and consent, and by the consent of the commonaltye of the same town, To have granted and concludede, and by theis presentes doo graunte and conclude and agre wth John Dalton, James Scolles, Richard Hargell, James Chapman, William Rooper, William Clarke, alias Sevyer, Herry hornecastell, and John Rycarhy, Berhruers:—

1\. The Berbruears to be one Company. To elect yearly one Warden. And two Stewards. And one Searcher if it be thought necessary. All to take their corporal othes.

That the Berhruears inhabitynge win the same town ffrom hensforth shalbe one companye or felowshipp, and that yerely and by yere appon Saynte Mathewe day befor the ffeaste of Saynt Mychaell, Archangell, The same occupacon shall nominate, Electe, and chose of themselves oon sohre and dyscrete person by their discreocon to be Warden of the same occupacon or mysterie of Berhruars, and two persons to be Stewardes of the same, to stonnd for one year. And yf yt be thought necessarye one conveyente person to be Sercher of the same occupacon, lykwyse to stond for one yere, And soo successyvely and yerly to be chossen apone the same Sainte Mathewe day, And after eleccon of the sayed Warden, Stewardes, and Sercher, they and everye of them t' appere befor Mr. Mayor for the tyme beyng, and ther to take ther corporall othes apone a book for the Due execution of all thinges conteyned and declared in this presente Composition or Wryting indented.

2\. None to brew except for his own use or to sell, unless apprenticed for seven years and a brother.

Itm yt ys covenaunted, concluded, and agreyed That noo person nor persons shall excercyse, occupye, or use the sayed mysterye of ber hruynge within the same town of Kingston apone Hull otherwise then for the provysion of his or ther howse or howses, neyther shall they hrewe to Sell, uttre by retaylle nore ingrosse, anny kynde of bere by lonnd or by water, excepte the same person or persons have bene pronntyse at the same occupacon by the space of viith yeres, or otherwyse having knowleg, be laufullye admytted by Mr. Maior for the tyme being, and his hrethern and the same occupacon, in payne of foriffactur for everye hoggeshed Barrell, demy harrel, kyldrekyn, fyrkyn, or other vessell of greatter or smaller measure, brewed or sold contrarye to this ordenaunce, xxs.; for every gallon potell, quarte, pynte, or gyll, vis. viiid., ffrom tyme to tyme to be levyed of the goodes and cattalls of the offendr or offendors by the mayer and his hrethern. And th' one moytye therof to be to the use of the townnes chambre of Hull, And th' oder moytye thereof to th' use of the same occupacon. Provydede always that every inhabitaunte w^tin the same town dwelling may lawfully brewe for the Provysyon and Serving of there own house or housses, puttyng non to Sale, noyther ingrose nore retaille.

3. Promise to serve all the inhabitants, strangers, and shipping with lastyng and helthsome bere.

Item the same occupacon of berbruars for them and there Successors Doo Covenannte, grannte, and promyse to and with the sayed Mayo^r and Burgesses and ther Successors, appene reasonable warnyng, to serve all th' enhabitaunntes w^thin the sayed town of Hull, and all Strangers Resortynge unto the same Bothe for Shippyng and otherwise, At all tyme and tymes lastyng and helthesome bere, At and by suche Reasonable Prices as shalbe lymyted unto them by Mr. Mayo^r for the tyme beyng, and his brethern Aldermen, wheder yt be for the tonne or other vessell of greatter or smaller measure, the prices in rysyng or fallyng of malte, hoopes, and other thinges belongyng to the said occupacon from tyme to tyme reasonably consydered.

4. Not to entice another servant.

Item it is ordeyned y^t noo person nor persons being of that occupacon doo allure or intyce anny servannte or servauntes reteynyng to or wth anny other being of the same Scyence to departe out of Servyce unto suche tyme as the same servannte or servanntes have fully and holly accomplysshed his or ther tearm or promyse mayed, in payne of every defaulte duely proved iij*s*. iiij*d*., to be levied to th' use aforsaied.

5. Ships to be served only by the Company.

Itm all maner of Shippes, Crayers, and Keilles, for ther necessary victnallyng(*a*), at the request of the owners of the same, shalbe served here in this porte by the same occupacon onely, and by non other person or persons, in payne of every tonne bere delyvered to the contrary xx*s*., and every other vessell under a tonne x*s*., to be levyed as is above rehersed unto the use aforsaied.

6. 6s. 8d. upsett.

Item that every person whiche from hensforthe shalbe admytted and allowed to be one of the same occupacon, and ys willing to have and enjoye the benefyte of this occupacon, shall furst agre withe the same Wardens and Stewardes, and pay unto them for his upsett vi*s*. viii*d*., whereof the one moytie to be to the use of the town chambre, And th'odre moytie to the saied occupacon.

7. No servant to be engaged unless he has been apprenticed 7 years. But Mr. Mayor, etc., may have one to ayd him in his own house.

Item that non of that occupacon shall releyve noo servannte in wages except that servannt have ben prentyse seven yeres at that occupacon. Provydede yf Mr. Mayor or anny of his brethern th' aldermen [or any other honest burgess, (interlined)] be dysposed to have helpp or ayd for brewynge of bere w^thin his or there own house

(*a*) The word "victualling."

or houses for ther own provyson wthin ther houses, that then appon requeste to the Warden of the same company he shalbe appoynted to have such oon for his ayd as shalbe thought mete for that purpose.

8. May make ordinances.

Item yt shalbe lanfull to the Warden and Stewardes, by cousent of ye occupacon, to make suche lanfull orders for ye occupacon as shalbe nothing prejudiciall to the commen welthe.

9. Mayor, etc., may sett the price of dohle bere and merchante or shipping bere.

Itm it shalbe lanfull to the Mayor and aldermen Justices at all tymes to sett price of dohle bere and merchante bere, oyerwise called shippe here.

10. Persons refusing to come to election or meetings, 3s. 4d.

Itm yf any persons or person being of the companye of the same occupacon doo obstynatly wthdrawe hymmselff, and will note come unto the same warden eyther at the eleccon tyme or at anny oyer tyme reasonahle when he haythe warnynge, then every suche person to foriffaite and losse to th' use aforsaied for every defaulte iijs. iiijd.

11. Warden to yield account within 14 days of expiration of office.

Itm that every Warden, wth the Stewardes of the same occupacon wch have remayned for one yer, shall yelde and make ther juste accomptez from yer to yer unto the newe Warden and his company within xiiith dayes next after the eleccion, and therapoonne to mayke payment of all suche Sommes of money as shall remayn or be fonde in his or ther handes, apponne payne of every defaulte xls., to be levyed to th' use aforsayed.

12. Every brother to be agreable to the Warden and the rest, or be expelled.

Item it is ordeyned aud agreyd that every broder of the same occupacon or mysterye shalbe agreable to & wth the Warden & other officers, wth the reste of the company of the same occupacon from tyme to tyme, in payne of foriffacture for the furst defaulte xijd., The Second defaulte ijs., And the thyrd defaulte iijs. iiijd., to be levyed to the usse aforsaied. And yf anny further variance, controversye, debate, or stryff do ensewe by reason of the sayed partye offending as hefor, then he to be clerely dysmyssed oute of ye saied company wth suche punyshment as by Mr. Mayor for the tyme beyng shalbe thought reasonable.

13. Brewers will pay 2d. for every ton of beer they brew.

Ffurther the sayed occupacon or mysterye of berbruers (videlicet), John Dalton, James Scolles, Rychard Hargell, James Chapman, William Rooper, William Clarke, alias Sevyor. Henry Hornecastell, and John Rycarby, for them and their successors, berbruars of ye same town, Doo covenaunte, promyse, & graunt to & wth the saied Mayor & Burgesses & yeir Successors, That they the sayed occupacon and yeir Successors, berbruars of ye same town, Shall for the having, usyng, & enjoyng of all and singler the promysses menccioned & declared in ye saied composicon, shall yeld and pay yerely and successyvely for ever unto the use of the chamber of Kingeston apon Hull aforsaid for every tonne of bere which they or anny of them shall brewe, to sell two pense ynglysshe money, and the same to be payed and answered quarterlye (videlicet), at Mychaelmes, Xpenmas, Easter, and Mydesomerre, appon the othes and consciences of hym or them yat soo shall brewe the same, unto the Chambrelayns of the same towne, and the commen officer for the tym being. And the same occupacon or mysterye of Berbruars always to be ordered, perswaded, and Ruled in matters of varyannce and matters tonching the publique welthe, by Mr. Mayor for the tyme being and his brethern th' aldermen of the same towne. In witness whereof to th' on partie of theis indentures Remaynyng wth the saied John Dalton, James Scolles, Richard Hargell, James Chapman, William Rooper, William Clerke, alias Sevyer, Henry Hornecastell, & John Rycarby, the sayed Mayor and Burgesses have putto ther Common Seall of the same towne. And to th' oder partey of theis indenturs Remaynyng wth the sayed Mayor and Burgesses the sayed John Dalton, James Scolles, Rychard Hargell, James Chapman, William Rooper, William Clarke, alias Sevyer, Henry Hornecastell, and John Rycarby have putte ther Severall Sealls. Datede at Kingeston apon Hull aforsayed, the ixth day of ffebruary, In the ffourte and ffyfte yeres of the Reigne of oure Soveraign Lord and ladie Philipp and Marye, by the grace of god King and Queue of England, Spayn, ffrance, Bothe Tytylls, Jerusalem and Ireland, Defendors of the ffaythe, Archeduckes of Austria, Duckes of Burgundy, Myllan, and Brabant, Counties of Haspurg, ffandres, and Tyrrol.

To be ordered and persuaded by the Mayor.

[The signatures are on the strips of parchment by which the seals are appended.]

John Dalton.	Jhayms Scolles.
Richard Hargyll.	Jhams Chapman.
Harry Hornecastel.	Wym. Roper.
William Clarke.	Jhou Rycarhoe.

[*Endorsed*]

Ber Browesers.

CHAPTER XXIII.

THE TAILORS' GILD.

To the tune of "Treason's Joy."

Then let all London Companies
  So highly in renown,
Give Merchant Taylors name and fame
  To wear the laurel crown:

For seven of England's royal Kings
  Thereof have all been free,
And with their loves and favours grac'd
  This worthy Company.

Ballad (227) *Written in Honour of the Entertainment of James I.*

This is he, whom sitting downcast, on the hard basis of his shopboard, the world treats with contumely as the ninth part of a man! Look up thou much injured one, look up with the kindling eye of hope, and prophetic bodings of a noble better time! Too long has thou sat there, on crossed legs, wearing thy ankle joints to horn!—*Carlyle.*

What too are all poets and moral teachers, but a species of metaphorical tailor?—*Ibid.*

IT is difficult to say on what grounds the tailor has been held to be only the part of a man. None of the mediæval trades have a more valiant and even turbulent record than this maligned fraternity. The records of the craft from the earliest times are full of stirring episodes. In London in 1226 we find the trade engaged in a great city tumult with the Goldsmiths, in which the combatants mustered upwards of 500, and many were wounded in the fray. In addition to the early importance of the Gild of the "Tailors and Linen Armourers," the "yomen taillours" or journeymen shew themselves in this trade at an early date vigorously striving to assert their independence. From a complaint of the date 1415 we learn that, "dwelling with one another in companies, they did hold and

(227) Herbert, II., page 432.

Silver Tankard.

Now in the possession of the Hull Trinity House.

The following are the inscriptions:—

"Concordia parvæ Res Crescunt"

"Ebenezr. Robson, Warden"

"This interesting Relic of the Ancient Guild of Merchant Tailors of Hull, was presented by George Hall, Esq., an Elder Brother of this Corporation, 1860."

inhabit divers dwelling houses within the city against the will of their superiors in the said city, and of the masters of that trade." Not only so, we read that they "had often assembled in great numbers, held divers assemblies and conventicles, and wounded, beaten, and maltreated many lieges of our lord the King, including one master," and wear a livery annually (228)." They are therefore forbidden for the future to be presumptuous, and told to obey the masters. But two years afterwards the "yomen taillours" rallied, and made application that they and others of their fraternity of yomen yearly may assemble at the feast of St. John Baptist, in the Church of St. John of Jerusalem, near to Smithfield, and make offerings for the souls of brethren and sisters, and do other things that they were wont to do (229)." The issue is not recorded, but the claim upon the ground of custom shews that the fraternity had existed, in fact, long previously, while the assumption of a livery seems to shew that it was a numerous and powerful body.

The classic ground, however, of the craft was at Exeter. There the long battle of the tailors against the city fathers deserves to rank as the Iliad and Nibelungen Lied of the fraternity. The origin of the Exeter Gild is not stated. Its interest begins with a royal charter granted by Edward IV. in 1466, incorporating with a common seal, a livery, and corporate privileges the "men of the said Craft," with a Master and four Wardens, under general control of the Mayor. This charter seems to have had a very stimulating effect upon the recipients. Their privileges seem to have induced several other crafts to join the Gild, as was often the case elsewhere. Their ambition ran high. From the Rolls of the Mayor's Court, 1475-6-7, it appears that a general attempt was made by them to bring all tailors by force under power of the Gild, and to compel payment of the Gild fees. In language which is probably unique in the history of literature, they went forth "modo guerrino arriati, vi et armis, videlicet jactis, doblettis of defence, swerdis, bokelers, gleyves,

(228) Riley, page 611.
(229) Riley, page 653.

and stavys, in domo" of the offender, beating and threatening. Still the arsenal is not exhausted. At other times they are provided with "arcubus, glayvis, baculis, et daggariis," or with "gladiis et daggariis." Scissors seem to be the only weapons not mentioned in this terrific warfare. No wonder the fathers of the city took fright. After great counsel, an elaborate case was got up, and emissaries were sent up to London to lay the complaint before the King. It was successful. A decree was obtained quashing the Gild, and "the Mayor, John Deuys, and the 24 after communication had in the Church of St. Peter with John Fortescue and John Courtenay, the King's Commissioners, jubilantly drank wine in the house of Matthew Tubbe at the expense of the town to the amount of viii*d*." The feasting, however, was premature. The Gild continued without intermission; a compromise was settled, and the King's final award defined more closely the extent of its authority under the Mayor, while in no way impairing its prosperity. The Gild remained in existence continuously for about four centuries, and only ceased in the present century, the last amended body of ordinances being dated 1716, and the books containing the entries of the Gild from 1477 to the second quarter of the 19th century are now in the possession of the Corporation of Exeter. They possessed a Taylor's Hall, with a parlor, buttery and chamber and outer chamber; on the dais in the hall was a painted cloth; there was kept also a box for the deeds and writings, a streamer and banner, and other effects; and lands were entrusted to it for religious purposes. In the 14th century there were master workers with shops, journeymen and workers by the year, month, or week, apprentices and serving men, all belonging to the Gild.

The Exeter Gild as thus pourtrayed will serve as an example of the Gilds of the same craft existing in probably every town of importance in England, and nearly everywhere taking a prominent place among the municipal organisations, although we may presume not everywhere with the same ferocious proclivities. The methods of working of tailors were then in many respects different from those of the present day. As in other trades, like the goldsmiths, the customer bought his own material, and the tailor wrought it up.

From the records of Exeter also we are able to gain an insight into the beneficial effect of the gild system of organisation which it is only fair to set forth by the side of the account already given. The honest fulfilment of a contract was a matter for the strictest surveillance. A customer complains that one John Rowter received four yards of cloth, and it was not all used. The "gowne was sene by the said crafte," and "there was fownde no cloth wasted, but ther wasse dewly proved III. quarteris of brod clothe convayed in peces, as hit apereth by patrons of blacke paper in our comen cofer of record, at any tyme to shew." At another time John Carter was similarly accused. It was found that none was stolen, but a quarter of broad cloth was wasted "for lack of konnynge," so John Carter was ordered to pay for the cloth and keep the gown. But if the tailor was not of the Gild the customer had no remedy but to sue for his damage at the common law. Thus both the power and the benefit of such gilds is evident. They constituted a kind of *imperium in imperio*; they could fine a dishonest member, and even put him in the stocks, while the customer had an easier remedy than he had in common law.

According to Stow, who was himself a merchant tailor, the London Tailors' Gild was licensed in the 28 Edward I. (1299-1300), though as already noticed we have the record of an affray between the Tailors and Goldsmiths as early as 1226, shewing this craft then as a powerful body; and they already possessed a hall before purchasing the present site in 1331. Their earlier title was "The Tailors and Linen Armourers of the Fraternity of St. John the Baptist," the latter term referring to the internal fitting of the armor of the period. They were, moreover, extensive dealers in and importers of woollen cloth, and in 28 Edward III. sent six members to the Common Council, this number of representatives being equal to that sent by the largest gilds. The date of their incorporation was 1466, the same year as the Gild at Exeter. The more ambitious title by which the craft was known in the 16th century, that of Merchant Tailors, dates from the time of Henry VII., who conferred it when he was himself initiated in 1503, "in consideration of their having immemorially exercised merchandise in all parts of the globe (230)." In the same year this King similarly chartered the ancient Gild of the Merchant Tailors at York, which still carries on its meetings in he fine Hall of the Gild, where the arms of the Company remain, and the well-known motto, "Concordia parvæ crescunt res (231)."

The patron saint of the tailors was almost universally St. John the Baptist (232), and the crest is a lamb in a glory. The reason assigned for this is curious. It might be thought taht the saint in question had little claim to patronise garments of purple and fine linen, and might have looked upon those who dealt in them with little favor; but the point of contact was in the fleece of the lamb, which was the staple of the trade. In Hull it will be noticed that the compositions all put the election day near the feast of St. Michael the Archangel, who, according to analogy, would be the patron saint of the Gild. On the other hand the crest and motto were, with some slight differences, the same as those of London and York. The question is involved in another of more curious interest. There is no account of a Tailors' Hall in Hull before the Reformation, although such an important craft must in all probability have possessed one. But upon the suppression of the gilds in 1550, a large part of their possessions passed into the hands of Henry Thurscross, whose name appears in the composition of the 4 Edward VI. Among these was the ancient hall of the Gild of St. John the Baptist, which was situated close to St. Mary's Church. Either Henry or Luke Thurscross shortly afterwards gave this hall to the Tailors' Company. According to Sheahan (p. 656) the front of the building exhibited a carved coat of arms, above which was inscribed, "This is Thorcross Armes," and below it the initials "J. H. T.," but no date. The hall itself was only demolished

(230) Herbert, *Tailors' Company*.

(231) See "Bricklayers' Ordinances."

(232) In Constantinople the patron is Adam.

in 1863. The question that suggests itself is, was there any special reason for this act of generosity?

Now the Gild of St. John the Baptist was founded about 1350, and in the full copy of the deed of foundation (see p. 112) we find the name of William, domestic tailor of Lord William de la Pole. The custom in Pre-Reformation times was for the crafts either to be closely connected with the religious Gild of their patron saint or to be merged in it. Thus the return sent from the Gild of the Tailors at Norwich in 1388 is that of a purely religious Gild. The tailors are not mentioned in it ([233]). On the other hand the clause in the Hull St. John's Gild relating to apprentices points to a connection with some craft. It is by no means improbable that it was really the religious fraternity of the tailors. The names of the founders would in that case be those of ordinary master tailors. The tailor of De la Pole was so specified because he was not a master tailor in the ordinary way. Again, in the ancient pageants of the town the tailors would group themselves under the banner of St. John the Baptist, borne by the St. John's Gild, shewing the crest of St. John. It was so at Carlisle, where the rule for the tailors on Corpus Christi Day was that "ye whole occupacion and banner was to be assembled by 10 a.m., and who comes not before ye banner be raised is fined *vid.*" At the funerals of tailors the light "with ye banner" was ordered to be used ([234]). If these indications are to be relied upon, the Hall of the Gild of St. John the Baptist would, in accordance with custom, be equally used by the Tailors' Craft, and when the Gild was suppressed the Tailors' Company would be left homeless. It would be at this crisis that Thurscross gave the Hall, as we are told, to the Company. But from the above considerations it is not unlikely it was really their ancient meeting place which was now restored to them. The connection with St. Michael may have been a change introduced at the time of the suppression, when the trades gilds were anxious to disown their

(233) *Early English Gilds*, page 85.

(234) Ferguson, *Cumberland*, page 206.

connection with the religious ones, so as not to run the risk of confiscation.

In a conveyance dated Dec. 14th, 1803, it is described as "All that messuage, tenement, and dwelling house, with the chamber over the same formerly used as a meeting house for the Company of Taylors, and commonly called Leaden Hall, or Taylors' Hall, situate in the town of Kingston-upon-Hull aforesaid, in a certain place there called Low Church Alley, near unto St. Mary's Churchyard." In a deed of 1774 the recital is the same ([235]). From this it would seem that the Hall was subsequently used as the "Leadenhall," the trade in lead of the Peak district being a very ancient and important one in the town.

The Compositions now extant in the Town Hall are dated 1550, 1563, and 1680. The books of the Company have disappeared.

Now Hadley, in his "History of Hull" (see p. 830), published in 1788, "inserts" what he calls "the preamble and a few extracts" from a composition of the Gild of Tailors, dated 1617. The first article speaks of the "Guilde" as containing "brethren and sisters." We read next of the "Alderman or Warden, and of his Stewards and Searchers and twelve Assistants." Then the following ordinances are given:—

> That no tailor should be made a free burgess of the town, or brother of the Guild till he has served seven years with a freeman of the town.
>
> That none should take a second prentice till the first has served four years; nor should take a third till the second had served five years; and that each apprentice should be twenty-four years old before his prenticeship should expire, under a penalty of £5, half for the Corporation and half for the town (on account of the number of the trade and scarcity of work).
>
> That none should entertain more than three prentices or servants (being strangers and no inhabitants) on pain of forfeiting two pence a day, but that it should be allowed to employ a tailor (an inhabitant) exceeding the limited number, warning thereof to be given to the Alderman or Warden, paying only four pence a day wages and his victuals; but if no inhabitant is to be got, it should be lawful to employ strangers, paying to the Guild four pence weekly for every one so employed, under a penalty of two shillings and sixpence.

(235) For the above I am indebted to Mr. R. H. Barker, Solicitor.

That the Warden should be acquainted when strangers were entertained or discharged. [Clause as to working in peoples' houses.]

That every brother should keep the secrets of the town according to his burgess oath, and be obedient to the Corporation.

That none shall swear, under a penalty of one shilling for the first offence, two for the second, three for the next, etc.

That on being admitted of the Guild they should set their hands and seals to the book of orders, and pay five shillings towards the maintenance of the stock.

"Every brother to bring his servants and prentices to Church on the Sabbath and other festival days," and to restrain them from unthriftily using taverns and alehouses and unlawful games, and that no brother should fit on or carry home any cloaths on the Sabbath Day, etc.

Now a comparison of these with the terms of the compositions which we give from the originals of 1550, 1563, and 1680, will show most remarkable differences. In the latter there are no sisters, and the Alderman is absent. In Hadley's document the ordinances relating to the freedom of the town are unlike any that occur either in the compositions of the tailors or of any other trade of the town. The rules for apprentices are different, and the limit of 24 years of age is introduced. The permission to employ strangers at 4d. a week fine, the wage of 4d. a day and victuals, are anachronisms. The ordinances that follow might have had place in "the Book of Acts" of the fraternity, but look strange in its composition. He adds that it was "signed by the Corporation," and "there are the hands and seals of three hundred of the Guild affixed thereto." No other composition that we know of was signed by anyone but the Mayor and the chief officials of the trade. And that there should have been 300 members in 1617 is extremely improbable.

No information is given as to the original of this document, and whether it ever had any existence at all is very doubtful. Possibly it was a traditional account given to the author by some old inhabitant who retained a memory of the general purport of similar ordinances. Yet this is the only body of ordinances of the Crafts' Gilds of the town which has ever been published.

His further statement that the old compositions of the Gild from 1590 to 1699 are extant, is, as will be seen, at variance with the dates of those which are now preserved in the Town Hall.

The first Composition which we give below is that of 4 Edward VI. It assumes the form of an indenture or agreement between the town and the Gild, and the elections are granted "as in tymes past." The Composition of 1563 is so nearly identical with it that the points of difference are simply noted below in their places.

COMPOSITION OF TAILORS, 4 EDWARD VI.

These are the articles and liberties grauntide by John Oversall, Mayor of Kinstowne upon Hull, and th' aldermen his brethern, Thomas Dalton, th' older, Henry Thurscroste, Elizander Stocdale, Willyam Clarke, John Thaccar, Walter Jobson, Willyam Jonson, Willyam Jaxson, James Stocdale, John Thornton, and Thomas Dalton the yonger, for them and theire successors, to ye wardyn, stewardis and serchars of the Tayllyors occupacion of Kingstoune upon Hull aforesaid, and to theire Successors, this sixte Daye of octobre in the fourthe yere of the Reigne of our Sofferagne Lorde Edwarde the vith, by the grace of god King of England, Fraunce, and Eyreland, Deffendar of the faythe, and in earth of the Churche of England and also of eyrelande suppreme heade, Anno Domini 1550.

1. Item in primis it is graunted by the said mayor and Aldermen to ye said wardyn, stewardes, and serchars of the said occupacon of Tayllyors that they shall have their eleccion amongest them Selves as they have had in tymes paste, and at the Daye of there eleccion shall electe two honeste men symyttede and Chossen by the said occupacion, th'one of these two to stande wardyn for that presente yere according as ye eleccion Shall fall, and the said wardin at the goinge owte of his yere shall nominate one man to be of th' eleccion, and the Reste of th' occupacion to nominate Another honeste man, owt of the whiche ij men the said wardin shall be chossyn, and ye said wardyn at the going onte of his said yere shall stande and be one of the serchers for ye yere folowing, and the said occupacion to chosse Another serchare to hym, and the said wardin entering in to his office shall Appoynte one of the same occupacon to stande stewarde for his yere being, and the Reste of th occupacion to chosse Another to hym. Providide always that ye said wardin, stewardis, and serchars shall yerelye be Chaungide, and other chossyn in their Romes within xiiijth Days next folowing ye feaste of saynte migholl th' arcangell, and for Lacke of so doing shall forfayte xxs. to ye towne's chambre.

To have their eleccion amongst themselves, as in tymes paste.

One Warden and two Searchers.

To be changed yearly.

2\. *To be sworn before Mayor.*

Item that the said wardin shall presente the ij serchars for the tyme being unto y^e^ mayor for that yere, being in the comen hall (*a*) of Hull Aforsaid, and their to take their othe that they shall Dewlye and trewlye presente to ye mayor of Hull Aforsaide, and to ye wardin of th' occupacon, all the forfayts and Defawts Donne within th' occupacon, and yf there be annye Defawte ffounde within the said occupacon, that the said serchars makithe not Amendis for it within them Selvis, That then they to presente it to the Mayor for the tyme being, praying hym that he will determyne it and correcte it Lyke as he thinkithe beste, according to the qnantite of the Trespace at A Resonable fyne, and that the same fyne be the one halfe to the chamber of Hull and the other halfe to the said occupacon.

Half fines to go to Mayor, and half to th' occupacion.

3\. *Fine for absence, 3s. 4d.*

Item That yf anny of the said occupacon with Drawe hym Selfe when he is warnyd to come to th'eleccion, and Do absente hym Selfe without lysence of the said wardyn for the tyme being, The said person or persons for everye tyme so offending shall forfayte and paye iij*s*. iiij*d*. (*b*) to the said occupacon.

4\. *Searchers to have 4d. for each upsett, and 4d. yf any gargmente be founde fawteworthye.*

Item that the said Serchars shall have of every Upsetter iiij*d*. (*c*), and yf anny gargmente be founde fawteworthye before the serchars eyther of them to have iiij*d*.

5\. *Not to employ another's servant.*

Item that no Tayllyor give no garmente to worke or sewe to anny other manis servante before he be departide frome his master's Servis upon payne of fforfayting for every tyme so doing xii*d*. to the said occupacon.

6\. *No wages to be detained above 14 days.*

Item that no master witholde no wagis that shalbe dewe unto yis servante over the Space of foretene Days (*d*) next after his Departing frome his master, and yf the said master will not paye his Servant let the same Servant complayne hym to the said Serchars, and they shall see yat he have his Dewtye.

7\. *Fine 3s. 4d.*

Item that yf so be that the said master Do make Delaye Agaynste the said Serchars, the said master or masters for everye tyme so offending shall forfayte iii*s*. iiij*d*., the one halfe to the Townis Chamber and the other halfe to the said occnpacion.

8\. *Fines for resisting Searchers.*

Item That yf anny of the said occnpacon make Reaystannce or Disturbaunce Agaynste the said Serchars or anny of them in there offices, Doing and Amending of the fawtes within the said occupacon, that he be fynede

(*a*) "Guylde hawll" in 1563.

(*b*) Article 8 of 1563 enacts vi*d*. fine in the case of ordinary meetings.

(*c*) 12d. for upsetts and 8d. for defaults in 1563 (Article 6).

(*d*) Six days instead of 14 in 1563 (Article 8).

the first tyme xij*d.*, the seconde tyme xx*d.*, the thirde iij*s.* iiij*d.* (*e*), to the said occupacon.

9. No aleaunte straunger to sett up a borde unless he paid 40s.

Item that no Aleaunte straunger Set up no borde to worke upon, upon payne of fortye shillings (*f*), xx*s.* to the Townis Chamber and xx*s.* to the said occupacon, for the whiche xl*s.* he shalbe ffree to occupye the said occupacon Amongeste us.

10. Searchers to make no extorcions.

Item that no Serchar nor Serchars take no extorcions of no manner of gatheringes other wise than they shall give A trowe Accompte upon be fore the said wardyn and the said occupacon upon payne of forfayting of v*s.* to the said occupacon.

11. Not to pledge the garments.

Item that no tayllyor laye anny maner of garmente in pledge, being another manis, or witholde or prolong any manis garmente or clothe Agaynst his will, he that makithe such defawte for every tyme so doing shall forfayte vj*s.* viij*d.* (*g*), to be Devydide as is Afforsaid, and to Restore the goods Agayne.

12. Master taking apprentice to paye vj*d.*, and seware to paye viij*d.*

Item that what tayllour that takyth Aprentis he shall paye to the said occupacon at his entring vj*d.* (*h*), and that no Tayllour take no seware to sewe excepte the same seware paye to the said occupacon yerelye viij*d.*

13. Every tayllour dwelling in the town to pay xij*d.*, & every aleaunte 2*s.*

Item that every master Tayllour that dwellithe within the said towne shall paye unto ye occupacon every yere xij*d.*, and every Aleaunte ij*s.*

14. No money to be deposited without proper account.

Item that no parcell of money or profyts belonging to the said occupacon he put in handis of no person or persons but suche as the same shall yelde up accompte to ye said wardyn and other officers of the same occupacon, upon payne of forfayting of xx*s.* to the townis chambre of hull, and to yelde Agayne all suche things as he or they hath in there handis, the fyne not with standing.

15. Workmen tayllors not to work in dwelling houses.

Item that no man within the Towne of Hull Dwelling shall kepe no maner of workman Tayllyor workyn within his house upon payne of iij*s.* iiij*d.*(*i*), and the workman to forfayte as muche the one halfe to ye townis chambre and ye other halfe to ye seaid occupacon.

16. Wardens, etc., to be burgesses.

Item that no persone or persons shalbe chosseyn to be wardyns, stewardis, and serchars of the said occupacon but suche as are burgesses of ye saide Towne of Hull, upon payne of fforfayting of xx*s.*, the one halfe to ye townis chambre and ye other halfe to the said occupacon.

(*e*) In 1563 the fines are discretional for the first three offences, and then expulsion (Article 9).

(*f*) In 1563 fine 53s. 4d. (Article 6).

(*g*) Fine 6s. 8d. in 1563.

(*h*) Apprentice 6s. 8d. in 1563.

(*i*) Employer fined 6s. 8d. and workman omitted in Article 15 of 1563.

17. Not to tice other men's sewares.

Item That anny Tayllyor having a sewer with hym by weke or by yere, that no other workman shall tyce the said Servante from his master upon payne of forfayting of iii*s.* iiij*d.* to the saied occupaccion.

18. No seware to depart without resonable warnyng.

Item that no Seware do Departe frome his master after that he is hyeride withont Resonable warnyng gevin to the said master before ye serchars of th' occupacon (*j*).

19. Searchers to prevent all suche as shall worke aborde of any shippe.

Item that the said serchars shall presente before the mayor for the tyme being all suche as shall worke aborde of any shippe or shippis in ye havin of the said Towne of Hull, and for every Defawte founde the shippe to forfayte to ye said chambre of Hull x*s.*, and ye workman as much to ye said occupacon.

20. No master to set up without licence and paying his upsets.

Item That no master Tayllyor Shall set up no horde as a master to work without lysence and over sight of the said Wardyn, Stewardis, and Serchars of the said occupacon, they to able ye said workman before he set up in payne of forfayting of xx*s.* to the chamber of the towne of Hull, and ye workman to paye for his upset vi*s.* viij*d.*, the one halfe to ye townis Chamber and ye other halfe to ye said occupacon, and viij*d.* to the serchars.

21. But Mayor and Alderman may have Aprentis at their comaundemente.

Item That it shalbe Lawfull for the said mayor and Alderman at anny tyme or tymes here after to have Aprentis of the said occupacon within ye Town aforsaid, at their comanndemente to mend suche certayne gere as they stande nede upon, they payeng them for there paynis.

22. Searchers may search any man's howse.

Item That it shalbe Lawfull for the said Wardyn, Stewardis, and Serchars, and their successors, at anny tyme or tymes here after to make serche in anny manys howse within the towne aforsaide for all suche persons or persons of the said occupacon that shall worke in anny manis howse other wise than is abone mencionede.

23. And the Gild will pay xxx*s.* yerely to the Town's Chamber.

And for the Accomplishemente of the grannts and premysis Abone Specified the said occupacon and there successors shall paye yerely and by yere unto ye townis chamber of Hull thirtye shillings, the which xxx*s.* to be always paide within xvi^th^ days next after the feaste of Saynte myghell th' arcangell.

[Seal cut off.]

[*Endorsed in error*]

Taylers Composi., 5 Eliz. Regni.

[This document is attached to the Composition of 5th Elizabeth.]

The remaining Composition, of the year 1680, is a very long one. Its provisions, moreover, though framed in many cases on

(*j*) Fine 3*s.* 4*d.* in 1563.

the same lines which had been traditional in the craft, afford so many points of difference that it has been thought desirable to give it in full. It is remarkable for its strained effort to present the form of an exact legal charter of the Company granted by the Mayor by virtue of several charters and letters patent (which did not exist), and also by ancient custom and usage. "Imprimis It is statuted, ordained, declared, and agreed That the said Company or Society of Tailers shall stand and be incorporated into a Brotherhood (236)." The Company since its earlier period had developed an order of Elder Brethren, such as we find also in the Coopers' Company and Trinity House. The fines are in many instances increased, and the regulations directed against strangers are more stringent. In spite of this, however, the "composition rent" paid to the Corporation is decreased from 30s. to 15s. This may be an indication of power, but more probably, in spite of the greater parade of these later ordinances, the spirit of the times was against them, and the brethren, in reality, although more exclusive, were really less numerous and powerful.

We cannot help being reminded of the Merchants' Company, who ended their career with a desperate effort to assert similar privileges.

Notwithstanding the involved and tedious length of the ordinances, a picture of the trade of the period could not be complete without them.

Composition of Tailors of the Year 1680.

In the honour of Almighty God, and as tending to the Good of the Weale Publique of the Town or Borough of Kingston upon Hull. And for the better Order, rule, Government, and direction of the ffraternity or Company of Tailers within the said Town of Kingston upon Hull and liberties thereof, At the humble and speciall instance and request of Tristram Berry, now Warden, Robert Graves and Francis Bartill, Searchers and Elder Brethren, Ffrancis Lampson and William Legard, Stewards of the said ffraternity or Company of Tailers, and John Stockson senior, William Temperance, John Toft, John Howdell, Andrew Rainer, John Ffryston, William Simpson, Robert Hoole, Thomas Coates, and Thomas Gray, Elder Brethren of the said Company, on the behalf of themselves and the rest of the Handy Crafts and Tradesmen in the Craft, trade, and mistery of

(236) On this "Incorporation" see the chapter on this subject below.

Tailers aforesaid. Together with the assent, consent, and approbation of the Right Hor[ll] George Crowle, now Maior of the said Towne, and the Wor[ll] the Aldermen his Brethren, And as well by vertue of several Charters and Letters Patent heretofore granted and confirmed unto the Maior and Burgesses of the said Town of Kingston-upon-Hull, As also according to antient Custom and Usage These Orders, Acts, Articles, Libertys, Priviledges, and Constitutions hereunder written were made, constituted, ordained, established, and agreed to, to th' intent that as well all and every the said Persons of the said occupacon herein named, As others which now are or hereafter shalbe admitted into the same, shall or may have, keep, observe, execute, maintain, and enjoy All and every the same Orders and Articles and Constitutions as followeth :—

2. Imprimis It is Statuted, ordained, declared, and agreed That the said Company or Society of Tailers shall stand and be incorporated into a Brotherhood by such name as heretofore of ancient time they have been, And that they shall consist of a Warden, Two Searchers, Two Stewards, and Twelve Assistants, of which Assistants the said Searchers are two, and the rest of their Brethren the Company, And that Tristram Berry, the now present Warden, shall so stand untill the day of Eleccon now next coming, hereafter specified, and likewise the said Robert Graves and Ffrancis Bartill shalbe Searchers, and Francis Lampson and William Legard shalbe Stewards of the said Company, untill the said day of Eleccon, unless that they or any of them shall before such day of Eleccon happen to dye, or for some Misdemeanour to be removed accordingly as hereafter in these presents is inserted. And that the same Warden, Searchers, and Stewards, and ffraternity of Tailers in Kingston upon Hull aforesaid, shall have their Eleccon amongst themselves, within Eighteen days after the ffeast of S[nt] Michael the Archangel, called Michaelmas day next ensuing, and soo yearly forever hereafter, And that upon the said day of Eleccion, two of the Elder Brethren of the said Company, to be named by the Warden and Elder Brethren, or the Major part of them shall go on for one to be chosen Warden for the year then next ensuing. Which Warden, after such his Eleccion and entry on the said office, shall that day immediately elect and choose one of the younger Brethren of the said Company to be Steward for his yeare, And the rest of the Company at the same time shall nominate and elect another Brother of their Company, to continue and be Steward with him so chosen by the said new Warden for the said year, And also That the old Warden shall stand and be one of the

Company to stand and be incorporated.

A Warden, two Searchers, two Stewards, and twelve Assistants.

Warden to be from the Elder Brethren.

Steward from the Younger Brethren.

Searchers for the year following the said day Eleccion of a new Warden, And the said Company shall elect and choose another of their Brethren to stand and be Searcher with him for the year ensuing such his Eleccion. And so all Elecciones of the said Warden, Searchers, and Stewards shall yearly hereafter be observed and kept within the time aforesaid, and the said Warden and Searchers shalbe sworn according as is herein expressed, Upon pain of forfeiting to the said Maior and Burgesses, their Successors and Assignes, the summe of Twenty Shillings of lawfull English money, to be respectively paid by him or the most offending herein. Provided That if any of the Officers dye within the year they are so chosen to serve, or be removed for any Misdemeanour or miscarriage contrary to these Orders and constitutions, That then it shall and may be lawfull for the said Company within ffourteen days next after such death or removall, to Elect others in their places so dying or removed to continue and serve in their severall and respective offices for the rest of that year. Which persons so elected shalbe sworne as is hereafter mentioned.

2.

Warden and Searchers to be sworn before the Mayor.

Item It is statuted, Ordained, declared, and agreed, That the said Warden elected shall yearly the next day after such his Eleccon be sworne by and before the Major of the Town of Kingston-upon-Hull aforesaid, for the time being to the Right and due execnton of his office for the year following his foresaid Election. And also That the said Warden shall then present the Searchers appointed and elected as aforesaid, before the said Major for the time being. And they then and there to take their Oaths that they shall duly and truly present to the Major of Kingston upon Hull for the time being, and to the Warden of the said Company. All the fforfeitures and defaults concerning the said Occupacon, happening within their year of being Searchers, and done within the said Town by any Inhabitant or other not free of the said Company thereof, they can by any good ways or meanes come to the knowledg: And that the said

Warden, Searchers, and Stewards to be bound in Sureties.

Warden, Searchers, and Stewards for the time being, shalbe bound with sufficient Surety or Suretys in a reasonable summe of money to such person as shalbe nominated and appointed by most part of the said Company, well and truly to execute their severall offices for that year, and also to make a just and true accompt of all their receipts and disbursements for the said Company during their year, and to pay and deliver up to the next Warden, Searchers, and Stewards of the said Company, all and every such summe and summes of money and other things, as in any wise shalbe remaining in their hands at their departure from their severall offices, And further, in Case any of the officers, vizt., the said Warden and Searchers elected within Eighteen days after Michaelmas as aforesaid, do happen to dye or be removed within the year, then such person or persons as shalbe new elected in his or their respective places, shalbe sworn by and before the Major of the said Town for the time being, within three days next after such Eleccion, well and truly to perform and execute their respective offices aforesaid, as is herein declared, upon the pain and penalty mentioned in this Article.

3. Item It is Statuted, Ordained, declared, and agreed That if any the said ffraternity or company shall be elected and chosen in manner and forme above expressed to the respective offices of Wardens, Searchers, and Stewards, or any of them, or that shalbe elected an chosen an Elder Brother or Assistant upon the death or removall of any of the said Company, by most voices thereof, and shall upon knowledge or notice of such eleccon refuse or neglect to stand to and execute the same respective Offices or Places, That then such Person or Persons so refusing or neglecting shall forfeit to the said Company the severall sums hereafter mentioned, viz.: The Warden ffour Pounds, the Searchers or Stewardes fforty shillings apeece, and the person or persons elected to be an Elder Brother or Assistant, ffour pounds, all of good and lawfull English money, The one half thereof to be to the use of the said Major and Burgesses, their Successors and Assignes, and the other half thereof to the use of the said Company, the better to increase their Stock, All which severall Sume and Sumes of money aforementioned, or any other summs of money hereafter expressed and sett down for breach of any order or Article in these presentes, shall upon refusall or neglect to pay the same upon demand, be immediately levyed by way of distresse and sale of the goodes and Chattelles of every Person or Persons dissenting or offending contrary to the true intent and meaning thereof, and the overplus, if any such be, shalbe restored to the owner thereof. Provided that no such distress be made but by Warrant under the hand and seal of the Major of the said Town for the time being, and in such cases the Officer of such Major or such other person or persons as he shall appoint shalbe aiding and assisting in the premisses, and the said officer of the Major to have only ffour pence for his paines. And further, That upon the refusall or neglect of persons chosen to serve in the respective Offices aforesaid, it shallbe lawfull for the said Company to choose other

Penalties for refusing to aid Warden, £4; Searcher or Stewards, 40s.; and Elder Brother or Assistant, £4.

To be levied by distress.

persons in their Roomes and places, Who shall serve as hath been accustomed, Upon the Penalties aforesaid.

4. Penalties for withdrawing or being absent.

Item It is further Statuted, ordained, declared, and agreed That if any of the said Company, being warned, withdraw himself and be absent from the Election or other common meetings without speciall licence of the Wardens of the said Company for the time being, he shall forfeit to the use of the said Company only ffor every time being so absent or withdrawing, vizt., ffrom the Eleccon three shillings and ffour pence, and from other common meetings six pence a time.

5. No one to be admitted but by apprenticeship and a Burgess, and none other to set up in the Town.

Item It is further Statuted, ordained, declared, and agreed that no Tailer without notice to the Warden and Searchers of the said Company (except such as shall have served with a Burgesse of the said Town and a Brother of the said Trade by Indenture as an Apprentice to that trade for Seaven years at the least) shalbe admiteed to be Burgess of the said Town of Kingston-upon-Hull. And further that no Taillor which is not a free Burgesse of the said Town, and a free brother of the said Company, shall sett up to worke as a Maister Tailer within the said Town of Kingston upon Hull and liberties thereof by any waies or meanes whatsoever, And that no Tailer whatsoever shalbe admitted to be a free Burgesse of the said Town and a free Brother of the said occupacion But such as within a year after their being bound to that trade have had their Indentures inrolled as well in the Town's Book as in the Company's book, and shall have served his Apprenticeshipp to the said Trade by the space of seaven years at the least, by Indenture as aforesaid, and according to the Statute in that behalf.

6. Setting strange tailors to work in houses.

Item It is Statuted, ordained, declared, and agreed That no Burgesse or Inhabitant of this Town or the liberties of the same (Other then the Brethren of the said Company) shall sett on work in his, her, or their house or houses any Straunger or Straungers whatsoever being a Tailer not free of the said Town and Company as aforesaid, such Burgesse or inhabitant having notice thereof, in pain to forfeit and pay in maner and form following, vizt., the Householder where any Stranger shalbe be found Twenty Shillings, and the stranger Tailer Tenn Shillings, The one half thereof to the use of the said Major and Burgesses and their successors, and the other half to th' use of the occupacion's stock, to be levyed in manner and forme above expressed. And that it shall and may be lawfull for the Warden, Searchers, and Stewards of the said Company, and such of the said Company as they shall think fitt, with th' assistance of one of the officers of the Major for the time being, or any other person or

Power of Search. persons he shall appoint, to make search in any man's house within this Town for such as shall work of the said Trade otherwise then is limited, and that according to warrant from the said Major for the time being to be made in that behalf. Provided always and nevertheless it shall be free and lawfull for any brother of this Occupacon and their Apprentices and Servants to amend any old apparell whatsoever for any Inhabitant of this Town where he or they shall think fitt to work, taking for his day wages six pence, with meat and drink convenient.

But a free brother may amend old garments and take 6d. a day, with meat and drink convenient.

7. Item It is Statuted, ordained, declared, and agreed That no Brother of the said Company of Tailers shall sett on work in his house, shopp, or other place within the said Town of Kingston upon Hull any stranger or strangers whatsoever being a Tailer not free of the said Town and Company as aforesaid, and is a marryed man, upon the pain and penalty of ffive pounds, to be levyed as aforesaid of the Goods and Chattels of the said Brother offending, To the use of the said Mayor and Burgesses, their Successors or Assignes.

No married stranger to work in any shop, on penalty of £5.

And that if any Man of the said Brotherhood or occupacon of Tailers or their Servants shall at any time or times work any manner of new Work in any Inhabitant's house within this town (on Apparel for Children and Apprentices untill the time of Marriage only excepted), He or they so working shall for every time forfeit and pay ffive shillings To th' use of the said Occupacon Stock, and the Inhabitant where any shall so work shall likewise forfeit and pay other ffive shillings To th' use of the said Mayor and Burgesses, their Successors and Assignes, Without drift or delay. Provided alwaies It is intended and thought fitting That no Wedding Apparel, either for Children or Apprentice, shall at any time hereafter be made in any Inhabitant's house of this town, but only in the Houses and Shopps of some of the Brethren of this Occupacon, under the Penalty aforesaid, And likewise Provided That any Inhabitant of this Town shall or may at their liking Hire or keep by the year any One Tailer which hath served his Apprenticeshipp or the greater part thereof in this Town to amend, make, or work up any Apparel whatsoever (Except Wedding Apparel) for themselves and their own Household only, and not otherwise.

None to work in private houses (Apparel for children and apprentices until tyme of marriage only excepted).

8. Item it is Statuted, ordained, declared, and agreed That every Master Tailer and others who are free Brothers of the said Company dwelling in this Town shall pay to th' Use of the said Warden and Company of Tailers every year for his Brotherhood ffourteen pence upon the day of Eleccon, And likewise that every Appren-

Free brother to pay 14d. on Eleccon Day.

tice which shall have served with a free Man of the same Trade and shalbe free Burgess and admitted to sett up his Trade as aforesaid, shall pay for his Upsett Three shillings and ffour pence, Twelve pence thereof To th' use of the said Mayor and Burgesses and their successors, and th' other Two shillings and ffour pence thereof To the Use of th' Occupacon, to be divided amongst th' Officers of th' Company aforesaid and To th' use thereof as heretofore hath been accustomed. And that either of the Searchers shall have of every One who maketh a Garment which is found insufficient or fault worthy vijd. lawful English money.

3s. 4d. for upsetts.

9\. Item It is statuted, ordained, declared, and agreed That if any Tailor shall work on board any Shipp or Shipps in the Haven of the said Town after warning given to the Master of the Shipp or such Workman they shall forfeit for every such default Ten shillings a peece, Marriners mending their own Apparel only excepted, Th' One half of th' said ffine to be to th' use of the said Mayor and Burgesses and their successors, And th other half to the Company's Stock, to be levyed in manner and form aforesaid.

Tailors working on ships without permission, 10s.

10\. Item It is statuted, ordained, declared, and agreed That no manner of person or persons being a Tailor not dwelling in the said Town (other than such as are free of the said Town and Company), shall come into the same Town or Liberties thereof, to fetch any work of the Inhabitants of the Town to th' end to work or make the same upon Pain that the owner of the Work shall forfeit for every time that such offence is made, five shillings, Th' one Half To th' use of the said Mayor and Burgesses and their successors, and th' other Half to the Company's Stock.

No strange Tailors to fetch work out of town to make, on pain of 5s.

11\. Item It is further Statuted, ordained, declared, and agreed That no Tailor in the said Town ffree as aforesaid, shall keep or take any Apprentices but according to the Statute, vizt., shall for the Third Apprentice keep one Journeyman, and for every other Apprentice above the said Number of Three, One Journeyman, Under the Pain and Penalty of the Statute in that behalf made.

Three apprentices to one journeyman as per Statute, under the penalty of the same.

12\. Item It is further Statuted, ordained, declared, and agreed That it shall and may be lawfull to and for the said Warden, Searchers, Stewards, Elder Brethren, or Assistants, or the Major part of them, To make and establish from time to time hereafter such good, lawful, and wholsom Orders agreeable to the Laws of the Land for the better help, support, and government of the said Company as they shall think most meet, profitable, and convenient, so as the same be first seen, liked, approved,

Power to make ordinances to be appointed by the Mayor.

and allowed of by the Court of Mayor and Aldermen of the said Town of Kingston upon Hull for the time being, Or the more part of them. And in Case Any of the Younger Brethren of the said Company shall come and appear at the Publique place of Meeting of the same Company, without the notice and warning given by the Stewards of the said ffraternity for the time being, He and they so coming whereby to make any disturbance or disorder among the Brethren of the said Society, shall forfeit each Man Twenty shillings, Th' one half to the said Mayor and Burgesses and their successors, and th' other Half To th' use of th' said Company, to be recovered as aforesaid. And if it happen That at any of the Publique and General Meetings of the said Brotherhood, That any of the Elder Brethren of the said Society shall abuse the Warden or any Brother of the same Society by any unseemly opprobrious or contumelious Words or carriage, he shall forfeit for every such offence Ten shillings. And if any Young Brother abuse any of the said ffraternity by the like Words or Carriage, he shall forfeit the sum of ffive shillings. Both the said sums to be levyed and divided as aforesaid.

Younger brethren not to meet and make disturbances, on pain of 20s. each.

If Elder brethren abuse the Warden, 10s.; if younger brethren, 5s.

13. Item It is Statuted, ordained, declared, and agreed That the said Company or ffraternity of Tailors may take and admitt into their Society, ffraternity, or Company, the Woollen Drapers, Linnen Drapers, Milliners, or any other Trade with the same Town relating thereto, not already of a Company, who shalbe desirous to come within their said Company (if the said Company can agree with them). And such Trades as shalbe so Taken and admitted in are to be ordered by these orders and ordinances. Provided That such person or persons so desirous to be admitted, and all other Persons of the said Trade and Mistery of Tailers that shall request to be made a Brother of the said Company by his Apprenticeshipp for the Term of Seven years, To one of the Brethren of the same Society shalbe first and before made a free Burgess of the said Town or Borough of Kingston-upon-Hull, upon the penalty and forfeiture of ffive pounds of currant English money ffor every person admitted into their Company to the Contrary, to be paid by the said Company To th' use of the Mayor and Burgesses aforesaid, their successors and Assignes, at their Town's Auditt.

Woollen Drapers, Linen Drapers, Milliners, or any other Trade not already of a company, may join if burgesses.

14. Lastly It is statuted, ordained, declared, and agreed That no Brother of the said Company by himself, Journeyman, or Apprentice, shall carry home to the House or Houses of any person or persons that employ him upon the Lord's day any work or Garments by him

No one to carry home garments on the Lord's Day, on pain of 10s.

made, On pain of forfeiting Ten shillings, And that no Brother of the said ffraternity nor his Journeyman or Apprentices shall work upon the said Trade or Mistery after nine of the clock on Saturday Nights, in Pain to forfeit for every such offence the Sum of Ten shillings, Both the said sums to be levyed as aforesaid, and to be divided, One Moiety thereof to the said Mayor and Burgesses and their Successors, and the other Moiety to the use of the said Company.

Not to work after 9 p.m. on Saturdays.

In consideration of all which said Premises The said Company of Tailers and their successors shall yearly yeold and pay Unto the said Mayor and Burgesses, their successors or assignes, At their Anditt to be holden at the Guildhall of the said Town of Kingston upon Hull, the yearly sum of ffifteen shillings of current English money in the name of Composicon Rent: And moreover At th' aforespecifyed Auditt They the said Company of Tailers and their Successors shall make and yeeld a just and true Accompt Of all the ffines, fforfeitures, penalties, sum and sums of Money that shall respectively become due and payable to the said Mayor and Burgesses and their Successors ffor, upon, or by reason of this said Composicon, And then pay the said ffines, fforfeitures, penalties, sum and sums of money due as aforesaid, To th' use of the said Mayor and Burgesses, their Successors and assignes. And in case the said Warden, Searchers, and Stewards of the said Company for the time being shall at any time hereafter neglect or refuse to pay the ffines, fforfeitures, penalties, sum and sums of money becoming due as is aforelimited and expressed, And the said Yearly Composicon Rent At the time and place herein before limited, or any of them: Or That the said Warden, Searchers, and Stewards, Elder Brethren and Assistants and Company of Tailers aforesaid, or any of them in their several and respective Places and Offices, shall any ways demean themselves contrary to the true intent and meaning of this Composicon as by the Court of the Mayor and Aldermen of the said Town for the time being shalbe deemed and adjudged: Or that the said Warden, Searchers, and Stewards, Elder Brethren, or Assistants and Company of Tailers aforesaid, or any of them, shall admitt any Person or Persons to be a free Brother or Brethren of the said Company unless he be a free Burgess of the said Town, as is before expressed, Then this Ordinary or Composicon shall utterly cease and become void and of none effect To all intents and purposes whatsoever, And any of the said Officers shalbe likewise removable for any Offence done contrary to the

Annual Composition Rent to town to be 15s.

true meaning hereof, At the pleasure of the said Court of Mayor and Aldermen.

In Witness whereof the said Mayor and Burgesses to this present Composicon have caused the Common Seal of this Corporacon to be affixed, And the said Warden, Searchers, Stewards, Elder Brethren or Assistants of the said Company To the copy or Counterpart of the same Composicon have sett their hands and seals the second day of September in the two and thirtieth year of the Reign of our Soveraign Lord Charles the Second, by the grace of God King of England, Scotland, France, and Ireland, Defender of the Faith, and Annoq. Dni. 1680.

Tristram Berry.	John Toft.
Robert Graves.	John Howdell.
Francis Bartill.	And. Rainer.
William Legard.	Robt Hoole.
John Stockton.	Thomas Coates.
William Temperance.	Thomas Gray.

[The seals remaining are repetitions of one another, and of little interest. The impressions are poor, paper being placed over the wax.]

[*Endorsed*]

Sealed and delivered by the within-named [here follow all the names] in ye presence of

W. Blansherd.	Thomas Williamson.
Tho. Snawsdell.	Benjamin Graves.
Lance. Smith.	

Chapter XXIII.

The Company of Joiners.

TWO Compositions of this Company remain, the one dated 1598, and the other 1629. Their relation to each other is explained below.

From the preamble we learn that the names of those petitioning for the grant of ordinances are those of "ancient brethren," and the same is probably the case in other compositions, although not generally expressed. The due payment of wages within six days is carefully provided for, and "stubborn resistance" to the Warden and Searchers fined "according to the quantitie of the faulte." "Cubbord bedsteads" and tables were common articles of manufacture, and "Rayles, sealinge boards, wainscott clappboards, and bedd tymber" their raw materials. The monopoly exercised by the Company, as in other trades, was suspended during fair-time, shewing that the old fairs extended to the more substantial as well as the lighter articles of sale, and this explains in great measures the importance of these fairs and their natural decadence in the times when freedom of trade was established. All the "stuffe" and workmanship of manufactured articles was viewed and tried by the Searchers, and defaulters fined in due measure. Apprentices served seven years, and no master was allowed more than two, being born or remaining in the town, and hired men, whose number apparently was not limited, though 8d. each was paid to the Company's stock on their employment. No carpenters, housewrights, or other wrights, might do joiners' work, on pain of forfeiting for each transgression, 10s.

These were the men whose oak bedsteads, chairs, and cupboards remain still firm and solid, while generations of showy and veneered suites have had their brief day and fallen to pieces.

In 1623 we read that Robert Wright, joiner, was accused of that he when sent for by the Mayor for using evil words, said "he wold not come till he had done his worke," and "shut the dore of him," and so came not at all. He was discovered in an attempt at deceiving the Company by affirming that an apprentice named Hugh Hewett had served his full time when he had not, and the Company of Joiners appears to have informed against him. The sentence was that the apprentice should pay 10s. to the town, 10s. to the Company, and 8s. 7d. to the master. The sum demanded by the Company appears to have been £4 10s.

THE JOINERS' ORDINANCES, 1598.

The Joiners' Ordinances of 1629 are copied without variation, except in two particulars, from the ordinances of 1598. The spelling is the same in both. The differences are: 1st., in the introduction of 1598.

Great complaint of Joiners of strangers and unskilled workmen.

"Whereas great Complaint is made to us the said Maior and Burgesses by Thomas Crawthorne, Richard Sherington, Richard Haslam, William Anderson, and John Lowman, Joyners and Burgesses of the same towne of Kingston upon Hull, for and in the behalf of themselves and others, which are or shalbe theire of the same occupacion or mysterie, that Dyvers disorders and unlawful attemptes are used in the said towne to their great hinderance, by many that use and exercise their trade there which never have bene apprentices nor brought upp therein, and which are strangers and unskilfull: We therefore, the said Maior and Burgesses, etc."

The other difference lies in the seventh paragraph, which reads—

None to set up unless apprenticed for seven years.

Item that no person or persons hereafter, otheres then such of the saide trade as nowe use the same in Kingston upon Hull, if they shalbe thereunto allowed by the Maior and Aldermen of the same towne of Kingston upon Hull, Doe sett upp and use the occupacion of a

Except those unfree who have served seven years with unfree men on payment of £3 6s. 8d.

Mr. Joyner within this towne, except he have served seaven yeares, at the least, as apprentice at that trade with a free burgesse of Kingston upon hull, saveinge such unfree men or straingers as have served seaven yeares as apprentices with unfree men of the same towne and occupacion, who will and shall pay before they sett upp in the samo towne and occupacion of Joyners, three poundes sixe shillinges eight pence to the towne and occupacion.

Signatures to Joiners' Ordinances of 1598.

Thomas Crathorne.	Robert bankes.
Richardi Sherington	John Lowman.
Willmi Anderson.	Will'm hodgson.
Rychard haslam.	

Ordinances of 1629.

To all Christian people to whome this present wrytnge Indented shall come. The Maior and Burgesses of Kingston upon hull send greeting in our Lord god everlastinge.

Whereas the Companie or occupacion of Joyners within the said Towne, being Burgesses thereof, have heretofore for many yeare past had and enjoyed dyvers grauntes and orders made and confirmed unto them by the Maior and Burgesses of the said Towne for the tyme beinge, under there common seale, for the avoydinge of sondre disorders and unlawfull attempts which were used in the said Towne, to the great hurt and hinderance of them the said Joyners, Burgesses, by manie that used and exercised their traid within the said Towne which never had bene apprentice nor brought upp therein, and which were straingers and unskilfull. And Whereas dyvers of the Auncient Brethren of the said occupacion of Joyners, nowe dwelling within the said Towne, and Burgesses of the same, by names Richard Haslam, Edward Haslam, Henry Nayler, Edward Thewlis, John Norman, William Lawe, John Anderson, Robert Buller, and Edward Marshall, have peticioned us the said Maior and Burgesses in the behalf of themselves and others which are or shalbe of there said occupacion or traid within the said Town, to renewe and confirme unto them the auncient grauntes and orders which they have formerlie enjoyed with some alteracion, for better explaynyng thereof, and for assigninge a newe daye for eleccion of their warden and other officers, more fittinge and convenient then formerlie. Wee therefore, the said Maior and Burgesses, beinge noe lesse carefull then our predecessors of the welfaire and good estaite of the said companie and occupacion, and desiringe withall the good observance of all laudable orders within this Towne, Doe by force and virtue of such charteres, Letteres Patentes, and grauntes, as have bene to us made and graunted, make, publish orders, ordeyne, and establish theise orders, articles, and acts hereafter followinge. And doe for us and our successors covenaunte and graunt to and with the said Richard Haslam [here follow the names as before], That they and all others which nowe are or which hereafter shalbe free of the said misterie or occupacion of Joyner's within kingston-upon-hull aforesaid, shall or maye keepe, use, exercise, mayntayne, and execute these said orders, articles, and arte, hereafter ensewing. That is to saye—

1\. *To choose a new Warden and two Searchers on Thursday next before St. Andrew's Day.*

Inprimis that the men of the said occupation of Joyners maye yearelie from henceforth elect and chuse amongst themselves on Thursday next before St. Andrewe daye, a newe warden and two searchers of some of there occupacion, to be and to contynewe in their said office for a yeare after there eleccion, And if the said warden and searchers or any of them soe choses doe dye within the yeare, That then they of the said occupacion maye within tenn dayes after chuse another in the roome of him soe dying, to contynewe in his place untill the next eleccion daye after that, and that the warden and two searchers shalbe sworne before the Maior of Kingston upon Hull or his lieutenante, the Morrowe after such eleccion for the time beinge, trewly to present to the Maior all the forfeictures, offences, and defaultes made or comytted by any of the said occupacion or by any other person or persons. And the said Maior and Burgesses have nowe elected and nominated William Lawe and Robert Buller and Edward Marshall, searchers of the said occupacion, to contynewe from hence untill the next eleccion daye.

To be sworn on the morrow.

2\. *Any Joyner not coming to the election to forfeit xiid.*

Item that if any of the companie of Joyners beinge warned withdrawe himself or be absent from the said eleccion without lycence of the warden he shall forfeict for everie tyme that he is so absent xij*d*. to the occupacion, or if any beinge warned shalbe absent from the other common meetings without lycence as afore shall forfeict vj*d*. to the said occupacion.

3\. *No maister to withhold his servant's wages over six days.*

Item that noe maister of the said occupacion withhold his servant's wages dewe to him over the space of sixe dayes after the same be dewe, and if he doe withhold ytt any longer, upon complaint to the warden he shall cause him to have his wages paid. And if the said maister doe denie to pay ytt agayne within sixe dayes after that, That then he shall forfeict to the said Maior and Burgesses and the said occupacion xij*d*.

4\. *Anyone stubbornly resisting to be fined according to the quantity of the fault.*

Item if there be any of the said occupacion that will not be ordered by the warden and other officers of the same occupacion, but stubbornly resiste them, that then he or they for everie such offence, att the discrecion of the wardens and searchers and more parte of the Companie of the said occupacion, shalbe fyned according to the quantitie of the faulte.

5\. *vid. to be paid for*

Item that everie Joyner that taketh an apprentice shall att his firste entringe to worke of the said occupa-

each apprentice, and viiid. for each hired man. cion paye vj*d*., and everie hyred man att his firste entringe viij*d*. to the Companie of the same occupacion.

6. Item that noe person or persons hereafter shall sett

No one to sett upp unless seven years apprenticed. upp and use the occupacion of a Mr. Joyner within this towne except he have served seaven years att the leaste as apprentice at that traid with a free Burgesse of this Towne of Kingston upon hull.

7. Item that noe persons butt such as be free of the

None but members to sell any newe and unoccupyed cubbord bedstead, or table. same occupacion, or there servants, shall sell any newe and unocoupyed Cubbord, bedstead, or table, or any other Joyner wayres within this towne (except in the faire tyme) upon paine to forfeict for everie tyme soe doeinge

6s. 8d. or sellinge of any iij*s*. iiij*d*. to the towne and iij*s*. iiij*d*. to to the said occupacion of Joyners.

8. Item that noe person or persons shall buye anie Rayles,

Nor bring anie rayles, sealinge boards or bedd tymber to sell again. sealinge boards, or bedd tymber to sell againe in this towne (except he be free of the said occupacon of Joyners, or other wise be a free Burges of this towne), or doe sell them to some of the same occupacion, or occupie them for his owne use upon paine everie buyer to forfeict for everie tyme taken sellinge of any vi*s*. viij*d*., th'one half to the Maior and Burgesses, and th' other half to the said occupacion.

9. Item that the warden and searchers shall present to

Warden and Searchers to present all offenders. the Maior of Kingston upon hull for the tyme beinge all such persons as are not free of the said occupacion, and which shall worke in any man's howse in this towne, And for everie daye that any is taken soe workeinge he that setteth him on worke shall forfeict to the said Maior and Burgesses xij*d*., and the workeman to the said occupacion xij*d*., and soe ratable.

10. Item that ytt shalbe lawfull for the warden and sear-

Power to view and trye all wares and worke, except in faire time. chers of the said occupacion to view and trye all wares and worke made by any Joyner in this Towne or brought into this towne by straingers (except in the tyme of the faire), that itt be made of good and lawfull stuffe and workemanlike, and to have for such there view and triall of waire and worke brought in by straingers iiij*d*. att the pounde accordinge to the valewe, and after that rate. And every defaulte founde as well of townsmen as straungers, the person makeing or sellinge the same to be fyned att the discrecion of the warden and searchers and of the more parte of there Company.

11. Item that ytt shalbe lawfull for any of the said occu-

To buy wainscott clappboards. pacion of Joyners to buye wainskott, Clappboards, or any of other stuffe belonginge to there said occupacion, and such onely as they shall worke and noe other, and broughte in by Anie straingers to be sold in this towne of kingston upon hull.

12. None to keep above two apprentices, or any but those borne or remayning in the town.

Item that noe Joyner in this towne keepe above two apprentice att one tyme, And that he take noe apprentice but such as are borne or remayninge in this towne if any such be sufficient to serve his torne, and everie seconde apprentice which any of the said Joyners shall soe take, the same to be taken by the consent of the Maior and Aldermen of this towne, or more part of them for the tyme being, and to take and receive from the Towne for takeinge of such seconde apprentices, but twenty shillinges lawfull english money upon paine to loose his freedom.

13. Power to make ordinances.

Item that yt shalbe lawfull for the warden, searchers, and others of the said occupacion of Joiners, to make and sett downe any good orders hereafter for the governement of the men of the same occupacion, not hurtefull for the common wealth of this towne, and agreable to lawe and equitie.

14. No carpenter, howsewright, or other wright to make any Joyner worke.

Item that noe Carpenter, housewright, or other wright within this towne, shall make any Joyner worke whatsoever upon paine and forfeicture for everie time soe doinge, x*s*. to the Maior and Burgesses and the said occupacion.

15. Moiety of fines and upsetts to go to the Mayor.

Item that the Moytie of all fynes and forfeictures not otherwise herein lymitted, and likewise the moytie of all Upsettes, incomes, or other receites or profitts whatsoever accrewinge or growinge to the said Companie or occupacion by means or reason of this Composicion, shalbe th' one half to the Maior and Burgesses, payable att the next Audite yearelie, and th' other half to the occupacion.

16. And 5s. yearly.

Item the said occupacion of Joyners shall paye yearelie att everie Audite, to the Maior and Burgesses of Kingston upon hull for this there Composicion, v*s*.

17. Mayor to help and aid the Warden.

Item that wee the said Maior and Burgesses and our successors shall from tyme to tyme hereafter, when any offence shall happen to be comytted against these orders, upon notice gyven to the said Maior of kingston-upon-hull for the tyme beinge, be helpinge, aidinge, and assistinge to such of the said occupacion as shalbe warden, to punish and correct the same offendors by any lawfull meanes which may be used or inflicted upon them. And the officer for bringing in of everie such offender to have for such his paines everie tyme, iiij*d*. And itt is ordered and agreed that the Warden and Searchers for the tyme beinge, may distreyne the goods and chattells of any offender for any the penalties or forfeictures aforesaid.

In witness whereof th' one parte of this wrytinge Indented, remayning with the said Joyners, Wee the said Maior and Burgesses have putt to our Common

Seale, and to th' other parte of the same remayning with us, the said Maior and Burgesses, the Joyners abovenamed, have putt there hands and seales, the sixe and twenteth dayo of November, in the fifte yeare of the reigne of our Sovereigne Lord Charles, by the grace of god, kinge of England, Scotland, ffrance, and Ireland, defendor of the faith, etc. Annoq domini, 1629.

Richard Haslam.	William Lawe.
Edward haslam.	John Anderson.
Henry Nayler.	Robte Buller.
Edward Thewlis.	Edward Marshall.
John Norman.	

[*Endorsed*]

Sealed and Delivered in the presence of William ffoxley, Henry Winchester.

[Joyners' Composicion renewed in Anno, 1629.]

CHAPTER XXIV.

THE FRATERNITY OF CARPENTERS.

THE carpenter was originally one who made the "carpent" (Latin *Carpentum*), or heavy covered carriage or cart, of which the old type of carrier's cart, still to be seen lumbering in to the market from some far off wold village, is the best modern exponent. From this the transition was easy to the meaning of a craftsman who wrought in all kinds of woodwork. The name, however, was early used to denote especially the worker in the heavier kinds of woodwork, such as that required in the timbers of houses and roofs. To the joiner belonged the doors and the smaller kinds of work. Although to an outsider the distinction between the two trades does not seem very definite, possibly the very narrow line of division was itself the cause of the strictness with which it was maintained. Carpenters, joiners, and shipwrights were thus early differentiated, and the line of demarcation was jealously safeguarded. To the present day the jealousy of these several trades is such that the Trades' Union Congress in this year (1890) has thought it necessary to pass a special resolution with a view to its allayment.

In the following ordinances the technical details are few. We should like to know in more detail the rules under which men shaped the old timbered houses, and set on their solid roofs. As an illustration of the material of these workmen at an earlier date, we give below some extracts from an inventory and valuation of stores belonging to the works at London Bridge, delivered to the Wardens thereof by the outgoing Wardens in the 24 Edward III., 1350.

400 great pieces of oak timber, value 40d. the piece; also timber for 14 shops fully wrought and framed for immediate building, £36; also 120 pieces of elm for piles, at 2s. the piece; also divers boards of oak and of "estrichesborde" [deal boards from the Eastland countries on the Baltic], value £6 12s. 4d.; also 57000 "hertlathes," value 4s. per 1000; also 30000 "saplathes," value 2s. per 1000 [laths from the heart of the wood and laths with the sap in]; also 7 barrels of pitch, value 4s. per barrel; also 12000 of "planchenail" [plank nails], value 4s. per 1000; also 3000 of "dornail," value 2s. 6d. per 1000; also 400 large nails for the drawbridge, at 12d. per 100; also one maser with a silver foot, value 10s.; also 2600 of "wyndonnail," at 2s. 6d. per 1000; also 23000 of "rofnail," at 12d. per 1000; also 9000 of "traversnails" [tree nails], at 8d. per 1000. In the same inventory, but not valued, appear two engines with three "rammes" for ramming piles, two cauldrons for melting pitch for cement, one presser for fixing, five pots of brass, and four posnets, old and worn out (237).

Such stores will serve with fair accuracy to bring to the mind of the reader those of the men who drove the stout piles of the old beam in High Street, or those which supported the merchants' stores and houses along the shipping banks of the river Hull. As to the houses themselves, one Simon de Canterbury, of the year 1308, furnishes us with some useful facts. This worthy, being a carpenter, on November 11th, came before the Mayor and Aldermen of the city of London, and acknowledged that he would make at his own proper charges, down to the locks, for William de Haningetone, pelterer [skinner], before the feast of Easter then next ensuing, a hall and a room with a chimney [camino], and one larder between the said hall and room, and one sollar [sun parlour, an upper room] over the room and larder; also one oriole at the end of the hall, beyond the high bench, and one step with an oriole (238) from the ground to the door of the hall aforesaid, outside of that hall; and two enclosures as cellars, opposite to each other, beneath the hall; and one enclosure for a sewer, with two pipes leading to the said sewer; and one stable [left blank], in length, between the said hall and the old kitchen, and twelve feet in width, with a sollar above such stable, and a garret above the

(237) Riley, *Mem.*, p. 261.

(238) Riley suggests that this word in the previous line means a recess with a bay window, and here a porch.

sollar aforesaid; and at one end of such sollar there is to be a kitchen with a chimney; and there is to be an oriole between the said hall and the old chamber, eight feet in width. And if he shall not do so, then he admits, etc. And the said William de Haningtone acknowledged that he was bound to pay to Simon before-mentioned, for the work aforesaid, the sum of £9 5s. 4d. sterling, half-a-hundred of Eastern marten skins, fur for a woman's hood, value five shillings, and fur for a robe of him the said Simon, etc. (239).

A Composition of the Carpenters, 1598.

A Composicon indented dated the neinth day of ffebruary in the one and forty yeare of the reigne of our soveraigne Laly Elizabeth, By the grace of god Queene of england, fraunce, and Yreland, defender of the faith, Etc, Made between the Maior and Burgesses of Kingston upon Hull on th' one parte, And Mathew Parkin, William Whelpdale, Henry Thompson, Thomas Holland, Alexander Robinson, Xpofer Walker, Thomas Thompson, George Silverside, William Terrington, Henry Chapman, Roberte Iveson, Roberte Tailer, Thomas Richardson, William Matthew, Carpenters, on th' other party, witnessethe that the Saide Maior and Burgesses for theim and their successors (as moch as in theim is), upon the desire and sute of the said Carpenters, and to the intente that the same trade may the better flourish within the towne of Kingston upon Hull aforesaid, Have geven and graunted theis ordenannces, grauntes, and clauses hereafter following and ensewing:—

1\. Imprimis that the said company within the towne of Kingston upon Hull shall from henceforth have emongst theim one warden and twoe Searcheres to be choseen yearly by most voyces emongst theimselves upon the Wednesday seunitt after Michaelmas day, and that twoe shalbe of elleccion for warden, whereof th' one shalbe chosen, and fower of eleccion for Searcheres, whereof two shalbe chosen, which warden and searcheres shall yearly for ever the morrow after the said eleccion day be sworne upon the holy evangelist of god befor the saide Maior or his lieutenant for the true and just using of their places and offices for one hole yeare, or to like effect. And if any of the saide of the said [*sic*] officeres of warden and searcheres shall happen to depart this lif in soch offices being, then other or otheres shalbe elected and choseen by most voyces amongst theimselves within viij daies next after the death of him or theim so dyeng, and in their rowmes and places to serve forth the rest of

To have one Warden and two Searchers elected yearly.

To be sworn on the morrow.

(239) Riley, *Mem.*, p. 65.

that yeare, and shalbe sworne in manner and forme above recyted. And the saide Maior and Burgesses doe nomminat, elect, and appoint Henry Thompson for first warden, and Thomas Holland and Thomas Thompson for first Searchers for the saide company till the saide eleccion day.

2. Bond to be taken.

Item that the said company shall take bonde or bondes of said warden and Searcheres from time to time, or of any otheres, in the name of the saide Maior and Burgesses, for the performance of any accomptes, debtes, or other thing, and yet not withstanding the saide company to have the benifift thereof, and not the saide Maior and Burgesses.

3. None to be admitted unless a Burgess or compound with the Mayor.

Item they shall receive none into their company as free of the same unles he be first free Burges of Kingston upon Hull or that he first agree with Mr. Maior and the warden of the Company.

4. No joiner or shipwright to worke Carpenters' worke. Penalty 12*d*. the man and 21*d*. the master.

Item that no Joyner nor Shipwright shall at any time or times in privat or publicke worke any worke appertevning properly to the carpinter to worcke, unles his or their owne worck, upon paine of everie day doing contrary to loose any pay for the same, xij*d*., and he or they within this towne that sett soch aworck everie day likewise to forfaite xxj*d*.

5. None but members to be set on work.

Item further no inhabitant within this towne other then the saide company of carpinters and any or everie of him without the consent of Mr. Maior for the time being shall sett on worcke any carpinter not free of the said company in paine of everie day xij*d*., and everie soch carpinter to pay for everie soch fault for everie day xij*d*.

6. Power to make ordinances.

Item that the saide warden, searcheres, and company, or the greater nomber of theim for that time being shall make any ordenannces or orderes from time to time for good rule, order, and government to be had emongst theim selves, Provided the same tend not to the hurt of the common weale of this towne at the Judgment of the same Maior and Burgesses if the same come in question, And provided further they make no order for taking above xx [?] for the upsett of carpinters or housewright sonne free of the saide company, or for the upsett of an apprentice that haith served seaven yeares by indenture with any free of the same occupacion.

7. Power to distrain for fines.

Item that the saide warden and searcheres or their sufficient deputy or deputies in their sicknes or absence occupyeng their rowmes or any of theim may distraine the goodes or cattelles of any offenderes in the premisses, or any parcell thereof, for the fynes, forfaitures, and paiments abovesett or to be sette according to the true meaning hereof. And if any resistaunc be, then they shalbe ayded by the officer or officeres of the saide Maior, which distresses shalbe kept till satisfaccion be made for their offenc, And everie soche officer ayding theim shall have iiij*d.* for his paines therein taken instantly paid him.

8.

And the Warden will undertake to see that everie inhabitant of this towne shall have carpenters to do honest worcke upon twoe daies warning.

In consideracion of all which premisses the saide Company of Carpinteres, doe graunt that everie inhabitant of this towne upon twoe daies warning or request to be made or geven at the dwelling house of the warden of the said company of [or] his deputy for the time being, at soch time and times hereafter as the said artificeres can not easiely be gotten, shall have assigned unto theim good and sufficient workmen to doe any worcke they wolde have done more or lesse, Which shall doe the same without deloying thereof, and that the saide company shall duely and justly doe their worck according to the lawes and statutes of this realme. And that they will take no apprentice without consent of Mr. Maior for the time being, and the greater nomber of the Aldermen his Bretheren, but soch as are borne or remaining within this towne, and that by their consent likewise if their be any soche sufficient to serve their turnes, and further that the one half of all the fines and forfaitures above sett or to be sett and more, vs. yearly for this composicion shalbe yearly paid by the saide company at the townes auditt for the use of the saide Maior and Burgesses, without any collusion. In witness whereof on th' one parte of this composicion indented remaining in the custody of the saide carpinters, the saide Maior and Burgesses have sett their common seale, and unto th' other parte hereof remaining in the custody of the Maior and Burgesses, the carpinters above named have sette their handes and seales the day and yeare first above written, and in the yeare of our Lord according to the computacion of England one thousand five hundred ninety and eight.

And one-half of fines and 5s. yearly be paid to the Mayor.

Mathew Parkin.	Tho. Thompson.
Henrici Thompson.	Wm. Terrington.
Walker.	Robart Iveson.
Robt. Tailr.	Thome Richardson.
George Silverside.	Wm. Mathewe.
Tho. Holland.	

[Seals conventional and the same as found on other ordinances herebefore printed. The strips of parchment by which the seales are attached, are fragments of a contemporary lease by William Tailer to Thomas Wilkinson and Margaret his wife, of a house in "Scaile lane," for 21 years, reckoning from the "feaste daie of Penthicoste, commonly called Whitsondaie"].

[*Endorsed*]

Sealed, subscribed, and delivered in the presence of us, vizt.,— William Dowsone. Wm. Bower.

CHAPTER XXV.

THE COMPANY OF GOLDSMITHS, SMITHS, PEWTERERS, PLUMBERS, GLAZIERS, PAINTERS, CUTLERS, MUSICIANS, STATIONERS, BOOKBINDERS, AND BASKETMAKERS

THIS curious combination of trades shows the strength of the tendency to organisation at the close of the 16th century. Both for municipal purposes and for mutual protection union was necessary, and the mere fact of the weakness of their independent position, irrespective of the natural connection of their trades, seems to have drawn them together into one society. The Goldsmiths must at this time, however, have fallen somewhat from their ancient importance. Some fine examples of their skill remain among the plate of the Trinity House and Corporation of the town, and many more were lost in the holocaust which was one of the first acts of the Reformed Corporation in 1835.

The pewter of those days was a product very different from the multifarious alloys which now flood the market with cheap imitations of silver. In the 14th century, "the good folks making vessels of pewter" in the city of London, petitioned the Mayor and Aldermen for the better maintenance of their trade. It was then stated to be founded on the admixture of copper, tin, and lead in due proportions. What these proportions were may be gathered from the regulations made at the time. "All manner of vessels of pewter, and other things made square or ribbed, shall be made of fine pewter, with the proportion of copper to tin as much as by its own nature it will take; and all other things wrought by the trade, such as rounded pots, of tin alloyed with lead in the proportion of 1 cwt. of tin to 22 lbs. of lead." Two years afterwards, however, in 1350, 20 "saltsellars" and 23 "potels" of pewter were presented as being "the greater part lead . . . whereas to 1 cwt. of tin there ought to be added only 16 lbs. of lead (240)." The proportion of the present day is about 4 to 1, though it is to be feared that if the ancient Searchers were to make their rounds, they would discover many articles answering to their description of the "saltsellars" and "potels" above quoted (240).

It is curious to find that the Smiths had at this time no gild of their own, as they must have constituted an important handicraft of the town. The nuisances caused by their fires were often the subject of regulation in London and elsewhere, and the flames belched forth from their furnaces, and the heat, smoke, and noise, are depicted by enraged neighbours in terms which would befit a pandemonium. They were consequently specially forbidden to work during the night. The Cutlers are here apparently the representatives of three trades. In 1408, the good men of the trade of London say that every knife is prepared by three crafts, the blade by the bladsmythes, the handle and other fitting work by the cutlers, and the sheath by the sheathers. Every maker was obliged to put his mark upon his work, and even in that day we read that knives were introduced with forged marks. There is a curious prohibition against cutlers selling on Sunday, "Seeing that their journeymen and apprentices have wasted and purloined the property of their masters while they have been attending at their parish church or elsewhere (241)."

The Plumbers are recorded in 1365, and the connection of these with the Glaziers points to the time when glass was generally set in leaden framework, such as is now mostly confined to ecclesiastical work.

The Painters included those who painted armorial bearings,

(240) Riley, *Mem.*, p. 260.

(241) Riley, *Mem.*, p. 218, etc.

of which we have an example in the Merchants' Book (p. 178), while special provision is made for the Musicians, who kept dancing schools. Doubtless these poor gentry fared badly in the coming days, when the Puritans held sway in the town. The heterogeneous list closes with "Stationers, Bookbinders, and Basketmakers." The Searchers of this Company must have been handy men, and when the smith and pewterer, who were the first Searchers under this composition, went their rounds, the musicians, dancing masters, plumbers, painters, stationers, and basketmakers must have exercised creditable restraint in allowing their work to be judged by these worthy officials.

COMPOSITION OF GOLDSMITHS, &c., 1598.

A Composicon indented dated the last day of ffebruary in the one and forty yeare of the reigne of our soveraigne Lady Elizabeth, by the grace of god Queene of Englande, ffraunce, and Yreland, defender of the faithe, Maide betweene the Maior and Burgesses of Kingston upon Hull on th' one party, and George Harwodd, James Watson, James Carlill, Martin Moone, Edmond Bussell, goldsmithes, Henry Hubbert, Thomas Smith, th elder, John Billop, Peter Thorneton, Thomas Tailer, Roberte Morris, James Graunt, John Gibson, Thomas Wilkinson, Richard Wright, and Thomas Smithe younger, smithes, Thomas Scupholme and George Marshall, pewtherers, John Clarcke, Thomas ffuller, John Barron and Arthure Hawardd, plummers and glasiers, John Gibson, Samuell Aplyne, Bartholomewe Aplyne, and George Todd, painters, Roberte Gretom, Edward Gorrell, Roberte Hollis, and Dennis Haworth, cutlers, Henry Smithe, William Burne, and Xpofer Thornetone, musicions, Thomas Barughe and Thomas Widdowes, stationers and bookbinders, and Xpofer Hubbert and Thomas Alburne, baskitmakers, of Kingston upon Hull aforesaid, on th' other party, Witnessethe that the saide Maior and Burgesses for theim and their successors (as moche as in theim is), upon the desire and suite of th said goldsmithes, smythes, powthers, plummers, glasiers, painters, cutlers, musicions, stationers, bookebinders, and baskitmakers, and to the intente that the said artes, occupacions and mistories may better flourish within the towne of Kingston upon Hull aforesaide, Have geven and Graunted and doe hereby give and graunte theis ordenaunces, grauntes, and clauses hereafter ensuing and following:—

1. First, that all and everie the severall persons within the towne of Kingston upon Hull aforesaide, of the saide severall artes, occupacions, and mistries, being free Burgesses of the saide towne of Kingston upon Hull, shall from henceforthe be but one intire company, and not severall companies, and shalbe called the company

All of these trades henceforth to be one Society.

of goldsmithes and smithes and others their brethren, which company shall from henceforth have emongest theim one warden and two searcheres, to be chosen yearly by most voyces emongst theimselves upon the monday next after St. Luke's day, And that twoe shalbe of eleccion for wardon, whereof th' one shalbe chosen, and fower of eleccion for searchers, whereof twoe shalbe chosen. And the saide Maior and Burgesses doe elect, appoint, and nominat James Watson for first warden, and Thomas Smith th' elder and Thomas Scupholme for first searcheres till the saide eleccion day. And that the warden and searcheres hereafter to be elected shall yearly the morrow after the saide eleccion day be sworne upon the holy evangelist of god before the Maior or his lieutenaunt for the time being, for the true, just, and upreight using, exercising of their places, rowmes, and offices for one whole yeare to soche effect, and if either warden or searcheres shall happen within their yeare to chaunge this life, or to refuse their place, being elected, then otheres shalbe elected and chosen by most voyces emongst the saide company in the stede and place of soche warden and searchers within eight daies following to serve forth the rest of the year, and to be likewise sworne. And if any warden nowe appointed or hereafter to be elected shall refuse to execute the saide place, he shall forfaite for soche refusall xx*s*. And if any searcher now appointed or hereafter to be elected shall refuse to execute saide place, he shall forfaite for soche refusall x*s*.

One Warden and two Searchers chosen yearly.

To be sworn the day after election.

2\. Bond to be taken.

And also that the saide company of goldsmithes and smithes and other their brethren shall take bonde or bondes of the saide warden and searcheres and of any otheres from time to time for ever in the name of the Maior and Burgesses of Kingston upon Hull aforesaide, for the performance of any accompt, debt, dammage, demand, or other thing or matter whatsoever, which bonde or bondes shall notwithstanding be to the onely behoof and benefitt of the saide company and not to the behof or benefitt of the saide Maior and Burgesses.

3\. Only Burgesses and Members to carry on these trades, except on Market Days and in Fair time.

Moreover the said company of goldsmithes and smithes and others their brethren, shall not receive any person or persones whatsover into their said company unles he be first a free Burges of the towne of Kingston upon Hull aforesaide. And that no goldsmithe, smithe of any sorte, pewtherer, plummer, glazier, painter, cutler, picture drawer, or armes painter not sufficiently authorised, stationer, bookebinder, nor basketmaker not free Burges of this town of Kingston upon Hull and free of their company, shall kepe any shopp or work within this towne or liberties upon paine of everie weke, x*s*., and so after that raite for more or lesse time, neither shall sell or offer to be solde any goodes or waires within this towne or liberties belonging properly to the said artes occupacions or mistries, but upon the tuisdaies and fridaies markitt daies in open markitt, and also in the faire time in paine of seizing and forfaiting the same goodes and waires in whose handes soevr the same shalbe founde, nor that no inhabitant within this towne other then of the saide company, shall buy or exchange any goodes or waires, newe or olde, within this towne belonging properly to the said artes, occupacions, or mistries to th' end to sell the same againe in paine of seizing and forfaiting the saide goodes and waires wheresoever the same shalbe founde (faire and markitt daies in markett time excepted). Neither that any musicion not free burgess of this same town and free of the saide company of goldsmithes and smithes and otheres their bretheren, shall within this towne kepe any daunsing schoole, neither that any musicion not free of the said company and not dwelling within this towne, shall here play at all without the consent of the Maior for the time being, and of the warden of the said goldsmithes and smithes and otheres their bretheren, unlese they be lycensed by the lawes and statutes of this realme.

No musicion not a Burgess and Member to keep a Dancing School.

4. And that no inhabitant of this towne shall within this towne sett on worke any goldsmithe, smithe, powtherer, plummer, glasier, painter, picture drawer, or armes painter not sufficiently authorised, cutler, stationer, bookebinder, or baskitmaker not free of the said company upon paine of everie defaulte, xs. Neither that any inhabitant of this towne shall within this towne demise or let any place or rowme to any musicion or otheres wherein any daunsing school shalbe kept, neither shall learne to daunse or play within this town with any musicion not free of the said company upon paine of everie default by the space of one weke, vs.

5. Furthermore the saide warden and searcheres for the time being, with the greater nomber more of the saide company of goldsmithes and smithes and otheres their bretheren, shall from time to time make any lawes, ordenaunces, and orderes for good rule, order, and government to be had, kept and preserved emongst themselves, which lawes, ordenaunces, and orderes, shall bind the saide warden, searcheres, and the whole company of goldsmithes and smithes and otheres their bretheren, And to set down paines, penalties, and forfaitures for breach of soch lawes, orderes, and ordenaunces, Provided alwaies the same lawes, orderes, and ordenaunces tend not to the hurt and harm of the common weale of this

May make Ordinances.

towne at the Judgment of the Maior for the time being, and the greater nomber of his bretheren the aldermen if the same come in question.

6. Power to distreyne.

And moreover that the said warden and searcheres or any of theim their or any of their deputy or deputies in sicknes or absenc may distreine the goodes or cattels of any offender or offenderes in the premisses or any parcell thereof for the fynes, forfaitures, and paines above sett or to be sett according to the true meaning hereof. And if any persone or persones whatsoever shall resist theim or any of theim, then the said warden and searcheres or any and everie of theim, their or any and everie of their deputy or deputies shalbe ayded by the officer or officeres of the saide Maior, And all distresses by theim taken shalbe kept till satisfaccion be made for the offenc with the chardges about taking of soche distresses, and the keping of the same and everie soche officer ayding theim shall have for his pains, iiij*d*.

Agree to take no apprentice without permission of the Mayor.

In consideracion of all which premisses the saide goldsmithes, smithes, pewtherers, plummers, glasiers, painters, cutlers, musicions, stationers, bookebinders, and baskitmakers doe graunt that they will take no apprentice without the consent of Mr. Maior for the time being and the greater nomber of the aldermen his Bretheren, but soche as ar borne or remaining within this towne, and that by their consent likewise if there be any soche sufficient to serve their turnes. And further that the one half of all the fynes and forfaitures above sett or to be sett which shall be levied and received, or the one half of so moche of the same as shalbe taken, and further *xs*. yearly for this composition shall yearly be paied to the towne's use at the towne's auditt withoute drifte or deley. In witnes whereof unto th' one parte of this composicion indented remaining in the custody of the saide goldsmithes, smithes, pewtherers, plummers, glasiers, painters, cutlers, musicions, stationers, bookbinders, and basketmakers, the saide Maior and Burgesses have affixed their Common Seale, and unto th' other parte hereof remaining in the custody of the saide Maior and Burgesses the said goldsmithes [etc.] have sett their handes and seales the day and yeare first above written, And in the yeare of our Lord according to the Computacion of England one thousand five hundred nenety and eight.

Half of fines to the town.

And 10s. yearly for the Composition.

George Harwadd.	Thomas Scupholm.
James Watson.	John baron.
J. Carliell.	Arthur Heyward.
Martin Moone.	Jhon gybsonne.
Edmond Russell.	Samuell Applin.

Henry Hubbert.	George Todd.
Thomas Smyth.	Robt. Greton.
John byllop.	Dionisii Haworth.
Robert Morris.	Willi Burne.
Jacobi graunt.	Ro. hollis.
Jo. Gibson.	thomas barcig.
Tho. Willeynson.	Henry Smyth.
Rici. Wright.	Chrystefer Thornton.
Thomas Taylor.	Xpofer hubbert.
George Marshall.	Thomas Alburne.

[*Endorsed*]

Lect, sigillat, et deliberat in pur, John Logan, F. Walter Cave, Peter Smeatonn, William Dewseye, Wm. Bower.

[Goldsmithes, etc., Composicon, 1598.]

Chapter XXVI.

The Fraternity of Bricklayers, Tilers, Wallers, Plasterers, and Pavers.

HULL contains some of the earliest mediæval brickwork in the kingdom. The absence of workable stone in the immediate neighbourhood, and the abundance of good clay, facilitated the manufacture, and the choir of Holy Trinity Church has long been famous for its fine work of this character. We are not surprised, therefore, to find the trade well organised, and supplying us with interesting records.

Nevertheless it is probable that the Plasterers were the more ancient of the two, and the Tilers with the old earthenware tiles must have been nearly contemporary. We have the agreement still extant which Adam the Plasterer made to plaster the great hall of the Earl of Richmond in London with plaster of paris and the tewel (chimney) in eight weeks for £24 ([242]). In 1329 Hugh de Hecham, a "lymbrennere," for extortion in asking 1½d. a sack for lime instead of a 1d., was ordered to lose his freedom and to go to prison ([243]). In 1356 we find that the Mayor has been given to understand "that divers dissensions and disputes have been moved in the said city between the masons who are hewers on the one hand, and the light masons and setters on the other, because their trade has not been regulated in due manner by the government of folks in their trade in such form as other trades are;" "so the Mayor caused all good folks of the said trade to be summoned before him, to have from them good and due information how their trade might be best ordered and ruled for

(242) Riley, page 125.
243) Ibid, page 176.

the profit of the common people; whereupon the good folks of the said trade chose from among themselves twelve of the most skilful men of their trade (six masons hewers and six light masons and setters), the which folks were sworn," etc ([244]).

The fraternity does not seem then, however, to have had any permanent status, for it was added that "the good folks of the said trade shall be chosen and sworn every time that need shall be, to oversee the trade," etc. In 1362 the Tilers are bidden not to ask greater wages by reason of the great tempest ([245]). About the same time, 1359, for repairing a house in Cornhill, a tiler was paid for two days 14d., his man 10d., and for their drink 2d.; while carpenters worked for 7d. a day.

In the case of Hull we are fortunate in possessing the Composition in the Town Hall, and the Book of Ordinances owned by the Gild itself for the same year, and are thus enabled to compare exactly the two bodies of rules. The only other case in which this occurs is that of the Coopers' Gild, and in the latter the Composition and the Book are not of the same year, and might therefore be supposed in the case of divergences to have varied in the interval. We can thus see plainly the relation between the two bodies of rules. They are mutually supplementary, and show that in the Composition, which is all that remains in the case of most trades, we have only a very partial and to some extent perfunctory revelation of the real fraternity. The orders as to behaviour, religious observances, burial customs, feasts, apprentices, drinking and gambling, trade customs and honest work, are found only in the Gild's own Book. The public side of the trade, the relation to the Town Chamber, are shewn in the Composition, while a few of the more important duties are common to both.

Among the curious allusions is that to the town's Kiln. This was situate near the old mouth of the River Hull, long known as Lime Kiln Creek, and provided ready means for burning the chalk from the neighbouring quarries of Hessle. The care taken

(244) Ibid, page 283.
(245) Ibid, page 308.

to provide for honest work, good bricks, and honest lime shews the beneficial work of the Gild. The following tragical document, which is in the Town Hall, shews another side, which the reader may not take so seriously as the authors evidently did.

Kingston upon Hull.

To the right worshipfull John Ramsden, maior, and the aldermen his bretheren, all happines with increase of worshipp in this life and in the life to come, the joyes eternall.

The humble petition of the wardon and brotherhoode of Breecklaiers of the saide towne.

Complainyng Sheweth unto yor woppe that whereas one James Hudson, an Englishman, and by occupacon a breeklaier, dwelling at Amsterdam, in Hollande, is of laite arrived at this porte, and here dothe remaine and worke, delndinge diverse of the inhabitants of the same, p'swading them that their chimneys be very insufficientlie made for avoiding of smooke, and that he can with a small cost amende them, although he doth not so, but raither makes them worse, to the cost of the owners, and the great hurte and discreditt of yor worpps petitioners, as wilbe justlie p'evd unto yor worpps, and the hinderance and impoverishing of them their wives' children and s'vants, whoe have no other meanes to live and maintaine themselves, but by their occupacon, And for that yor worpps have graunted us a composicon under the towne's seale, and confirmed or book of orders under yor sev'all handes for the avoiding (among other things) of straungers and interlopers, and for the better living and maintenance of us or wives and families, and having no other meanes for redresse of theis and suche like wrongs, but from yor worpps (as helpers and defenders of us and others in such like caises). Therefore we are bolde to laie open or greifes and become most humble suters unto yor worpps, Desiring yor worpps for godes cause (the p'misses duelie considered) to avoide the saide James Hudson and such others, and com'aunde him to forbeare working in such sorts as he doth, and not to scandalize and wrong yor poor pet'ioners, but that we have and enjoye all oure p'viledge according to our saide composicon and true meaning of our orders as heretofore we have hadd, and as we hope is yor worpps true intent and meaning. And we according to bounden duetie shall dailie praie unto god for the good and p'sperous estaite of yr worpps ev' to endure.

Yor worshipps peticoners, the warden and companie of Breeklaiers within Kingston upon Hull.

To the reighte worshipfull John Ramsden, maior, and his worshipfull bretheren the aldermen.

The names of suche neighbours as have hadd their chimneys to have ben mended by one James Hudson, breeklaier, a stranger, for the avoiding of smooke, but they prove raither worse then better, to the discreditt of th' occupacion of breeklaiers in this towne, and their greate hinderance in wourke, as followethe, vizt.:—

Inprimis Mr. Goodman haithe a chimney which the said Hudson did take in hande to amende, and haithe not onelie made it worse but putt the gentleman unto greater chardge as he affirmeth, althoughe he is loathe to complaine on him because he is a poore man.

Robart Ashedon, blacksmithe, affirmeth the like.

Katherine Grimbald, wedowe, saith the like.

William Mathew, draper, affirmeth the like.

Mrs. Chapman, wedowe, saith the like.

Besides diverse others whose names we omitt for being too troublesome unto your worshipps, for which wronges we desier redresse at your worshipp's handes.

Robart Harison.

Elziabeth Baker, at Tripot.

Your worshipps at comaunde, the warden
and companie of breeklaiers.

Among the curious customs bearing upon this trade was one at Reading. In 1443, for shaving anyone after 10 p.m. from Easter to Michaelmas, or 9 p.m. from Michaelmas to Easter, the fine for a barber was 300 tiles. One, John Bristo, was actually fined 2100 tiles for shaving seven customers, but the number was remitted to 1200 on the score of poverty. The object was to encourage tiling the roofs, and so to obviate the danger from fire arising from thatch (240).

We will now give the Composition of the Hull Bricklayers' Gild.

BRICKLAYERS' COMPOSITION, 1598.

A composicon indented, dated the fowerteenth day of ffebruary, in the one and forty yeare of the reigne of or soveraigne Lady Elizabeth, By the grace of god, Queene of England, fraunce, and Yreland, defender of the faith. Betwen the Maior and Burgesses of Kingston upon Hull on th' one parte, And Richard Hitchcocke, Moyses Stones, John Dove, Xpofer Maxwell, John Buttle, John Waddy, John Webster, Thomas Bilton, James Wright, Richard Kitching, John Young, and Gyles Kircke, of Kingston upon Hull aforesaide, bricklaiers, tylers, wallers, plaisterers, and pavers, on th' other part. Witnessethe that the saide Maior and Burgesses for theim and their successores (as moch as in them is) upon the desire and sute of the saide artificers, and to the intent that the saide severall artes or trades may the better flourishe within the towne of Kingston

(240) See *Reliquary*, July, 1890. *The Guilds of Reading*, by Rev. P. H. Ditchfield, M.A., F.R.H.S

upon Hull aforesaid, Have geven and graunted theis ordeuntes, grauntes, and clauses hereafter following and ensewing.

1. One Warden and two Searchers, the Monday Sennet after St. James' Day.

Ffirst that the saide artificers within the towne of Kingston upon Hull shall from henceforth have emongst theim one warden and twoe searchers, to be chosen yearely by most voyces emongst themselves upon monday sennet after St. James' day the Apostle, And that twoe shalbe of eleccion for warden, whereof th' one shalbe chosen, and fowar of eleccion for searchers, whereof two shalbe chosen, which warden and searcheres shall yearly the morrow after the saide eleccion be sworne upon the holy evangelist of god before the saide Maior or his lieuteunte for the true and just using of their places and offices for one whole yeare, or to like effect. And if any of the saide officeres dye, then other shalbe chosen within xii daies in the rowme or place of him so dyeng, to serve forth the rest of the yeare, and to be sworne as aforesaide. And the saide Maior and Burgesses doe appoint and nominate Richard Hitchcocke for first Warden, and Xpofer Maxwell and Moyses Stones for first searcheres till the saide eleccion day.

To be sworn the morrow before the Mayor.

2. Bond to be taken of Warden and Searchers.

Item that the saide company of Breicklaiers, Tilers, Wallers, plaistereres, and paveres shall take bond or bondes of the saide warden and searcheres or of any others from time to time in the name of the saide Maior and Burgesses for the performance of any accompt, debte, or other thinge. And yet no profitt thereby shall come to the towne, but onely to the saide company.

3. None to be admitted but Burgesses, and none to work unless free of the Company.

Item that they shall receive none into their society as free of their company unles he be first free burgess of Kingston upon Hull, and that no inhabitant within this towne shall sett on worke any soch articifer not free of their company upon paine of everie day xij*d.*, and soche artificer himself for everie day to lose xij.

4. All bricks or tiles made in town or country to be viewed by the Searchers; if bad, to be forfeited, and if good, 3d. per 1000 to be paid.

Item that if any breickmaker make any breicke or tyle within this towne or countye to sell here in Hull, the same shalbe vewed by the saide Searcheres, and if the same be not good and sufficient it shalbe seized and forfaited by theim, and if it be good they shall pay to the saide searcheres for use of the saide company for everie thousand viewing iij*d.*, and soe after that raite for more or lesse nomber.

5. All brought into the town 2d. per 1000 if bad.

Item that if any persone or persones bring any lattes, breick or tyle To this towne to be solde, the same shalbe vewed by the saide searcheres, and if the same be not good and sufficient it shalbe likewise seized by the said searcheres, and if it be not good yet ij*d.* for vieweng everie thousand shall likewise be paied for the same, and so after that raite for more or lesse.

6. Only to be sold to brethren.

Item that the same agane within the towne, but onely to the free men of the occupacion, in paine to forfaite for the vallew of everie shilling so bought *id.* in the shillinge.

7. Only brethren to burn lyme, unless in Town's Kilne.

Item that no persone or persones shall burne any lyme for the use of the towne or any inhabitant therein unles he be free of the said company, or have the townes Kilne (*a*), upon paine of everie default ij*l.* [£2], unlesse that the saide company doe not sufficientlie serve the towne and Burgesses with the same, then yt shalbe lawfull for any.

8. No lime to be bought but of brethren.

Item that no inhabitant buy any lyme within this towne on any persone not free of the saide company, in paine of everie default xij*d.* of a chalder (*b*), and so after the raite, provided alwaies they have enough to serve the towne and burgesses at the pryse sett downe by Mr. Maior and his bretheren.

9. May make Ordinances.

Item that the said company of Breicklaieres, tyleres, walleres, plaistereres, paveres, or the most parte of theim, shall from time to time make any orderes for good government and rule to be kept emongst theimselves or otherwise concerning their traid, So as the same tend nott to the hurt of the comon weale of this towne [at the judgment of Mr. Maior, the greater nomber of his brethren, if the same come in question—(*interlined*)] nor against the lawes of this land, and so sett downe paines and forfaitures for breache of soche orderes.

10. May distrain for fines.

Item that the saide Warden and Searcheres, or their sufficient deputy or deputies in their sicknes or absenc, or any of theim, may distreine the goodes or cattells of any offenderes in the premisses or any parcell thereof for the fynes, forfaitures, and paimentes above sett, or to be sett, according to the true meaning and intent of theis presentes. And if any resist theim, or any of theim, then they shalbe ayded by the officer or officeres of the saide Maior, which distresses shalbe kept till satisfaccion be had for the offence, and chardge paied about the distresses taking and kepinge, and everie soche officer aydihg theim shall have for his paines, iiij*d*.

The Mayor to assist them.

In consideration of which premisses, Warden will provide workmen upon two days' warning.

In consideration of all which premisses, The said Breicklaieres, Tileres, Walleres, Plaistereres, and Paveres, doe graunt that everie inhabitant of this towne upon ij daies warning or request, to be had or given at the dwelling house of the warden or his deputy for the time

(*a*) The Town's Lime Kiln gave the name to Lime Kiln Creek, the ancient mouth of the river Hull. The Kiln was a wise provision of the Corporation, in early days, to supply the town with a reliable means of burning the convenient products of the neighbouring Hessle quarries. It was let out as a yearly farm, and the rates at which the inhabitants were to be served were fixed by the Corporation.

(*b*) "Chalder" for chaldron is yet current in the district.

being, at soche time and times hereafter, as the saide workmen can not easilie be gotten, shall have assigned unto theim sufficient workmen to do any worke according to the lawes and statutes of this land, and shall and will teache or procure to be taught their servauntes and apprentices, aswell to pave as other partes of their traide, which shalbe likewise covenaunted by theim in the indentures of apprentishipp. And that they consent likewise if their be any soche sufficient to serve their turnes, And further that the one half of all the fines and forfaitures above sett or to be sott, and more, vs. yearly for this composicion shall yearly be paied to the towne's use at the towne's auditt, without drift or deley. In witnes whereof unto th' one parte of this composicion indented, remaining in the custody of the said artificeres, the saide Maior and Burgesses have setto their common Seale, and unto th' other parte hereof remaining in the custody of the saide Maior and Burgesses, the said artificeres have sett their handes and seales the day and yeare first above written, and in the yeare of o^r Lorde according to the computacion of England, one thousand five hundred neinty and eight.

Half the fines and 5s. yearly to go to the town's use.

Rici (His Mark).	Tho. Bilton.
Xpofer Maxwell.	Ric Kitching.
Moyses Stones.	Jo. Dove.
Jo. Webster.	Gylles Kyrcke.
Jo. Buttle.	Jacobi Wright.
Jo. Waddy.	Jo. Young.

[There are more seals than names, and they are evidently lawyers' stock seals. The devices are: a fleur de lys, a sun, a boar's head, stag's head, dove, Tudor rose, and dragon-bird].

[*Endorsed*]

Sealed, subscribed, and delivered, in the presence of us, viz., William Dowson, Walter Cave, William Bower.

Bricklayers.	Plaisterers.
Tylers.	Pavers.
Wallers.	

[Bricklayers' Composicon, 1598].

The Book of Ordinances, finely engrossed on vellum (now in the possession of the Hull Subscription Library), begins as follows:—(247)

S. John, 1, 2, 3, 4, 5.

In the beginning was the worde, and the worde was with God, and God was that worde. The same was in

(247) The marginal abstracts in this case are from the original.

Christ is God before all tyme. the beginnyng with God. All things were made by it, and without it was made nothing that was made. In it was life, and the life was the lighte of menne. And the lighte shineth in the darkness, and the darkness comprehended it not.

Plato. All men are by nature equall, made all by one worckman of lyke myre; and howsoever we deceave ourselves, as dere unto God is the poorest begger as the most pompous prince living in the worlde.

Plato. Of all the giftes of God wisdom is the most excellent. She geveth goodnes to the good, and forgiveth the wicked their wickednese. She ordreth the mind, shee directeth the life, and ruleth the worckes thereof, teaching what oughte to be done and what to be lefte undone

"Concordia magna res crescunt, discordia maxima dilabuntur."

Then follow the Ordinances as held by the fraternity. It will be noticed that some are stated in the margin to be not allowed, but at what date does not appear.

The Book of Orders made for the utilitie and good government of the occupation of breeklaiers, tilers, wallers, plaisterers, and pavers, within the towne of Kingston upon Hull. Being incorporated into brotherhoode by composition in writing, from the right worshipfull the maior, aldermen, and burgesses of the saide town, under their anciente seale of the same towne [maister John Graves, then mayor], established and confirmed under their handes with the whole consent and liking of the said brotherhood, the twentie daie of June, in the yeare of our Lorde God, one thousand five hundred neinetie and neine, and in the one and fortie yeare of the reigne of our moste gracious Soveraigne ladie Elizabeth, by the grace of God, Queene of England, Fraunce, and Ireland, defender of the faithe.

All which orders are in manner and forme as hereafter perticulerlie ensewth.

Election of Wardon and Searchers. Im primis yt ys decreed that the saide brotherhood shall have one wardon and twoo searchers, to be chosen yearlie, for ever upon mondaie Sennitt after Sainte James daie the apostle, by most voices emongst themselves, in paine of forfaiture of their compositions.

And that the wardon and searchers shalbe sworne the morrowe after their election daie, before the maior or his lieutennant for the time being, without further drifte.

1\. Reverence towards the worshipfull of this towne. Item yt ys ordered that all the saide brotherhood and their successors, shall reverence and dutifullie use and behave themselves unto all the worshippfull of this towne, as to good maners and Christianitie dothe apperteine, in paine of every defaulte, 12d.

2. Secretes of the town not to be disclosed.

Item that yf any of this brotherhood shall disclose the secrets of this towne (being proved), he shall forfate everie tyme, xii*d*.

3. Reverence towardes the Wardon.

Item that everie one of this brotherhood shall reverence and obey the wardon at all times and in all places, in dutifull manner, in paine of every defaulte, to paie ii*s*. vi*d*.

4. The Wardon and Searchers not to be missused in wordes or deeds.

Item anie of this brotherhood doe at anie tyme, in private or peulic, missue the wardon or searchers, with anie manner of unsemlie wordes or deedes (if proved), he shall paie for every suche offence, ii*s*.

5. One brother shall not in anie wise misuse another in wordes.

Item that if anie brother of this companie shall misuse one another in the presence of the wardon, or at anie other tyme, with anie unsemelie worde, he shall paie for such abuse, xii*d*.

6. Not to departe withoute any licence.

Item that yf anie of this brotherhoode doe departe from anie meetinge without licence of the wardon, he shall paie for his contempte, for everie tyme so doinge, vi*d*.

7. Silence and keypnge of places.

Item that yf anie shall be misordered, and will not kepe his place and silence, at the wardon's comaundment, shall paie for everie such contempt after warninge, vi*d*.

8. Absence from meetinges and at the howre appointed.

Item If anie of this brotherhoode, which shall be warned to anie meetinge by the wardon or his deputie, doe absent himselfe, and not come at the howre and appointed place, withoute leave of the wardon, or doe show insufficiant cause to the contrarie, shall paie xii*d*.

9. Not to be absent upon the election daie, nor from the election dinner.

Item That yf anie of this brotherhoode be absent upon the election daie, from the election, or from the election dynner, without licence of the wardon, shall paie vi*s*. viii*d*.

10. Not to lawe out with another for small debts owyng, and other small controversies. Not allowed.

Item If anie brother of this occupacion shall owe anie debte one to another (not being above five shillings), they shall not go to lawe for the same, but first shall make complaint thereof unto the wardon, and then the warden shall take to himself twoe indifferent bretheren of the companie, and they three or twoe of them shall order the matter betwixt them. And so in all other small controversies. And the parties or partie that shall refuse, and not stande unto such order so to be made, shall paie to this of the stocke, xii*d*.

11. The Wardon not to forbeare anie man offendinge.

Item yf the wardon shall forbeare anie person or persons which shall offende or breake anie the orders of this booke, made or to be made, and doe not his best endevor to take their fynes herein expressed, shall paie the same himselfe.

12. Servantes for to learne good manners.

Item That every brother of this saide brotherhood shall bringe up reverentlie their servanntes in the feare of God, and teach them good manner, so far forth as in

and to resorte unto divine service and sermons.

them lioth. And that every maister shall bring his servant to the Church upon Sondaies and holie daies, to heare devine service and sermon, if they be able to come, and not forth of towne, or can shewe sufficient cause of their absence to the wardon, in paine of everytyme making defaulte, to forfait and pay vid.

13. Servantes not to take chardge before he hath been allowed by the Wardon so to do.

Not allowed.

Item That no brother of this companie shall sett his servant to worcke, and take chardge in his companie, nor oute of his companie, excepte he shalbe allowed by the wardon, and beinge allowed, the maister shall paie for such his allowance to the use of the companie, xii*d*.

14. Secretts of the brotherhoode not to be opened or disclosed.

Item yf anie of this hrotherhoode shall disclose or make knowen anie of the secretts of this societie, he shall forfaite and paie for every such offence, iii*s*. iv*d*..

15. No apprentice to be taken for less time than seaven yeares.

Item That none of this brotherhood shall take anie apprentice for lesse tyme than seaven yeares, and that by indenture, in paine of everie one herein offendinge, to forfaite and paie for everytyme, x*s*.

16. Not above two apprentices at once.

Item that noue of this hrotherhoode shall have above twoe apprentices at once, and that th firste apprentice shall have served fower yeares of his tearme before the seconde be taken to serve as an apprentice, in paine of everie one doeinge to the contrarie, to paie for everie tyme so doing, iii*s*.

17. Apprentices to paie their brotherhoode.

Item that everie apprentice which shal be borne in the towne, and serve forth his apprenticeshipp here with a free brother of this companie, the maistor for his parte shall paie towardes the brotherhoode or freedom of his saide apprentice, twoo shillinges and sexpence, and everye such apprentice shall for his parte paie three shillinges. And for every apprentice not borne in this towne, the maister shall paie twoo shillinges and sexpence, and every such apprentice so servyinge as aforesaide, shall pay for his admittance or upsett, five shillinges unto the wardon for the use of the saide companie, and to the clarcke of the saide companie, iiii*d*.

18. Laborers working not being townsmen.

Not allowed.

Item That yf anie of this hrotherhoode shall hier or retayne anie laborer to worcke by daie or otherwaise, not beinge a towneesman, he shall paie for every daie so workinge to the occupacion, vi*d*.

19. None to resorte to the alehouse nor cardes in time of their worcke.

Item yf anie of this hrotherhoode, being at worcke with any man, doe in the tyme of his worcke, resorte unto the ailehouse, or doe plaie at diyce, cardes, or anie other unthriftie game (and duelie proved), he shall forfaite and paie for everie time so doinge, viii*d*.

20. [Erased entirely and left blank].

21. None to do any

Item That none of this brotherhoode shall doe anie worcke hy greate or hy daie taile, being above the

worcke before he have ended his first worcke. Not allowed.

valeue of twentie shillinges, until he have made an end of his firste worcke (excepte that the wardon and owner doe allowe him), in payne of everie daye so departynge, for to forfaite and paie to the use of the occupacion, iis.

22. None to be free unless he have served seaven yeares by indenture as an apprentice.

Item That no man shall be free of this brotherhoode, unless he have served as an apprentice seaven yeares by indenture.

23. Everie man to worcke, and to kepe his and their servants from filchinge.

Item that all worckemene of this brotherhood shall worcke his or their worcke truelie and faithfullie, accordinge to workmanship, and put good stuff in their worcke, and make good morter (so far forth as the owner shall allowe stuff). And shall have regarde unto all places where neede standeth. And shall keepe themselves and their servants from filching of other men's goodes. In paine of being put forth of this brotherhood, or otherwise punished at the discretion of the maior and his brethren for the tyme beinge.

24. Resorting to the buriall of anie brother or sister dieinge.

Item yt ys ordered that when yt pleaseth God to take to his mercie forth of this worlde, anie of the bretheren of this companie, or anie of their wives, children, or servantes, that then everie one of this brotherhood shall (upon warning given) resorte together, and goe with the wardon in decent manner to the buriall of everie suche dead corpes, at the hower appointed. And yf anie doe make defaulte, and absent himselfe, and not come accordinglie (without licence of the wardon), he shall forfaite and paie for everie time so offendinge to thuse of th occupation, xiid.

25. Inrolling of indentures and paieing duties.

Item That everie maister of this brotherhood shall enrole into their booke of inrolment his apprentice indenture, within his firste yeare, and shall paie to thuse of this occupation for suche his inrolment (yf he be borne in this towne), twelve pence, And if he be a straunger, twoe shillings, And to the clarcke of this companie, twoe pence, And for his indentures, twentie pence. And that none of this brotherhood shall putt his apprentice indenture to anie to make but to the clarcke of this companie. And that he shall have for everie one that shall be made free brother of this companie, after that he hath served his apprentiship as befower, fower pence, upon paine of everie one offendinge in anie pointe of this order to forfaite and paie for everie tyme so offending, iiis. ivd.

26. Indentures to be brought in to be seen and perused at the commaundement of the Wardon.

Item That everie brother of this brotherhood shall (upon commaundment of the wardon) bringe in his apprentice's indentures for to be seene by the wardon and his assistance, and redd and perused if occasion serve, in paine of everie one doinge the contrarie to paie for everie tyme, iiis. ivd.

27. Burninge of Plaister. Not allowed.

Item that all such as shall burne anie plaister and putt anie rubbishe or lime therein, shall forthwith forfaite and lose all the same plaister, unless they doe agree with the wardon and companie for ye same without drifte or delaye.

28. Sellinge of lyme.

Item That whosoever shall burne or sell lyme, and shall put anie rubbishe or drosse into the same to the ende to make it more, or otherwaise to hurte it, he shall forfaite and lose the same lyme, unless he doe agree for yt.

29. Wrightes not to have nor sawe anie timber.

Item That no joyner nor wrighte shall have or cutt anie postes or sawe timber, excepte it be on the grounde or above tenne foote from this occupation their worcke (having warning), wherunto the contrarie in paine of every defaulte, iii*s.* iv*d.*

30. The Wardon offendinge to be doble fined.

Item If the wardon of this companie shall offende in anie of the orders that ar contenied in this booke (being proved), be shall be fined doble for every suche offence, accordinge to the fines herein limitted and sett downe.

31. Thomas Burie, clarcke and free brother to and with this occupacion.

Item It is agreed that Thomas Burie shall be clarcke unto this brotherhood, and is a free brother of the same, and hath paid his dues. And that he shall have paied him yearly at whit sondaie for his yearly fee, five shillinges. And be freed at all times with them in their feastes and generall meetings. And shall have for the inrolling of everie stranuger that shall obteine his freedom of this brotherhood, xii*d.*

32. Viewinge of bricke and tyle, as well good as badd.

Item it is ordered that if anie breckmaker doe make anie breeke or tyle within this towne or the liberties thereof to sell againe, the same, shall be viewed by the wardon or searchers or their sufficient deputie or deputies. And yf the same be not good and sufficient, yt shall be forfaited and by them seised. And yf yt be good and sufficient yet there shall be paid by the seller of the saide stuf unto the saide wardon or searchers, or their deputy or deputies to the use of the said companie, for everie thousand viewinge, threepence of a thousand. And so after that raite be the stuf in number more or less.

33. Viewing of latte, bricke, and tyle, which shalbe solde or broughte to this towne for to be solde.

Item yt ys decreed that yf anie person shall bring or sell into this towne any lattes, breeke, or tyle, or anie to be solde to anie whomsoever, the same shalbe viewed by the wardon or searchers or their sufficient deputie or deputies, and yf the same shalbe founde not good nor sufficient, yt shall be forfaited and by them seised. And yf yt be found good and sufficient, there shalbe paied by the seller of the saide stuf unto the said to the wardon or searchers or their deputie or deputies for the use of the said companie, for everie thousand viewing, twoepence of a thousand, and so after that raite, be the stuff in nomber more or lesse, and whether the same stuf were bought beforehand or not.

34. Item It is confirmed that no straunger shall worcke within this towne or corporatiou, except he componnde with maister maior and the wardon for the tyme beinge, in payne of everie day for the straunger so worcking, twelve pence, and likewise other twelve pence for him that so setteth him on worcke, according to the order of the composition of this brotherhood. The one halfe to the town chamber and the other halfe to the use of this brotherhood.

[Signatures of mayors from 1621 till 1629, then 30th August, 1630—]

I do approve of these orders, so far forth as they are agreeable to the laws of this Kingdom, and warrantable by the charters of this Incorporation.—John Lister, maior.

And this is repeated with signatures till 1740 inclusive, and from 1699, Warden and Searchers as well, excepting the year 1700. The entry follows till 1743, but is not signed.

Then towards the end of the volume occur these additional ordinances under their respective dates.

Kingston super Hull.

Orders made and agreed upon by the warden and company of Breeklayers, at their meeting in the hall, the 28th day of December, 1665, John Low, being then wardon, to be observed and kept by and amongst the said company as followeth:—

1. That no person of the Company shall at any tyme take any married man to be his apprentice, in paine of fifty shillings fyne.

2. That no master or free Brother of this Society shall give or sell his Apprentice any part of his tearme, in paine of five pounds fyne.

3. That if any master or brother of this Society do happen to dye (his apprentice not having served his tearme), that then such apprentice shall not be admitted to become contributor, but be turned over to some other free Brother of this trade. And that no apprentice shall be admitted and be made a free Brother of this Companie unless he have first served out the tearme of seaven yeares.

4. That no younger Brother shall take any apprentice till he himself have been fower yeares free of their Company, in paine of a fyne, five poundes; and the first apprentice shall have served fower yeares before a second be taken, in paine of five pownds fyne.

5. That no brother of this Company shall take any worke at an undervalue at the judgment of the warden and maior part of the

Company, upon paine of five shillings fyne at the pound, and soe ratably according to the value of the worke.

6. That noe person of this Society or trade shall take any worke out of another man's hand in paine of five shillings fyne at the pound for every pound, that the said worcke is of value, and so ratably.

7. That if any of this Company being chosen by the maior part thereof to be warden doe refuse to stand and officiate as warden he shall forfeicte and pay to the Companye for a fyne the sum of fower pounds, or if any being chosen for Searcher doe refuse to observe or stand to such office, he shall forfeict and pay to the Company for a fyne the sum of forty shillings.

8. That every one of this Company shall upon demand of the warden for the tyme being pay all suche fyne or fynes as he is liable to, or which shall be imposed on him for any breach or default upon any order or otherwise, shall pay for the first refusal vid., for the second 1s., for the third 2s., and be further proceeded against according to the quality of the offence, as the warden and maior part of the Company shall thinke fitt.

August 3rd, 1713.

9. Ordered that noe person free of this Company shall at any time from henceforth be absent from the audit dinner upon paine of everie default to forfeit and pay one shilling.

12*th November*, 1729.

Ordered and agreed by a great majority of the Company of Bricklayers, then present, that every person that shall hereafter be absent from the audit dinner, provided for this company, shall pay for his being absent, three shillings.

At a general meeting of the Company of Bricklayers, the fourth day of August, 1735.

Ordered and agreed by the consent of the said company, that no brothers which now are or which hereafter shall be made brothers of the said company, shall for the future employ any person whatsoever being a bricklayer now or which shall belong to this company to work in the said trade within the town of Kingston upon Hull and liberties of the same, that refuse to pay what owing by him to the said company to the then present warden when demanded by him. Every brother of this company employing any such person shall for every day that he shall so employ him or them, pay respectively to the present warden then being, for the use of the said company, the sum of 12d., for every day every person that he or they shall so employ in the said trade.

Then follows a register of the names of all the Mayors, Sheriffs, and Wardens from the year 1598, the Mayors' names being in some cases signatures, but generally engrossed, and that for 1696 being omitted; also the Sheriff's entry for 1690, 1696-7-8, and the Warden's for the same years are wanting. The last entry of a Warden is in 1735, when Joseph Berry is enrolled, and the entries of Mayors and Sheriffs have been continued to the present day.

Chapter XXVII.

The Fraternity of Coopers.

HULL must always have been a place with a strong body of the men of this craft. Even before the chartering of the town by Edward I., there was a considerable trade in wine, which must have given employment to Coopers. The imports of Baltic merchandise included several articles, such as tar, generally brought in casks; the fish, the various kinds of oils, and the famed ale of the town must have kept the craft busy from century to century, as it is a busy one with an active trades' society to-day. As it was one of the earliest, so the fraternity was the last of the old trades' gilds which survived. The representatives of its last members are still familiar to us, and it is the more interesting that we are able to follow pretty closely their proceedings for a period amounting to a little short of 300 years.

Our sources of information are, first, two Compositions between the Mayor, etc., on the one party, and the representatives of the Gild on the other, now in the Town Hall, and dated 1598 and 1668 respectively. These, which are given below, contain the rules and ordinances formally licensed by the Town Chamber, and which gave the fraternity the status of an authoritative court for the regulation of the craft. But secondly, we have in this case a much rarer record in the Book of the Company, in which the private minutes and ordinances of the members were recorded for the Company's behoof. This Book ([248]), presented by Daniel Thompson, Warden of the Company in 1681, is a folio bound in vellum, and contains the ordinances

(248) Now in the possession of Mr. Councillor Fewster.

in full, entries up to the year 1766, the signatures and seals of members, an account of lands and leases belonging to the Company, and an inventory of plate and furniture in its possession. We are thus in this case enabled to supplement the bare rules of the Composition, which is all that we possess in the case of most of the other crafts, with some account of what the fraternity was in its own inner working, and the insight thus afforded us must be of great service in studying the compositions of the other trades.

The first point which comes out very clearly is this, that though as viewed from the Town Hall, these companies were invested with a kind of municipal authority, and were, so to speak, a part of the town government so far as regarded their own compact handicraft, yet that, viewed in their essential character, they constituted independent and self-governing societies. They had their hall, their tenements, their seal and their plate, and their common trade interests, which amounted in some important particulars to a partnership in the purchase of goods. They constituted, if we may use the expression, a sub-estate of the community. They could not only fine, but distrain for the fine if the delinquent refused to pay.

Another very curious point comes out, namely, that the ordinances contained in the public Composition [249] and those in the Company's Book shew differences of a rather remarkable character. What these were in this case will appear directly. Certainly, the ordinances in the White Book are signed by the Mayor. On the other hand, it is noticeable that they were the secrets which members were bound on oath and under penalty not to reveal. It is impossible to say how far this difference in other cases extended.

The following is the Composition of 1598. From the clause which gives the nomination of the first Warden until the regular election day to the Mayor, it would seem that the Company had been for some time lacking in complete organi-

(249) It will be observed that the term "Composition" is used in the Gild Book of the rules therein. Its proper use, however, was for the deed executed with the Mayor.

sation. The cause of this is unknown to us. It is very improbable that so ancient a trade had been without its Gild. Possibly it had been disorganised by the dissolution of some religious fraternity with which it had been closely connected. During the reign of Elizabeth, we can trace a growing tendency towards the closer organisation of the various trades and their delimitation from each other, and of this tendency the Coopers seem to have had their share.

A Composition of the Coopers, 1598.

A Composicon indented dated the seaven and twenty day of January in the one and forty yeare of the reigne of or Soveraigne Lady Elizabeth, By the grace of god Queene of England, ffrannce, and Yreland, defender of the faithe, and Betweene the Maior and Burgesses of Kingston npon Hull on th' one party And George Thompson, Thomas Wighton, William Jackson, John Blaydes, William Ingledew, John Harlande, William Browne, Thomas Mownteine, William Murton, Rafe Gawtree, Henry Williamson, Edwarde Walker, William Teale, Richard Lilforth, William Wilkinson, and James Nornavell, of Kingston upon Hull, aforesaide, cowperes, of th' other party, Witnesseth that the saide Maior and Burgesses for theim and their successors (as moche as in theim is), npon the desire and sute of the said George Thompson [here follow also all above names], and to the intent that the occupacion and traide of the cowperes may better flourishe within the town of Kingston upon Hull afore saide; Have given and graunted theis ordenaunces, graunntes, clauses, and orderes hereafter ensewing and following :—

One Warden and two Searchers to be chosen the Monday before St. Luke's Day.

1. ffirste, that the Company of Cowperes within the towne of Kingston npon Hull aforesaide shall from henceforthe have emongst theim one warden and two searcheres to be chosen yearly by most voyces emongst theimselves, upon the monday next before St. Luke's day yearly, and that twoe shalbe of eleccion for warden, whereof th' one shalbe chosen, and fower of clecion for searchers, whereof twoe shalbe chosen, Which warden and searchers shall yearly the morrowe after the saide elecion day be sworne upon the holy evangelist of god before the said Maior or his lieutenaunte for the true and just usinge of their places and offices for one hole yeare, or to like effect. And if any of the saide officers dye, then anewe shalbe chosen within tenne daies in the place or rowme of him or theim so dyeing, to serve for the rest of the yeare, and to be sworne as aforesaide. And the foresaide Maior and Burgesses doe nominate and appointe George Thompson for first warden till the saide eleccion day, and th' aforesaide Thomas Wighton and William Ingledew, Searchers.

On the morrowe to be sworne upon the holy evangelist of god before the Mayor.

The first Warden and Searchers to be nominated by the Mayor.

2\. Bond to be taken of the Wardens, but no benefit to acorue thereby to the Mayor.

Item that the saide company of cowperes shall at their liberty take bond or bondes of the saide Warden and searchers, or of any otheres from time to time in the name of saide Maior and Burgesses for the performance of any accomptes,̧ debts, or other thinges, which yet notwithstanding no benefit shall thereby accrewe to the saide Maior and Burgesses, but onely to the saide company of cowpers.

3\. No one to be admitted or to keep a shop unless a burgess, on pain of 5s weekly.

Item that they shall receive none into their socyety as free of their company nules he be firste Burges of Kingston upon Hull. And that no cowper nules he be a free Burges of the saide towne and free of their company shall kepe any shopp there upon paine of five shillinges weekly.

4\. No wage to be detained beyond six days on pain of 12d. to the Company.

Item that if any m^r^ of the saide company doe deteyne the waiges of his servaunte by the space of six daies after the same be due, The saide warden and searcheres shall upon complaint thereof see the same be paied, And if the saide M^r^ doe not upon request thereof repay the same, Then he shall not onely within six daies after repay the same, but also shall forfaite for soche his wilfulness for everie weeke the same is unpaied twelve pene.

5\. All to come to meetings in pain of 12d. for any election meeting, and 6d. at other times.

Item that all and any of the said company being warned to come to any meting in the name of the warden, whether it be to the eleccion or other affaires, shall without delay, having no lawfull excuse of absence, appeare at the time appointed, of forfaiture for everie defaulte on the eleccion day, twelve pence, and everie other time, six pence. And if any of the said company

If stubborne, wilfull, or forwarde, or use himself unseemly, to be fined according to the quantity of the offence.

be stubborne, wilfull, or frowarde, or use theimselves unsemely, contrary to good rule and order, he shall pay soche fine as shalbe assessed by the warden, searchers, and company, or the most part of theim for the time being, according to the quantity of the offence.

6\. Master to pay 6d. on taking an apprentice, and 8d. yearly for hired servant.

Item that everie cowper that taketh an apprentice shall pay to the company at the time of his entrie day, vid., and for everie hyred servaunte, viiid. per yeare.

7\. No one to carry on the trade unless apprenticed seven years. Penalty, 6s. 8d.

Item that no persone or persones (except in faire times and in markitt daies in markitt time) shall sell any hogsheade or barrill, or any other new vessell within this towne, except he have served seaven yeares as an apprentice by indenture with a Cowper, upon paine of everie time so selling to forfait vis. viijd. And that no

No strange houpes to be sold by strangers.

straunger or otheres not dwelling within this town shall bring any houpes to this towne to sell to any other straungers or otheres not dwelling in this towne. And that no inhabitant within this towne shall buy any houpes to the end to make saile thereof, save onely to the cowpers of this towne.

8.

No one unfree of the Company to worck or meddle a shippe boarde or elsewhere on pain of 3s. 4d. from the cowper and 3s. 4d. from his employer.

Item that no persone or persones not free of the company shall worck or meddle in that occupacion either a shippe boarde, or other vessell in the haven or roade, or in any man's honse, upon paine everie defanlt he so working to forfaite for the same, iii*s*. iiij*d*., and he or they that shall sett him on worcke, other iii*s*. iiij*d*.

9.

No cowper to packe fishe unless appointed by the warden. Penalty 12d. within the town; a shippe boarde 3s. 4d.; and 6s. 8d. per 1000 for selling houpes.

Item that no cowper shall within the towne packe any fishe, herringes, or salmon, except he be appointed by the wardin for the time being, upon paine to forfaite for everie soche default within the towne, xii*d*., and for everie soche defanlt a shipp board, or other vessell, iii*s*. iiij*d*. And that everie persone above lymitted selling honpes here contrary to the order above graunted, shall forfait for everie thonsande, vi*s*. viij*d*., and so after that raite for greater or less number.

10.

Searchers to seise all badd stuf.

Item that the said warden and searcheres shall from time to time search, viewe, and trye all hogsheades, barrill's, kilderkines, and all other vessell made by any cowper in this towne, or by any other brought to be sonld within this towne, if they be made lawfnll, workmanlike, and good, without any sapp or other badd and insufficient stnf, and to seize the same if the same be not good, or otherwise to assesse fynes for soche badd stnf at the discrecions of the saide warden and searcheres, according to the statnt, And that the saide company of cowpers shall at their liberty and pleasure bny clapboardes or any other stnf belonging to their traid brought into the towne by any persone or persones to be solde, straungers or others.

Company to buy stuf belonging to their trade.

11.

No cowper to keep more than two apprentices at once, and by the consent of the Mayor and Aldermen.

Item that no cowper within this towne shall kepe above twoe apprentices at once npon paine to be fined by the warden, searchers, and saide company, or the most parte of them, And that the said cowpers nor none of theim shall take any apprentice withont the consent of Mr. Maior and the most parte of the aldermen, but soche as ar borne or remayninge within this towne, and that to be by the consent of theim likewise, if ther be any soche snfficient to serve their tnrnes.

12.

Have the right to make ordinances, but not to the hurte of the common weale of the towne, nor disagreeable to law.

Item that it shalbe lanfnll for the said warden for the time beinge, and searcheres, with the greater number of the saide company of cowpers, to make any ordores from time to time for good government and rnle to be had emongst theimselves or otherwise concerning their traide, So the same tende not to the hnrte of the common weale of this towne [at the Jndgment of Mr. maior and the greater nomber of his brethren, if the same come in qnestion (*inserted*)], nor disagreable to lawe, And to sett downe paines and forfaitnres for Breach of soche orders.

13.

The Wardens or

Item that the saide warden and searchers or their snfficient depnty or deputies in their sickness or absence

Searchers to distrain for fines.

occupyeng their rowmes or any of theim, may distraine the goodes or cattelles of any offenderes in the premisses, or any parcell thereoff for the fynes, forfaitnres, and paiments abovesett or to be sett according to the trne meaning hereof, And if any resist theim or any of theim then they shalbe ayded by the offycer or officeres of the saide Maior, And all distresses by theim taken shalbe kepte till satisfaccion be made for the offence, And everie soche officer ayding theim in the premisses shall have for his paines theirein paiod by the warden and searcheres iiij*d*., without deley.

The halfe of all fines to be paid to the Mayor.

In consideracion of all which premisses the cowperes above named doe grannt to the said Maior and Burgesses that the halfe of all fines, paines, and forfaitnres above mencioned shall by the warden an searchers be paiod over to th' use of the Maior and Burgesses at the next auditt yearly then following without drift or deley, And further that the saide Warden, Searcheres, and Company shall yearly for ever paie to the Maior and Burgesses aforesaide at everie auditt for this their composicion, vj*s*. viiij*d*. In witnes whereof unto th' one parte of this composicion indented remaining in the custody of the saide cowpers, the saide Maior and Burgesses have sette their common Seale, and unto th' other parte thereof remaining in the custody of the saide Maior and Burgesses, The cowpers above namd have sett to thier handes and seales the day and yeare first above written, And in the yeare of our Lorde according to the computacion of England one thousand five hundred ninety and eight.

And a fee of 6s. 8d. for this Composition.

George tomson.	Edwardi Walker.
thomas weton.	Raufe Gawtre.
John Blaydes.	Henry Williamson.
So. harland.	Jacob. [?] Nornavell.
Willam Ingledew.	Wm. murton.
Wm. teale.	Richard Lilforth
Thomas mountayn	

[*Endorsed*]

Scaled, subsribed, and delivered in the presence—Willm. Dowsone, Wm. Bower, Walter Cave.

Md. that the wordes, viz. :—markitt daies in markitt times being interlyned within, was done before th' ensealing and deliverie hereof. And also theis presentes were sealed and delivered.

Coopers' Composition, 1598.

[On two pieces of parchment, fastened together by the seal strips].

The next document remaining is another Composition, dated 1668. It begins as follows :—

COOPERS' COMPOSITION, 1668.

A Composition Indented, made, dated the Eight and Twentieth of May, in the Twentieth yeare of our Soveraigne Lord, Charles the second, by the grace of God, King of England, Scotland, France, and Ireland, defender of the faith, etc. Annoq. dni., 1668.

Betweene the Mayor and Burgesses of the Towne or Borough of Kingston upon Hull on the one parte, And Christopher Fanthorpe, William Bewley, Thomas Bambrough (*b*), William Seamer, Edward Cosens, Thomas Stephenson, Robert Cannaby, Robert Squire, Edward Rooke, John Tnrner, John Wright, John Cooke, and Robert ffowler, of the Towne and County of Kingston-upon-Hull, aforesaid, Coopers on the other parte.

The ordinances themselves turn out on inspection to be almost exactly the same as those of 1598. They are signed by the following :—

Christopher Fawthrop, Warden.	Thomas Stephenson.
William Bewley.	Robert Squier.
Thomas Baumbrough.	John Cooke.
William Seamer.	Edward Rooke.
Edmond Cossin.	John Wright.
Rob'rt Cauiby.	Robert ffowler.
John Tnrner.	

[Seals unimpressed, poor, or illegible].

[*Endorsed*]

Sealed and delivered by the within-named Christopher Fawthrop, warden, William Bewley, William Seamer, Robert Caniby, Robert Squire, and Edward Rooke, in the presence of

Char. Vaux (*c*).

Sealed and delivered by the within-named Edward Cosens, Thomas Stephenson, and John Wright, in the presence of

Char. Vaux.
John Bewley.
John Graves.

Sealed and delivered by the within-named Thomas Baumbrough, John Cooke, and Robt. ffowler, in the presence of

Char. Vaux.
John Bewley.
John Graves.

[Counterparte of A Composiccion granted to Company of Coopers, 1668].

(*b*) His widow, Clare, founded a hospital for poor widows, in Salthouse Lane; her tombstone is still to be seen in Holy Trinity Churchyard.

(*c*) Town Clerk.

We now give in full the White Book of Ordinances contained in the Company's Book, which it will thus be seen contains in one the Court Book and Book of Acts. The marginal summary and numbers, in this case, are taken from the original. In the Compositions they are added for the convenience of the reader. The date is 1681, or 13 years after the last extant Composition; but there is no reason to suppose that it differed materially from the body of rules which existed in the older Book which it succeeded. That being so, it is remarkable that with the exception of the payment for "upsett," or starting business, all the fines in this book go direct to the Company, instead of being divided between the Mayor and the Company as is the stated rule in the Composition. Whether the Company kept an exact account of these, and paid the moiety to the Mayor in lump, sums does not appear, and cannot now be decided. The discrepancy is curious.

The White Booke of Ordinances, made, enacted, and established by the Warden, Searchers, and Elder Brethren of the Societie or Companie of Coopers, within the Towne of Kingston upon Hull, with the whole assent and consent and agreement of the rest of the Brethren of the said Company, for the good Government, Benefitt, and Publick weale of the said Company, and with the approbacion and allowance of the Right Worshipfull the Major of the said Towne of Kingston upon Hull, and the Worshipfull the Aldermen his brethren, The Fifth day of May, in this Three and Thirteth yeare of the Reigne of our Soveraigne Lord, Charles the Second, by the Grace of God, King of England, Scotland, France, and Ireland, defender of the faith, etc. Annoq. Dni., 1681. In the yeare of Daniell Thompson, Warden, and Anthony Payley and George Wilkinson, Searchers of the said Company.

I.

Eleccion of the Warden & Searchers.

Imprimis It is ordered and established By the said Warden, Searchers, and Elder Brethren, with the consent of the Brethren as aforesaid, That the said Society or Companie of Coopers, shall have amongst them one Warden and two Searchers, to be chosen by most voices of ye Elder and younger Brethren of ye said Companie yearely and every yeare, upon the second Wednesday, which shall be in the moneth of October. And that two of the Elder Brethren of the said Companie shall be then putt on by the present Warden or Elder Brethren, or major part of them, for Eleccion for Warden, whereof one shall be chosen, aud ffower for Eleccion of

Searchers, whereof two shall be chosen, which said Warden and Searchers shall yearely the morrow after the said Eleccion day be sworne upon the Holy Evangelists, before the Major of this Towne or his deputie for the time being, ffor the true and juste useing of their said places and offices for one whole yeare, or to the like effect, and if any of ye said officers die within the said yeare, then a new one shall be chosen in ye place of him soe dieing, within tenne days next after such death, to serve for ye rest of the yeare, and to be sworne as aforesaid.

2. Comeing to the Eleccion and accompanying the Warden to Dinner.

Item it is ordered and decreed That every brother, ffree of this Societie, shall upon the Election day come unto the Eleccion of the Warden and Searchers, in their best apparell, and not be absent at the place and houre appointed without a lawfull excuse or cause, first made knowne and allowed of by the Warden for the time being, and att ye said Eleccion shall take his place in order, and give but one vote to one, and not prompt any of his fellowes. And after the said Eleccion, shall in decent Manner accompany the said warden to such place to dinner as the said warden shall appoint and give notice of. And shall pay for his dinner soe much as the warden, takeing with him the major part of ye Elder Brethren, shall agree upon, for the said Company, in paine of every man ofending herein, to forfeit and pay to the use of the said Company, v*s*.

3. Obedience to ye Mayor of this towne, and to the Warden of ye Companie.

Item it is ordered and agreed That every brother of this Societie shall reverently and dutifully behave themselves to the Right Worshipfull the Major and Aldermen of this Corporacion. And also that everie brother of this Companie and their servants shall be obedient to the Warden duering his yeare, and reverently behave himselfe towards him att all meetings and att all other times and places. And in noo wise misuse the Warden and Searchers or their deputies, by or with any unseemely wordes or gestures in their presence or absence, in paine of every one offending in this order to pay to the use of ye said Company, v*s*.

4. Fine for not comeing to meetings.

Item it is established and agreed That noe brother of this Societie or company, being warned by the Warden or Searchers, or their deputie or deputies to come to any meeting or other assembly of the said Company, doe absent himselfe from any such meeting or assembly, in paine of every one being absent (without a lawfull excuse to be allowed of by the Warden for the time being), to pay as is herein mencioned (vizt.), Elder Brother offending to pay to ye use aforesaid, 1*s*., and every Younger Brother, 6d.

5. Departing from meetings without leave of the Warden, or being disordered there.

Item it is ordered that if any brother of this Societie doe departe from any meeting or assembly of ye said Company, before he shall have leave of the Warden soe to doe, or be disordred then and there, and will not keepe his place according to his ancientie, and keep silence att ye commaund of the Warden for the time being, and give diligent care and attendance to what shall be spoken by the Warden or his depnty, or by any other by their appointment, or that any yonnger Brother doe come in att any meeting of the Warden and Elder Brethren, without being warned by ye Warden. That then every one offending in this or any branche thereof, shall forfeit and pay fforthwith to the use of the said Company, iis. vid.

6. Comeing to Burialls.

Item it is ordered That every Brother ffree of this Companie shall (upon notice given by the Warden) in decent manner accompany the Warden to the Buriall of any brothers of the Company, or their wives, children, or servants, att such house as the Warden shall appoint (if the Relacions or —— of the partie to be buried, desire the Warden to warne the said Companie to the funerall), in paine of every one offending herein to forfeit and pay to the use aforesaid, vid.

7. Youngest Brother to warne the Companie.

It is ordered and decreed that the youngest Brother ffree of this Societie shall from time to time, att the comandment of the Warden for the time being, without deley give warning to the rest of the rest of ye Brethren of the same Societie, to come to every meeting and assembly att the houre and place appointed by the Warden. And if the said youngest Brother refuse to warne the said Companie, or be Sick, or forth of the Towne, That in such case such of the younger Brethren shall warne the said Company as the Warden shall appoint. And if any of the younger Brethren shall neglect or refuse to warne the said Company att the request of the Warden or his deputie, The partie soe neglecting or refueing shall forfeit and pay to the use aforesaid, vs.

8. The Companie to be governed by the Warden and Ancients.

It is ordered, agreed, and concluded that the said Society or Company shall as formerly be ruled and governed by the Warden and twelve Ancients of the said Company for the time being. And that the said Warden, Ancients, or any six of the Ancients, with the Warden, are hereby impowered from time to time as shall be thought necessary and convenient to them, to make, enact, and execute such laws, orders, and ordinances, as are or shalbe made for the well governeing of the said Societie or Company. And that when the said Warden and Ancients shall have occasion to meet upon any business which shall concerne the Trade, each man shall beare his own charges, and alsoe that when any of the said Ancients departe this life, there shalbe a ffree eleccion of the whole Companie, or the major parte of them, for the chuseing another in his place. And if any of the Ancients shall wilfully refuse or neglect to meet amongst his said Brethren three times together (having lawful warning thereof, and not showeing some reasonable cause for his absence to the Warden) that then such Ancient shalbe displaced, and another to be chosen in his roome by the Warden and Companie, or the major of parte of them. And that the Warden for the time being, and the major parte of the Ancients, shall have libertie att any of their meetings to give to the poore of their Companie as shalbe thought by them convenient.

9. Not to disclose the secrets of the Companie.

Item it is ordered and established that if any ffree of this Societie doe att any time disclose the secretts of this companie or of these orders, he shall forfeit and pay for every time soe offending, to the use aforesaid, *viz.* viiid.

10. Not to misuse one another.

Item it is decreed that noe Brother ffree of this Societie shall misuse or slander one another with any unseemely wordes or carriage, either in ye presence or absence of the Warden and Searchers, or their deputy or deputies, in paine for every one offending herein to forfeit and pay for every such offence, to the use aforesaid, *vs.*

11. None to buy ffatt hoopes or pind hoopes, but to let the rest of the Companie have parte.

Item it is established and ordered that noe brother ffree of this Societie shall buy for himselfe onely any ffiatt hoopes, or any other sorte of Pind Hoopes, brought to this Towne to be sold, if there be above twentie of any such sorte of hoopes. But he shall lett every brother of this Company that shall be desirous have parte of the same hoopes, upon paine to forfeit and pay to the use aforesaid, one shilling.

12. Colourably taking of hoopes brought to this towne to be sold, and letting the rest of the Companie have parte.

Item it is decreed, ordered, and established that noe brother ffree of this Companie shall colourably take any hoopes into his howse or celler of any wares brought to this Towne to be sold, to hinder any of the Brethren to have their proporcion. And that if any hoops of what sorte soever shall happen at any time to be brought to this Towne to be sold, That then noe free brother of this Companie shall buy above halfe a thousand of the same hoops onely for himselfe, without makeing the Warden of the said Companie for the time being first acquainted therewith. And then if he buy any more hoopes than half a Thousand of a sorte, he shall lett every brother of the said Societie have parte of them, att such price or prices (they bearing their equall parte of all charges) as he or they shall buy the said hoopes att, if there shalbe above half a Thousand Hogshead hoopes, Barrill hoopes, or ffirkin hoopes, upon paine of every time doing the contrary to forfeit and pay to the use aforesaid, two shillings and sixpence.

13.
Buying of Close boards, pipe staves, etc., to lett the rest of the Companie have parte.

Item It is ordered, established, and agreed that if any Brother of this Company shall hereafter buy any Close boards, Pipe Staves, Ash Staves, Hogshead Staves, Barrill Staves, Puncheon Staves, or any other such like stuffe, which shall happen to be brought into this Porte or Towne of Kingston upon Hull, to be sold by any person or persons whoesoever, that then every such Brother shall make the Warden of the said Companie privie thereto. And then if such Brother buy one hundred of Close Boards, Pipe Staves, Ash Staves, Hogshead Staves, barrell Staves, Puncheon Staves, or such like stuffe, hee shall lett the rest of the Companie have ffower score of the same. Iff hee buy two hundred, hee shall lett the rest of the Company have 140 of ye same. Iff hee buy 300, hee shall lett ye reste of the Company have two hundred of the same. And soe after that proportion for a greater or lesser number of such close boardes, Pipe Staves, and Ash Staves, Barrill Staves, Puncheon Staves, or such like stuffe belonging to the said occupacion of Coopers, each man paying for the said stuffe to the Warden of the said Company for the time being, an equall parte or proporcion of the price the same were bought att, and bearing rateably and proportionablie, thus equall partes and proportions of all other charges which shalbe laid out about ye buyeing of the said stuffe, In paine of every offending in this order to forfeit and pay to the use of the said Companie, the ffine hereafter expressed (viz.), ffor every hundred of Close boards which hee shall buy above halfe a hundred, Tenne shillings lawful English money; for every hundred of pipe staves, if he buy above a hundred, five shillings like money; ffor every Hundred of Barrill Staves, if he buy above three hundred, two shillings sixpence; ffor every Thousand of Ash Staves, which he shall buy above a Thousand, five shillings lawful English money; ffor every Hundred of Puncheon Staves and Hogshead Staves which hee shall buy above a hundred, two shillings sixpence; And soe after that rate for a greater or lesser quantity of the stuffe above mencioned, or such like stuffe belonging to the said occupacion. And that every Brother upon Receipt of his parte of the stuffe, or when the Warden shall order, shall pay into the Warden's hands his proportion of what is due to be paid for the same. To the end the same may be paid according to the intent hereof, upon paine of forfeiting every weeke to the use aforesaid, five shillings.

14. Filling or driveing wine or oile.

Item it is ordred and decreed that every Brother ffree of this Society, That shall ffill or drive any wine or oile of any person not a free Burgess of this Towne of Kingston upon Hull, and which shalbe brought into this Towne or Porte from beyond the seas, or shall ffill or drive any wine or oil bought in this Towne by any not ffree of this Towne, That such brother shall acquaint the Warden of the said Companie for the time being, of such wine or oile which he shall soe fill or drive, And shall pay to the Warden for the use of the said Companie, fforth of every five Tonnes that he soe filleth or driveth, sixpence; forth of every tenne Tonnes, twelve pence; and soe after that rate for a greater or lesser number, upon paine of every time doeing ye contrary to forfeit and pay to the use aforesaid, iis. vid.

15. Ordering of Debts and Controversies.

Item it is ordred That if any pettie or small controversie shall happen to arise Betwixt one brother of this Societie and another, or any small debt be oweing by one of them to another, the partie grieved shall before he goe to law for the same, make complaint thereof to the Warden for the time being. And upon such complaint, the Warden takeing to him two, three, or ffower of the Ancients of the said Companie, shall decide and order the matter betwixt them, and if either of the parties shall doe contrarie, or refuse to stand to such order and end as they shall make, hee soe refuseing shall forfeit and pay to the use of the said Companie, tenne shillings.

16. Opening shopp and selling casks.

Item It is ordred that noe cooper, unlesse he bee first free Burgesse of this Towne, and free of this Companie, shall keep any shopp in this Towne, upon paine of 5s. weekly. And that noe person or persons whatsoever, not free of the said Companie (except in faire times and markett days in markett time) shall sell any Hogshead or Barrill, or any other new vessell within this Towne, upon paine of forfeiting to the use of the said Company, vs.

17. Working on shipp-board.

Item It is ordred that noe person or persons not ffree of this ffellowshipp, shall worke or intermeddle in ye occupacion of coopers, either on board of any shipp, or any other vessell in the haven or Roadstead of this Towne. Nor in any man's house in this Towne, upon paine to fforfeit and pay for every defanlt for the use of the said Companie, by him that worketh contrarie to this order, Three shillings and ffower pence, and by such as sett him on worke, other three shillings and ffower pence.

18. Packing of ffish.

Item that none of this brotherhood, nor any Cooper whatsoever, shall within this Towne, or on shipp board, or on other vessell in this haven or Roadstead, packe any Fish, Herrings, or Salmon, except he be appointed soe to doe by the Warden for the time being, upon paine to forfeit for every such default within this Towne, iii*s*. iiii*d*., And for every default on board of any shipp or other vessell, alsoe iii*s*. iiii*d*.

19. Keeping of Apprentices.

Item it is ordred that noe Cooper ffree of this Companie shall kepe above two apprentices att once, upon paine to forfeit and pay for every such offence to the use of the said Company for every weeke herein offending, 10s.

20. Enrolling of Apprentices in towne's booke and Companie's booke, and Clarke's dues.

Item it is ordred and agreed that all apprentices and hired servants shalbe enrolled in the Companie's booke of enrolments, And that every master shall enroll his apprentice Indenture within the first yeare of his apprentishipp, in paine to forfeit for every such default to the use of the said Companie for every weeke after the said year, iis. As alsoe every master shall enroll his apprentice in ye townis Booke of Enrolments within one yeare after his takeing bound such apprentice, in paine to forfeit to the said Major and Burgesses Tenne shiilings. And that Richard Winchester, of this towne, Scrivener, shall be Clarke to the said Brotherhood and Society, and that hee shalbe ffree att all ffeasts, drinkings, and other meetings amongst the said Society, And that the said Clarke shall have the making of all Indentures of Apprentices for the Brotherhood of this Companie, in paine of any offending herein to forfeit and pay to the use aforesaid Three shillings and ffower pence, And shall have for every paire of Indentures making twenty pence, and for enrolling of any apprentice or hired servant into the Companie's Booke ffower pence, and for every Brother that shalbe made free of this Companie sixpence. And that the said clarke shall put the master in minde that he cause the said Indenture to be enrolled in the townis Booke of Enrolments, pursuant to an order of the bench.

21. Paying to the Companie so enrolling Apprentices and servants.

Item that every apprentice that shalbe enrolled in the said Companie's Booke of Enrolment shall pay to the warden for the time being for the use of the said Company, sixpence, and every Hired Servant soe enrolled shall pay att his enrollment, to the use aforesaid, eight pence, and that none shall hire any journeyman not ffree of this Companie for lesse time than one whole yeare, without consent of the warden and Elder brethren, or any six of the ancients with the warden, in paine of every weeke offending herein to pay to the use aforesaid 1s.

22. Payeing of uppsetts to ye Company, and 8s. 4d. to the towne yearely.

Item it is ordred and agreed that every one whoo hath served his apprentishipp with any ffree Brother of this Companie, att the time of his takeng his ffreedome of this society shall pay for his uppsett to the said Companie six shillings and eightpence, and not to worke as a ffreeman till then, in paine to forfeit to the use aforesaid for every weeke doeng the contrary, viz. viiid. And that the said Companie shall pay to ye said Major and Burgesses att the townes anditt Three shillings and fower pence every yeare, in the name and in lieu of all the uppsetts received hy them for that yeare.

23. Payeing the fines and forfeitures.

Item it is agreed and concluded that all the dues, payments, and forfeitures before in these orders expressed, or which hereafter shalbe due and payable, shalbe paid unto the warden of this society or his deputie for the time being, upon demand of the same by the said warden or his deputie, upon paine of everyone offending to forfeit and pay to the use aforesaid xs. And that if the warden for the time being shall forbeare any person or persons offending in any orders now made or hereafter to be made touching the said Companie and the weale and Governement thereof, And doe not doe his best endeavours to Levie, Collect, and gather the fines, uppsetts, and other dueties due to this Companie by virtue of their composition and orders, without using partialitie or slackness therein, the said warden herein offending shall pay all the said fines, uppsetts, and other dueties himselfe without any further deley, And if he doe offend himselfe, or shall doe contrary to the orders of this Booke and the true meaning of this Composition, he shalbe fined double for every such offence, and pay the same without deley upon paine to pay to the use aforesaid xs.

24. Assistance of the Mayor's officer.

Item it is ordred and decreed That the said Warden and Searchers, or their sufficient deputie or deputies in their sickness or absence occupyeing there roomes, or any of them, shall or may (upon request unto the Major) have the Major's Officer to goe with them to distreine the goods and chattells of any offenders in the premisses, or any parte thereof, ffor the fines, fforfectures, and payments above sett or to be sett, according to the true meaning hereof, and if any resistance be they shalbe aided by Major and Aldermen of this towne for the time being ffrom time to time. Which distresses shall be kept untill satisfaccion be made for the offence. And every such officer goeing and distreining as aforesaid shall have for his paines therein taken instantly paid him by the offender ffower pence.

25. A brother offending by refuseing to pay to have no benefitt by pakeing Fish or haveing stuffe.

Item it is ordred and agreed that if any brother ffree of this Companie be refractorie, and will not stand to the orders now made or which shalbe made for the weale and governement of the said Company, or doe refuse or deley to pay such fines, dues, and dueties as are sett upon him, That then the partie so offending shall have noe benefitt or advantage either by packing fish, haveng parte of stuffe bought by any of the said Company, or any other benefitt or advantage whatsoever by the said Company, untill such brother doe conforme to the orders of the said Companie, and doo pay such fines, dues, and dueties as he ought to pay, and as are sett upon him, upon paine of forfecting to the use aforesaid vs.

26. Reading ye orders yearely. Noe alteracion without approbacion of ye Mayor and Aldermen, and appeals to them.

Item it is ordred that these orders shall yearly be read over (upon the Eleccion Day for the said Companie) to the whole companie then present, to the end they may take notice of and the better observe the same, And that noe alteracon be made in these orders, nor any of them, or any new ones made without the approbacion and allowance of the Major and Aldermen of the saide towne of Kingston upon Hull for the time being, or the major parte of them, according to this Composition, And that if any small difference arise betwixt one Brother of this said Company and another, which cannot be decided by the Warden and Elder Brethren, or major parte of them, as is above mencioned, then the partie grieved shall appeale to the Major and Aldermen to have redresse therein before any proceedings be at Law.

These orders are approved of and confirmed by us underwritten, May 5th. 1681.

Simon Gibson, Mayor.
Chr. Richardson.
Geor. Crowle.
Humphrey Duncalfe.
Ben Maister.
Robert Mason.
Joseph Petre.

"Att a generall meeting," held "The second Day of December, 1693," an ordinance was agreed upon to the following purport:

27. Order for payment of quartridges quarterlie.

Whereas the Co. have formerlie by ancient custome amongst them paid quartridges towards increase of their Stock, Wardens and Elder Brethren iii*d*., and younger ii*d*. a quarter, Now Agreed, for the better increase of stock and relief of widows, Warden and Elder Brethren pay xii*d*., and younger vi*d*. quarterly for 3 years, and so to continue if thought advisable.

Confirmed by Mayor 7th Dec., and sealed by Co. on the 8th.

Then, after some other entries, occurs the following heading:

In testimonie hereof And for the ffurther confirmacion of the orders in this Booke, wee the Brethren of the Societie or Companie of Coopers in Kingston upon Hull,

> whose names or marks are hereto subscribed and seales sett, Doe promise to conforme ourselves to and observe the orders of the said Companie.

Then follow 64 names, seals, and marks, apparently under the above date, four under 1693, three under 1694, one under 1696, one under 1697, two 1708, and so on, 173 in all, the last being John Voase, without date, apparently about the middle of the 18th century.

The reader who wishes to gain a thorough insight into these early Trades' Unions has now, in these bodies of rules, a full statement of their constitution. It remains to supplement these by giving an account of the property of the Fraternity, and the ordinary mode of conducting its business.

The most important possession was the hall, which was on the second storey of a building in Hales' Entry (250). It had a lower storey, and also a garret, both of which were let at the annual meetings for a sum varying from 20s. to 15s., and the rent added to the Company's stock. Over the doorway were the arms of the King and Coopers; above was the legend, "Fear God, honor the King, love the brethren," and below were the words, "Richard Hudson, Warden, 1714 (251)."

The hall itself was a considerable source of income, as it was let for meetings to various other trade societies of the town, who do not appear to have had halls of their own. In 1685 we find that "the Shipwrights have a lease from this companie for their meeting place, and to pay xxvs. if Translaters and Weavers disturb them, but if they may enjoy it without disturbance, then to pay xxxs." The "Translaters" were cobblers. Shortly afterwards, the Cordwainers rent it. In 1687 the "Translaters" pay "seaven shillings" for the same. In 1689 the Companie of Weavers have it. In 1692 the Companie of Bricklayers. In 1693 the Translaters again. In 1710 the Bakers, and in 1714 the Companie of Barber Chirurgeons and Perukemakers. Probably these societies had it on different days, in the same way as a modern Friendly Societies' Hall.

(250) Now Whitehorse Yard, adjoining Messrs. Peck & Son's establishment.

(251) Sheahan, p. 657.

In addition to the hall and its appurtenances, the Company possessed apparently five houses in Blanket Row, one, of which the floor door opened upon the walls, having been bequeathed by John Harrison for the dwelling of "two poor widdowes, late wives of some of this companie." The following is an inventory of the plate and other articles of furniture. Among these is a silver tobacco pipe and a silver stopper. The Company evidently had its merry feasts, when the punch bowl was well filled, and the silver tobacco pipe, according to the old custom, was passed from mouth to mouth, in the same manner as the loving cup still goes round. According to Sheahan, "this Gild, as indeed did most of the fraternities, made annual processions, exhibiting their plate." The Book, however, contains no reference to these; possibly they were of earlier date.

21 Octob., 1686 — An account of such plaite and other Goodes as belong to ye Company or ffraternitie of Coopers of Kingston upon Hull.

Imprimis one silver Tankard, ye gift of Samuell Kingdon, Esq., one of the Burgesses of Parliament ffor this towne, weighing 23 ounces and a halfe.

Item one other silver Tankard, ye gift of S. Willoughby Kirkman, Baronett, and John Hampdene, Esq., Burgesses of Parliament for this towne, weighing 23 ounces and a quarter.

Item one silver beaker, the gift of Mr. Christopher ffawthropp, an elder Brother of this Companie, weighing 4 ounces.

Item one other silver beaker, the gift of William ffowler, an Elder Brother of this Companie, weighing 4 ounces.

Item one other silver beaker, the gift of Mr. George Mawson, of this towne, weighing 3 ounces and fower penneweight.

Item one silver tumler, the gift of Mr. John Bowley, of this towne, whose ffather was twice warden of this Companie. Weight of this plaite, 3 ounces wanting a three pennie weight.

Item one silver seale, with the Companies arms Ingraven upon it, bought by the Company.

Item a carpett for the warden and elder brethren's table, the gift of Robert Squire, an elder Brother of this Companie.

Item two peuter fflagons, marked C.F., the guift of Mr. Christopher ffawthropp to the Companie the 19th of October, 1687 [this entry erased].

Item two plaites of Tynn for pipes, the gift of Robert Squire.

Item ffower brasse Candlesticks, weighing eight pound two ounces, two pair of Brasse Snufflers, and pewter Chamber pott, the guift of Daniell Thompson and Wm. Best, Elder Brethren of the said Companie (changed for 6 new ones).

A pair of tongs and fire shovell, two brushes, and a pair of bellowes, the guifft of ffrancis Watson, an elder Brother of ye said Companie. (Gone.)

A silver spoone, the guift of Samuel Watson, an elder Brother of the Companie, weighing one ounce and an eight pennyweight.

A silver spoone, the guift of Thomas Norfolk, an elder brother of the said Company, weighing two ounces wanting a six pennyweight.

Two table clothes for the long table, the guift of Mrs. Alice E. Berisford, sometimes wife of Mr. John Harrison, late a ffree brother of this Companie. (One.)

Itm two dozen of Huggaback napkins, the gift of the said Mrs. Alice Berisford—one napkin lost in Geo. Wilkinson's time. (Gone.)

A large wainscott chair, the gift of William ffewler, an elder Brother and twice warden of this Companie.

A Dozen of huggaback napkins, one towell, and a pewter bason, the gift of the said Mrs. Alice Berisford. (Gone.)

Itm a dozen knives, ye gift of Mrs. Beresford [erased and added "lost," (this in another hand) "or worne away."]

Item Mrs. Berisford gave the companie in Matthew Craven's yeare of being warden *xxs.*, and to Richard Cook in his yeare of being warden, *vs.*, in all *xxvs.*, which by her was intended and suitably disposed in buying a large Bible with annotations, with the harmony of the Gospell by the said Richard Cook, now warden, October, 1696.

Itm a silver tobacco pipe, the gift of Matthew Craven.

A silver stopper, the gift of John Shorte.

A silver tobacco box, given by Mr. Henry Winchester, the 5th of Aprill, 1709, Richard Cook being the second time warden.

Onely now remaining, 20th Oct., 1709, a dozen [the words "a dozen" erased] and ½ of table napkins, two table cloths, a dresser cloth, and a towell.

The Coopers' arms over the hall door, the gift of Mrs. Sapsford, in remembrance of her ffather, Christopher ffawthropp, decd., sometime an elder brother of this Companie.

The Coopers' arms in the hall now painted, the gift of Samuell Thompson, warden of the said Companie.

The Queen's arms now sett on the Coopers' Hall door was the gift of John Short, Junr.

Mem. the setting up of the Queen's Armes and Coopers' Arms, the support and peddiston and Cornich pollishing, painting, and guilding over the Coopers' Hall, was at the Company's own charge and cost, in all £2 11s. 6½d.

Oct., 1729.—Two silver saltes (weighing 2 oz. 18 pennyts), the guift of Mr. Joseph Pease. Wm. Stannage, warden.

1730.—Itm six new brass candlesticks and three p. of new candle snuffers, a peuter chamber pott, and a peuter bason.

8 Oct., 1733.—Itm a silver headed punch ladle, the gift of Ald. Leonard Collings.

Oct., 1739.—A Large Chamber Pot Peuter, bought by the Trade. (Erased.)

Oct., 1755.—A new large Chamber pott, bought by the trade in liew of the old one changed, which cost in exchange 8s. 6d.

Oct., 1756.—A new Turkey Carpet cost £3 5s. 0d.

The entries in the Company's Book are largely taken up with the enrolment and admittance of apprentices. In these appears the old custom of an apprentice being obliged to execute his "masterpiece" of work before being admitted to full membership. In 1701, "Hee hath his certificate upon a iis. stamp."

Some of the later entries shed a curious light upon the life of the time. In 1759 a great discussion took place on a proposition to give half-a-guinea each to the brethren to save them from serving in the militia, and the motion was lost by one vote, but on the same date it was decided to give the half-guinea to seven of the younger brethren. But on March 25th, 1763, it is ordered "That the Warden make a Treat on account of the generall Peace." The entries continue somewhat irregularly till 1788, when William Good was Warden, John Voase, Deputy Warden, Mr. Witty and Mr. Wilkinson, Stewards. And so the Book ends.

Sheahan states that Mr. Voase was the last surviving member, and it is supposed that he transferred the property of the Gild to the Corporation of the town. None of the plate, however, is to be found among the town's collection. Probably it went in the holocaust of ancient silver with which the said Corporation celebrated its reform in 1837.

From the records of the Corporation we learn that the Hall at one period of the last century was used as a schoolroom, and also as a place where one of the Town's Waits taught music. Such, however, was the noise, that objection was lodged by the neighbours. On the 2nd February, 1806, a Trust was declared by Alderman Osbourne upon a conveyance of certain tenements in Hales' Entry and on the walls, belonging to the dissolved fraternity of Coopers, which property was taken from John Witty, the surviving member of the said brotherhood in trust for the Corporation, in consideration of the weekly sum of 10s. 6d. to be paid to John Witty, and Susannah his wife, for their lives and the life of the survivor.

It is a curious fact that the printed rules of the modern Coopers' Trades Society, established in 1853, bear the old Coopers' arms upon the title page.

CHAPTER XXVIII.

THE COMPANY OF BAKERS.

THE Bakers, like the "Berbruers," the Taverners, and other retailers of standard articles of food, were from the earliest times the object of special supervision by the authorities. The assise of bread is the subject of one of the earliest of our statutes after the great Charter. In 51 Henry III., the great assise of bread and ale tried to fix the measures for the kingdom; and in all our local records, as well as in the statutes of the realm, the regulation of the Bakers was a matter of frequent concern. Many were the odd expedients by which these old bakers evaded these ordinances, and cheated the King's lieges.

In 1316 we read of a baker put in the pillory in London, for making "pain demaign" of bad dough within and good without. Ten years later several of the trade were detected having "skilfully and deceitfully made holes in their molding bordes," like mouse traps, through which they put lumps of dough, and thus defrauded the citizens. Their punishment was to stand in the pillory with lumps of dough round their necks ([252]). In 1331 was a large assembly of the citizens, by reason of the "immense loss by the city in times past, incurred through the malignity of bakers withdrawing themselves, and hiding in their mills and elsewhere without the city, so that they cannot be brought to justice, and there placing and assigning their men and servants in their stead to make loaves that are false, as well to the dough as the measure thereof." At the end of the same

(252) Riley, *Mem.*, p. 165.

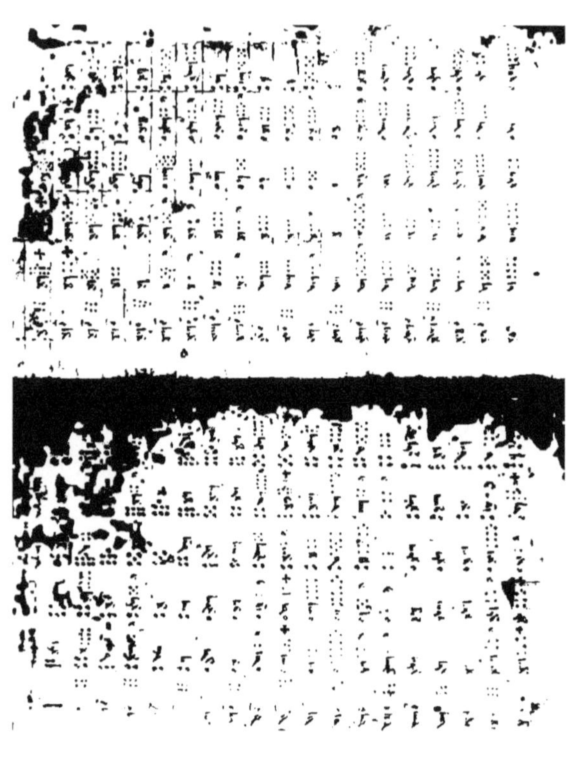

century, Robert Porter was convicted of the clumsy method of putting iron in his loaves, and pilloried with a loaf and piece of iron round his neck ([253]). It is probable that in this persistent tendency to fraud, we have the result in part of the attempt to fix the price in the assise at less than the real value. Nevertheless, the penalties were at times very severe, the cruel punishment of the hurdle being not uncommon. It is curious that so early as 1365, in London, we meet with the same municipal ordinance which occurs in the Hull Compositions of 1598 and 1618. Horse-bread was not to be made by hostelers and herbergeours, but by bakers, "each loaf being stamped with the mark of the baker of whom the same was bought ([254]).

At Easter, in 1483, the Bakers' ordinances fix "two horse loaves to a penny, and of clean beans." But the Assise of Bread, 1468, says, of "al maner of corn," and this seems to have been the general custom. This horse bread was the common artificial food of horses in the Middle Ages. In Elizabeth's time the assise was three loaves a penny, and thirteen pennyworth for 12d.; every one of the three loaves to weigh the full weight of a penny white loaf ([255]). The modern dog biscuit is its nearest equivalent.

The curious Tables in the illustrations are from the ancient Bench Book of the town, and shew the Assise of Bread in accordance with the Act 51 Henry III., 1266-7, which states "when a quarter of wheat is sold for xii*d*., then wastel bread of a farthing shall weigh vi*li*. and xvi*s*." The reader will observe that pounds shillings and pence are used to represent weights. The key to the symbols is as follows: The round mark = a pound, a dot = a penny, a crescent with dot = ½ penny, a cross = a farthing; shillings are written in figures, and a cross in a circle = ten pounds. Hence the significance of the first line of entries is as follows, when price of wheat was 1s. for the quartern.

(253) Riley, *Mem.*, p. 498.

(254) Riley, *Mem.*, p. 328.

255) See *Early English Gilds*, pp. 334 and 366.

The farthing	wastel loaf	was to be		*6lbs.*	*16s.*
,,	white	,,	,,	6	18
½d.	white	,,	,,	13	16
½d.	wheat	,,	,,	20	14
½d.	horseloaf	,,	,,	27	12

So the price of bread did not vary, but it represented a varying weight ([256]).

Universal as was the Bakers' craft, the Gilds were not everywhere so prominent as we might expect. They had too much of the character of public functionaries to be independent in their organisation. The position of the Mayor is evidently in this case more authoritative than in the other ordinances which we have given. Nevertheless, it was here a true society, although limited in its independence.

Two Compositions remain in the Hull archives, dated 1598 and 1618. They are almost exactly similar in context, and that of 1598, which is here given, must serve for the two. The later one, however, is a very fine and neat example of the caligraphy of the period.

A Composicion of Bakers, 1598.

A Composicion indented dated the nenith day of ffebruary in the one forty yeare of the reigne of or sovereigne Lady Elizabeth, By the grace of god Queene of england, fraunce, and Yreland, defender of the faithe, etc., Made betwene the Maior and Burgesses of Kingston upon Hull on th' one party, And John ffox, Thomas Barton, Thomas Ramsdaile, Henry Hubbert, William Jackson, Edward Blythe, William Murton, Matthew Storme, William Johnson, younger, Nicholas Patteson, widowe Arnold, John Hall, William Thompson, and John Dickonson, Bakeres, on th' other party, Witnessethe that the saide Maior and Burgesses for theim and their successores (as moche as in theim is), upon the desire and sute of the saide bakeres, and to the intent that the same traid may the better flourish within the towne of Kingston upon Hull aforesaid, Have geven and graunted theis ordenaunces, grauntes, and clauses hereafter followinge and ensewinge.

1. ffirst that the company of bakeres within the towne of Kingston upon Hull aforesaide shall from henceforth have emongst theim one warden and two searcheres, to be chosen yearly by most voyces emongst theim selves upon the monday sennet after Michaelmas daie, And that two shalbe of eleccion for warden, whereof th' one shalbe chosen, and fower of election for searcheres, whereof twoe

May have one Warden and two Searchers elected yearly.

(256 See *Reliquary*, October, 1890, by R. C. Hope, F.S.A.

shalbe chosen, which warden and searcheres shall yearly the morrow after the saide eleccion daie be sworne upon the holy evangelist of god before the saide Maior or his lieutenannt for the trne and jnst usinge of their places and rowmes for one whole yeare, or to like effect. And if either warden or searcheres dye then other shalbe chosen in their place so dying within viij daies followinge, to serve for the rest of the yeare, and to be likewise sworne. And the saide Maior and Burgesses dotho elect and appoint Edward Blytho for first warden, and Henry Hnbbart and John ffox for first searcheres till the saide eleccion daie, and if any warden chosen or hereafter to be chosen refnse his place, he shall forfaite for soche refnsall xx*s*.

To be sworne the day following.

2. Bond to be taken.

Item that the saide company of Bakeres shall take bond or bonds of the saide warden and searcheres, or of any otheres from time to time, in the name of the said Maior and Bnrgesses for any accompt, debte, damage, or other matter whatsoever, which notwithstanding shalbe for their own behoof and benefitt, and not for the Maior and Bnrgesses.

3. Only freemen admitted.

Item they shall receive no man into their saide company of bakeres, nor woman nnles her hnsband have bene a free burges, and componnd with Mr. Maior and the warden of the company.

4. No inholder, etc., to take bread to sell; penalty, x*s*.

Item that no inholder or alehousekeper or other inhabitant within this towne not free of the saide company of bakeres shall bake any kindo of. bread to sell againe npon paine of x*s*. everie default:

5. Or to serve their guests.

Item that no inholder or alehouskeper within this towne shall bake any kinde of breade for serving their gnestes, or horsebread, npon paine everie defanlt x*s* (*a*).

6. No inhabitant to bake cakes to sell, unless a member.

Item that no inhabitant within this towne not free of their company shall bake any cakes to th' end to sell againe, npon paine of everie time ij*s*.

7. No person from outside the town, except on Market days, and not to sell again.

Item that no persone or persones dwellinge withoute this towne shall sell any breade or cakes within this towne otherwise then on the Tewisdaies and fridaies, marckitt daies, in open marckitt, and that to soche as shall not sell the same againe. And no inhabitant within this towne shall bny any soche to th' end to sell the same againe of any person dwelling without this towne npon paine soche buyer to forfaite for everie time so offending ij*s*.

8. May make ordinances.

Itom that the saide company of bakeres, or the greater nomber, shall from time to time make any manner of orderes for good rule and government to be kept emongst theimselves or otherwise concerning theire

(*a*) See corresponding ordinance in the Inholders Composicion, Chapter XXXI.

traide. So as the same harme not the common wealth of this towne at the Judgement of the Maior and Burgesses if the same come in question. And to sett downe paines and forfaitures for breache of soche orderes.

9. Warden, etc., may distrain for fines.

Item that the said warden and searcheres or their deputy or deputies in their sickness or absence, or any of them, may distroyne the goodes or catteles of any offenderes in the premisses or any parcell thereof, for the fynes, forfaitures, and paiments above sett or to be sett, according to the true meaning of theis presentes. And if any resist theim, or any of theim, then they shalbe ayded by the officer or officeres of the saide Maior, And everie soche officer ayding theim shalbe paied by theim for that canse, iiijd. Inconsideracion of all which premisses the bakeres abovenamed doe graunt to the saide Maior and Burgesses that they will serve the towne well with all kind of bread, and kepe th' assize, and that the halfe of all paines, forfaitures, and seizures above lymmited, shalbe payed by the saide company unto the Maior and Burgesses at the towne's auditt yearly, and further xs. yearly for this their camposicion. And that they will not take any apprentices without the consent of the Maior for the time being, and the greater nomber of the aldermen his bretheren, but soch as are borne or remaining within this towne, and that by theire like consent, if their be any soche sufficient to servo their turnes. And that the warden and searcheres shall once everie weke repaire and come to the Maior for the time beinge, to take their assize to sell by, and that all the saide company will deliver forthe their breade from time to time xiijten to the dozen to the poore women, and other of this towne to retaile the same again.

Bakers promise they will serve the town well, with all kinds of bread, and keep the Assise.

Pay 10s. yearly.

Warden and Searchers to come weekly to the Mayor, to take their Assise to sell by.

And deliver to poor women 13 to the dozen to retail again.

In witnes wheroof unto th' one parte of this composicion indented, remaining in the custody of the said bakeres, The saide Maior and Burgesses have sette their common Seale, and unto th' other parte thereof, remaining in the custody of the saide Maior and Burgesses, The bakeres above named have sette their handes and seales, the day and yeare ffirst above written, And in the yeare of our Lorde, according to the computacion of Englande, one thousande five hundred nenity and eight.

Edward Blyth.	Wiliam marston.
Henrye Hubbert.	Willm Thompson.
Thomas Ramsdale.	Mathew Storme.
Thomos Barton.	Widow alnold.

John Hall. John foxe.
Nichols Patteson. Wm. Johnson.

[*Endorsed*]

Md. that at the time of the sealing of theis presentes, the Bakeres whoe sealed theis presentes, did promise the Maior and Aldermen that the Maior for the time being, and the greater nomber of the aldermen his bretheren, shall at their discrecion appoint more Bakeres from time to time, Any thing within conteyned notwithstanding, And also theis presentes new sealed and delivered.

Sealed, subscribed, and delivered in the presence of us, viz.,

John Coupland.
Henry Fullwad.

[Bakers' Composicon, 1598].

CHAPTER XXIX.

THE BROTHERHOOD OF COBLERS.

THE estate of the Coblers seems to have been the lowest in the scale of the craftsmen of Hull in the reign of King James. In the first of their Compositions of 1622 they stand alone as having no right of free election of Warden or Searchers. The Mayor of the town yearly was to name and appoint one of the most discreet of the said Company to be Warden, and two to be Stewards or Searchers. The fines which were levied went one half to the Mayor and the other half to the informant, a custom of which we have no other example in Hull. In the ordinances of 1622 we find no mention of apprentices, though it is possible they existed(257); but the rule relating to cordwainers who took up the trade of a cobler, and had to cease cordwainery, seems rather to point to the fact that coblers were chiefly recruited from the less successful of the higher class. In 1680 the ordinances shew that apprentices were taken in cobling as in other branches of the trade.

The struggle of coblers for existence was of old standing. As early as 1395 the King issued a decree in response to a piteous complaint from "Cobelers from beyond sea, that they could not gain their living as they had gained it beforetime by reason of the disturbance by the Wardens of the Cordwainers." This was in London, and the King's decree was that the "cobelers" should be allowed to gain a living. The Mayor therefore after due consideration proceeded to take the following very practical course. He called together twenty-four men from

(257) Mr. Wildridge informs me that in 1769 Robert Gale, of Kingston-upon-Hull, took an apprentice in the "Art, Trade, or Mistery of a Heelmaker."

the whole trade, twelve to be new workers (or cordwainers), and twelve to be old workers (or "cobelers"), and of the latter six were to be aliens and six English. With these as assessors, he then ordained that making things of new leather is to appertain to new workers, and of old to old workers, "excepting in mending old boots and shoes, that is to say, in quareling before and behind, cloutling and pecyng and ryvetting and lyning, in doing which they may take new leather or old." The overseers, or Searchers, were to be cordwainers. Thus the King's decree was satisfied ([258]).

On the 29th Jan., 1622, the first of the extant ordinances was granted, it being ordained in the 10th article that "this graunt shall have continuance and stand in force forever." On the 19th Dec., however, in the same year, appears another Composition somewhat more precise, but not differing materially from its predecessor. The ordinances continued in force till 1680, doubtless with due renewal from time to time, and in the latter year another Composition was granted which remains. It is almost exactly similar to the later one of 1622. Those articles which are of additional interest, are given here after the first composition. The effect of them was to safeguard more effectually the work of the craft from the intrusion of cordwainers and shoemakers, and to regulate the taking of apprentices.

> To all xtian people to whome this present Indenture of composicon shall Come. The Maior and Burgesses of the towne or borough of Kingston uppon Hull sendes greetinge. Knowe ye that the said Maior and Burgesses, uppon the peticon of the Coblers, inhabitantes of this towne, And for the common good of them and others that shall succeed them of that trade, Have by vertue of the Charters and Letters Patentes to us graunted from the Kings's Majestie that nowe is, and his progenitours, Agreed, ordered, established, and sett downe, That these Articles and orders hereafter mencioned shalbe held, kept, observed, and performed by the Coblers within this towne, and others whome they shall concerne as followeth.
>
> 1. Inpremis it is ordered, established, and agreed that the Maior of Kingston uppon Hull for the time beinge, shall yearlie or otherwise, name and appoint one of the

Mayor yearlie to appoint one of the Company to be War-

(258) Riley, *Mem.*, 540.

den, and two to be Stewards or Searchers. most Discreete of the said Companie to be warden, and two to be stewardes or searchers, which warden, with the assistants of the said stewards, shall have the Government of the said Companie, And to see to the performance of these orders and Levyinge of forfeictures for breache of anie of them, and to Doo and execute suche necessarie Duties as belonges to their offices, for the weale and good of the said trade.

2. No showmaker to exercise the trade of a cobeler.

Item that noe showmaker, or other person or persons, shall use or exercise the trade of a Cobler for mendinge of shoes within this towne, But such as nowe are or hereafter shalbe admitted there unto, by the Consent of the Maior of Kingston uppon Hull and the greater parte of the Alderman for the time beinge, uppon paine of everie one doeinge to the Contrarie, to forfeict for everie offence the Somme of iij*s* iiij*d*., to be levied and converted as followeth.

3. A showmaker may become a cobler, but must use that trade of coblinge onely.

Item that anie that is a free man of this towne, being a showmaker, and leaveinge of his said trade of showmakinge, may have libertie to use the trade of a cobler, observinge their orders soe longe as he useth that trade of Coblinge onelie and noe longer, uppon penaltie aforesaid.

4. No cobler to amend shoes or bootes with bad stuffe, or at unreasonable rate, or keep them longer than two daies.

Item that if anie Cobler shall hereafter amend anie shoes or bootes insufficiently, or with bad stuffe, or at anie unreasonable rate, or shall keepe anie worke brought to him anie longer than Two Daies, withoute consent of the owner thereof, That then everie one offendinge in in anie of these pointes, shall forfeit for everie offence the Somme of two shillinges and sixepence.

5. No stranger to be sett on worke unless allowed by the Mayor.

Item that noe Cobler shall sett anie strainger or other on worke within this Towne of that trade, But such as shalbe firste allowed of by Mr. Maior for the time beinge, in paine to forfeict for everie offence for everie Daie, twelve pence.

6. No cobler to use the trade of a showmaker.

Item that none of that trade of Cobblers shall for or within the time that he useth that trade, use or exercise the trade of a showmaker or showmakinge, uppon paine to forfeict for everie offence, two shillinges and sixepence.

7. Noe cobler to abuse another on pain of 6d.

Item that noe Cobler of the said Companie shall abuse one another by evill or rayllinge wordes, upon paine of forfeicting sixepence.

8. Fines to go half to the Mayor and half to the informant.

Item it is further ordered and agreed by the consent aforesaid, that all forfeictures, which shall growe Dewe by force of these orders, shalbe Converted, and be the one half thereof to the Maior and Burgesses of Kingston-uppon-Hull and their successours, And the other half to such person and persons as shall first present and give notice thereof to the Maior of Kingston uppon Hull for the time being, And that all and everie the said forfeictures shall be levied or taken by such of the said Coblers or others, as shall have orders soe to Doe by the Maior of Kingston uppon Hull for the time beinge, by way of Distresse of the goodes and Chattells of everie offender, which shalbe Deteyned and kept till the forfeictures be satisfied and paid.

9. But a showmaker or cordiner may soale new boots with their own leather.

Provided alwaies that it shalbe lawfull for anie show-makers or Cordiners useinge that trade onelie to soale anie shoes or Bootes, as also to underlay anie shoes or bootes by them made newe with their owne Leather, and not with other, withoute anie forfeicture aforesaid.

10. This graunt to have continuance and stand in force forever.

And that this graunt shall have continuance and stand in force forever. In witness whereof to the one parte of these present Indentures remayninge with the said Companie of Coblers The said Maior and Burgesses have affixed their Common Seale, And to the other parte of these Indentures remayninge with the said Maior and Burgesses The Coblers now beinge have herounto sett their handes and seales, the Daie and yeare after written, That is to saie, the neine and twentie day of Jannarie in the one and twentith yeare of the Reigne of our sovereigne Lord James, by the grace of god Kinge of England, ffrance, and Ireland, Defender of the ffaith, etc., and of Scotland the lvijth, 1622.

Robeart pylland.	Xpofer Peto.
Mathew Gurden.	Bire. Bloud.
John Pattison.	Richerd Kitching.
Edward Bonieosse [?]	William Wright.
James Leckonbie.	

[The seales are curiously grouped upon the slit strips of a central parchment attachment.]

[No endorsement.]

Additional Articles in the Composition of 1680.

And that it shall not be lawfull for any Shoemaker or Cordwainer using that trade onely to amend any shooes or bootes for any person whatsoever, but only for their owne family, under the penaltie of forfeiting for every offence the summe of three shillings and four pence.

And further it is statuted, ordered, and agreed upon that no free brother of the same trade shall take or entertaine a Second Apprentice untill the first Apprentice hath served as an Apprentice for the space of ffour yeares, under the penalty of forfeiting thirty shilling, to be levied, taken, received, and divided as aforesaid, and their Apprentices to be enrolled within twelve moneths after the date of their Indentures, in the Towne's booke prepared for that end, upon the penalty of five shillinges for everie offence. And that this Graut shall have continnance and stand in force during the pleasure of the Conrt of Major and Aldermen.

Signatures to the Coblers' Ordinance of 1680:—

Thomas Willson.	John Proctor.	Robert Robson.
John Tripp.	George Watson.	John Ellers.
Walker Procter.	Samllus Tiplin.	

[*Endorsed*]

Sealed and delivered in the presence of

George Shaw.
Tho. Snawsdell.
Char. Vaux.
Benjamin Graves.

Counterpart of the Indenture, etc., 1680.

[The seals, some of which are the same as used for other Compositions a century earlier, are covered with paper.]

Chapter XXX.

The Fraternity of Cordwainers and Shoemakers.

CORDWAINERS were originally workers in Spanish or Cordovan leather, generally tanned and dressed goat skins or split horse hides, and the craft was one of the most common in all our ancient cities. The craft in Hull was evidently an influential one, and three of the Compositions remain in the Town Hall, one for 1564 and others for 1606 and 1624. The one for 1606 contains rules too similar to the earlier document to need repetition. Those for 1564 and 1624 are distinct, and are given in full.

In the earlier one the regulations as to inspection of leather and the technical details of the trade are interesting, and shew the care of the old workers in leather. Approved goods were stamped with a mark, just as was a ship when it had passed the shipwrights' search. The later Composition is remarkable for its very stringent, and, as we should say, inequitable provisions against external labour. It seems to mark a strong attempt to limit the benefits of the trade to a close circle of the Gild.

Cordwainers' and Shoemakers' Composition, 1564.

To all trewe xpian people to whom those presentes shall come, John Smithe, maior of kingston npon hull, and the burgesses of the same towne Sendes greatinge in our lord god everlastinge.

I. *To be one Company or feloweshippe.* Knowe ye that th' afforesaide maior and burgesses of one assent and consent, for dyvers good and holsome cawses and consyderacions at this present them specyallie movinge: and for th' advancement and settinge forwarde of the publick wellbe within ye town and countie of kingston upon hull afforesaid, and in all other playces nere adyoning the same, at the humble petycon, praier, and request of men of th' occupacion or mysterie of cordwayners inhabytinge within the same towne of kingston upon hull, That ys to saie of John Hewytt, William Maugham, John Veroo, George Anderson, Robert Isaac, John todde, Robert barnabye, William Corke, William Pellam, Richard duffell, William tomposon, henrye Smithe, Alexander hewytt, Robert pattison, and Richerd Roger have covenaunted, concluded, graunted, and by these presentes confirmed unto th' afforesaid occupacion or mysterie of cordwayners inhibitinge and dwellinge within ye sayd towne of kingston upon hull and there successores from hencefurthe for ever, to be a companye or feloweshippe of themselves, and yat hereafter no alien straunger beinge of the same occupacion shall woorke within ye said towne of kingston upon hull without agrement and lycence of ye same feloweshippe upon peyne to forfeyt for every weak yt he settithe uppe and workithe for himselfe iij*s*. iiij*d*., to be levied of his goodes and cattalls ffrom tyme to time, th'one moytie thereof to be to th' use of the same maior and burgesses and there successours, th' other moitie to be to th' use of the said felowshipp or company of cordwayners and their successors, And yf the same alien strainger or straingers be Sett on woorke by any other person or persons inhibitinge within the same towne: then the same penaltie of iii*s*. iiij*d*. for everie weake to be levyed upon his or there goodes or cattalls so Settinge ye same strainger on woork, unto th' uses above wryten.

And no one to woorke at the occupation unless approved, on pain of 3s. 4d. weekly.

2\. Item yt is graunted and by these presentes ordeyned and concludyd by the same maior and burgesses yat the same feloweshippe and companye of cordwayners and there successours for ye tyme beinge yerelie and every yere at the feaste of Easter or within xv daies after, may and shall have a free election emongst them selves, and in the same election shall nominate, elect, and choose one sobre and dyscrete man to be there wardein, one stewarde, and two searchers of the same occupacion and misterie of cordwayners, which said wardein, together with the stewarde and Searchers, within eight daies after there election, shall yerelie be sworne before Mr. Maior for ye tyme beinge to execute and doe there deweties and offyces trewlie in all thinges, as to men havinge such offyces in ye said occupacion or misterye apperteanithe.

To elect at Easter one sobre and discrete man to be Warden, one Stewarde, and two Searchers.

To be sworn.

3\. Item that from tyme to tyme the said searchers elected and sworne as before shall diligentlie and trewlie viewe and searche all kinde of tanned letther brought to the markytt of the said towne, and yf the same searchers finde the same lether well and sufficientlie tanned in all pointes as yt owght to be, and throwghlie dryed accordinge to the statute thereof provyded, That then they marke and seale yt with there stamp and seale accustomed for

Searchers diligentlie and trewlie to view and search all kind of tanned leather.

And to marke and seale it with there stamp and seal.

yat purpose, and suche as thei finde defectyve and not sufficientlie tanned and dryed, or solde before ye same be searched and sealed trewelye and uprightlie, thereof to make seisor and presentment to Mr. Maior and other ye quene's majestie Justices of peace for ye tyme beinge, without color, favor, or affection of any person or persons, the forfeytours whereof to be imploied accordinge to the statute thereof provyded and ordeyned by acte of parliament, And yf the same searchers fynde any oxe hyde, stere hyde, or cow hyde sold, exchaunged, or profferred to be sold or exchaunged, or otherwayse departed with, but onlie whole, without cuttinge any bellies, called wombes, or other peaces from yt (slowtinge letther to be cutt into three or fower bendes or peaces, overwhert th' ole hide onlye excepted) before the same be searched and sealed to make seysor and presentment thereof as before, And lykewise to sease and present all horse hides, bull hides, and shepe skynnes as they shall fynde tanned and putt to saile, yat th' offendors therein may be orderid accordinge to ye tenour of ye same estatute.

4\. A curriour curryinge any lether in the house of a shomaker, and not in his owne howse, scytuate in a corporate or market towne.

Item that the same searchers shall diligentlie and trewlie search whither ye curriours or any of them shall currie any lether in the howse of any shomaker or other person, but onlie in his owne howse scytuate in a corporate or markit towne, and whether same curriours or any of them doe currie any lether, but suche as before ys well and perfytlye tanned, and woorke and currie the same perfitelie, sufficientlie, and substancyallie in all pointes and respectes, according to the statutes thereof provyded, and such as thei shall fynde defectyve or offendinge contrarie to the premyses trewelie to present yat thei may be ordered accordingelie, and such lether as thei finde well, perfytelie, and substancyallie in all poyntes and degrees curried, to seale with a marke and seale therefore ordeyned.

5\. A currier refusing to currie for an artificer within a reasonable time.

Item the same searcheres shall dyligentlie and trewlie searche whither any courriour refuse to currie any lether to him or them for yat purpose brought by any artyficer beinge a cutter of lether, or doe not currie the same with as convenient spede as maie be not excedinge fyve daies in sommer and tenne daies in winter, after yat he shall or may take in hande and present th' offendors therein to Mr. Maiour for the tyme beinge.

6\. To search all bowtes, shoes, buskynes, startuppes, slippers, and pantoffles.

Item the same searchers shall well and dyligentlie searche and trie all bowtes, shoes, buskynnes, startuppes, slippers, and pantofles, maide by any Cordwayner or Shomaker, whether yat they be maide of any lether but of lether well and trewlie tanned and curried, or of lether well and trewlie tanned onlie, and well and substancyallie sowyd with good threde, well twysted and maide and sufficientlie waxte with waxe well ltosened, and the stitches harde drawen with hande lethers, without minglinge or mixinge of overlethers, yt ys to saie parte of the overlether of neates lether and parte of calves lether, and whither any cordwayner putt into any parte of any shoes, bowtes, buskynnes, startuppes, slippers, or pantoffles, or into ye nether parte of any bowtes (th'inner sole and th' ele of ye shoe onlie excepted) any parte of any hide from whiche ye sole lether ys cutt, called the wombe, necke, shanke, flanke, poll, or cheke, nor shall putt into ye utter sole any other lether then ye best of ye oxe or stere hide, nor into the inner sole any other then ye wombes, necke, polle, or cheke, nor into ye treswells of ye doble solde shoes, other then ye flankes of any of the hides afforesaid, And also shall well and trewlie searche all other thinges perteaninge to the same occupacion or misterie of cordwayners. And yf any defawlt be lawfullie fownde to make presentment in manner and forme as ys above recyted and declared, and ye forfeitures yereof to be ordered accordinge to the statute.

7. Searchers to viewe and search all leather waire, to seise all bad work, which is to be tried by the oath of six expert men, within 15 days.

Item yt ys also ordeyned and establyshed by the same maior and burgesses that the said searchers shall ffrom tyme to tyme make trewe searche and veiwe of all the kinde of waire and stuffe and other thinges whatsoever maide of tanned lether in all and every howse and howeses, plaice and plaices within ye precinct and liberties of this towne, and after every suche serche and veiwe had to sease as forfeyted all such thinges, waire, and stuffe, as shalbe maide of lether contrarye to the trewe meaning of th' estatutes of this Realme, and to Reteyne the same in there custodye untill ye same be tried by the othe of vj expert men appointed by ye said maior for ye tyme beinge, the same tryall to be within xv daies after such seysor.

8. One Searcher to keep the seales for sufficient leather.

Item yt ys ordeyned and establysshed by the same maior and burgesses, yt one of the same searchers shall have the custodye of the Seales or markes, ordeyned to seale suffycient lether, and with ye same seales or markes shall seale all suche lether as shalbe in all respectes good and suffycient and none other, upon peyne to forfeyt for every tyme yt they refuse or doe ye contrarye to ye use of ye said townes chaimber, vl*s*.

9. Any person obstructing the Searchers to forfeit £6.

Item yt is ordeined and establisshed by ye said maior and burgesses yt yf any person doe wilfullie withstande or deny any suche serche to be had, or will not suffer ye same searchers appointed and sworne to enter into his or there howse or howesys, or other plaice, to veiwe and serche at there will and pleasour, all manuer of tanned lether, and all manner of bowtes, shoes, males, saddells, and all manner of waires maide and wrought of lether, and to sease and carry awaie all suche lether, shoes, and waires, as thei finde insufficientlie tanned, curryed, and wrought, or maide of ill stuffe, That every such person so denyinge and withstandinge shall lose and forfeyte for every tyme yt he doithe so denie and withstande, v*li.*, th' one moytie whereof to be levyed to th' use of ye townes chamber, and th' other moytie thereof to th use of ye said occupacion.

10. Searchers to diligently do their duties; fine, 6s. 8d.

Item yt ys ordeyned and establysshed by ye said maior and burgesses yat the said searchers and eyther of them shall dyligentlie, trewlie, and faithfullie doe and execute there deweties and offyces in and by all thinges thereto apperteaninge and appointed by ye lawes of thys Realme, upon peyne to forfeyte for every defawlte, vj*s.* viij*d.*, to be levyed to th' usys afforesaid.

11. Searchers to keep a book, and enter particulars of all bargains in leather.

Item it is ordeined and concludyd yat the same searchers and sealer shall kepe one Register or booke wherein (beinge Required) by ye bier or Seller, thei shall enter all suche bergaynes as shalbe maide for lether, hides, or skynnes, duringe the tyme of the markytt, and ye prices also of suche lether bought and solde, and ye names and dwellinge plaices of ye bier and Seller, takinge for hys or their paynes for ye sealinge of suche lether, cuttinge of the wombes, and for regystrainge thereof of the Seller of every dycker of lether, ij*d.*, and so after ye Rayte, and for every vj doossen calves skynnes, ij*d.*, and of ye byer after ye same raite, upon payne to forfeite for not entringe for every dycker of lether, iij*s.* iiij*d.*, and for every dozen of calves skynnes, ii*s.* iiij*d.*, and so after ye Raite, to be levyed to the uses afforesaid, And the seller to forfeyt the valewe of the lether so solde and not registered, and also ye byer to forfeyte the same lether or ye valewe thereof, bowte and not searched, and sealed or carryed awaie and not registred, all whiche forfeytours shalbe levyed to the uses afforesaid.

12. Wombes to be cut off before hides are curried.

Item yt ys ordeyned, establysshed, and concluded by the said maiour and burgesses yat no cordwayner, shomaker, or cobler, shall carry or cawse to be carryed any oxe or stere hides (whereof any sole lether shalbe cutte of) owte of ye markyt whole before ye wombes be cutt of, upon peyne to forfeyt for every hide in suche sort carryed owte of ye markytt, vj*s.* viij*d.*, and ye hide or ye valewe thereof to be levied to the us' afforesaid.

13. Every brother to be

Item yt ys ordeyned, concluded, and fullie agread by the same maior and burgesses yat the every brother of

confirmable and agreable to the ordinances

feloweshippe or companie, shall be so confirmable and agreable and with th' orders of yat occupacion, upon peyne of forfeitour for the first tyme, vj*d.*, for ye second tyme, xij*d.*, and for ye third tyme, iiis. iiijd., and so fowrthe for every default in obstynacye, iij*s.* iiij*d.*, to th' uses afforesaid, to be levyed upon his goodes or cattalls so founde defectyve.

14\.
No person to sett uppe unto suche tyme as he shall have settled with the Mayor and Warden.

Item yt ys ordeined and graunted by ye sam maiour and burgesses yat no person or persons of that occupacion or mysterye shall Sett uppe or open any shoppe to th' intent to occupie ye same within ye said towne, unto suche tyme as he or they have agreyd with Mr. Maiour and ye wardein of the said occupacion, felowshippe, or companye for ye tyme beinge, in payne to paie vi*s.* viij*d.* for everie weake yat he or they shall so use ye same, to be unto th' uses afforesaid, And that every strainger being dysposed to Sett uppe Shoppe and occupie the said occupacion within ye said towne, shall paye for hys upsett, xxvj*s.* viij*d.*, viz., xiij*s.* iiij*d.* to the said maiour and burgesses to th' use of there townes chamber, and th' other xiij*s.* iiij*d.* to th' use of the sayd occupacion.

Every stranger to pay 26s. 8d.

And also yat every man servinge in this towne vij yeres as an apprentice with a free burgesse of this towne, being dysposed to Sett uppe shoppe, shall pay for his Upsett, vi*s.* viij*d.* unto th' uses afforesaid.

An apprentice to pay 6s. 8d. on setting up.

15\.
No shop windows to be opened on Sabbaothe daies, on pain of 8d.

Item it is ordained and agreed by Mr. Maior and ye burgesses afforesaid and ye said feloweshippe, yt no shoppe wyndowes of yat occupacion shalbe opened upon the "Sun-" [crossed through] Sabbaothe daies, in payne of every default, viij*d.*, and yat no person or persons of yat feloweshippe shall by any meanes allure, persuade, nor entyse the servaunt or servauntes of other men ffrom his or there service, unto suche tyme as they and every of them have fullye and trulye accomplysshed there services and former promises made accordinge to the lawes of this Realme, on peyne of every default proved, iij*s.* iiijd. unto th' usys afforesaid.

No servant to be allured from his work.

16\.
Not to dight or dress any searchable leather into the country, until seen by searchers.

Item yt ys ordeyned, concluded, and fullie agreyd by the same maior and burgesses, yat no curryer inhibiting or dwellinge within ye same towne shall dight or dresse any kinde of searchable lether unto the countrey, but suche tymes as the searchers of ye same occupacion or mysterie of cordwayners have had intelligence and knowledge of the same, to th' intent they may perfytelye knowe whither the same be able stuffe and sufficientlye dressed and curryed or no, upon peine of every default, iij*s.* iiij*d.*, to be levyed of the goodes and cattalls of the same curryours so offendinge, to be to ye usys above mencyoned.

17. No cordwainer to be a tanner or currier, and *sic versâ*.

Item the said feloweshipp or companye of cordwayners for them and there snccessonrs, doe covenaunte, promysse, and grannte to and with the same maior and hurgesses yat none of yat feloweshippe shall occnpie ye crafte or misterye of a tanner or curryer, nor permytt or suffer any tanner or curryour to use or occupie ye mysterye of a cordwainer, or any other artyficer usinge cnttinge of lether npon peyne of pnnishment and of suche losse and forfeite as hy the lawes of this Realme Therefore be ordeyned and provyded.

18. Company to pay 20s. yearly to the town.

ffor the havinge, injoinge, and nsinge of all and singnler the premysses above named and declared, the said John hewytt and others, th' abovenamed cordwayners, for them and there successoure, doe covenaunte, promysse, and graunte hy these presentes to and withe the same maior and burgesses and there successours at all tyme and tymes reqnieyte, havinge th' aide and th' assistance of Mr. Maior for the tyme beinge and hys brethren th aldermen, that the same feloweshippe or companye of cordwayners and there successonrs, shall well and trewlie paie or cawse to be paied yerelie and hy yere unto the same maior and hnrgesses and there snccessours, nnto the use of their Chamber, xxs. of good and lawfnll englishe money, at Whit sondaie and martynmas by even porcions. Provided alwaies yt yf there fortune any contencion, controversie, debayte, or stryfe to arryse emongest the feloweshipp or company afforesaide, which can not be ended emongst them selves, that then they and every of them to be persuaded, Rewled, and ordered by the dyscretion of Mr. Maior and his brethren th' aldermen, not onelie in these matters of controversie, debate, and strife, but also in all and singular other thinge and thinges conserninge or in any wyse touchinge ye premysses or any artycle thereof, and therewithe be contented and pleased in such sorte, manner, and form as though this composicion and wrytinge indented had not been mayde nor graunted. Provided also yt the said companye of feloweshippe of cordwayners and there successours, shall yerelye and hy yere at the ffeastes afforesaid, content and paie to the said maior and burgesses and there successours, all such forfeytures and somes of money as shalbe then dewe to ye same maior and hurgesses for upsettes, or any other cawse or matter above specyfied and declayred.

Any dispute to be settled by the Mayor.

All due fines to be paid to the Mayor.

In witnes whereof to th' one partye of this wrytinge indented, remayninge with the said feloweshippe and company of cordwainers, the said maior and burgesses have putto there seale of the said towne of Kingston npon Hnll, and to the partyo remayninge with the said maior and burgesses, the said John hewot and others, th' abovenamed cordwainers for them and thero successours, have pntto their seales the ixth daie of marke, in ye Sixt yere of tho Reigne of owor Sovereigne Ladye Elizabeth, yo grace of god, of england, ffrance, and Ireland, queno defendor of the ffaitho, etc.

Willm maughm.	Willm thompson.
Rbert Bornbye.	Henry Smith.
John Vero.	Willm Cortt.
George Anderson.	Richard Roger.
Robert Isaac.	William Pyllm.
Alisander hewit.	Ric. Dnffeild.
John Todd.	Robt. Pathyson.

[*Endorsed*]

Connterpart of Composicion of Cordwyners, vj° 2 Eliz.
Shoemakers' Composicion, vj° 2 Eliz.
Tho Shomakers' Composicion.

CORDWAINERS' COMPOSITION, 1624.

A Writing Indented dated the 20 day of May, and in the yeare of the reigne of our Sovereigne Lord James, by the grace of God of England, Scotland, ffranco, and Yreland, Kingo, defender of the faith, etc., vizt., of England, ffrannce, and Yreland tho xvij, and of Scotland the lvijth, Made betweeno the Mayor and Burgesses of Kingston npon Hull on th' ono parte; and Edward Waller, now warden, Myles Todd, Robert Peckett, William Clarke, Peter Turner, Henrie Etherington, Richard Stringer, Robert Stevenson, John Ombler, Launcelott Jegger, Hngh Wilson, George Blaydes, Edward Burden, John Skarth, John Kitching, George Peckett, Christopher Etherington, Thomas Ingleduo, William Jogger, and Robert Basforth, Cordwaynores, on th' other partie, Witnesseth that the said Mayor and Burgesses for them and their successors (as mnch as in them is) upon the desire and sute of the said Cordwayners, and to the intent that the same trayde may the better flourish within the town of Kingston npon Hnll aforesaid: Havo gyven and graunted these ordinances, articles, and clauses hereafter following and ensewing.

1\. First that none of this traydo or followshipp of Cordwayneres within Kingstone upon Hull, shall sett on worke anio Journeyman, straunger, or hyrod servant, that hath Wife, childe, or children, of his or theire knowledge from and after the daio of the date hereof, npon payne of everie ono so offending herein, to forfaite and loso his freedome, and be quite disfranchessed therof.

That none of the trade sett on worke any man that hath wife, childe, or children, on pain of forfeiting his freedom, & being disfranchised.

2\. Item it is likewise ordored and agreed by the said Mayor and Burgesses, that if anie of this fraternitie or brotherhoodo of Cordwayneres that now havo or hereafter shall have anie Journeymen or hyred men, which is single and

Any brother suspecting any journeyman of getting married, to report to the Mayor, and discharge him

forthwith on paine as aforesaid.

unmaryed, and doe perceyve in them anie signes of contract or marriage with anie woman Within this towne or Without this towne, That then everie Master of such servant shall gyve notice thereof to the Mayor (for the tyme being), and withall discharge him of his service, upon payne to lose his freedome as aforesaid, and no brother of that companie to sett him on worke, upon the like payne.

3\. No brother to engage a journeyman for more than two years on pain of disfranchisement.

Item it is likewise ordered that if anie brother of this fellowshipp shall sett on worke anie straunger, Journeyman, or hyred servant for more tyme then two yeares from and after the date hereof, shall forfaite to the Towne his freedome, and quite be disfranchessed thereof,

And a journeyman departing within two years not to be entertained or given work.

And if in case anie such Journeyman or hyred servant doe depart from theire said master within the tearme of two yeares aforesaid, by reason of anie cause, collour, controversie, or otherwise; then no brother of the said Companie shall intertayne him, or gyve him anie Worke at all, upon the like payne.

4\. Every journeyman within ten days of their intertaynement to have his name enrolled in the White Book, and pay 4d., on pain of 10s.

Item it is further ordered that everie m^r^ of such Journeymen or hyred servantes within tenne dayes after theire intertaynement, shall present theire names to the warden (for the tyme being), and therewithall cause theire names to be regestered in theire white booke or booke of recorde, with the day and yeare accordingly, to the ende they may the better remember how long they have served, and how long they have to serve, for the avoyding the daunger abovesaid; and therewithal shall pay for his regestering, iiij*d*., upon payne to forfaite for everie tyme so offending herein, tenne shillinges.

5\. No brother to take any boy or child for his second apprentice, but such as are born and remayning in the town, and to receive 20s. from the town.

Item it is further agreed by the same Mayor and Burgesses, that no brother of this Companie from and after the date hereof, shall take any boy or childe for his second apprentice; Otherwise then such as are born and remayning within this towne (If there be anie such to serve theire turnes), and with him to receyve from the towne the summe of xx*s*. lawfull English money, upon paine to lose his freedome.

Item it is likewise ordered that no brother of this Companie from henceforth, shall take anie apprentice for lesse tyme then that at the ende of his tearme he shall be complett and full the age of 21 yeares, according to the statute provyded therein.

Lastly it is ordred and agreed that the warden and Searcheres (for the time being) shall have full power and authoritie to distrayne the goodes and chattels of anie offender touching the breach of anie such articles as is mentioned and expressed in theire Composition and booke of orderes, And if anie resist them, then shall they be ayded by the officer or officeres of the said Mayor;

and everie such officer ayding them shall be payed by them for that cause, iiij*d*.

In witness whereof unto th' one part of this present writing indented, remayning in the Custodie of the said Cordwayneres, The said Mayor and Burgesses have sett to theire common seale, And to th' other part thereof remayning in the custodie of the said Mayor and Burgesses, the Cordwayneres above named have sett to theire handes and seales, The day and yeare first above written, And in the yeare of our Lorde God, according to the computation of England, 1624.

Edward Walker, Warden.	John Omblers.
W. Clarke.	George Blaydes.
Peter Turner.	Edward burden.
Henry Eatherinton.	Christopher Etherington
Richard Stringer.	Robert Basforth.

[*Endorsed*]

Sealed and delyvered in the presence of [blank].
[Counterpart of Cordwainers' Composicion, 1624].

CHAPTER XXXI.

THE COMPANY OF INNHOLDERS.

NOWHERE does the ancient system of trade organisation, as shewn in the Hull records, shine out to better advantage than in the ordinances of the Innholders. The monopolizing tendencies which acted with injustice or injury in the case of other crafts are here seen at their best. Their trade was ever considered one specially of public concern, "for the better safeguard of the King's Majesty's liege people repairing to the town," and remains one under public control until the present day. M. Jasseraud has shewn in his entertaining work that alongside the guest houses of the monks, which catered especially for the extremes of rich and poor, there were in the 14th century wayside inns on all the great highways of the country to supply the traveller's needs (259). The Act, 23 Edward III., compelled "hostelers and herbergers" to sell their food at reasonable prices; and when the social life of the people is revealed to us in the national literature no character is more remarkable than "mine host."

The following Composition shews the innholders, dames, mistresses, and hostlers of Kingston-upon-Hull, banded together under the eye of the Mayor for the due performance of their duties, and the safeguarding of their legitimate interests. It was not simply the interests of the trade, but the due filling of an honorable position in the life of the town which governed their conduct. Over the fraternity sat one Master and Warden, "honest, skilful, and discreet," ruling as well as governing, and assisted by two Searchers, substantial burgesses as himself.

259) *English Wayfaring Life*, pp. 126-129.

On entering into office the one gave bond for £50, the others of £40, for the due performance of their duties. When the fraternity met at the "prime guild," at the old sign of the "White Horse," when the plate was brought out of the three-locked chest, and the clerk sat at the table with the books of the Gild—all sworn men to do loyally and honorably, and keep the secrets of the fraternity—there was something more than the spirit of a trade protection society to animate their doings. None had repaired to tavern or tippling house on Sunday or holiday during time of divine service; none said to another "Thou lyest" or "Art false;" all behaved themselves comely and decently, and kept silence at the Warden's word—at least if they did otherwise there was 3s. 4d. or 6s. 8d., which might be distrained for or claimed at the Court of Record in Hull, or in those of Westminster, with no chance of escape or diminution.

The rules give us an idea of a standard of comfort and utility for which we look in vain in our own day. Wherever the traveller saw the "hinging sign," which every member must shew at his door, he knew there were at least "four comely and decent guest bedds," one of which he might claim. For his horse there were certainly at all times "four bottles of hay" ready at hand, and a hostler who was sworn to report at once the least suspicion of robbery or dishonesty. There was bread made by members of the Bakers' Gild for himself, and good horse bread for his beast. Such were the inns which entertained Abraham de la Pryme and his contemporaries, and the others whose names remain to this present.

Peace be to them: may their descendants cater as industriously and well, and the dark days of Permissive Bills and Prohibition will pass over and leave them unharmed.

In the honour of Almighty God, And tending to the Good of the Weale-Publique of the Town or Borough of Kingston upon Hull, And for the better Government, Order, rule, and direction of the Inholders, now residing and dwelling, and hereafter to reside and dwell within the said Town of Kingston upon Hull and the Liberty's thereof, At the humble and speciall instance and Request of William Riley, John Winspeare, John Rawim, Joseph Towerson, Morgan

Roberts, and Elizabeth Boys, widow, men of the said Company, Occupacon, or ffellowshipp of Inholders, Together with the Assent, consent, and approbation of the Right Worshipfull Thomas Johnson, now Major of the said Town of Kingston upon Hull, and the Worshipfull the Aldermen his Brethren, And as well by Vertue of Severall Charters and Letters Patents heretofore granted and confirmed unto the Major and Burgesses of the said Town of Kingston upon Hull. As also according to anciente Custome and usage Time out of mind of man, These Orders and Constitutions here underwritten, were made, Constituted, Ordained, established, and agreed upon the nineteenth day of the month of December, in the foure and Twentieth yeare of the reign of our Soveraign Lord, Charles the second, by the grace of God, King of England, Scotland, ffrance, and Ireland, Defender of the ffaith, etc. Annoq. Domini, 1672.

1.

All Inholders to be one Society.

Imprimis It is statuted, Ordained, declared, and agreed that from henceforth that all and severall the Tradesmen in the Trade and Mistery aforesaid, now dwelling and residing, and which shall hereafter dwell and reside within the said Town of Kingston upon Hull And the Libertys thereof, shall from henceforth remain and be one Society, Brotherhood, ffraternity, and Company. And that they shall hereafter from time to time have power and authority yearly and every yeare upon the ffeast day of All Saints, if it be not Lord's day, then the next day following, to Elect, Choose, nominate, and appoint Of from and amongst themselves, One honest, skilfull, and discreet Person, who shalbe Master and Warden of and for the said Society, Brotherhood, and Company for one whole yeare then next following, and that Mr. William Riley shalbe the now present master and Warden of and for the said Society, Brotherhood, and Company, soe to abide and continue untill the ffirst day of Election now next comeing (If he shall soe long live). As also upon the said day of Election to elect, Choose, nominate, and appoint Of from and amongst themselves, two honest, skilful, and discreet Persons, who shalbe Searchers Of and for the said Society, ffraternity, and Company for the yeare following, And that Mr. John Winspear and John Rawlin shalbe the now present Searchers Of and for the said Society, ffraternity, and Company, and soe abide and continue untill the day of election now next comeing (If they shall soe long live). And if at any time it shall soe happen, That such master and Warden or Searchers of the said Company, and soe to be nominated, chosen, and appointed as aforesaid, or any of them to dye or be removed from his or their Office or Officers, Place or Places within the yeare for which he or they is or are to serve, or shall refuse to stand and accept of such or their office or

Have power to elect yearly one honest, skilfull, and discreet Person to be Master and Warden.

And two honest, skilful, and discreet persons to be Searchers.

And vacancies to be filled up.

offices, place or places, That then and soe often it shall and may be lawfull to and for such of the said Society, ffraternity, and Company as shalbe for the time being, or the major part of them, to choose of from and amongst themselves some other honest and discreet Person or Persons in his or their place or places, stead or steads, for the yeare or residue of the yeare then remaining. And if any of the said ffraternity and Company hereafter shalbe elected, nominated, and chosen to such place or places, Office or Offices of Master and Warden or Searchers, or any of them, and haveing notice of such Election, and not haveing served in the said office or imployment to which he is soe elected and chosen by the space of Two yeares then next before, shall refuse as aforesaid to take upon him or them, and to exercise any such Office or Place whereunto he is soe elected, and shall deny to stand to and accept thereof, or to become bound or sworn as herein and hereby is declared and sett down, shall for every his or their contemptuous Refusall be amerced and forfeit and pay in manner and form following, namely, The Warden for every Refusall to forfeit Twenty Shillings, And the Searchers for every Refusall, either of them, to forfeit Thirteen Shillings and ffoure pence, To the Use, benefit, and behoofe of the Major and Burgesses of the said Town of Kingston upon Hull. All which Penaltys and forfeitures are to be sued for and recovered by Way of Bill or Action of Debt, and prosecuted in the name of the Master and Warden of the said Company for the time being, As well in his Majesties Court of Record, holden before the Major and Sheriffe of the Town of Kingston upon Hull, as in any of his Majesties Courts of Record at Westminster, or otherwise to be levied by distresse and sale of the Offenders' goodes upon Warrant from the Major or any Two of the Aldermen of the said Town (*a*), Restoring to the Partys the Overplus.

Anyone refusing for his contemptuouse Refusall to be amerced.

Warden, 20s.

Searchers, 13s. 4d., to go to the Mayor.

2. Item It is Statuted, etc., That the aforesaid Master and Warden for the time being shall have the Custody and keeping of all and every such Plate, Bookes, and goodes as are belonging to the said Society, Brotherhood and Company, And the same shall yearly and from time to time be delivered and transmitted over by the old Master and Warden to the new; And to that end every Master and Warden new elect shall yearly from time to time, immediately upon his Election and acceptance of his said Office and place, become bound by Writing Obligatory in the penall summ of ffifty pounds unto the old Master and Warden then

Master and Warden to have the custody of all Plate, Bookes and Goodes.

To deliver over on leaving office.

To enter into bond in the penall summ of fifty pounds.

(*a*) The Aldermen by virtue of their office were Justices of the Peace till 1835.

living and next preceeding before him, with Condition to deliver All and every such Plate, Bookes, Stocke, and Goodes of and belonging to the said Society, ffraternity, and Company unto the Master and Warden which shalbe then next succeeding. As also th' aforesaid Master and Warden for the time being shall have power and authority, And it is his Office to Order, rule, guide, and govern the said Society, Brotherhood, and Company, according to the Orders and Ordinances herein and hereby sett down and agreed upon, or which hereafter shalbe made and agreed upon by the said ffraternity, Brotherhood, and Company, as also according to the Laws and Statutes of this Land and Nation. And them to congregate in the Lorde's Chamber, at the White horse (*b*) of the said Town, or some other convenient Place within the said Town, at such times and times as to him shall seem meet for and dureing his said yeare for which he is soe elected as aforesaid, And at such Guildes, Congregations, and Assemblys, together with the said ffraternity, Brotherhood, and Company, or the Major part of them, to consult, advise, agree upon, and ordain from time to time Any such further Order or Ordinances as to them in their discrecon shall seem meet for the well Ordering, Government, and Guidance of the said Society, ffraternity, and Company, touching the Craft, trade, or mistery aforesaid. And whosoever of the said Society, ffraternity, and Company shalbe disobedient to any lawfull command of any such Master for the time being, or shall abuse the said Master and Warden in any place or at any time by any unseemly, opprobrious, or contumelious wordes or carriage, in the doeing or executeing of his Office or any thing tending thereto, shall for every such offence forfeit and pay the summ of Tenn Shillinges of lawfull moneys of England, to be levyed to the Use aforesaid. And also That the said Master and Warden within Two days after his Election, be sworn by and before the Major of the said Town for the time being, well and duely to execute and discharge the same Office for the yeare next ensueing, or untill such time as he be thereof legally discharged.

To order, rule, Guide, and govern the said Society, Brotherhood, and Company

The Society to congregate in the Lorde's Chamber, at the White horse Inn.

And settle the affairs.

Disobedience, unseemly, opprobrious, or contumelious Wordes or carriage, to be punished by a fine of 10s.

The Master to be sworn before the Mayor two days after his election.

3. The duty of the Searchers.

Item It is Statuted, etc., That the said Two Searchers for the time being shall have power and authority, And it is their Office and Duty to be most especially at the Commandment of the Master and Warden for the time being, and to sue, prosecute for and demand, levy and receive All and every the Penaltys and forfeitures herein

(*b*) The White Horse Inn, in the Market Place, said to have been, or to have been upon the site of, one of the castellated houses of the De la Poles. The site is the present No. 10.

and hereby assessed and imposed, and which at any time hereafter shall become forfeited and due, and to be the Receivors and Disbursers Of all Moneys, Receipts, and Disbursements touching and concerning the said

To render account at the first Guild, Assembly, Congregation, Meeting, of all moneys.

Company in Generall, and shall yearly and every yeare At the ffirst prime Guild, Assembly, Congregation, or meeting of the said Society, ffraternity, and Company which shall happen and be after the Expiracon of the yeare for which they or either of them were soe Searcher or Searchers, make and yeeld up to the said Society, ffraternity, and Company, a true and perfect Accompt in Writing of all the moneys they or either of them have received and paid within their yeare ffor or by reason of their said Office or Offices, namely, of whom, What, and for what received, and to whom, what, and for what paid. And if any overplus doe remain in their or either of their Handes, to pay the same over to the succeeding Searchers for the year then in being, for the use of the said Society, Brotherhood, and Company.

To summon and convene all meetings.

As also from time to time at the Command of the Master and Warden to summon and convene all the Congregations, Guildes, and Assemblys of the said Society, ffraternity, and Company soe to be as aforesaid, and to be attending thereon, and to travell and goe about all the necessary affaires and businesses touching and concerning the said Society, ffraternity, and Company. And

Anyone abusing the Searchers to pay 6s. 8d.

that whosoever of the said ffraternity, Society, and Company shall resist or abuse the said Searchers, or either of them, in any place or at any time by any unseemly, opprobrious, or contumelious wordes or carriage, in the doeing or executing of their or either of their Office, or anything tending thereto, shall for every such Offence, forfeit and pay the summ of six shillings and eight pence, to be levyed to the use aforesaid.

4.

earchers to become bond in £40

Item To the end the said Searchers may make a true and just Accompt of all such moneys as they shall receive of or belonging to the said Society, Brotherhood, and Company. It is Statuted, declared, ordained, and agreed That the Searchers new elect shall yearly and from time to time upon every their Election as aforesaid and acceptance of their said Places or Offices, become bound by Writing Obligatory in the Penall summ of fforty Pounds to the Two old Searchers then leaving their Office, Or to such Searchers or Searcher as shalbe then living and next preceeding, with Condicon to yeeld and make a true Accompt of all such money as they shall receive Of, for, or belonging to the said ffraternity, Brotherhood, and Company At the end of their yeare, and in the manner and form as in and by these present Orders is afore directed and sett down.

5. Power and duty to make search in the houses of all they shall suspect or know to keep any Inn, Hostry, or taking in of horses.

Item It is statuted, etc., That the said Two Searchers for the time being shall have power and authority, and it is their Office and imployment to make search in all things that Concern the Weale of the said Society, ffraternity, and Company, within the houses of them that they shall suspect or know to keep any Inn, Hostry, or takeing in of horses, dwelling within this Town or Borough, or the Suburbs, or precincts of the same, At all times of the day time for the Weale and good order of the said Company, and Profitt of the Kings Majesties People. And that whosoever will not suffer the said Searchers to enter into their houses or other places to make due and true search as is aforesaid, or be disobedient thereinto the said Searchers, shall forfeit for every time for offending, the summ of Six shilling Eight pence, to be levyed to the Use aforesaid. And of all and every particular offences which shalbe against any of these Orders and Bylaws contained and declared in and by these presents, And which shall in any wise come to the Witt and knowledge of the said Searchers Or either of them, thereof to make due Informacon at the next Guild, Congregation, or Meeting of the said Society, Brotherhood, and Company, after they shall soe have witt and knowledge of the same. That soe due course and redresse may be made and taken in such cases as the Law shall provide and by these Orders and Bylaws is expressed and mentioned. And to the end such Searchers may make due Informacion and presentment Of all such offences in the said Craft, mistery, or occupacion as shall soe come to their Witt and Knowledge, It is Statuted, declared, and agreed That the said Two Searchers within Two days after their Election be sworn by and before the Major of the said Town for the time being, well and duely to execute and discharge the Office of Searchers for and dureinge their yeare, or untill such time as they shalbe thereof legally discharged. And true presentment and informacion to make of all and every Offence, matter, and thing as is declared and required of them in and by these Orders.

At all times in the day time.

Anyone resisting or disobedient to forfeit 6s. 8d.

To be sworn before Major within Two days of their election.

6. Any brother misbehaving, saying "Thou lyest," or "art false," or such like; not keeping silence, going without leave, to forfeit 6s. 8d.

Item It is Statuted, etc., That if any Brother of the said Society, ffraternity, and Company of Inholders, at their appointed meetings and assemblys, or at any other time, when the Master and Warden, Searchers and Company shalbe together, shall not use himselfe orderly, quietly, peaceably, and Brotherly, or doe miscall any of his Brethren of the same ffelowshipp by any uncomely or slanderous speeches, so to say (Thou lyest, or art false, or such like;, and will not keepe silence at the commandment of the said Master and Warden and Searchers, or otherwise shall depart from the said meeting or assembly before the generall breakeing up of the same Company, without Licence granted to him by the Master and Warden, That he or they offending in any part herein contrary to the intent of this Article and order, to forfeit for every Offence six shillings and eight pence, to be levyed to the Use aforesaid.

7. Every Inholder to pay 3s. 4d. admittance, according to Statute, and 4d. to the clarke.

Item It is Statuted, etc., That every Inholder that hereafter shalbe allowed within this Town or Borough and the Libertys and precincts thereof, shall pay for his admittance into the said Society, Brotherhood, and Company, into the hands of the Master and Warden or Searchers, to the Use of the Company, Three shillings and ffoure pence, according to the Statute as hath been accustomed. And also shall likewise pay ffoure pence to their Clarke for the entry of the same admittance. And likewise the party soe admitted shall receive and take an Oath appointed and sett down in this ordinary for him to take before the Major for the time being, And also That noe person shall keep any Inn or Hostry, or take or receive in any horse into there back sides, stables, houses, or garths within this Town or Borough and precincts of the same, and take any money for the same, unless they have a hinging sign at their Doore, and be admitted to keepe an Inn, upon pain of forfeiture for every horse soe found, Twelve pence a peece, to be levyd to the Use aforesaid.

And take an oath.

No person to take horses in unless he has a hinging sign at his Doore.

On penalty of 12d. for each horse.

8. No person to sett up or keep any Inn, or receive Guests for profitt, unless he can make and furnish foure comely and decent guest bedds, and be a brother and burgess.

Item It is statuted, etc., That from henceforth hereafter noe manner of Person or Persons within this Town or Borough of the Libertys and precincts of the same, shall settup or keep any Inn, or receive Guests for their profitt or gain as an Inholder (Except every such person can make and furnish ffoure comely and decent Guest bedds upon their own provision), And also be admitted and allowed by the Master and Warden and Searchers of the same Company to keepe an Inn within the same Town or Borough and the Libertys and precincts thereof, he being first made free Burgesse of the Town of Kingston upon Hull, upon pain That every one herein haveing first warning of the same given them by the Master and Warden and Searchers of the same Company or some of them, shall forfeit and pay for every such offence Contrary to this Article, Order, or Bylaw, the summ of fforty shillings, to be levyed to the Use aforesaid.

40s. fine.

9. No brother to resort to any Tavern, Inn, Alehouse, or Tipling-

Item It is statuted, etc., That noe Brother of the said Society, ffellowshipp, or Company of Inholders shall at any time resort to any Tavern, Inn, Ale-house, or Tipling-

House, on Sonday or other Holiday, during time of Divine Service or Sermons, on pain of 3s. 4d.

honse npon any Sonday or other Holidays dureing the time of Divine service or Sermons, npon pain of every one offending, to forfeit and pay for every such offence, the summ of Three shillings ffoure pence, to be levyed to the use aforesaid; neither shall any Brother of the said Society, Brotherhood, and Company receive any other Person or Persons on Sabboth days dureing the time of Divine service or Sermons; other then their Guests being Strangers or Travellers, nnder the penalty of Tenn Shillings for every offence, to be levyed to use aforesaid.

Or receive any other person.

The *bond fide* traveler.

10s. penalty.

10.

No Baker making Horse-bread to take in horses.

Item Whereas It is enacted, and accorded by Act of Parliament, That noe Inholder or Hostler shall make any Horse-bread within his house or elsewhere, And for the better observing thereof, It is Statuted, etc., that no Baker within this Town or Borongh, or the Libertys and precincts thereof, shall keep any Inn or Hostry, or take in any Horses into their Honses or precincts thereof, to the hindrance of the said Society, ffellowshipp, or Company of Inholders, upon pain of forfeiture of fforty shillings for every horse or mare soe found, to be levyed to the nse aforesaid; neither shall harbour or lodge any Guests of whom they shall take money for their Victualls, upon pain and forfeiture for every default, Six Shillings eight pence, to be levyed to tho use aforesaid.

Penalty, 40s.

11.

Every Inholder to have ready made foure bottles of hay, to be shewed to the Searchers, penalty, 4d.

Item It is Statuted, etc., That every Inholder that shalbe admitted within this Town or Borough, and the Libertys and precincts thereof, into the said Society, ffellowshipp, and Company, to keep an Inn, shall have in his or their Houses, ready made, ffonre bottles of hay, to be showed to the Searchers at all times when they shall come to make search, upon pain of every Default, foure pence, to be imployed Only to the use of the said Company.

12.

No one not free of this Company, Inholder, Hostler, or other keeping Hostrie, to take guest horses on Market days or otherwise, penalty, 12d. a piece.

Item It is Statuted, etc., That if any Person or Persons whatsoever being not free of the said Company, Society, or ffellowshipp of Inholders shall receive Gnest horses dureing the Markett time or the Markett days, or otherwise at any other time into their own houses, stables, backsides, garthes, or grounds, or their neighbours, takeing any money for the same or any consideracion, shall forfeit and pay for every horse soe found, Twelve pence, And also if any inholder, Hostler, or other, keeping any Hostrie in this Town or the Libertys thereof, shall by himselfe, Servant, or other person whatsoever, goe into the Markett and bring any Markett horse into his Hostry or stable, shall forfeit the summ of Twelve pence for every horse soe taken, To be levyed to the use aforesaid.

13. All Hostlers and other Servants to be approved by the Company.

Item It is Statuted, etc., That noe Master, Mistresse, or Dame, occupying or keeping any Inn or Hostry within this Town or Borough, or the Liberty thereof, shall take or receive into their service any person to be an Hostler within their Houses, without the Consent of the Master and Warden and Searchers of the said Company for the time being, nor for any lesse term then for one whole yeare, upon pain of fforfeiture of six shillings and eight pence, to be levyed to the use aforesaid, And the said Master, Mistress, or Dame shall present his, her, or their Servant to the Master and Warden and Searchers of the said Society, Brotherhood, and Company for the time being, at the place of their Assembly, and upon his admittance to be brought by the Searchers to the Major for the time being, and to be sworn according to their Ordinary for the better safe guard of the King's Majestie's Liege People, repairing to the said Town or Borough within Twelve days next, after the takeing of any such Servant into their said Service for that use, or shew some reasonable cause to the Contrary; And that the said Servant being an Hostler shall pay for Entry of his Admission Two pence, To the use of the said Society, Brotherhood, and Company, And also other Two pence to the Clarke of the said Company for the entring of him into their booke, and every Master, Mistress, and Dame doeing contrary to this Order or Article, to forfeit and pay three shillings and ffourepence, to be levyed to the use aforesaid.

Hostler to pay 2d. admittance, and 2d. to the clarke.

14. Dissentions to be settled by four, six, eight, or ten persons, that have been Masters and Wardens or Searchers; fines not to exceed 3s. 4d.

Item It is Statuted, etc., That it shall and may be lawfull to and for the Master and Warden and Searchers of the said Company for the time being, at any time when they shall think it convenient for the Weale and benefitt of the said Society, ffraternity, and Company, when any Dissention or complaint shalbe made by any of the Brethren of the said Company, to take and appoint to them ffoure, six, eight, or Tenn persons of their Brethren, That have been Masters and Wardens or Searchers, to the end they may Order and determin all causes of Variance between Party and Party of the said Company for any cause or matter touching or concerning the said Company, And also if they shall find or perceive in their Judgments That there shalbe just cause to punish either of the said Partys, then the Master and Warden and Searchers to take such ffine of the Offender as they shall think reasonable, Soe that there be not taken above Three shillings and ffour pence for any such at one time, And what other causes shalbe by them determined, touching the Good and benefitt of the said Society and Company, shall continue and stand good without controulment of others of the said Company, without sufficient cause to the Contrary shewed to the Major for the time being.

15. Quarter Days to be kept.

Item It is statuted, etc., That every master and Warden of the said Company That shall hereafter be elected and chosen, shall yearly observe and duly and orderly keep quarterly every Quarter of a yeare a Quarter day, At the Common place of assembly, At such ordinary time or times as heretofore hath been used or accustomed, And also shall cause lawfull Warning to the same Company to appeare at the said Assembly or Quarter daye, upon pain of every Master and Warden neglecting to observe and keep the same Quarter days, to forfeit for every such Offence or default Three shillings ffour pence, to be levyed to the use aforesaid, And if any Brother, being lawfully warned, doe not appeare at such time, and do not ask leave of the said Master and Warden, or in his absence of the ancient Searcher of the said Society, ffellowship, and Company for the time being, shall forfeit and pay for every such absence or Default Six pence, to be levyed to the use aforesaid.

16. Every brother at the feast of All Saints', for his brotherhood, to pay the Brotherhood twelve pence.

Item It is statuted, etc., That for the better increase and maintenance of the Stock belonging to the said Society, ffellowship, or Company, every Brother of the said Company shall pay yearly at the ffeast of All Saints, to the hands of the Master and Warden and Searchers of the said Company for the time being, or their assignee or Assignees, Twelve-pence, for and in the name of their Brotherhood Twelve pences, and what Person or Persons soever shall refuse to pay the same Contrary to this Act or Order shall forfeit and pay Two shillings to the Use of the Company.

17. Inholders may sett on the table boulted-bread of their own making, for their family or retainers, but bakers' bread for guests.

Item It is statuted, etc., That it shall and may be lawfull ffor any ffree Inholder within this Town or Borough, or Libertys and precincts of the same, haveing himselfe, his wife, Children, Retainers, or ffamily, or any of them sitting at the Table with his or their Guests, to sett upon his or their Table boulted-bread of their own makeing, Soe that there be sufficient of the Bakers' Meat-bread or boulted-bread for their Guests then at the Table, Notwithstanding any Article or Order in the Bakers Ordinary to the Contrary.

18. Fines below 3s. 4d. to go to the fraternity. Fines above that to be divided between it and the town.

Item It is statuted, etc., That the Master and Warden and Searchers of the said Society, ffraternity, and Company for the time being, shall from henceforth receive, take, and have to the only Use of their Company, All ffines sett down by their Ordinary amounting to Three

10s. yearly for the Composicion. shillings and ffoure pence or under. Provided That the said Master and Warden and Searchers, or some of them for the time being, shall yearly and every year hereafter well and truely pay unto the said Major and Burgesses and their Successors, at the Townes Auditt, the Moiety or One halfe of all the aforesaid ffines, fforfeitures, and penaltys to be levyed or received by force and vertue of th' aforesaid Orders or Ordinances, exceeding the Summ of Three Shillings and foure pence as aforesaid, And also Tenn Shillings more over and above the Moiety or one halfe of the same ffines, forfeitures, and penaltys exceeding Three Shillings and ffoure pence as aforesaid, ffor and in the name of their Composition Rent.

10. Item It is Ordained That the Master and Warden and Searchers of the said Company or ffellowshipp for the time being, shall have and receive the one halfe or moiety of all and singular Summ and Summs of money, ffines, or fforfeitures, by reason of the breaking of any of the Articles or Orders mentioned in this Ordinary, as they shall hereafter happen or become due or forfeited, at the discretion of the Major of the said Town of Kingston upon Hull for the time being, And if the said Master and Warden and Searchers of the said Company for the time being shall at any time hereafter neglect or refuse to pay the Moiety or one halfe of all the aforesaid ffines, and the said yearly Composicon-Rent, at the time and place herein before limited, or that the said Master and Warden, the Searchers and Company aforesaid, shall any ways demeane themselves contrary to the true intent and meaning of this Ordinary or Composicion, as by the Court of Major and Aldermen of the said Town for the time being shalbe deemed and adjudged, then this Ordinary or Composicon shall utterly cease and become void and of none effect to all intents and purposes whatsoever.

The Oath of Warden and Searchers.

"You doe Sweare That from henceforth you shalbe true to our Soveraign Lord the King's Majestie, his Heires and Successours, And to the Major and Burgesses of this Town or Borough of Kingston upon Hull, And all such Good Ordinances, Usages, and Customes as are or hereafter shalbe lawfully made, ordained, and sett down ffor the Company and ffellowshipp of Inholders within this Town by their Ordinary, And by you as Master and Warden and Searchers of the said Company to be observed and kept, you shall to the best of your powers, witt and cunning, support, maintain, and keepe, and all other things doe and execnte which belong unto you, to be done as Master and Searchers of the said Company or ffellowshipp, Soe helpe you God."

OATH OF THE CLERK.

"You shalbe true to our Soveraign Lord the Kings Majestie, his heires and Successours, You shalbe lawfully obedient to the Master aud Searchers of the Company of the Inholders within this Town for the time being, and soe from time to time you shall read all these Ordinances contained in their Ordinary when you shalbe commanded by the said Master and Searchers, which are now or hereafter shalbe, and make duo and true Entry's as the Master and Searchers shall command you, without sparing any person or persons for love or affection, or to hurt any manner of person or persons by any manner of Entry, Otherwise then of right you ought to doe And you shall not deliver Coppy of any Booko or any Notes concerning the same fellowshipp, without licence of the Master of the Company, or of any Articles whereby the ffellowship may take any hurt, neither shall you reveale nor shew tho said Bookes to any person without the Commandment, consent and agreemeut of the Major of this Corporacion for the time being, or of the Master and Searchers of yonr Company for ye time being, Soe help you God."

OATH OF HOSTLERS AND SERVANTS.

"You sweare to be true, just, and faithful to our Soveraign Lord the King's Majestie, his Heires and Successours, you shall obey the lawfull Commandments and request of the Master and Searchers of your said Company for the time being, you shall duely on your part observe, keepe, and obey the lawfull Ordinances, actes, and articles anthorized for the good rule and government of the same ffellowshipp, Or else to pay such penaltys and ffines as be assessed and appointed by your Ordinary to pay, to the use of the said ffellowship, as the Master of the Company for the time being shall sett down. And moreover you shall disclose and shew to the Major and Justices within this Corporacion, all such suspected persons disobedient to his Majestie's Lawe as from time to time shall resort unto your house, or to the Houses of any Inholders for the time being. And if your Master or Mistresse with whom you dwell and serve use any subtilty or crafty dealing with any of his or her guests, in any thing belonging to them, to the disturbance of the King's peace, you shall utter and descry the same and all the Circumstances thereof that you know. And further, if you have knowledge or intelligence of any ffelons, murderers, or suspicious persons resorting to your Master or Mistresse house, or to the houses of any other of the said Company or fellowshipp, you shall with all diligence first disclose and shew the same as soon as you shall know or heare thereof, unto the Major of this Corporation for the time being, or to some of his Majestie's Justices of the peace within the same Town. You shall not willingly or wittingly receive, harbour, or cherish any Thiefe, Robber, or other suspicious persons, nor you shalbe of Councell with any such person of misdemeanour for the setting of any Robbery, doinge of any violence, Theft, or fraud to any person or persons whatsoever, nor you shall know the like to be intended for any without discloseing the same as aforesaid, Soe helpe you God."

In Witness whereof the said Major and Burgesses of the Town or Burough of Kingston upon Hull, at the instance and Speciall Request of the Master and Searchers and ffellowshipp, or Company of Inholders within the said Town or Borough, to this present Ordinall have caused the Common Seale of this Corporacion to be affixed, And the said Master and Warden and elder Brethren of the said Company to the Coppy or Counterpart of the same Ordinall have sett their handes and seales the nineteenth day of December, In the ffoure and Twentieth yeare of the Reign of our Soveraign Lord, Charles the second, by the grace of God, King of England, Scotland, ffrance, and Ireland, Defender of the ffaith, etc. Annoq. Dni., 1672.

Will. Riley. Joseph Towerson.
John Winspeare. Morgan Roberts.
John Hawkins.

Counterpart of Composicion of Inholders, 1673.

EAST (Size of original, 12½ in. by 13½ in.)

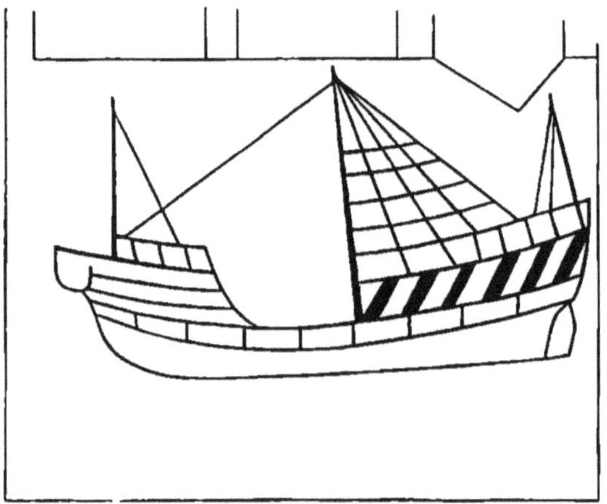

WEST (Size of original, 12 in. by 8½ in.)

Ships of late 15th Century,

Incised in the stone jambs of a tomb arch in the South Aisle of Holy Trinity Church, Hull, from rubbings kindly lent by Sir Henry Dryden, Bart.

Chapter XXXII.

The Society of Shipwrights.

THE rules of this Society are of more than local importance. From the time of Chaucer to the present day Hull has been famed for the excellence of its ships. The case of Taverner has already been mentioned, and in the early days, when the Royal Navy consisted mainly of merchant ships requisitioned on occasion, the number and size of the Hull ships are conspicuous in the lists which have come down to us. In 1359 the port sent 16 ships with 466 seamen to the fleet of the third Edward. At the same time London sent 25 ships with 662 men, and Newcastle 17 ships with a complement of 314. Twenty years later two large and well-manned ships were sent to the aid of Richard II. In 1414 several ships of large burden were sent to assist in Henry V.'s expedition to France (260). Nor were the stout ships of the Humber absent on the memorable days of the Great Armada. The records of their number and equipment still remain in great part, though of the exact details of their achievements in the contest we have no knowledge (261). Another great ship was sent forth to fight the Spaniard in 1597.

Coming down to later times, many of the "wooden walls" of Old England, during the 17th and 18th centuries, were built by

(260) Sheahan's *History*, pp. 71-72.

(261) The ships were the "Griffin," 75 tons, with a complement of 85 men, commanded by John Dobson; the "Marigold," 150 tons, with a complement of 70, commanded by Francis Johnson; and probably (Mr. Wildridge writes me) the pinnace "Little Hare." Another ship sent out at this time was the "Marie Rose," belonging to Walter Pecke, merchant adventurer.—See the *Hull Illustrated Journal*, 1888, Ed. T. Tindall Wildridge, p. 164.

the men who worked under the rules which are here first made public. The Trinity House still preserves a silver tankard presented by the Admiralty, in the reign of William and Mary, to commemorate the launching of their Majesties' 80-gun ship, "Humber," March 30th, 1693, built at "Hazel Cliffs" by Mr. John Frome. Sheahan gives (p. 367) from MSS. in the possession of Captain G. S. Walton, the names of 36 ships of war built here between the years 1739 and 1814. Now, the massive ironclads are launched upon the water of the Humber in their stead. Nor is it only for their warships that the Hull Shipwrights were famous. They built as well the earliest fleets for battling with the ice floes in the whale fishery of the Northern Seas.

The following document shews the internal organization of the craft in the time of Charles II. In no case should we more wish to have the corresponding Book of Ordinances of the Gild itself, with its detailed rules of the trade; but the Composition, as it remains, is of great interest.

The importance of the Company is shewn by the number of the Searchers or Assistants, which in this case is 12. It is noticeable also that they were appointed for life. In these ordinances we have substantially, without doubt, the traditional maxims of the Shipwrights whose work we have traced for so many centuries. They were shipwrights who all served a seven years' apprenticeship to the craft. Some were master workmen: these could have one apprentice only; some had yards of their own, and could have four; and the training of these apprentices was a matter of careful technical education. A ship carpenter was a registered and approved shipwright. Once monthly the Master of the Gild, accompanied by some of the Assistants, inspected all work in progress. If it was found sound and honest the vessel was marked with the mark or seal of the Company. If any part was insufficiently or deceitfully made, the bad work was ordered to be taken out and replaced to the satisfaction of the Master and his Assistants. Quarterly meetings were held, payments made for the stock of the Gild, and for every vessel launched 2d. a ton was paid for the support of the poor, aged, and decayed Shipwrights. It is impossible not to regard this organization with admiration. The trade did for itself what Parliament and self-interest together fail to accomplish at the present day. Doubtless the secret of its possibility lay in the more limited sphere of its field of labor, but it is a question well worth asking, whether it is altogether beyond the capacity of the men of to-day to accomplish something which can do for the artisan and manufacturer of this time what such a society did for the 17th century.

SHIPWRIGHTS' COMPOSITION, 1682.

A Composition Indented dated the ffirst day of March, In the ffive and Thirtieth year of the Reign of our sovereign Lord Charles, by the Grace of God King of England, Scotland, ffrance, and Ireland, Defender of the ffaith, etc., Annoq. Dni. 1682, made between the Maior and Burgesses of the Town or Burrough of Kingston upon Hull of the one part, And Benjamin Blaydes, William Simpson, Thomas Ffrench, Richard Lemmon, Peter Bond, Thomas Doughty, John Cannaby, John Atmarr, Stephen Thompson, Samuell Freeman, James Moody, and James Atmarr, Lawrance Walkington, Samuell Drambam, William Hodgson, Joseph Hoyles, William Newlove, John Warde, John Mosse, William Dunning, Robert Atmarr, Joseph Harris, Richard Gleadow, Ralph Walker, Robert Earatt, Joseph Harley, Nathaniel ffellows, Joseph Rawson, John Read, Richard Clarke, Nathaniel Harley, William Story, Richard Long, William Peacock, Thomas Clifford, Marmaduke Bell, John Doughty, Joseph Ffarmer, ffrancis Violett, and Jonathan Stockwell, of the Town of Kingston upon Hull, Shipwrights, on the one part, Witnesseth that the said Major and Burgesses, for them and their successors, as much as in them is, upon the desire and suite of the saide Artificers, and to the intent that a Society or Company of Shipwrights, Ship-builders, or Ship Carpenters, may the better flourish within the said Town of Kingston upon Hull, and for the Prevention of strangers or aliens to come to worke or inhabit within the Town of Kingston upon Hull that are not of this society, and Burgesses of this Incorporation, have given and granted the Ordinances, grantes, and clauses hereafter following and ensueing, for the better regulating and governing of the said society and their successors for the future.

1\. *To have one Master Warden, twelve Assistants, and four Auditors.* Inprimo That The said Artificers within the town of Kingston upon Hull shall have amongst them one Master Warden and Twelve Assistantes and ffour Auditors, two of them to be chosen out of the Assistantes

and the other two out of the Comminalty, for the taking up of the old Warden's Accompt for and during the year of his Wardenshipp, aswel of such expenses by him laid out and expended for the weal and Worshipp of the said ffraternity, as also for the all other sums of moneys and other profits whatsoever as he hath or might have received for such dues as shall belong to the said Society, And also to elect one Beadle to remaine in his respective place for and during the tearm of his natural life, if not removed for some just cause by the Major vote of the said Master Warden and Assistantes, whereof any Seven of them to make a Hall.

And one Beadle for life.

2.
Mode of elections.

Item It is Ordered That from henceforth the ffeast day of St. John the Evangelist yearly be the general day of the eleccion of these Officers hereafter following, and likewise be their ffestivall day, except the same shall happen to be on Sunday, and then to be on the next day following, the old Warden and the Twelve Assistantes or the Major part of them shall first choose Two out of the Twelve Assistantes, whereof one of them Two shall be chosen Master Warden for the ensuing year by most Voices amongst the whole Society that shall be then present, and then the said Master Warden and Assistantes shall the same day proceed to elect Eight Auditors, ffour to be of the Assistantes, ffour of the Comminalty, out of which Eight, Two of the Assistantes and two of the Comminalty to be elected Auditors for the taking up of the last yeares Accompt, and that the said Master Warden the next day after this eleccion shall be sworne before the Major of the Town of Kingston upon Hull aforesaid for the time being, or in the absence of the Major then before the eldest Alderman of the said Town upon the holy Evangelist, duly to execute his said place or office for one whole year next ensuing. And the Major and Burgesses do hereby appoint and nominate Benjamin Blaydes for the ffirst Master Warden, and Joseph Blaydes, William Simpson, Thomas French, Richard Lemmon, Peter Bond, Thomas Doughty, John Cannaby, John Atmarr, Stephen Thompson, Samuell ffreeman, James Moody, and James Atmarr for the ffirst Twelve Assistants, and Lawrance Walkington, Beadle, the said Benjamin Blaydes, Master Warden, to remain in his said office of Master Warden until the next day of eleccion appointed as aforesaid, and the Twelve Assistants to remain in their respective offices for and during the tearm of their natural lives, and upon the death of any one of the officors above mencioned, the others shall be chosen in their roomes by the said

Master Warden to be sworn next day before Mayor.

Benjamin Blades appointed first Master Warden.

Warden to be elected yearly; Assistants for life.

ffraternity within Twelve days, to serve and be sworne as aforesaid.

3. Bond to be taken of the Warden.

Item That the said Company of Shipwrights shall take bond or bondes of every Master Warden upon the eleccon from time to time in the name of the said Major and Burgesses, for the performance of any accompt, debt, or other thing, and the forfeitures happening thereby to come to the use of the said Company.

4. Conditions of Membership.

Item That they shall make none free of their Company before they be first made a free Burgesse of Kingston upon Hull, and produce their Burgesse Oath to the said Company. And that no free brother of this Society, nor any ffreeman or inhabitant within this Town, at any time hereafter shall sett on worke any Shipwright not free of the said Company or apprentice of such, except he be hired or Shipt to goe a voyage in such Shipp as he shall work upon, upon paine of payment every day Twelve pence, and every such Artificer for every day so working to loose Eighteen pence, and that no Shipwright or Shipcarpenter shalbe admitted into the said Company unless he hath served his time or was borne in the said Town, or at present hath a family resident in Kingston upon Hull.

5. Power to make ordinances.

Item That the said Master Warden and Assistantes of the Company of Shipwrightes or the Major part of them shall from time to time make any Orders for good government and rule to be kept amongst the said Society or otherwise concerning their trade, so as the same be not against the common Lawes of the Land, nor tend to the hurt of the common weal of this Town, and also allowed and approved by the Major for the time being and the greater of the Aldermen his Brethren, who are to sett down paines and forfeitures for breach of such orders.

6. Members not attending 12d, and tarde 6d

Item It is ordained that if any Person of the said Company, being at any time summoned to appear at their Common hall or any other place for their meeting respectively, doth not come at the day, time and place accordingly, having no just cause of excuse, shall forfeit to the Master Warden for the use of the said ffraternity, Twelve pence, and if Tarde after the Roll of names be called over, Sixpence.

7. 5s. penalty for going to law without first laying the matter before the Company.

Item It is Ordered that if any person of the said Company should quarrel, beat, or abuse one another, and thereupon commence a Suit at Law without first acquainting the Master Warden and Assistantes or the Major part of them, who are hereby ordered to imploy their true and best endeavour to order, compound, and appease all complaintes and controversies between any members of the said fraternity, to the end to prevent all occasions of Suites in Law by One of them against another, he or they who shall offend herein shall forfeit to the use of the said Company, ffive shillinges.

8. 3s. 4d. for abusing each other.

Item It is Ordered That no person of the said Company shall openly or privily revile, miscall, misuse with evil speech of reproach any of the said Company, or use any uncivil or undecent tearm against any of them, upon paine to forfeit and pay for every time so offending to the Master Warden, to the use of the said ffraternity, Three shillinges and ffour pence.

9. 3s. 4d. for going without leave.

Item It is Ordered that every person of the said Company at any of their assemblies or meetinges being then and there mett that shall depart from such assembly without leave first had of the said Master Warden and the Major part of the Assistantes, shall forfeit and pay for every time so offending, to the said Master Warden, for the use of the said Society, Three shillinges and ffour pence.

10. Contribution of 2d. in the £ on wages for stock and charity.

Item It is Ordered that for the better supporting of the said Society, and for the maintenance and reliefe of the poor, aged or decayed persons of the same, Every person of the said Art or Mistery or their Apprentices that shall from henceforth be hired to Sea for wages or shares shall pay and contribute to the said Master Warden Two pence for every Twenty shillinges that his wages or share shall amount unto, And that whosoever shall refuse to pay the same upon demand or before he go to Sea upon another voyage, shall forfeit to the said Master Warden of the said Society double the value and ffive shillinges over.

11. No Carpenter to go to sea without registering & being approved.

Item It is Ordered That no freeman of the said Company shall at any time hereafter be hired to serve or goe forth to Sea as a Carpenter in any Shipp or Vessel unless he shall first give notice thereof and register his name with the Clark of the said Society, upon paine of ffive shillinges, to be forfeited to the use of the said Society, for everie time doing the contrary, And that no Servant or Apprentice to any of the said Company shall serve or goe to Sea as Master Carpenter of any shipp or Vessell except his sufficiency be first certifyed by the Warden under the Common Seal of the said ffraternity, upon forfeiture of ffive pounds, the one Moiety thereof to be paid to the Major and Burgesses of Kingston upon Hull, and the other moiety residue thereof to be paid to the said Warden for the use and common profit of the said Society.

12. Quarteridges to be paid on quarter days.

Item It is Ordered That the Monday next ensuing the ffeast of th' Annunciation of the blessed Virgin Mary.

the Nativity of Snt. John the Baptist, of Snt. Michael the Archangell, and of Snt. John the Evangelist, being the ffeast day of, if they or any of them happen to he on a Snnday, then on the day following, be yearly and every year qnarter days, where and at which time every person of the said Company being in Town and not having a snfficient excnse to the contrary, shall appear at the Hall npon Snmmons, and their pay their qnarteridge, to witt, every yard keeper or Master builder One shilling a piece a Qnarter, and every other person of the said Company ffonr pence a piece a Quarter.

13. Substantial chest with three lockes to be kept.

Item It is Ordained That the said Company shall at all times hereafter have one snbstancial chest with Three lockes and Keyes for the keeping of all moneys, plate, goodes, evidences, ordinances, accomptes, and writinges to the said Society belonging or appertaining, which three keys shall always he and remain in the several enstody of the said Master Warden, the eldest Assistant, and the eldest Auditor, who shall be all present at every opening of the said chest, and if any by necessary occasion shall he letted that he cannot be then present, he shall appoint one of the Assistantes to take his key and supply his room in his absence.

14. All ships, &c., to be inspected monthly while building.

Item It is Ordained That the said MasterWarden or any Two or more of the Assistantes shall once every month, or oftner if need require, diligently view, search, and snrvey aswel all Shippes, Pinkes, Ketches, Hoys, Keels, Boates, Barges, Lighters, and all other Vessells whatsoever now bnilt or that hereafter shall be built or repaired in any place or places within the Town and County of Kingston npon Hnll, and all timber, plank, and other stnffe provided fitt or prepared for the bnilding, makeing, triming, or repairing of any such Shippes, Boates, or any Vesselles whatsoever, as also all and every the workes and workmanshipp of all and every person and persons whatsoever used or imployed in the said Art or Mistery, or anything therennto appertaining, And all snch shipps, boates, and other vesselles whatsoever which upon any such search, view, or survey they shall find to he snbstantially wronght or framed, they shall pnt the marke or seal of their Company in some convenient place if they thinke fitt to testify the same, And such of the said Shipps or other vesselles which they shall find upon their view in any part to be insnfficiently or deceiptfnlly made and wronght, or repaired, they shall charge the bnilders or owners thereof forthwith to take the same insefficient wood, timber, stnff, or other materialles away, and to snpply it with others that shall he good and snfficient, which if within convenient time after such charge or

If approved, the marke of the Company to be put in some convenient place.

If insufficiently or deceitfully done to be replaced, on penalty of £5.

warning they shall deny, deferr, or neglect to do, That then it shall be lawfull to and for the said Master Warden and Assistantes, or any two of them, or any two of their depntyes aforesaid, to impose and assesse npon every offender for every such offence ffive poundes of lawful money of England, or less at their discretion, the one Moiety of which fine assessed shalbe paid to the Major and Burgesses of Kingston upon Hull aforesaid, and the other moiety thereof to the present Warden for the common profit of the said fraternity.

15. Every master must himself serve seven years and be approved to take an apprentice.

Item It is Ordained That no person or persons of the said Society, Art, or Mistery, shall from henceforth keepe any Apprentice at all until he himself hath served as an apprentice Seven yeares or more in the said Art or Mistery, and shall be allowed to be a sufficient workman by the said Master Warden and Assistants or the greater part of them; Nor any Master Workman of this Society shall have or take above the number of one Apprentice, and that no Master Workman of this Society shall take an Apprentice till he hath been half a year out of his time, and until that Apprentice hath served ffive years or dye. That no yard keeper shall have above ffour Apprentices at any one time, being first one year for himself. And who of the said Society shall offend this ordinance shall forfeit and pay to the said Master Warden, fforty shillinges of lawful money of England, the one moiety thereof to be paid to the Major an Burgesses of Kingston upon Hull, and the other moiety to the present Warden for the use and common profit of the said Society.

Master workman to take one apprentice.

Yard keeper may have four apprentices.

16. Apprentices to be enrolled at the Town Hall.

Item It is Ordained That no person of the said Art or Mistery shall retaine or keep any person in the said profession as an Apprentice above three months before he bring him first to the Town's Hall to be there enrolled, and then to the Hall or place appointed for the said Society, to be there also inrolled by the Clark of the Company, or his Deputy or Deputyes, and to be done before the said Master Warden or his deputy, paying two shillinges and six pence for presenting to the Warden, and six pence to the Clarke for inrollinge, and four pence to the Beadle, and whosoever shall offend in binding his Apprentice else where, or any other of the said offences, shall forfeit to the Master Warden Tenn shillinges, and for every weeke that he shall keepe him unbound Tenn shillinges.

And in the Company's books, and to pay 2s. 6d. to Company; 6d. to the Clarke; and 4d. to the Beadle.

17. Fees to clerk.

Item It is Ordained That all Indentures for Prentices of the said Company shall be from henceforth made by the Clark of the said Company for the time being, or his deputy, for which he may receive and take the usuall allowance of sixteen pence a pair, upon paine of forfeiting for every paire made elsewhere to the use of the said Clarke three shillinges four pence of lawfull money of England, And it is further ordered that the foresaid charge of presenting, binding, and enrolling shall be paid by the friends of the Prentice, except the Master be otherwise contented.

18. **Due care in transference of Apprentices.** Item It is Ordained that no person or persons of the said Art or mistery shall bargain, sell, give, or sett over his Prentice or Prentices without the speciall privity, licence, and consent of the said Master Warden and Assistantes, or their deputy, in remote places, to the end they may foresee that they may be sett over to such as may lawfully take them, and shall be able to teach them in their Trade, and finde them all thinges necessary, upon pain to forfeit for every such offence fforty shillinges of lawful money of England, the one half to be paid to the Major and Burgesses of Kingston upon Hull, and the other Moiety to the present Warden for the use and common profit of the said ffraternity. And if it happen any person of the said Company to dye and depart this life, leaving any Apprentice who hath served two yeares or above of his tearm, It is ordained that it shalbe lawful for the widow of the party deceased, with the consent of the Apprentice, his parentes or guardians, to make her best benefitt of him, during her widowhood, that she can, And that upon request made to any master workman of the said art or Mistery that he hath meanes to imploy him, he shall sett him to worke for such reasonable wages as he is able to earne, But if at the time of his Master s decease hee shall not have served the full time of Two yeares, or that the widow die before the expiration of such Apprenticeshipp, or that his Master shall give over his profession, That it shalbe lawful for the said Master Warden and his Assistantes to assign and sett over every such apprentice to such persons as they shall thinke convenient, So as it be with the consent and liking of the parentes or guardianes of the said Apprentice.

19. **Inticing of Apprentices and Servants.** Item It is Ordained that no person of the said Company shall at any time counsail, intice, procure, or perswade any servant or apprentice of the said profession to any disorder or dishonest unlawful action, or to leave or forsake his trade or calling, or unlawfully to depart or runn away from his Master's service either before or after he is bound, And whosoever shall offend therein shall forfeit and pay for every such offence the sum of fforty shillinges of lawful money of England, the one half to be paid to the Major and Burgesses of Kingston upon Hull,

and the other moiety to the Warden for the common profitt of the said Society, or else to be corrected according to the quality and condition of the person.

20. No workman to leave work improperly.

Item It is Ordained That if any person of the said profession shall be lawfully retained in worke or service by the day or great (*a*) and shall unjustly and unlawfully leave or depart from the same until such time as the same worke shall be fully finished, he shall forfeit and pay to the said Master Warden and Assistantes for ever such offence fforty shillinges of lawful money of England, the one half to be paid to the Major and Burgesses of Kingston-upon-Hull, and the other moiety to the Warden for the time being, for the Comon profitt of the said Society. And it is further ordained that if any yard keeper or Master Workman of the saide Art or Mistery, after he hath retained any of the said Society into his worke or service, shall withoute just or reasonable cause, to be approved and allowed by the Master Warden and Assistantes, put him away and entertainte another, he shall forfeit and pay for every such offence to the said Master Warden and Assistantes, to the use of the said Company, tenn shillinges of lawful money of England.

Or master to dismiss his men.

21. Mode of enforcing penalties.

Item It is Ordained That if any person or persons using or exercising, or which hereafter shall use or exercise the said Art or Mistery, or any thing thereunto appertaining in any place or places within the precincts aforesaid, do or shall infring, break, or not observe any Act or ordinance in these pointes expressed, and do or shall deny, refuse, delay, or deferr to pay any such sum or sums of money as shall happen at any time hereafter to be forfeited or due, to be paid to the said Major and Burgesses of Kingston upon Hull, the said Master Warden and Assistantes for any paine, penalty, or forfeiture touching any of the ordinances in these presentes expressed, That then it shall and may be lawful for the Warden of the said Company for the time being, to bring his action in his own name in any of the Courtes at Westminster or in the Court of Record held within the Town of Kingston upon Hull, against any that offendeth, for the recovery of all such pains, penalties, forfeitures, or any other sum or sums of money menciond and expressed in the same, having been first demanded and to this present Composition refused or delayed to be paid. Provided alwayes that the said Master Warden shall not prosecute the same withoute the consent and Major vote of the Assistants, and of the bench of Major and Aldermen of Kingston upon Hull for the time being, nor after any suit is

Warden to sue in his own name.

Consent of Mayor requisite.

(*a*) Piece work.

commenced shall he release or desist prosecuting the same without their and every of their consentes first had and obtained, and such suites shalbe maintained at the common charge of the said Society, and the said Society shall indemnify the said Warden for all costes and damages that he shall happen or sustain in and about the prosecution and recovery of the same.

And the Society to indemnify the Warden.

22. For support of the poor, aged, and decayed persons, 2d. per tunn on all ships built above 100 tons.

Item It is ordained for the better supporting of the said society, and for the maintenance and relieving of the poor, aged, and decayed persons of the same, every person of the said Art or Mistery that shall hereafter make or build any new shipp or vessell of the burthen of one hundred Tunns and upwards, shall pay and contribute to the said Master Warden and Assistants, to the use of the poor, aged, and decayed persons of the said Society, two pence of lawful money of England for every Tunn that every such shipp or Vessell shall contain in Burthen. And that every person of the said Company that shall hereafter make or build any new shipp, Lighter, or any other Vessel or Vessells whatsoever, from one hundred Tunnes downwardes to Tenn Tunns, shall pay to the Master Warden and Assistants, to the use of the said Company, two pence for every Tunn that any such shipp, Lighter, or Vessell shall containe in burthen, and for every boat that he shall build under Tenn Tunns to pay to the use of the said Society ffour pence.

2d. per ton for every ship from 100 to 10 tons

And 4d. for every boat under 10 tons.

23. 20s. yearly to be paid to Town Composicion rent for the year, and afterwards 40s. yearly, and the moiety of all fines so reserved.

In consideration of all which before mencioned premises the said Company of Ship wrightes or Ship Carpenters and their successors shall yeerly yeeld and pay, and they do hereby covenant and promise to yeeld and pay unto the said Major and Burgesses, their Successors or Assignes, at the Auditt to be holden at the Guildhall of the said Town of Kingston upon Hull for this present yeare, the sum of Twenty Shillinges of lawful money of England, and from hence forward yearly at the Towne's Auditt the sum of fforty shillinges of lawful money of England, in the name of a Composicion Rent, And then also the moiety of all such fines as are above reserved, so long as they remain to be a Society. And in Case any person who is admitted a free burgesse of this Town of Kingston upon Hull do demand his freedome of the said Society of Shipwrightes, they shall receive him into their Society upon the payment of ffour ponudes ffine or under, the one moiety thereof to be paid to the Major and Burgesses of Kingston upon Hull aforesaid, and the other to the use of the said Society, Provided always that if any person or persons of the said Society shall do or act anything against the weal and Worshipp of this Incorpora-

Fine of £4 to be paid on admittance to the Society by a member.

tion, that then this present Composition to be void and of none effect.

Mayor reserves power to revoke the ordinances.

And Lastly, The said Major and Burgesses, being parties to these presentes, do reserve to themselves and their successors power of revocation or alteration of all or any thing heretofore mencioned or granted at their owne will and pleasure, as they see most convenient for the well governing of the said ffraternity.

In Witness whereof to the one part of this present Composition remaining with the said Company of Shipwrightes the said Major and Burgesses have caused to be affixed their Common Seal, and to the other part of the same remaining with the said Major and Burgesses the said Company of Shipwrightes have sett their handes and seales the day and year abovesaid.

[The signatures and seales have never been affixed].

[Upon three skins fastened together by the seal-attachments.]

[*Endorsed*]

Shippwrightes Composition, 1682.

CHAPTER XXXIII.

THE BARBER-CHIRURGEONS AND PERUKEMAKERS.

ALTHOUGH the most recent of the Hull Ordinances, the following yield to none in their singularity and antiquarian interest. The annals of the Barber-Surgeons abound with quaint and striking episodes illustrative of many sides of ancient life (262).

This union of trades, so grotesque to modern ears, seems to have existed to some extent from the earliest period. In London in 1307 we find an ordinance forbidding barbers to put blood in their windows, a prohibition which had to be repeated at a much later period; and in the following year, 1308, appears Richard le Barber, the first Master of the Barbers' Gild. There was nevertheless even in those days a clear distinction between Surgeons proper and Barbers, although the distinction was not one which commends itself to modern ideas. The Gild contained two classes of members—those who practiced barbery proper, probably including also blood-letting and tooth-drawing, and those who practiced surgery proper, and who were for distinction's sake called Barber-Surgeons. Outside this gild were other Surgeons, having a gild of their own.

In 1388, when the Barber-Surgeons again emerge from obscurity, their history is invested with a peculiar interest. Readers of Mr. T. Smith's work on Gilds will remember that among the returns sent in to the writ of 12 Richard II. those of the Trades Gilds are to a large extent lost. Alone among the London Companies the Barber-Surgeons preserve among their records a copy of the return sent in by their Gild in 1388. It

(262) See the *Annals of Barber-Surgeons of London*, by Sydney Young, Esq., 1890; a store of information admirably set out.

was extracted from the records in the Tower in 1634, and remains in a vellum book of ordinances which was written out fair fourteen years later. For the text of it the reader is referred to Mr. Young's work (see p. 28). It is in fact almost identical in type with those with which we are already familiar. The Gild is governed by Masters and "Surveyors"; the ordinances against opprobrious words, enticing another man's servant, refusal of office, are there; quarterages are paid, and the poor who have been seven years in the Company are paid 10½d. a week. It appears that in 1369 the Surgeons had obtained power to present all unskilled surgeons. Not to be behind hand, in 1376 the Barbers got similar powers. In 1390 we find four men admitted before the Lord Mayor as master surgeons, and sworn to make faithful scrutiny of others, both men and women, undertaking cures and practicing the art of surgery, and to present their defaults, and to be ready to examine persons hurt or wounded, and others, whether they are in peril of death or no ([268]).

The jealousy of these two rival bodies continued for a considerable period, the Barber-Surgeons, doubtless by weight of numbers, gradually coming to the fore, and succeeding about this time in wearing a livery, while the Surgeons had none. The predominance of the former still further appeared in 1462, when they obtained a royal charter, the preamble of which sets forth in solemn quaintness the serious climax of affairs. From the practice of unskilled sons of Esculapius we are told "Many and infinite evils have before this happened . . . from which cause some of our liegemen have gone the way of all flesh;" and others are given up as incurable; and "it is to be dreaded that similar or greater evils may in future arise." To prevent this the Barber-Surgeons are to have the supervision of all surgeons within the city, and they are to be examined by the Masters and presented to the Mayor as approved. Thirty-one years later an agreement was come to between the Gild of the Surgeons and the incorporated Barber-Surgeons, whereby they were to be ruled by joint ordinances, and each was to choose two Wardens. This, however,

(268) Riley, *Mem.*, p. 519.

was a purely informal agreement between the two bodies, intended to secure some uniformity of action and to avoid friction.

The reign of Henry VIII. was a momentous one for the craft. In their Hall still hangs the famous picture of the great monarch by Holbein, and on their table stands the great grace cup presented by him on the union of the two companies in the year 1540. We are accustomed to think of him as the great reformer of men's souls, but to the Barber-Surgeons he appears in another form. The dedication of the painting may be translated as follows :—

> Grievous the Plague had ravished England's realm,
> Rending the souls and mortal frames of men ;
> God from on high repenting of the scourge,
> Sent thee to work the good physician's part (264).

Nor was this altogether undeserved. He seems to have made an honest attempt to put some limit to the boundless quackery which doubtless still sent many of his liegemen "the way of all flesh." That he did not succeed in persuading our forefathers to confine their trust to the duly qualified barber-surgeons was a result for which perhaps the orthodox surgery of the day must take its share of the responsibility. According to the statute 3 Henry VIII., c. 11, that mystery stood in urgent need of reform. The preamble states that—"The science and connyng of physyke and surgerie, to the perfecte knowledge whereof bee requisite bothe grete lernyng and ripe experience, ys daily within this Royalme exercised by a great multitude of ignoraunt persones, of whom the grete partie have no maner of insight in the same, nor in any other kind of lernyng; some also can no lettres on the boke, soo far furth that common artificers, as smythes, wevers, and women boldely and custumably take upon theim grete cures and thyngys of grete difficultie, in the which they partely use sorcery and which-crafte, partely applie such medicine unto the disease as be very noyous and nothyng metely therefore, to the

(264) Tristior Anglorum pestis violaverat orbem,
Infestans animos corporibusque sedens ;
Hanc Deus insignem cladem miseratus ab alto,
Te medici munus jussit obire boni.—Young, *Annals*, p. 82.

high displeasoure of God." So everyone wishing to practice in London or seven miles round must be examined before the Bishop or Dean of St. Paul's, assisted by four "doctors of phisyk." In the country the examination will take place before the Bishop of the diocese or his Vicar General. In 1540 the same prince united the Corporation of the Barbers and the College of Surgeons, and granted each year to the new association the bodies of four condemned criminals for the study of anatomy. But the hold which the traditional medicine-lore of the country had upon the population was too strong to be dissolved by Act of Parliament. So the statutes 32 Henry VIII., c. 42, and 34 and 35 Henry VIII., c. 8, turn the tables, and re-authorise the old quacks, who are called "Divers honest persones, as well men as woomen, whom God hath endued with the knowledge of the nature, kinde, and operacion of certeyne herbes, rotes, and waters (265)," etc. So the infusions of toads' legs, cockroaches, and the like had again free course for a season.

The Act of 1540, comprising as it did the union of the arts of barbery and surgery, nevertheless took care to separate them in actual practice, though for reasons different from those which would weigh with a modern Parliament. No one using the art of surgery should practice barbery, and no barber should practice any point in surgery, the drawing of teeth only excepted, as it was "veraie perillous" on account of contagious diseases. Thus the Barbers and Surgeons settled down in peace, and lived in this ill-assorted union for over 200 years. One of the chief members, honoured with a place next the Master in the Livery, was the King's Barber. The following is the ordinance relating to this worthy under Edward IV. (266):—"A Barbour for the Kingis most highe and drad person to be taken in this Court, after that he standeth in degree gentleman yoman or groome. It hath bin much accustomed to one or two well knowne officers of the Livrie in household Daily of such as bene for the monthe sergeant or othir. Also we find how this hath bene used

(265) *English Wayfaring Life*, pp. 183-4.

(266) "Liber Niger, Domus Regis"—Young, *Annals*, p. 91.

amonge by a wele betrusted yoman of the Chambre ffor lacke of cunning of these other men. It is accustomed that a Knight of the Chambre or elles squire of the bodie, or both, be present every time when the Kinge wolle shave. This Barbour shall have every Satterday night, if it please the Kinge to cleanse his head, leggs, or feete, and for his shaveing, two lovis one pitcher wine. And the Usher of the Chamber ought to testifie if this be necessary dispensed or not." Thus the "Satterday night" tub has ancient and royal sanction.

Under Henry VIII. the ordinances were less rude (267):—"Item It is alsoe ordeyned that the King's Barbor shalbe daylie by the King's upriseinge readdye and attendant in the King's Privye Chamber, there haveinge in reddynesse his Water Basons, Knyves, Combes, Scissours, and suche other stuffe as to his Roome doth appertaine for trymminge and dressinge of the King's heade and bearde. And that the sayd Barbour take a speciall regarde to the pure and cleane keepinge of his owne person and apparell, useinge himselfe alwayes honestlye in his conversationne, withoute resortinge to the companye of vile personnes or of misguided woemen, in avoydinge such daunger as by that meanes hee might doe unto the King's most Royall person, not fayling thus to doe upon payne of looseinge his Roome and farther punishement at the King's pleasure." In 1543, however, by 35 Henry VIII., no person "having a greate bearde of notable perplexitie and length" was to be admitted to the liberty of the City.

Certainly the Barbers were a very numerous and important body, heading the list in 1537 with 185 freemen, as against the skinners 151, haberdashers 120, mercers 55, weavers 30, and bowyers 19. These Barber-Surgeons had also a monopoly of the gruesome art of the "opening, searing, and imbalmeinge of the dead corpses." For their demonstrations in anatomy they had, as we have seen, a lien upon the bodies of criminals, and the following entries shed a lurid light upon the customs of the last century:—"1720-1: Paid the Hangman for the dead man's cloths which were lost in the scuffle, and for his Christmas Box, 15s."

(267) Ibid, p. 90.

"1739: Paid the Beadles for their being beat and wounded at the late execution, 4li 4s. 0d."

It was an old complaint of the Church, dating at least from Archbishop Arundel, that the Barbers shaved customers on Sunday, and the Court of the Company had much trouble in repressing this inveterate habit. The following entry is not without its humour:—1566: "In Thys Courte William Gylam was discharged and released oute of warde, and hath paid his averages, and he hath confessed yt Richard Boomehead doth shave the Vyear of Stepney in his house every Sondaye."

The custom seems to have been for patients to bargain with the Surgeons to be cured for a lump sum, while any egregious failure rendered the unlucky practitioner liable to be presented before the Company. Thus on the 7th of September, 1874, "Here was John Griffen complayned upon William Pownsate for giving him a powder which loosed all the teeth in his head, which John Griffen had the dissease which we call Demorbo Gallico." Quacks were rigorously suppressed when caught, and in 1627 the Lord Mayor solemnly submits a case of a monstrosity having two heads, four arms, and three legs for decision by the Company as to whether it was naturally born. The Barber-Surgeons reply that they think it is put together from children or apes, monkeys, and the like.

It was not till 1745 that the union between the Surgeons and Barbers was dissolved by Parliament in spite of the opposition of the latter. The Company of the Barber-Surgeons still flourishes on its old premises in the City.

The combination of these with the Peruke-makers which we find in the Hull ordinances never obtained in London. In 1753 the Company made an attempt to absorb the Peruke-makers, but were foiled. Eleven years later the latter themselves sued for admittance, but being in a very forlorn condition, were then politely refused.

In the reign of Queen Anne and the period of the Hull ordinances it was a craft requiring no small amount of technical skill. There was the black "riding wig," the "bag wig," the night-cap wig," and a little later the "Ramilie wig," the "bob wig," the "tie wig," and the "pig-tail," which the reader may reconstruct in imagination if he will.

From the Coopers' Book we learn that in the year of this Composition the Perukemakers held their meetings in the Coopers' Hall, in Hale's Entry.

Among the apprentices' indentures recorded in connection with Ferris' Charity, are two to Barbers and Perukemakers, of 1782 and 1786.

Barber-Surgeons' Composition, 1714.

In the Honour of Almighty God And as tending to the good of the Weale, publick, and that of the Towne or Burrough of Kingston upon Hull, and for the better Government, order, rule, and direction of the Barber Chirurgeons and peruke makers now resident and dwelling, and hereafter to reside and dwell within the said Town or Burough and the liberties thereof, at the humble and Speciall instance and request of John Knipe, Matthew Redhead, George Hodgson, William Chambers, William Goodwin, John Knipe, junior, John Dawson, Samuel Ombler, William Nelson, John Carey, George Campbell, William Adams, Thomas Bradley, Henry Phillipson, and Nathaniel Nelson, Inhabitants of the said Town, Together with the assent, Consent, and approbation of the Right Worshipful John Collings, Esqr., present Mayor of the aforesaid Towne or Burrough, and the Worshipfull the Aldermen his brethren of the same Town, by virtue of several Charters and Letters Pattents heretofore granted and confirmed unto the Mayor and Burgesses of the said Town or Burrough of Kingston upon Hull. These orders, Rules, and Constitutions hereunder written, were made, constituted, ordained, established, and agreed upon the Ninth Day of September, in the first year of the reigne of our Soveraigne Lord, George, by the grace of God, of Great Britain, France, and Ireland, King, Defender of the faith, &c. Annoq. Domini, 1714.

1\. *All the craftsmen to be one Society, Brotherhood, Fraternity, and Company.*

Imprimis It is statuted, ordained, declared, and agreed that from henceforth all and every the Craftsmen and Tradesmen of and in the said Crafts, Trades, and Misteries, now dwelling and residing and which shall hereafter dwell and reside within the Town or Burrough of Kingston upon Hull aforesaid and the liberties thereof, shall be remain and Continue one Society, Brotherhood, Fraternity, and Company. And called by the name of the Company of Barber Chirurgeons and Peruke makers in the same Towne, and that hereafter they shall have power and authority yearly and every year upon the first Munday next after the Eleventh day

To elect one Warden yearly, an honest and discreet person.

of November, commonly called Martinmas day, to elect, Choose, nominate, and appoint of, from, and amongst themselves one honest and discreet Person who shall be Warden of and for the said Society, brotherhood, and Company for one whole year then next following. And that Matthew Redhead shall be the present Warden of and for the said Company, and so to abide and Continue untill the first day of Election now next coming if he shall so long live. And also upon the said day of Election to elect, choose, nominate, and appoint of, from, and amongst themselves two honest and discreet Persons who shall be Searchers of and for the said society, Brotherhood, and Company for the year then next following, and that Henry Philipson and Nathaniel Nelson shall be the now present Searchers of and for the said Company, and also to abide and continue untill the said day of Election next coming if they shall so long live, and if at any time it shall so happen that such Warden and Searchers or any of them to dye or be removed from his or their office or offices within the year for which he or they is or are to serve, or shall refuse to stand and accept of such his or their office or offices, that then and so often it shall and may be lawfull to and for such of the said Society, Brotherhood, and Company as shall be for the time being or the Major part of them, within Eight days after, to Choose of, from, and amongst themselves some other honest and discreet Person or Persons in his or their place or places for the year or residue of the year then remaining, which said Warden and Searchers within three days after their Election, and taking upon them their respective offices shall be sworne by and before the Mayor of the said Town or Burrough for the time being or his Deputy in that behalf, well and truely to execute and perform their said offices according to the tenour of the oath in these presents incerted. And if any of the said Society and Company shall hereafter be Elected, nominated, and Chosen to Such office or offices of Warden and Searchers or any of them, and having notice of such Election, and not having served in the Same office to which he is soe Elected and Chosen by the Space of two years then next before, shall refuse as aforesaid, take upon him or them, and to execute any Such office or Place wherein he is so elected, and shall deny to stand to and accept thereof or to become bound or sworne as herein and hereby is declared and Set Down, shall soe be by his or their Contemptuous refusall be amerced and forfeit and pay in manner as followeth, that is to say, The Warden for such refusall, fourty shillings, and the Searchers for

And two honest and discreet persons to be Searchers.

To be sworn within three days of election.

A Warden refusing to stand, 40s.; a Searcher, 20s.

every such refusall, each of them the sume of Twenty Shillings, The one half of Such Penalties and forfeitures to goe and be to the use and benefit and behoofe of the Major and Burgesses of the said Town or Burrough of Kingston upon Hull, and the other half thereof to the use of the said Society and Company, towards the defraying of their reasonable Charges and expenses touching the same. And the said penalties and forfeitures and all other the penalties and forfeitures herein mentioned, are to be Sued for and recovered by way of bill or action of debt, and prosecuted in the name of the Warden of the said Company for the time being, or otherwise to be levyed by distress and Sale of the offenders goods, restoring to the Parties the overplus.

This and all fines, etc., to be sued for in the name of the Warden, by way of bill or action of debt.

Or levyed by distress.

2.

Warden to order and guide the Company.

Item it is statuted, ordained, declared, and agreed that the said Warden for the time being shall have power and authority, and it is his office to order, rule, guide, and govern the said Society, Brotherhood, and Company according to the orders and ordinances herein and hereby set down, or which shall hereafter be set down and agreed upon by the said Society, as also according to the Statutes and Laws of this Land and Nation. And them to Congregate in Some convenient place in the said Town, and at such time and times as to him and the major part of the said Company shall seem meet for and during his said year for which he is so Elected as aforesaid, And at such guilds and meetings together to consult, advise, agree upon, and ordain from time to time upon any such further orders and ordinances as to them in their discretion shall seem meet for the well ordring, governance, and guiding of the said Society, touching the Trades or Misteries aforesaid, And whosoever of the said Brotherhood or Company shall be disobedient to any lawful and reasonable commands of Such Warden for the time being, or shall abuse the said Warden in any place or at any time by any unseemly, opprobrious, or Contumelious Words or Carriage in the doing or executing of his office, or anything tending thereto, shall for every such offence forfeit and pay the sume of tenn shillings lawfull money, to be levyed, Sued for, recovered, and disposed as aforesaid, And further that the said Warden for the time being shall have the Custody and keeping of all and every Such Plate, Books, and Goods, as are belonging to the said Society, Brotherhood, and Company, and that the same shall yearly and from time to time be delivered and transmitted over by the old Warden to the New, And the said Warden for the time being to be the receiver and disburser of all monys, Receipts, and disbursments touching the said Company in generall, And

To congregate in some convenient place.

At such guilds to consult and make ordinances.

Any brother disobedient, or abusive by unseemly, opprobrious, or contumelious words or carriage, to be fined 10s.

Warden to keep the plate, books, goods, and moneys.

And render accounts at the prime guild after his year expires.

shall yearly and every year at the first Prime Guild assemhly or meeting which shall happen after the expiration of his year make and yeild up to the said Society, Brotherhood, and Company a true and perfect account in writing of all the moneys by him received and paid within the year for and by reason of his office, namely, of whom what and for what received, and to whom what and for what paid, and if any overplus remain in his hands, to pay the same over to the succeeding Warden for the year then in being, to the use of the said Company, And for his

Warden to become bound by bond in the penal sum of £50.

the said Warden's faithfull performance of this article he shall become bound by bond or Writing obligatory in the penal Snme of Fifty pounds, or such other sume as the Major Parte of the said Company shall think fit to the old Warden then living and next preceding before him, and to the eldest brother of the said Company for the time heing, with condition to deliver all and every Such Plait, Books, Goods, and Money as shall appear to be in his hands on the account to he passed as aforesaid, of and belonging to the said Society, or unto the Warden which shall be then next Succeeding, to and for the use of the said Fraternity. [etc.]

3.

Searchers to view and search all defects, defaults, offences, and abuses in the said crafts.

Item it is statuted [etc.] that the said two Searchers for the time being shall have power and authority, and it is their office and Employment to view and Search all and every the defects and defaults in the said Trades or misteries committed, happening, or omitted by any of the said Society, Brotherhood, or Company, or any other person or persons within the said Town, or any the liberties or precincts thereof, And for the discovery of offences and abuses in the said Crafts or Misteries, It shall and may be lawfull to and for the said Searchers and either of

And to have right of search in houses and shops.

them to enter in the day time into the houses and shops of every Brother of the said Company or any other person whatsoever useing or exercising the Trades or Misteries aforesaid within the same Town or liberties thereof, and there search and view whether any thing be done or acted against the Laws and Statutes of this Land and Nation respecting the said Trades or Misteries, and what offences shall come in any wise to the witt and knowledg of the said Searchers or either of them during their year in Relation to the premises, they the said Stewards to pre-

And to present offenders at the next Quarter Sessions for offences against the laws.

sent the same at the next Assizes or Quarter Sessions to be holden for the said Town or Burrough of Kingston upon Hull and County of the same, or which of them shall first happen after the said Searchers or either of them shall so have knowledg, and of all and every particular offences which shall be against any of these orders and bylaws Contained and declared in and by these presents, and which shall in any wise come to the Witt and Knowledge of the said Searchers or either of them, thereof to make due information at the next meeting of the said Society or Brotherhood after they shall so have knowledg of the same, And further the said Searchers to summon and convene all the guilds, Congregations, and meetings of the said Company from time to time at the Command of the Warden for the time being, and to be attending thereto and to travell and go about all the necessary affairs and business touching and concerning the said Society, And that whosoever of the said Fraternity or Company shall resist and abuse the said Searchers or either of them in any place or at any time by any unseemly or opprobrious words or Carriage in the doing of his or their Offices or anything tending thereto, shall for every such his offence forfeit and pay six shillings eight pence to be levied, recovered, divided, and disposed as aforesaid, And to the End that due information may be made of all offences Committed as well against the Rules and orders of the said Company as against the laws and Statutes of this Nation in matters relating thereto, the said Stewards shall go along with and attend the Warden to be Sworne as aforesaid by and before the Mayor of the said Town or Borough for the time being, or his deputy in that behalf, well and duly to execute and discharge the office of searchers for and during their year, or untill such time as they shall be thereof legally discharged, and true presentment make of all and every offence, matter, and thing as is declared and required of them in and by these orders.

And to the next meeting of the Company for offences against these ordinances.

And to summon all guilds at the command of the Warden.

Abusing the Searcher, 6s.

4. Abusing a brother at a meeting, 5s.

Item it is statuted [etc.] that if any Brother of the said Company shall abuse any other of his bretheren at any assembly or meeting of the said Brotherhood by any unseemly, opprobrious, or Contumelious Words or Carriage, he shall forfeit and pay for every such offence the sume of five shillings, to be levied, recovered, and bestowed as aforesaid, And if any Brother of the said Society shall absent himself from any guild, Congregation, or Assembly to be Convened and Appointed as aforesaid, or from the buriall of any Brother of the said Company, having notice or warning the day or night before (unless good cause or matter of Excuse be shewed to the Warden and by him approved), shall for every such omission forfeit and pay the sume of two Shillings Six Pence, to be levied, recovered, and disposed as aforesaid.

5. None to practice the trades unless apprenticed for 7 years, and a free Burgess.

Item it is statuted [etc.] that no person or persons whatsoever shall in the said town or liberties thereof exercise, practise, or use the said Trades or Misteries of Barber Chirurgeons and Peruke makers, or either of them, other then such as are at present of the said Society and Company, Except they shall have served to the said Trade, or one of them within this Town, by the space of Seven whole years at the least as an apprentice to the same, and have first made himself a free Burgess of the said Town of Kingston upon Hull, upon Pain of everyone keeping a Shop or Working within this Town or the liberties thereof Contrary hereto to pay Ten Shillings per week, and after that rate for more or less time so long as he shall continue obstinately so to do, the said monys to be levyed, recovered, and divided as aforesaid. And for and in order to the more due Regulation and Carriage of the Masters of the said Trades or Misteries in this behalf, every Brother of the said Society shall from time to time give in the name to the Warden and Clarke of the said Company for the time being, and cause a due entry to be made in a book for that purpose of all such Journeymen and Apprentices as he or they shall reteyne or take into their service or Apprenticeship within one month after such Reteyner, upon penalty of Five shillings for every omission herein, to be levyed, recovered, and disposed as aforesaid, And every Brother of the said Company shall pay to the use of the same brotherhood for the entry of every such his Apprentice the Sume of Two Shillinges Sixpence, and for every Journeyman Quarterly the Sume of Sixpence, And for the Entry or Admission of any person into the said Society, Brotherhood or Company who hath served his or their Apprenticeship, or is capable of such admission, the sume of three shillings four pence, and no more, which respective sumes shall be for the use of the said Fraternity and Company, and to be levyed and recovered as aforesaid, And the Clarke of the said Company for the time being shall have the making of all the said Indentures of apprentiship and the enrolling of the same, as also the entry of all journeymen in the said book for that purpose, and of all the persons made free Brothers of the said Company, and shall receive such fees for the same as is Customary, upon the penalty of any offending in this case to forfeit and pay six shillings eight pence, to be levyed and recovered as aforesaid, And Further the said Clarke for the time being shall have a reasonable yearly Sallery for his pains to be taken in attending the said Warden and Company at their meetings, and for his transcribing the accounts and other business of the said Society.

Any one defying this order to pay 10s. a week.

All brethren to report to the Warden and Clarke the names of all Journeymen and apprentices within the month on pain of 5s.

2s. 6d. for the entry of an apprentice and 6d. quarterly for each journeyman.

3s. 4d. for the enrolment of a brother after apprenticeship.

Clarke to have all the work, fees,

And a reasonable yearly sallery.

6\. Item it is statuted [etc.] that every brother of the said Society, Brotherhood, and Company shall yearly and every year upon the said day of Election give and pay

Every brother to pay 1s. yearly, to be called Brotherhood-pences.

towards the increase of the Stock belonging to the same the sume of one shilling, which shall be called Brotherhood Twelve pences, on pain to forfeit two shillings, to be levyed, etc. And also that no Brother of the said Society exercising the Crafts or Misteries of a Barber or Perukemaker shall upon the Lord's day, commonly called Sunday, either out or in time of divine service, work on either of the said Crafts, Callings, or Trades, or keep open his Shop, on pain to forfeit for every time he shall be found so doing the sume of Ten Shillings, to be levyed, etc.

No Barber or Perukemaker to keep his shop open on Sunday on pain of 10s.

7\. No brother to take more than one apprentice until the first have served four years, on pain of £5. No apprentice for less than seven years, or teach any other person, on pain of £20.

Item it is statuted, etc., that no Brother of the said Society or Company who hath or shall have one apprentice, shall take a second untill the first have served a space of four years at the least of his time, upon pain of every Brother offending herein to forfeit and pay the sume of Five pounds, And that no Brother of this Society shall take any Apprentice for less time than seven years, nor teach nor instruct, or Cause or procure to be taught or instructed any person or persons whatsoever in the Trades or misteries aforesaid, or either of them, or in anything concerning the same, other then such as shall be bound Apprentice thereto as aforesaid, under the penalty of Twenty pounds, to be forfeited and paid by him or them that shall offend in either of the premises, the said penalties and forfeitures to be levied, etc., and to be divided and disposed, viz., the one half to the use of the Town's Chamber, and the other half to the use of the said Company.

8\. Power to make further Ordinances.

Item it is statuted, etc., That the Warden and Searchers and the major part of the said Company for the time being shall have power and authority, according to a branch in the Second Article of this Composition, to make any further ordinances and orders from time to time for the good rule, order, and Government to be kept and preserved amongst themselves, which orders, rules, and Ordinances shall bind the Warden, Searchers, and whole Company aforesaid, And shall and may set down pains, penalties, and forfeitures for breach of such orders and ordinances, provided always the same orders and ordinances tend not to the detriment or harm of the Common weale of this Town at the Judgment of the Mayor for the time being, and the greater number of his brethren the Aldermen, If the same come in question.

9\. One moiety of fines to be paid to the Town.

And lastly it is statuted, etc., that the said Warden and Searchers of the said Brotherhood and Company for the time being shall yearly and every year hereafter well and truely pay unto the said Mayor and Burgesses of the said Town or Burrough of Kingston upon Hull and their successors, at their Town's Audit, the moyety or one half of the aforesaid fines, forfeitures, and penalties aforementioned to be paid into the Towns Chamber, or to the use of the said Town, or the Mayor and Burgesses thereof, to be levyed or received by force and virtue of the aforesaid orders or ordinances, And the same of Fifteene shillings more over and above the moyety, or one half of the same fines, etc., in the name of their Composition Rent.

And 15s. for Composition rent.

The form of Oath for Wardens & Searchers.

The form of the Oath to be administered to the Warden and Searchers of the said Company for the time being, vizt., You shall swear to be true and faithfull to our Soveraigne Lord the King, and to this Town or Burrough of Kingston upon Hull, and to the Fraternity or Company of the Barber Chirurgeons and Peruke makers within the same town, and well and truely to execute, performe, and discharge the offices of Warden and Searchers for the year ensuing, and untill you be legally discharged thereof according to the Composition or ordernary granted to the said Crafts or Misteries by the said Mayor and Burgesses, and all the good orders, ordinances, and bylaws now made or which shall be made, touching the same Arts or Misteries, you shall support, maintaine, observe, and keep at all times, to the best of your power, skill, and knowledge, so long as you shall be brethren of the said Company, So help you God.

In Witness whereof to the one part thereof remaining with the said Company, the said Mayor and Burgesses have affixed their Common Seale, and to the other part of the same remaining with the said Mayor and Burgesses, the present Warden and Searchers and brethren of the said Company have sett their hands and seals the day and year first above written.

Matt. Readhead, Warden.
John Knipe.
George Hodgson.
William Chambers.
William Goodwyn.
John Knipe.
John Dowson.
Samuel Ambler.
William Nelson.
John Carey.
Geo. Camwell.
William Adams.
Nathaniel Nelson.
Thomas Bradley.
Henry Phillipson.

[The seals are covered with paper and inserted by the side of the respective signatnres. The same seal has been used for all.]

[This document is stamped with three sixpenny stamps and endorsed.]

Stampt according to Law, sealed and delivered in presence of

Tho. Peacock.

Compositions.

[Thomas Peacock was the Town Clerk of this period.]

CHAPTER XXXIV.

ANCIENT GILDS AND MODERN ECONOMIC PROBLEMS. LOOKING BACKWARDS AND FORWARDS.

THE reader who has followed the foregoing narrative will have already largely formed his own conclusions as to the relations between the ancient Gilds of this country and modern trade combinations, and as to what lessons may be learned from the past. What remains for us now is to give a short summary of the results arrived at, and to bring out the fundamental elements of the industrial problem into relief.

The first point which must be brought out is that the modern Trades' Union can only very partially be said to be a descendant of the ancient English Gild. One distinction is fundamental. The Trades' Union is a combination of artisans, laborers, and journeymen amongst themselves. The employer of labor is outside the Union, and enters into separate combination with other employers. On the other hand the ancient English Gild up to the 18th century was an association of all the workers in the craft [268]. Employers and employed, masters, journeymen, and apprentices, all had their part in the same union. Thus as every craft, even the smallest, was organised within itself, the opposing interests were not hired laborers and employers, but each particular trade and the public. The underlying opposing social

(268) The limitation to *English* Gilds is necessary. France presents us with a very curious development of the Gilds on lines which run more nearly parallel to the modern English relations of employer and employed. There were the ancient Craft Gilds proper, masters' fraternities, journeymen's fraternities, and the curious organisation of the *Compagnonage*, or the secret organisations of the crafts for the whole country. It does not appear, however, that this differentiation exercised any influence upon this country. A competent history of the French Trade Gilds would be of great interest and value.—See Gould's *History of Freemasonry*, Chapters IV. and V.

tendencies of rich and poor were kept out of view, and the question was one of the supply and demand for the products of the craft. The fraternity possessed within itself and kept the secrets of its particular craft; admittance was strictly limited to the apprenticeship for seven years; allied trades were rigidly confined to their own departments; no carpenter could do the work of a joiner or shipwright; no cobbler could make shoes; intruders from other towns were carefully excluded. Had these organisations been independent, the public would have been at their mercy. But on the other hand this danger was avoided by admitting every fraternity to a recognised position in the larger Corporation of the town. Along with public recognition went necessarily public control. Their ordinances were practically incorporated into the bye-laws of the borough, and made operative by process of law; but all their actions were subject to the supervision of the Mayor. Under the ægis of the Town's Chamber they became bound to supply the needs of the public in reasonable time and at reasonable rates. The mode in which this was accomplished has been fully set forth in the foregoing chapters, and need not be repeated here. If the market was an artificial one, and prices unnatural, on the other hand neither Government, municipal or sanitary inspectors, nor a clerk of the works, was needed. The Searchers of the craft saw to all that; and if bad leather was put into the Aldermen's boots, shaky timber used in a roof, or unhealthy beer sold to the King's lieges, the respective Wardens were sent for and soundly rated by the Mayor. The completeness of this system has been already noted.

But it will be seen to what another world the whole organisation belonged. The adoption of machinery, scientific methods of manufacture, the development of finance, the Protean fluidity of capital, the railway and the steamship and the telegraph, rendered a continuance of it as impossible as they would forbid its revival. But the fundamental elements nevertheless remain, though changed almost beyond recognition, and the great task which is threatening to baffle all the ingenuity of modern statesmen and economists is how to deal as successfully with these 19th century problems as their forefathers did with theirs.

The enormous difficulty of the task will be better realised by asking ourselves what form an organisation would have to take to-day which would reproduce a system as complete and effectual as that of 300 years ago. In consequence of the practical unity of each trade over vast areas, as governed by the rapidity of communication, and the markets of the world, the isolation which made it possible for each to be self-contained in each town must give place to wide-spread national or even international associations, in which local trade societies would occupy their several places on a system of federation. Each trade or manufacture must be sufficiently fixed and stable in its products and method of production as to be capable of having its procedure reduced to certain general rules. Those employed in the trade must be united in a common interest, either by certain fairly stable sliding scales of wages, or by a vast system of co-operation. Thus would be produced associations resembling the American Oil Trust, or the Chemical Union in this country, with the important difference that the classes of clerks, laborers, and employees generally would have definite positions and life interests in the Union. Thus would be arranged a united and organised trade of producers against the world of consumers and co-related trades. Then would arise the necessity, no longer chimerical, of self-protection on behalf of the public. Municipal regulation would be powerless. National regulation on the lines of the old Trades' Statutes of the later Middle Ages would be needed. It is true that this, strictly speaking, would be the introduction of no new principle in modern legislation. The laws against restraint of trade still hold good. In the case of Railway Companies the State has never relinquished its right to regulate rates, and to insist on due provision being made for public safety and convenience. Nevertheless the change of policy implied would be revolutionary, and the possibility of its successful application would be doubtful in the extreme. But supposing this organisation effected, the international character of trade would necessitate further measures. Protection and commercial treaties would be essential, pending at least an international organisation of trade and manufacture, which would fall hardly short of a federation of the nations in more ways than one.

Such is the task which awaits him who would revive under modern conditions the ancient symmetrical organisation of trade. It will be seen how each step bristles with obstacles which at present are insurmountable. But perhaps the most fatal of all is in the inherent spirit of progress which pervades modern industry. Such a system of organisation is conditioned by some permanence in the materials and method of production. But with the constant advance in machinery, in chemical technology, and in the course of trade, this condition ceases to exist. Either the new organisation must have an elasticity altogether foreign to the old spirit, or it must give place to the struggle for the survival of the fittest.

It will be seen then that the idea of attempting anything like a revival of the ancient system, if it exist, is chimerical. It still remains, however, to point out the extent of the existing tendencies to organisation, and the possibilities which lie before them.

We must recognise first the fact that the present economic condition, though symmetrically far behind the old, is, viewed from the standpoint of general utility, an advance. Around us flows the volume of an industry and commerce which is the more marvellous the more it is studied. Whatever its faults, and they are many, more people live in a higher state of comfort and prosperity than ever in these islands before. When men broke loose from the old Gild trammels, it was at the impulse of forces which opened out new eras of power and intelligence for mankind. It is not to be wondered that this era of change and expansion, still in the full flood of its development, should not yet have hardened or crystallised, so to speak, into fixed and definite forms. This hardening process belongs to maturity, and the epoch is young. Moreover, crystallisation belongs properly to inanimate forms, and society is an organism.

Turning now to the bodies which present the most points of similarity to the old Gilds—the Trades' Unions—we find the following features, besides the points of fundamental difference above noted. Modern Trades Unionism finds its closest analogy not in the old English Gilds, but in the widespread trade societies of ancient France and Germany. In this country the Gilds were local. On the Continent they were in many cases national. A journeyman went from North to South of France and found himself among the brethren of his own craft. The elements of secrecy, and also of licence, have gone; but the member of the Amalgamated Society of Engineers or the Seamen's and Dockers' Unions, or the Knights of Labor, aims at finding himself among brethren wherever he goes. There can be no doubt that this is the only form of union likely to be effective under modern conditions. It is impossible in this time of rapid extension of Unionism to give any figures which will be fairly correct a year hence, but it is safe to say that as yet the Unionists constitute still a far less proportion of the artisan and laboring population than was included in the Gilds. Until they are able to include the great mass of the workers, their work cannot be seen in its possible application and effect. Although in a more limited sphere, as excluding the employers, the same problems confront them as confronted the Gilds. Can they accomplish this first condition of success? It may be laid down that the State will not aid them in the task as it did the old Gilds. There are left to them, then, the sphere of legitimate influence and of social excommunication, or "boycott." The latter, if legal in some of its phases, passes off very imperceptibly into phases distinctly illegal, and it may safely be predicted cannot be ultimately successful.

The great difficulties of the position are evidently two: the want of stability in the methods or kinds of labor, and the constant influx of fresh swarms of men anxious to earn their bread, but apprenticed to no special trade, and continually tending to swamp the older hands. A few words of explanation are necessary on the first head. It would no doubt be incorrect to say that apprenticeship has ceased to exist, but it is true to say that its influence is limited to the older and more permanent kinds of skilled labour. On the one hand we see a minute subdivision of labor in manufactures which not only makes work more productive, as Adam Smith shewed in his famous illustration of the pins, but which also requires certain men or women to devote themselves entirely to accurate and rapid repetition of actions which become almost purely mechanical. The cramping effect of this kind of labor on mind and body is evident. But its bearing upon the point we are now illustrating is very marked. While this system produces marvellous skill in its own department, it unfits its victim to a great extent for any other than the unskilled departments of other work. When then the rapid advance of invention and change of method revolutionise an industry, the transition must be marked by the disuse of the superseded manual skill, and the reinforcement of the ranks of unskilled labor, at any rate for a considerable time. Thus the attempt to crystallise the several trades into close corporations, however liberal their terms of admission, in our present chronic state of progress must prove a mistaken one. If successful for a time, it must be modified by means of periods of disruption, and in so far as it is successful in opposing the change from less to more perfect production, it is easily seen to be hurtful to beneficial development. The leaders of the Trades' Unions do not seem to have sufficiently foreseen these results.

The remedy for the danger is two-fold. The mass of the people must receive a thoroughly practical technical and general education, which, while it does not prevent their becoming skilled in any one department of manufactures, yet affords a basis for change of application when required; and the hours of labor and means of recreation must be such as will allow the healthy development of the whole faculties, so as to counteract the cramping effect of devotion to one series of mechanical acts. The other remedy is one in which even less progress has been made, namely—the trades' organisations must be less exclusive, so as to afford natural means of transition from one trade to another within certain limits. The opposition to any such change of organisation would be great, but it is easy to see that only by some such provision can the Union include all the laborers, or protect themselves in the ultimate issue against the just demand of their fellow-men to be allowed to earn their bread. These seem to be the necessary conditions for the success of the attempt to place all laborers within the circle of the Unions. It remains to be seen how far this attempt will be pursued. The difficulties of its realisation are great, and there are signs that the leaders of the new Unionism are already contemplating the closing of their organisations of unskilled labor against new comers. Should they thus turn aside from the pursuit of their ideal, they will no doubt have under their control a power easier to wield, and will gain temporary successes; but the power which would result from a really complete organisation will not be attained, and they will simply fall into the line of the older Unions as against the swelling tide of new and unskilled laborers.

If, however, the great object be attained, and laborers be gathered into Unions federated and directed by skilful men, the old questions of the public welfare will be forced into prominence. The natural result must ensue of the federation also of employers wielding the immense power of capital, with the prospect of an ultimate trial of strength between immense social forces, which would entail results truly terrible to contemplate. In old times in many towns, especially on the Continent, the crafts not only gained the recognised position we have seen existing in Hull, but became truly estates of the governing bodies, sitting by means of class representation in the Town's Chamber. And the same principle of estates still theoretically exists in our national constitution. It is curious to see that were the demand for labor representation in our own day successful, a somewhat modified form of the same principle would be realised. The fact that all class representation is scouted does not alter the case as it stands However this may be, all analogy teaches us that with the completion of the Trades' Unions and the combinations of employers, some form of national recognition and control would come within the sphere of practical polities.

But it is better to realise the fact that not only are the natural obstacles to such a symmetrical organisation so great as to make the possibility of its enduring realisation very doubtful, but that also in itself it would be an unnatural and artificial basis to work from. Instead of following the lines of stratification, it would be better to make use of those of cleavage. The natural Union is evidently that of those engaged in a common industry. Without pursuing the ideal of such wide-spread association as that pourtrayed on p. 368, the consolidation of the interests of employer and employed in each factory, or under each company or firm, is practicable enough. A certain minimum wage being guaranteed, co-operative production can be attained by giving each workman a share in the profits of the concern. But the minimum wage is a *sine quâ non*, for the workman must have the means of livelihood as the condition of work. It would be easy to exaggerate the effect of this arrangement, but it is just as impossible to deny its benefit. It would not abolish Trades' Unions, nor is it desirable that it should. It would not supersede the struggle for life or competition, neither is that end desirable. It would alter the competing parties, and each factory united in interest would compete with its neighbour. There would be the natural tendency of a body of compact artisan shareholders to close their ranks and become as exclusively alive to their own interests as employers are in some cases to-day. But the effect of economy in labor and material, in the material prosperity of the laboring classes, and in the larger unity of social interests, would be an immense gain. And to this might succeed in the future a federation of these great co-operative companies for the purpose of checking the evils of that kind of competition which is really excessive and injurious.

Meanwhile the position of the Trades' Unions will be immensely strengthened if one of the most attractive features of the old Gilds be introduced, or made more prominent in their rules and ordinances. We have seen that in every trade fraternity of old the quality of the work done was one of the chief objects of solicitude. Not a single body of gild ordinances can be quoted in which this feature was absent. In the private books of the Gild, as in the Bricklayers' Book, we see how minute these provisions were. The same object was sought in apprenticeship. The old institution of the master-piece,—in German "meister stück,"—or the final example of the thoroughly acquired skill of the apprentice before he qualified as a journeyman, prevailed down to the beginning of the 18th century, and all through life the same thoroughness of workmanship and honesty of material was exacted by the Searchers of the Gild. It is true that the question is now largely one for manufacturers and contractors rather than artisans, but it is also, as we are continually reminded, perforce one for the artisans as well. Although the rules of Trades' Unions, levelling the work of its members to one dead mediocrity, may have had a justification in the necessities of a war time of struggle for existence, that time has gone. In its stead has come a period when the position of the Unions must be justified by their capacity to promote excellence of workmanship, and to call forth the best individual effort that each man is capable of putting forth. When the employment of Union men means the employment of a body of workmen who will be bound by their rules to do the best work, and this is ensured by the regular supervision of skilled overseers of their own Union, there will be no need to resort to other means of inducing or compelling the employment of Union men. An employer careful of the reputation of his products, would of himself choose that class of men as naturally as he chooses the best machinery, and his goods would command a price which would re-imburse him if he paid a higher wage. No reflection is here intended on the work of Union men, which is admittedly of a high class, but the feature is one which must be developed into far more prominence and efficiency before it attains the position which is its due. There is already a movement in this direction, such as that which has been so successfully instituted by means of the registration of plumbers, and it is noticeable that this is a case in which it is simply a revival of the ordinances of one of the surviving Gilds of London. For the mass of unskilled labor the case is somewhat different, and the scope is less, but here sobriety, industry, and capacity may be made a condition for Union employment. What are really to a large extent the objects of these Unions, namely, social improvement, and the fuller equalising of the position of the poor in comparison with the rich, do not properly belong to the sphere of purely industrial questions. They are social, and must, of course, develope into political organisations when they seek political and social change, and must be judged by the maxims proper to themselves.

Chapter XXXV.

The Incorporation of the Gilds.

IT is essential to the thorough appreciation of the position and work of the Gilds in this country to determine, as far as possible, their legal and constitutional position at the most important periods of their history. The knowledge of this will show in what degree they were fixed and permanent institutions of society, or merely temporary associations of men and women for ephemeral or convivial purposes. And the enquiry involves two separate though converging lines of investigation.

1. To what extent were the Gilds, in the proper sense of the word, corporations?

2. To what extent could they call themselves into existence, and, if the license of authority was needed, with whom did the power of granting this license rest?

On all these points our present authorities are very conflicting. The Introduction to the Early English Text Society's volume on Gilds lays it down broadly that the Gild was certainly a corporation, and that the King's license was not necessary, "as is wrongly alleged," to the foundation of a Gild (200). Dr. Freeman, in his Introduction to the series of hand-books on "Historic Towns," tells us that one of the duties of the Mayor and Council of a mediæval borough was to incorporate Gilds.

In the first place, then, it will be necessary to explain what is the actual constitutional position of a corporation as it has been understood in this country, at any rate since the 15th century. Writers have recognised five sources of legal corporations. They may exist by common law, prescription, Act of Parliament,

(200) Introduction, xxi. and xxvii.

charter, or implication. In theory these are mostly resolvable into Royal grant, in accordance with the ancient rule that "None but the King can grant a Charter (270)." The direct method is by charter or letters patent of the Crown, as in the case of the Merchants' Company on p. 164. The grant by Act of Parliament is held to fulfil this condition in the Royal assent. Prescription is held to imply an original grant. Implication is held when the purposes of a legally-constituted society cannot be carried on without corporate powers. Subjects who held the "jura regalia" could by virtue of this right exercise the same power as the Crown. Thus the Prince Bishops of Durham granted charters to that city as late as 1565 and 1780. In certain other cases a delegated power exists. Thus the Chancellor of Oxford may erect corporations by charter, but this power is not absolute. The characteristics of a corporation are that it is a body politic and corporate, may hold lands, possess a common seal, sue and be sued. The possession of a common seal is an incident of a corporation, but is not conclusive as to its existence. Thus on the one hand the Inns of Court have a common seal, but are voluntary societies; on the other hand, in France, on the dissolution of a commune the seal was formally destroyed (271).

So much is clear, but the application of these maxims is complicated by the further question how far they were understood and technically applied in the earlier period from the 12th to the 15th century.

The subject, as Dr. Gross remarks, has never been worked out, and what is here stated must to some extent be acknowledged to be tentative only Nevertheless, we can lay down some landmarks which will be of considerable service in the enquiry. On the one hand it must be remembered that the idea of a corporation as fully developed in legal theory was not one likely to be found in the earliest ruder attempts at government. On the other hand, it was developed with great refinement in the Roman civil law, and was early brought into prominence by the

(270) Blackstone, I., 473.

(271) Luchaire.

great ecclesiastical establishments, which took their models from sources which were still permeated with civil law principles. There was thus the ruder practice of the governments in dealing with the towns and Gilds, and on the other hand the gradual attempt of the lawyers to apply the refinements of the Civil Code. There were undoubtedly towns from a period before the Conquest possessing corporate rights by implication; but the attempts which were made in the 12th century to assume these rights were checked by the legal principles which were beginning to be more clearly recognised, and were used by the lawyers to strengthen the prerogative of the Crown. These, broadly speaking, were the causes of the changing usages with regard to the crucial words "communa" and "communitas," which were used generally of both boroughs and Gilds, which render the exact meaning doubtful in particular cases. The definition of Dr. Stubbs ([272]) is as follows:—"An organised body possessing rights and property in common, applied sometimes to a chartered town, sometimes to the community in general." In interpreting the use of these words in Early English documents, too much weight apparently has been allowed by our historians to the idea of the French municipal commune. The words properly in this country meant a community in general, and only in a secondary sense the chartered corporation of a town. It is doubtful if the exact conception implied by the French commune was ever anything but an exotic in this country. There is a well-known passage in Glanvil ([273]) which has done more than any other to confuse the whole subject. It is that in which he says that a "nativus" who remained a year and a day "in eorum communam scilicet gildam," shall be free. Whatever be the exact meaning ([274]), it is evident that the word "communa" did not alone carry the definite meaning of a borough corporation, but required the further explanation which he adds in the

(272) *Select Charters*, Gloss., s.v.

(273) Stubbs, *Select Charters*, p. 162.

(274) In our view *communa* means here the "community" of the town in its widest sense, and "gilda" is used to connote the full participation of the communitas by payment of scot and lot.

succeeding words. "Communitas" was a word early applied to boroughs, but also to Gilda Mercatoria, villages, counties, and hundreds.

The common opinion hitherto has been that advanced by Merewether and Stephens, that boroughs in this country were not properly incorporated until the 15th century, and that Hull and Plymouth were the first to obtain the distinction in 1439-40. Dr. Gross (275) shews conclusively that this view is only tenable on the supposition that the greater precision of technical language introduced at that period was essential at an earlier time. The charter of Edward III. to Coventry in 1345, "That they, their heirs and successors, may have 'communitatem' among themselves, and may of themselves elect and create yearly a Mayor and fit Bailiffs," must have carried with it the essentials of a charter of incorporation; and the grant to the town of Hedon in the 22nd year of the same King, in the same words, was equally significant. But there is no doubt as to the words of 12 Richard II. to Basingstoke, "Concessimus, pro nobis et heredibus nostris, hominibus ville predicte quod ipsi, heredes et successores sui unam communitatem perpetuam de se ipsis, et unum commune sigillum habent in perpetuum." As early as Henry III. Bracton applies "universitas" to towns. In 4 Edward II. Lynn is spoken of as a "corpus"; and in the year books of Edward III. London is described as "un Cominaltie come un singuler person qe puit aver action per nosme de common, come un sole person averoit." These quotations are conclusive as to the essentials of incorporation. What is true seems to be that the necessity for more exact definition of the incorporation of the "free boroughs," with their varying degrees of autonomy, was not widely felt before the 15th century. Dr. Gross thinks this was probably due to the extension of the Act of Mortmain to cities and boroughs by 15 Richard II. These facts will enable us to understand more clearly the position of the Gilds.

It is true that the origin of many Gilds was like that of Stratford, "whereunto the memory of men reacheth not." We

(275) *Gild Merchant*, 1890, p. 93.

have seen reason to believe that they dated from times when there was no central authority capable of licensing their foundation. But it is also certain that no sooner did the Government of England begin to centre in strong hands, and the organisation of justice and finance begin, than the King's prerogative in this respect was clearly asserted and acted upon. We should be going too far to attribute this jealousy to a conscious guarding of the right of incorporation. It was rather that of the right of association when the distinction between an association and a corporation was not clearly drawn. The form which this control took was the exaction of an annual tax or fine in return for the King's license. The following are examples :—

The weavers of London pay the fine to the King in Henry I. In the reign of Henry II., weavers of York, Lincoln, Huntingdon, London, Winchester, Nottingham, and Oxford, the fullers of Winchester, the men of Marborough, the bakers of London, all pay for the privilege of having their Gild, and the men of Andover for having the same liberty in their Gild as the men of Wilton and Salisbury. In 9 Richard I. the fullers of Winchester pay five marks to have a charter from the King; in 5 Stephen the weavers of Lincoln that they may have their customs as the King ordered by his letter ("per brevia sua"). We have also in the reign of Henry II. the account of eighteen Gilds in London fined for being set up without lawful authority, and of Gilds at Gloucester, Lidford, Colbern, and Eggulf. The burgesses of Totnes, and those of Bodmine were fined for the like offence. Ailwin of Gloucester and Thomas from beyond the Ouse at York were fined for setting up a "Communa (276)." In 1287 the Mayor and Commonalty of Bedfordshire were called upon to shew by what warrant they held their privileges of Gild Merchant, etc. (277).

As this old custom of taxation gave way to more modern necessities, we find the Royal prerogative more clearly defined. In 1349 the old Gild of Whitawyers in London entered upon a tenement which had been devised. Their right to do so was

(276) Rot. Pip., 16 Henry II.

(277) Merewether and Stephens, p. 529.

disputed, and it was decided in Court that a Commonalty to sue and be sued could not be affirmed but by order of the King [278]. Forty years later the Statute of Mortmain was extended to Gilds. Now on the same page of "Early English Gilds" in which it is laid down that the Gilds were true corporations, we are shewn that "the first founding of a Gild was generally by some body of the folks themselves," though sometimes by the "communitas" of a town. But this is conclusive evidence that they were not really incorporated, for at the period to which this refers—the 14th century—it was quite clearly understood that people could not set up corporations as they liked. The same principles were extended in greater detail by the Courts in after times. Thus in the reign of Queen Elizabeth, 1575, an order by the Mayor, Aldermen, and Sheriff of Newcastle incorporating the Fellowship of the Cooks was declared by the Court to be void, for "they could not make a corporation." Chief Justice Holt said, "These sort of bodies were not corporations, but brotherhoods, to meet and drink and talk together; they are only voluntary corporations [279]." Again, in the great City of London case, 1609, it was decided "That the customs of London, and their ordinances founded on it, were good, but that they would not be good by grant, and therefore no corporation made within time of memory can have great privilege unless by Act of Parliament." And it was adjudged "That a grant to restrain trade and traffic was void, because trade and traffic is the life of every commonwealth, and especially of an island. And therefore the King might erect Gildam Mercatoriam, *i.e.*, a fraternity, or society, or corporation of merchants, to the end that good order and rule should be by them observed for the increase and advancement of trade and merchandise, and not for the hindrance and diminution of it [280]." These examples will shew clearly in practice the constitutional principle that if the Gild was to be a true corporation it must be so by creation of the King.

(278) Merewether and Stephens, p. 638.

(279) Merewether and Stephens, 1328.

(280) Merewether and Stephens, 1486.

Thus the distinction between an ordinary Gild and an incorporated Company or Gild was clearly understood and acted upon by the end of the 14th century. The full technical grant of corporate powers appears first to the Gild at Bristol in 1416, and in the following year to the Gild of St. George at Norwich. In 10 Henry VI., c. 6, Gilds, etc., are referred to as incorporated, and eight years later the full grant of incorporation to a borough was first made to Hull.

The position of the unincorporated societies, however, can only be understood by reference to their relationship to the municipal government. How far the early Gilda Mercatoria had the power to license or regulate special Craft Gilds is doubtful. It is certain, however, that as the chartered towns obtained their liberties and grow in power, the control of these Gilds became subordinated to the Mayor and governing bodies of the towns. The power does not seem originally to have been expressly granted by charter, but to have been implied in the general power of regulation of municipal affairs. The licenses thus granted to the trades by the Mayor, of which the Compositions given in this work are examples, deputed to the Gilds certain powers of trade government which only existed by virtue of the charters of the town itself, but conferred no corporate existence upon the Gilds as such. Some of the later charters givə this power in very express terms. As an example may be given the charter of Elizabeth to Winchester in 1587 ([281])—" And further we will and by these presents grant for us, our heirs and successors, unto the said Mayor, Bailiffs, and Commonalty, and their successors for ever, that they shall and may from time to time ordain, create, and establish a society, guild, or fraternity of one master and wardens of every art, mystery, and occupation used or occupied, or hereafter shall be used or occupied within the said city and the suburbs thereof, And that they, with the assistance of the wardens of the said arts and mysteries, may make, constitute, ordain, and establish laws, constitutions, and ordinances for the public utility and profit, and for the better rule and regiment

(281) Milner, App. II., 800.

of our city of Winchester, and of the mysteries of the citizens and inhabitants of the same. And the said Mayor and Commonalty, so often as they shall make ordinances and establish such laws, constitutions, etc., may limit and appoint such like pains, punishments, and penalties as shall seem to them to be requisite and necessary for observing of the said laws and constitutions, all which punishments may be inflicted and levied without the leave of us, our heirs and successors, so as the same be not contrary or repugnant to the laws of our realm of England."

The matter had before this claimed the attention of Parliament. In 1376, and again several times in the next century, complaints were made of the ordinances and usurpations of the crafts, and in 1437 it was provided that all such should be submitted to the Justices or the Mayor. In 1503 they were ordered to be approved by the Lord Chancellor or Justices of Assize. So the Statute 17 Charles I. orders that they shall be approved by the Lord Chancellor. This applied as well to those which were actually incorporated, and does not seem to have produced any change in the ordinary custom of the boroughs. In one case, indeed, that of Cork, A.D. 1631, the charter expressly gives the power of incorporating the several arts, mysteries, and trades into several corporations, which, being so incorporate, might exercise their several mysteries in such sort as the commons of the city of Dublin used and were accustomed to use according to the ancient customs of any corporation within the kingdom of Ireland (282). The exceptional language of this charter must, however, be interpreted by what has just been laid down. A similar use of the term "incorporate" occurs in the statement of the Composition of the Hull Tailors in 1680 (see p. 241), and by the evident attempt to simulate the terms of a charter of incorporation, it is evident that this was a mere conventional use of the word. The only incorporated societies in Hull were the Merchants' Company and the Trinity House. It was everywhere the aim of the more important crafts from

(282) Merewether and Stephens, 1679.

the 15th century to obtain charters from the King, and this true incorporation rendered them to a varying extent independent of the Mayor and borough chamber ([283]). Thus at York there were three companies or gilds whose officers were exempt from the jurisdiction of the Lord Mayor, the Masters and Searchers of all others being sworn before him. These three were really six, but the Mercers, or Merchant Adventurers, and Apothecaries were incorporated as one company, the Drapers and Merchant Taylors as another, and the Linen Weavers as the third, all meanwhile remaining distinct, and having their own coats of arms. The reader will pardon us if we quote one more case which was contested in London in 1703, in order to bring out clearly the point in dispute. There had been a bye-law made by the Common Council of the city of London, "That the Company and Fellowship of Porters having been time out of mind a company and fellowship, it was ordained that they still remain and continue for ever a company and fellowship, and that no master of any boat, etc., should unload or send on shore any goods but by such persons as were free of the Company. It was objected—(1) That the city of London could not make a corporation, only the Crown; (2) that a corporation could not make a bye-law to bind strangers unless founded on public convenience. It was held that a corporation may make a fraternity. A corporation is properly an investing the people of the place with the local government thereof, and therefore their law may bind strangers; but a fraternity is some people of a place united together in respect of a mystery and business into a company, and their laws and ordinances cannot bind strangers, for they have not a local power of government ([284])." Although the more usual custom was for the Trade Gilds to be subject to the control of the Mayor and Town's Chamber, other customs prevailed in those quasi-boroughs such as Sheffield where the privileges were held under the Lord of the Manor. In the case of the Cutlers' Company, the Earl of Shrewsbury occupied a higher position

(283) See the history of the successive Merchant Companies.

(284) Merewether and Stephens, 1967.

than the Mayor of a free town like Hull. The ordinances granted by him in the 32 of Elizabeth are stated to be (285) :—"As well by the hole fellowshippe and company of cutlers and makers of knyves within the Lordshippe of Hallomshire, in the countye of Yorke, whose names are particularlye expressed in a sedule hereunto annexed, As alsoe by th' assente of the righte honorable George, Erle of Shrewsburye, Lorde and owner of the said Lordshippe of Hallomshire, for the better relief and comodytie of the poorer sorte of the said fellowshippe." The fines were half to the fraternity and half to the Earl, and article 16 states, "At the great Court of the Earl holden at Sheffield in Easter week, 12 men of the said scyence or mystery are to be nominated by the Earl or his learned steward, to inquire into offences and to punish offenders." Article 17 provides—"If these ordinances do not prove as beneficial as is expected to the poorer sort, the Earl may make them or any of them void." It was not till 1624 that the Company, which was then a very powerful body, obtained its incorporation by Act of Parliament.

These facts seem conclusive that the statements of the Introduction to "Early English Gilds" and Professor Freeman above-quoted cannot be accepted as accurately describing the true position of the Trade Gilds. It is even a question how far the religious Gilds before the Reformation could be founded without the consent of the Mayor. In those deeds of foundation which we have remaining, the Mayor's name appears among the signatories. It is true the word used in the deed is constantly "for us and our 'successors,'" which in modern times would not be the technical term for a private body of men to use, but the usage is evidently not in the more exact sense, and in some instances would in modern use be "heirs (286)."

(285) Hunter's *Hallamshire*, p. 110.

(286) See Gross, *Gild Merchant*, 1890, for these words as applied to borough

CHAPTER XXXVI.

THE GILD SYSTEM AND THE CHRISTIAN CHURCH.

WE have reserved for separate treatment the subject of the peculiar relation existing at various periods between the Gild, using the word in its widest signification, and the various institutions of the Christian Church. The subject is indeed far too wide for anything more than a brief indication of the several points of contact. In some directions it opens out questions of fascinating interest, which we must leave untouched. From the earliest dawn of Christianity down to the present day; from the Collegia of Rome to the Monasteries of the Middle Ages; from the Gild Chapels of our churches to the Religious Societies of the 17th and 18th centuries, some of which are in full vigour to-day, the influence may be traced; and while we can but touch the crucial points of the relationship, it would be impossible to leave it altogether unnoticed.

The reader will bear in mind what has already been said of the wide-spread prevalence of the Collegia and Sodalicia of the first centuries of the Christian era. They were not only trade societies, but also religious and funeral associations. Theirs was the general form of association which was familiar to the Imperial world. Now apart from the question, so ably treated by Dr. Hatch (287), as to the extent to which the early Christians availed themselves of the details of existing Pagan forms of organisation, it is evident that they had no choice but on the one hand to conform to such general features of association as were permitted by the laws, or on the other to be regarded by the heathen as one of the many religious societies which flourished

(287) Bampton Lectures

during the same period. This is evident from the celebrated letter of Pliny to Trajan, in which he says that some of the recreant Christians tell him they had deserted from going to the services in consequence of his having issued an edict forbidding the meeting of clubs and assemblies ([288]). The struggling Christian assemblies would be ranked with the various other heathen or Asiatic cults which were constantly springing up. Still bearing in mind the evidence of the Lanuvian Gild and the bequest on the Appian Way (see p. 26), let the reader follow the words of Tertullian in his "Apology ([289])," and note the evident allusion of the apologist in view of the aspersions of the heathen of his day—"The presidents or bishops among us are men of the most venerable age and piety, raised to this honor not by the powers of money, but the brightness of their lives: for nothing sacred is to be had for money. That kind of treasury which we have is not filled with any dishonorable sum, as the price of a purchased religion; everyone puts a little to the common stock, commonly once a month, or when he pleases, and only upon condition that he is both willing and able; for there is no compulsion upon any. All here is free will offering, and all these collections are deposited in a common bank for charitable uses, not for the support of merry meetings, for drinking or gourmandising, but for feeding the poor and burying the dead, and providing for girls and boys who have neither parents nor provisions left to support them, for relieving old people worn out in the service of the saints, or those who suffered by shipwreck, or are condemned to the mines, or islands, or prisons, only for the faith of Christ: these may be said to live upon their profession, for while they suffer for professing the name of Christ, they are fed with the collections of His Church." The meaning is evident. The Church too, so to speak, viewed externally, was a Collegium or Religio, but with objects which were Christian and benevolent. The general analogy descends into more striking particular. The honor paid by the Christians to the relics of the saints and martyrs, and the

(288) Pliny, Epistle x., 96.

(289) Chapter 39, Reeves' Translation, Griffith & Farran.

observance of their anniversaries or "feasts," offered a parallel with the heathen funeral observances above noticed. The question of the earliest forms of Christian architecture is a large one, but we know that the meeting places which preceded the incorporation of the Basilican form into the typical church were either the large private "upper rooms" or the "Cellæ," or memorial chapels of the cemeteries, and closely analogous to the latter were the "Scholæ" or regular halls of the Collegia, with the apsidal end which became a marked feature of the church, but which was wanting in the pure Basilica (290). It is by no means unlikely, though proof is not yet forthcoming, that the Schola was really the most common meeting-place of the Church in the second century. Take the following inscription found at Cherchel, in North Africa, the country of Tertullian, and dating from the third century:—"A worshipper of the Word (291) presented a space of ground for a sepulchre, and out of his own means built a cella, which he left as a memorial to the holy Church. Hail brethren, from a pure and guileless heart Euelpius salutes you, ye who are born of the Holy Spirit," and compare it with one of the bequests to a heathen Collegium, and it is easy to see the analogy (292). De Rossi, who is probably better qualified than any other man, gives his opinion as follows—"It is evident to me that the Christians made use of the privilege of the funeral colleges, and that the emperors who were well disposed to them, or at any rate not persecutors, availed themselves of this pretext to tolerate the assemblies of the faithful, and to permit the Church to establish itself little by little as a corporation in the bosom of the Empire."

Thus closely was the Early Church connected with the Roman Gilds, a connection which has even left traces among the accidental features of its constitution to the present day. After the final victory under Constantine, this relation necessarily ceased. The Church had need of no cloak under which to hide.

(290) See Baldwin, *From Schola to Cathedral*, passim.

(291) "Cultor verbi."

(292) Baldwin, *From Schola to Cathedral*, p. 25.

There were already churches under the reign of Severus, and the Schola and Cella and their adjuncts gave way to the splendid Basilica and the Memorial Church.

Meanwhile the Collegium proper, as we have seen, took its own course under Christian influences. The face of the Imperial world changed. Italy herself was overrun by barbarians, and the countries of Europe slowly laid the foundations of their mediæval nationalities, but the Collegia lived on.

How far the early monastic brotherhoods had any of their features in common with the later Collegia is a question which seems never to have been investigated, but which is worth some enquiry. The name is the same. Both were fraternities, and both were collegia. No exact line of demarcation can be drawn between the rules of a gild and the rules of a monastic fraternity. In the one case the community of life necessitated an extension of the system, but on the other hand, on the Continent, the same community of life was practiced, as we have seen (p. 142), for secular purposes such as trade. The "Confréries" and "Frairies" of old France, either the pure lay religious brotherhoods or those of the trades, answering to the English Gilds and Fraternities, corresponded very closely with the orders of the "Friars," while the "Collegiate" Churches, and the Gilds of the Kalendars, as at Bristol, shew in other respects points of close analogy. If we take, for example, the Franciscans, on closer study the relationship becomes more marked. In 1221 St. Francis founded the Confrérie of the "Brothers of Penitence," known from 1230 as "the third order," for men and women who lived the ordinary life of the world in the cities of Italy. This association bound together rich and poor, men and women, in one common fraternity for the works of piety and benevolence. Its progress was extraordinary. In a few years its members spread over Europe, and formed part of the vast network of organisation with which the Franciscans astonished the world of their day (203).

It is not possible here to pursue the study further. The points of difference were, of course, not less marked than those

(203) Gebhart, *L'Italie Mystique*, p. 126.

of similarity. Enough, however, has been said to shew that in the eyes of contemporaries there could not have been a very clear line between the Confréries of St. John or St. Michael and the Confrérie of Penitence, or between the Brothers of St. Benedict and the Fraternity of St. George. The great lay brotherhoods of St. John of Jerusalem, of the Templars, and the German Orders suggest themselves readily as other branches of the same great system of association.

When we come further down the stream of history, and cross the dividing line of the Reformation, another set of phenomena confronts us. The religious Gilds were, as we know, destroyed. Only the Trades' Gilds, and those which could take refuge under some form of public utility or corporate protection, such as the Trinity House at Hull, or the Gild of St. George at Norwich, survived. But the old principle lived on in the institutions which remained, and in the great trading companies which then came into prominent life. Abroad, in the countries which remained Roman Catholic in creed, and which were in constant intercourse with England, the old religious Gilds flourished as before. Then in this country followed the time when the old principle of one great society or church gave way to the congregational principle of a number of separate and independent ones, each an association in itself, and purposely avoiding the forms of mediæval tradition. But when the stormy days of the Puritan struggles were over, and the religious life of England began to settle down under the ægis of the National Church, we find at the close of the 17th century, and in the days of Queen Anne, religious societies springing up in various parts of England not dissimilar, considering the change of circumstances, to the old religious Gilds. De la Pryme tells us that on May 5th, 1698, he attended the visitation of the Archbishop of York (294)—" He gave us a great deal of most excellent advice, and talked severely against drunkenness, loos living, keeping of company, and such like; desired us all to beware of the same, and begged on us to enter into

(294) Sharp.

religious associations one with another [295]." Of such the Society for Promoting Christian Knowledge and the Society for the Propagation of the Gospel, which had their prototypes under the Commonwealth, were well-known examples. Such also was in its origin the brotherhood or society founded by John and Charles Wesley, which has had such momentous consequences for English Christianity. In these later examples no doubt the traditional form of association loses itself in the general tendency which is natural to humanity, but it should be observed, nevertheless, that the historic sequence has been continuous. They should be placed alongside the great trading companies, such as the East India Company, as the historical descendants in a different sphere of the same spirit and to some extent of the same form of association which we have traced through so many centuries of the past.

The forms of the past have disappeared, but its spirit lives on, and the genius of the ancient brotherhoods still animates many of the most fruitful tendencies of modern life.

Above all, we must recognise in the Gild, so far as it was antecedent to Christianity, and afforded an element which was assimilated to it in its progress, one more example of that tendency of mind "naturally Christian" which lights up the darker period of heathenism like the rays which precede the dawn. The bond of brotherhood was to give way to the wider brotherhood of Christian man; the re-union of brethren round the tomb of the departed, to the memorial of the saints which sleep; the monthly contributions to pious objects, to the sum laid by weekly as the Lord prospered each; the deeds of kindness to the Gild brother, to charity to all men, and especially to those of the household of faith.

(295) *Diary*, p. 178.

Appendix I.

Memorials of Merchants Adventurers, Staplers, and Members of the Eastland Company in the Churches of Kingston-upon-Hull.

[To the kind aid of Mr. John Bilson, F.R.I.B.A., I am indebted for being able to give the following list of the monuments of members of the old Merchant Companies trading in Hull, either recorded or still to be seen in the Churches of Hull.]

JOHN RAMSDEN lies buried in the north chancel aisle of Holy Trinity Church, in the fourth bay from the east. In the centre of the floor slab is his merchant's mark, with the date 1637. The inscription runs:—"Here lieth the body of the Worshipful John Ramsden, twice Mayor of this town, and Merchant Adventurer, who departed in the true faith of Christ the xxi. December. Mors omnibus communis."

A sculptured stone, formerly in the buildings at the corner of Chapel Lane Staithway and High Street (No. 32, High Street), and now refixed in the Globe Warehouses, bears this same merchant's mark, a combination of the 4 form so common in merchants' marks of this period and the letter R, over a coat of arms, of which the charges have disappeared, but which, from the supporters (two pegasi), was evidently that of the Merchant Adventurers. There is an illustration (rather a poor one) of the stone in Greenwood's picture of Hull. It seems certain, therefore, that John Ramsden lived at the corner of High Street and Chapel Lane Staithway.

William Ramsden lies buried in the north chancel aisle of Holy Trinity Church, near John Ramsden. The inscription on the floor slab is :—" In this vault lieth interred the body of | the Worshipfull William Ramsden, sometime deputy to the right | worshipfull company of Merchants Adven | turers of England, Alderman and Maior of this towne, twice a | Member of Parliament for the same | Corporation in the honourable House of Commons. He departed | this life in the true faith of Christ | the second day of September, Anno 1680, in the 63[d] yeare | of his age, waiting the morning | of the resurrection." It is to be noticed that while John Ramsden's slab bears his merchant's mark, William Ramsden's has a coat of arms—Argent on a chevron between three fleurs-de-lis sable, as many rams' heads couped at the neck of the first. His wife, Ann Ramsden, daughter of Thomas Boynton of Rockliff, Esq., lies near him; she died 1667, and her slab bears the arms of Ramsden impaling Boynton.

In the north transept of Holy Trinity Church is a floor slab, now being rapidly defaced, which bears a merchant's mark and the following inscription :—"Here liethe James Clarkson, thrice | Maior of Kingston-upon-Hull, Marchant Adventurer and free of | Eastland, who died the 17 day | of November, an. dom. 1585, in the trew faithe of Jesus Christ."

In the north chancel aisle, in the third bay from the East, is a floor slab with a merchant's mark and the following inscription :—" Here lyethe in peace Walter Pecke | Marchant Adventurer | who departed this | lyfe in the faith of Christ, ye 8 of July, A[no] D. 1598."

In the south chancel aisle, in the second bay from the East, is a floor slab with the following inscription :—" Here lyeth Thōas Dalton, thrise Mayor of Kingston-upon-hull, Marchante of the Staple a | nd venturer | who dyed viiii. day of January | Ano. dmni. 1590, in ye faith of Chrste and ful hope of resurctiō to lyfe eternall." The arms are much defaced, but appear to be those of the Staple of England.

In the eastern bay of the south aisle of the nave is a slab, formerly on an altar-tomb near the south porch, bearing this inscription:—"Here lieth the body of | the Worshipfull Joseph Feild, twice Maior of | this towne, and Marchant Adv | enturer, who departed in the true faith of Christ." Below is the date 1627, and "æt. 63," and other inscriptions, and the arms of the Merchant Adventurers of England with the supporters (pegasi) and motto.

Gent gives also the following inscription as to be found in the chancel:—"Here lieth the Body of the Worshipful Francis Dewick, Merchant-Adventurer, once Mayor of Kingston-upon-Hull, who departed this Life the 2nd of May, 1663. And also Margaret his Wife, who departed this life the 15th of February, 1661." Also the following as "on an inward south pillar at the west end" (and very near the same words are on the grave-stone in the great aisle):—"Near this monument are interred the Bodies of Mr. Henry Maister and Anne his wife, Daughter of Mr. William Raikes. They had issue 9 Sons and 2 Daughters, 7 of which survived them. He was twice Mayor of this town, and Deputy Governor to the Hamburg-Eastland Companies. He died 5th of April, 1699, aged 67. She died Dec. 14, 1685, aged 48. Hodie nobis cras vobis."

In St. Mary's Churchyard, near the south wall, is a floor slab bearing the following inscription:—"Here lieth the Body of | the Worshipfull William Dobson, Merchant Adve | nturer, twice Major of | this towne, who departed this life the 20th Day | of October, 1666, and of Sibyl his Wife, who departed this Life the 19th Day of August, 1668." In Gent's day it would appear that this was within the Church. See also the particulars of the monument and epitaph (Gent, p. 58). In the Churchyard also is a slab with the following inscription, apparently having shared the same fate as the preceding one:—"Here resteth in Peace | Mr. Thomas Swan, Marchant-Adventurer, Maior of | this towne, who depted to the Mercy of God the 20th of January, 1629." Gent adds:—"This Gentleman lies buried within the Rails of the

Altar; whose effigy, with that of his Lady, are neatly placed on the stone." From the same historian we learn of the following inscription:—" Here lieth the body of the Worshipful Thomas Thackray, twice Mayor of this town, and Merchant Adventurer, who departed in the true Faith of Christ, 1630. Quod sum fueris." Also that " He lies buried within the Altar Rails, over whom is his effigy, with those of his wife and children."

APPENDIX II.

THE ARMS OF THE MERCHANT COMPANY.

WHILE this work is being completed for the press, I am enabled to point out two surviving relics of the old Hull Merchant Company of curious interest, and of the existence of which, when writing the account in chapters xvi. and xvii., I was unaware.

It will be remembered (p. 177) that on the 4th August, 1650, it was ordered "that with all convenient speed the arms of the Commonwealth and the Merchants' arms be got made and put up in the Hall," which was accordingly done. Ten years afterwards, in 1660, we read that "the late Parliament of England's armes, now hanging in the Merchants' Hall," were taken down, and John Smeadley was employed "to draw the King's arms upon the same table, and hang them up again."

Mr. Bilson having heard of a coat of arms which he suspected to be that of the Merchant Adventurers, preserved in the New Municipal Hospitals, we went (Feb. 20th, 1891) on a visit of enquiry. Among other interesting relics brought from the Old Grammar School in 1882, we were shewn two framed oak tablets, 3ft. 5in. square, which had been hung by a staple at the corner. The figuring is very indistinct with age, but the heraldic skill of my companion soon recognised on one the arms of the Merchant Adventurers of England with two slight variations (see below), and on the other, rather more distinct, the royal arms of Charles II: Mr. Bilson has kindly sent me the following description.

"The Merchant Adventurers' arms are the same as those on the seal engraved in the lower part of Plate IV. of Frost's 'Notices,' viz., 'Barry nebulée of six argent and azure, a chief quarterly gules and or, in the first and fourth quarters a lion of England, and in the second and third quarters two Lancastrian roses;' but with two points of difference. The first is that the quarters in the chief are reversed, the first and fourth being two Lancastrian roses, and the second and third a lion of England. The same reversing of the quarters in the chief occurs on the brass of John Terri and his wife, 1524, in St. John's, Maddermarket, Norwich, and on the brass of John Clark, 1527, in St. Andrew's, Norwich (see Cotman's 'Sepulchral Brasses of Norfolk and Suffolk,' 1839). It possibly arose from copying the matrix of the seal. The second difference is in the motto, which in the arms of the Merchant Adventurers proper was 'Dieu nous adventure donne bonne,' but in the Hull tablet is 'God be our friend.' The Royal arms on the other tablet are those borne by the Stuarts, 1603 to 1689, viz.:—Quarterly, 1st and 4th grand quarters, France modern and England quarterly; second grand quarter, Scotland; third grand quarter, Ireland, with the initials 'C.R.,' used by both Charles I. and Charles II."

The upper storey of the Old Grammar School, whence the tablets were brought to their new abode, was the Merchants' Hall of the Company. It would appear, then, that when the plate and books of the Company were taken to the Town Hall, on Feb. 22nd, 1706, in pursuance of an order of the 13th Feb. (see p. 183), the tablets were left in their old position, as not worth removal, and so passed into the possession of the trustees of the building, now represented by the Charity Trustees. On the sale of the old buildings in 1882, they were carefully removed and preserved by the Secretary, R. G. Smith, Esq., and will no doubt add to the historic embellishments of the New Grammar School.

It appears, therefore, that although having a distinct seal (see

p. 177 and illustration), the Hull Merchants' Company used the arms of the Merchant Adventurers of England, for the seal was made in 1648, and the arms painted in 1650. The other seal above referred to was in all probability used by the local members of the Merchant Adventurers of England, who were also in most cases members of the Hull Company, although the latter was distinct, and had a Royal Charter of its own.

Mr. Bilson observes that Frost, on page 37, note, is in error as to the arms of the Merchant Adventurers of England, as they had no sceptre on an inescutcheon, this being borne by the French Company.

Bibliography.

THE following has been kindly compiled for me by Mr. W. G. B. Page, Sub-Librarian, Hull Subscription Library. It contains a list of those works and contributions to various classes of literature which are not included in the very full account contained in Dr. Gross' "Gilda Mercatoria" and "Gild Merchant."

ASHLEY, W. J., M.A.—An Introduction to English Economic History and Theory. London, 1888, pp. xiv., 228.

Chapter II. deals with the "Merchant and Craft Gilds" (pp. 67-129).

BONE, J. H. A.—Old English Guilds and Trade Unions. *Atlantic Monthly*, xxxix. (1877), pp. 278-287.

BULLOCK, John—The Pynonrs: Historical Notes on an Ancient Aberdeen Craft. Crown 8vo. Only 400 copies printed.

CLODE, C.M.—The Early History and Memorials of the Merchant Taylors' Company and its Associated Charities and Institutions, with Lives of some Eminent Members.

Printed for private circulation.

CUNNINGHAM, Rev. Wm., D.D., F.R.H.S.—The Formation and Decay of Craft Gilds. *Transactions of the Royal Historical Society*, 2nd series, iii., pp. 371-392.

A paper read before the members of the Royal Historical Society, May 20th, 1886; republished, with additions, in his "Growth of English Industry and Commerce during the Early and Middle Ages." Cambridge, 1890; Book III., chapter iv. (pp. 309-318)

——— Gross's Gild Merchant; a Review. *Economic Review*, i. (April, 1891).

DITCHFIELD, Rev. P. H., M.A., F.R.H.S.—The Guilds of Reading. *Reliquary*, new series, iv. (1890), pp. 141-149.

DRINKWATER, Rev. C. H.—Merchants' Gild of Shrewsbury, 1260-1304. *Shropshire Archæological Journal*, ii., Part I. (1890), pp.

FAIRHOLT, F. W., F.S.A.—Guild Processions and Observances.

A paper read before the British Archæological Association, August 2nd, 1850; and a *resumé* of it appears in the *Journal* (vol. L., pp. 314-316).

FALLOW, T. M., M.A.—Notes on the Plate of the Guild of the Trinity House, Hull. *Reliquary*, new series, I. (1887), pp. 212-217, ii.; with plates from drawings by D. A. Walter, of Hull.

GREGO, Joseph—Decorative Plate of the London Livery Companies. *Leisure Hour*, xxx. (1881), pp. 373-377, 495-497, 568-570, 632-634.
These articles are illustrated with nine engravings of the plate belonging to the various Companies.

GROSS, Charles, Ph. D.—Gilda Mercatoria. Ein Beitrag zur Geschichte der englischen Städteverfassung. Gottingen, 1883; demy 8vo., pp. vi., 110.
This work contains a long list (pp. 102-109) of books referred to for compilation, and as authorities.

——— The Gild Merchant. A contribution to British municipal history. Oxford, 1890; 8vo., 2 vols., pp. xxii., 332; xi., 448.
Vol. I. contains (pp. 301-331) a long list of authorities, which forms a bibliography of the subject of "Gilds," and to which this list forms a supplement.

——— Le Gilde Inglesi. Studio storica del Dott. G. B. Salvioni; Firenze, 1883. A review in *English Historical Review*, i., pp. 780-784.

GUILD, *Encyclopædia Britannica*, eighth edition, xi. (1856) p. 87.

GUILDS, English, *Edinburgh Review*, cxxxiv. (1871) pp. 342-360.

HOBHOUSE, Arthur—The City [London] Companies; *Contemporary Review*, xlvii. (1885) pp. 1-24.

HOPE, R. C., F.S.A.—Ordinances of the Company of Goldsmiths of Norwich, 1565. *Reliquary*, new series, iv. (1890), pp. 208-211.

——— English Goldsmiths. Scarborough; 8vo. (1890), pp. 76.

——— Old English Pewter. *Reliquary* iv. (January, April, 1891), pp. 21-26; 72-80.
The second article contains the Ordinances of the Pewterers of York.

HOWELL, George, M.P.—The Conflicts of Capital and Labour Historically and Economically considered; 2nd and revised edition, 1890.
Chapter I. deals with Part I.—"Guilds—their Origin, Essence, and History;" Part II.—"Religious and Social Guilds;" Part III.—"The Merchant-Guilds and Town-Guilds;" Part IV.—"Craft-Guilds;" Chapters II.-III.—"Trade Unions—their Origin, History, and Development."

JEAYES, J.H.—Confraternities. *Journal British Archæological Association* vol. xxxvii. (1881), pp. 13-21.
Read before the British Archæological Association, Jan. 7th, 1880.

KERRY, Rev. Charles—Discovery of the Register and Chartulary of the Mercers' Company, York. *Antiquary*, xxii. (1890), pp. 266-270; xxiii. (1891), pp.

KINGSTON-UPON-HULL—The Book of Orders of the Guild of Bricklaiers, Tilers, Wallers, Plaisterers, and Pavers. Folio, 106 pp., parchment.
This is the original MS. which belonged to the Guild, now the property of the Hull Subscription Library, in whose possession it has been since 1886. It contains the Rules, Orders, Register of the "Maiors," "Sheriffes," and "Wardens;" also the autograph signatures of the Mayors from 1630 to 1740.

LAMBERT, Rev. J. M., M.A., LL.D.—Some Lincolnshire Gilds. *Bygone Lincolnshire*, 1891, pp. 160-180.

LEICESTER Guild Rolls. Thompson's *History of Leicester*, 1849.

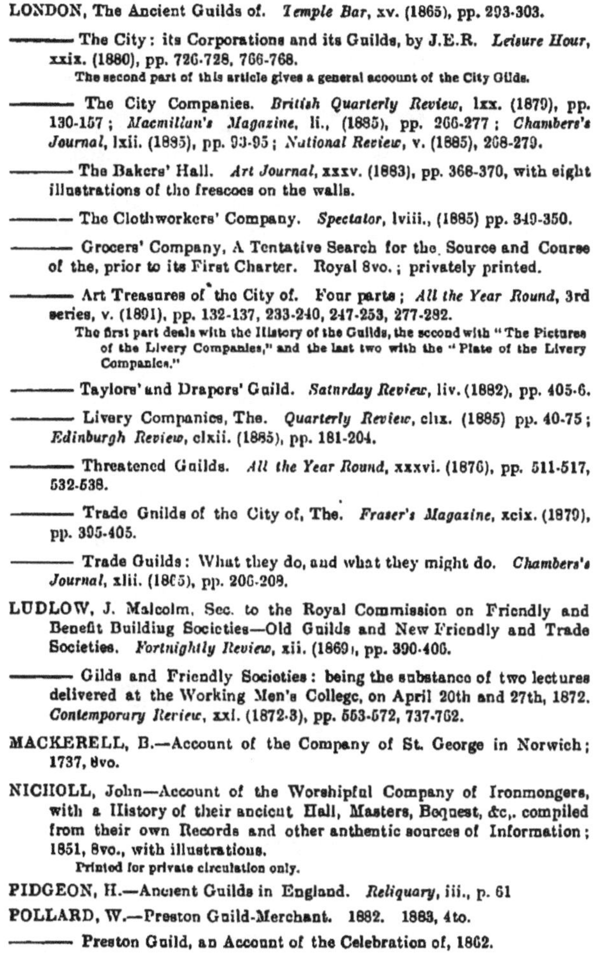

LONDON, The Ancient Guilds of. *Temple Bar*, xv. (1865), pp. 293-303.

——— The City: its Corporations and its Guilds, by J.E.R. *Leisure Hour*, xxix. (1880), pp. 726-728, 766-768.

The second part of this article gives a general account of the City Gilds.

——— The City Companies. *British Quarterly Review*, lxx. (1879), pp. 130-157; *Macmillan's Magazine*, li., (1885), pp. 266-277; *Chambers's Journal*, lxii. (1885), pp. 93-95; *National Review*, v. (1885), 268-279.

——— The Bakers' Hall. *Art Journal*, xxxv. (1883), pp. 368-370, with eight illustrations of the frescoes on the walls.

——— The Clothworkers' Company. *Spectator*, lviii., (1885) pp. 349-350.

——— Grocers' Company, A Tentative Search for the Source and Course of the, prior to its First Charter. Royal 8vo.; privately printed.

——— Art Treasures of the City of. Four parts; *All the Year Round*, 3rd series, v. (1891), pp. 132-137, 233-240, 247-253, 277-282.

The first part deals with the History of the Guilds, the second with "The Pictures of the Livery Companies," and the last two with the "Plate of the Livery Companies."

——— Taylors' and Drapers' Guild. *Saturday Review*, liv. (1882), pp. 405-6.

——— Livery Companies, The. *Quarterly Review*, clix. (1885) pp. 40-75; *Edinburgh Review*, clxii. (1885), pp. 181-204.

——— Threatened Guilds. *All the Year Round*, xxxvi. (1876), pp. 511-517, 532-538.

——— Trade Guilds of the City of, The. *Fraser's Magazine*, xcix. (1879), pp. 395-405.

——— Trade Guilds: What they do, and what they might do. *Chambers's Journal*, xlii. (1865), pp. 206-209.

LUDLOW, J. Malcolm, Sec. to the Royal Commission on Friendly and Benefit Building Societies—Old Guilds and New Friendly and Trade Societies. *Fortnightly Review*, xii. (1869), pp. 390-406.

——— Gilds and Friendly Societies: being the substance of two lectures delivered at the Working Men's College, on April 20th and 27th, 1872. *Contemporary Review*, xxi. (1872-3), pp. 553-572, 737-762.

MACKERELL, B.—Account of the Company of St. George in Norwich; 1737, 8vo.

NICHOLL, John—Account of the Worshipful Company of Ironmongers, with a History of their ancient Hall, Masters, Bequest, &c,. compiled from their own Records and other authentic sources of Information; 1851, 8vo., with illustrations.

Printed for private circulation only.

PIDGEON, H.—Ancient Guilds in England. *Reliquary*, iii., p. 61

POLLARD, W.—Preston Guild-Merchant. 1882. 1883, 4to.

——— Preston Guild, an Account of the Celebration of, 1862.

PRESTON Guild Rolls. Record Soc. Lancashire and Cheshire, 1884.

SMIRKE, Edward, M.A., Vice-Warden of the Stanneries, and Recorder of Southampton)—Ancient Ordinances of the Gild Merchant of the Town of Southampton (in French). *Archæological Journal*, xvi. (1859), pp. 283-296, 343-352.

The Latin text is given in Houard's "Coutumes Anglo-normandes," ii. (1776), and the English translation in Davies' "History of Southampton" (1883).

SMITH, Miss Lucy Toulmin—Guild. *Encyclopædia Britannica*, ninth edition, (1880), xi., pp. 259-262.

TOMPKIN, H.—Greek and Roman Guilds. *Foresters' Journal.*

TOTNES Guild Rolls. *Third Rept. Hist. MSS. Comm.*, 1872.

WALFORD, Cornelius, F.I.A., F.S.S., F.R.H.S.—Outline History of the Hanseatic League, more particularly in its bearing upon English Commerce. *Transactions of the Royal Historical Society*, ix. (1881), pp. 82-136.

———— Gilds: their Origin, Constitution, Objects, and later History; new and enlarged edition, London, 1888, pp. xii., 272.

Reprinted, with additions, from Edward Walford's *Antiquarian Magazine*, and by Mrs. Cornelius Walford. Parts I. and II. treat of Gilds generally: Part III., Geographical Survey, arranged in Counties.

WILHELM, L.W.—The Origin and Decay of Mediæval Guilds. *Overland*, new series, i. (1883), p. 421.

WILSON, J.—The Cordwainers and Corvesors of Oxford. *Archæological Journal*, vi. (1849), pp. 146-159.

WINCHESTER Trade Guilds. *Archæological Journal*, ix. (1854), pp. 87-88.

YOUNG, Sydney—Annals of the Barber-Surgeons of London. Compiled from the Records and other sources; with illustrations by Austin T. Young. 1890, 4to., pp. xii., 624.

Reviewed in the *Antiquary* (Sept., 1890), pp. 96-101. Illustrated with 5 engravings.

ZIMMERN, Helen—The Hansa Towns [Story of the Nations]; 1889, 8vo., pp. xvii., 390.

Period I., Chapters I.-III., treat of "The Dawn of a Great Trade Guild;" "Federation;" and "Foreign Trade;" and Period II. and III. of "The History of the Hanseatic League, from 1370 to the Public Peace of 1495, decreed in Germany by Maximilian I.," and of "The Decline and Fall of the Hansa."

INDEX.

www.ingramcontent.com/pod-product-compliance
Lightning Source LLC
Chambersburg PA
CBHW032257280326
41932CB00009B/603

* 9 7 8 3 7 4 4 7 2 3 8 8 6 *